FAIRY TAIL

37

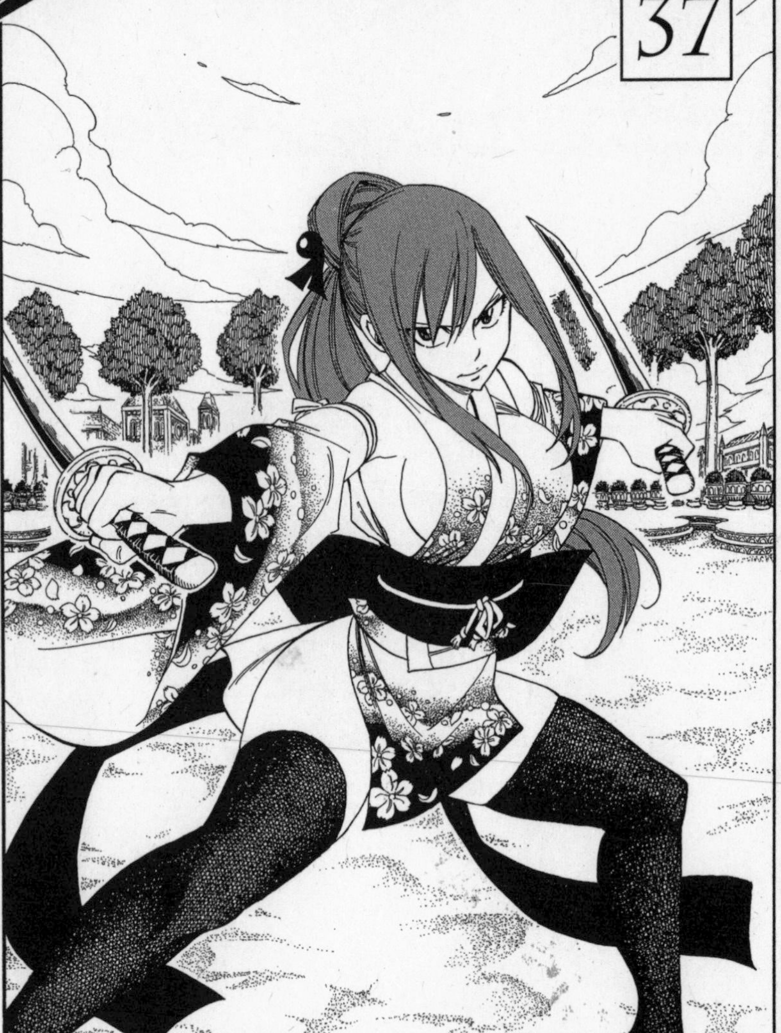

HIRO MASHIMA

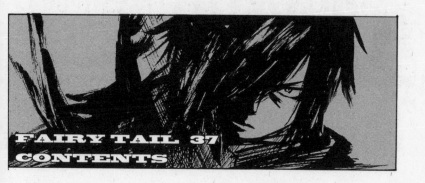

FAIRY TAIL 37 CONTENTS

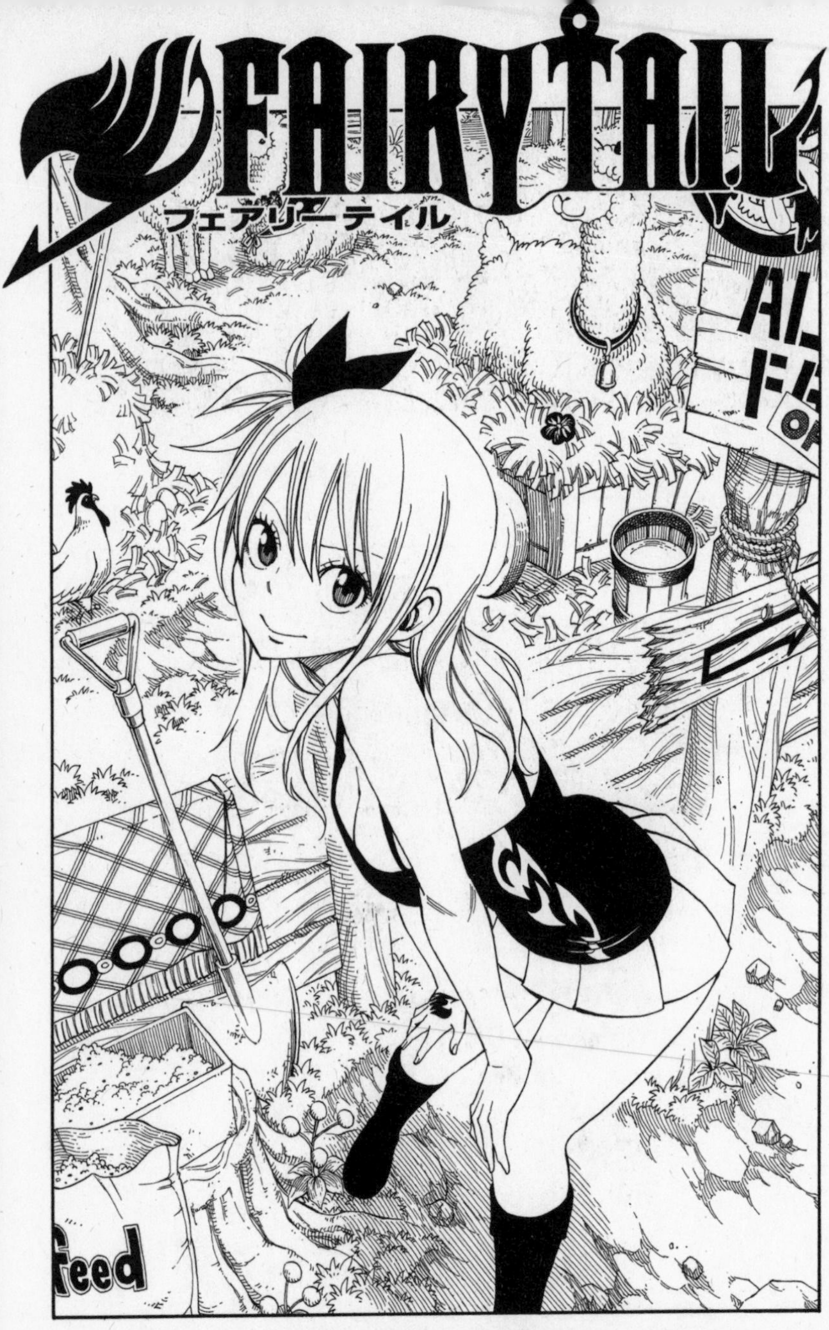
FAIRY TAIL
フェアリーテイル
feed

Chapter 309: The Burning Earth

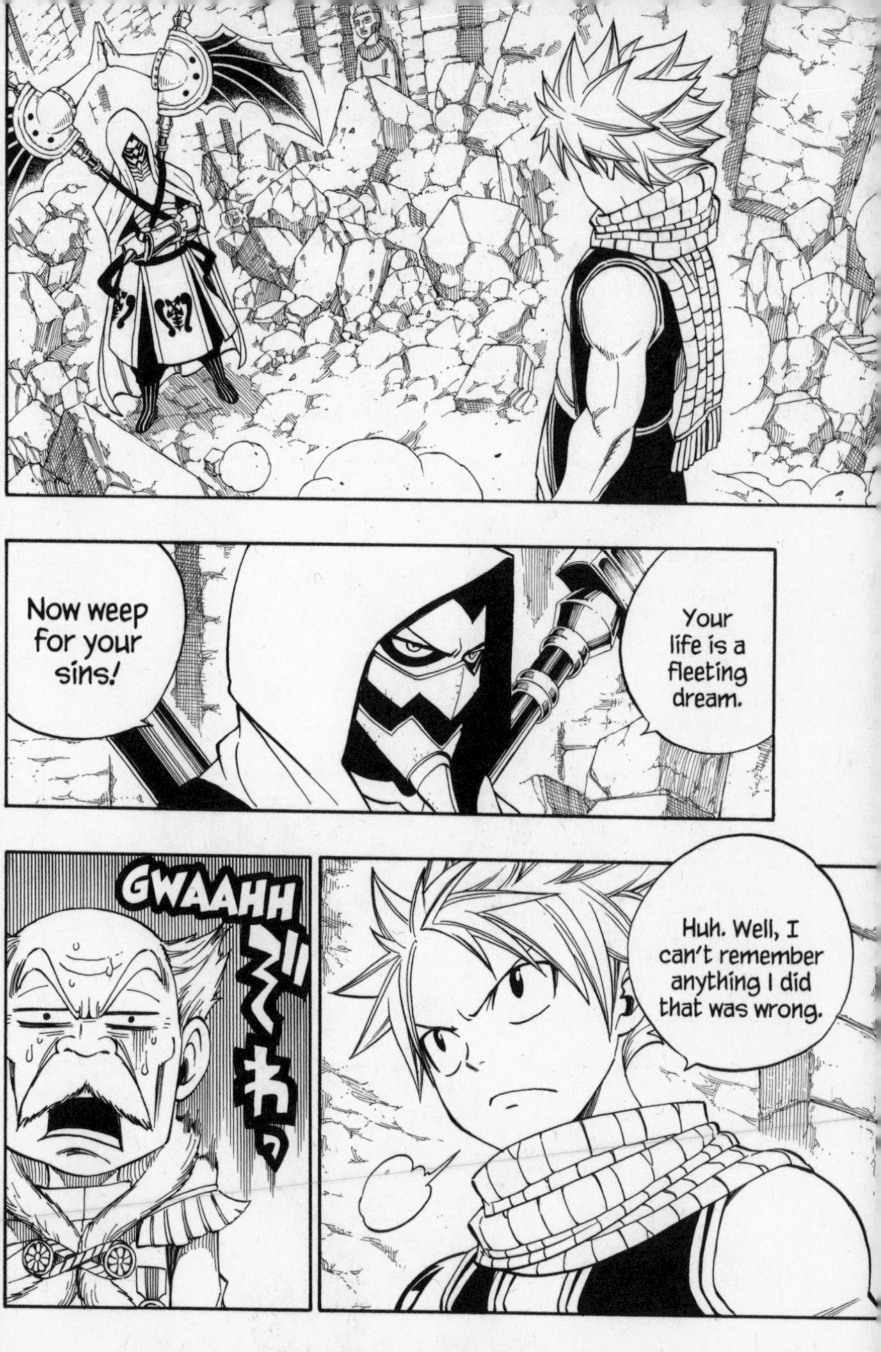
Your life is a fleeting dream.
Now weep for your sins!
Huh. Well, I can't remember anything I did that was wrong.
GWAAHH

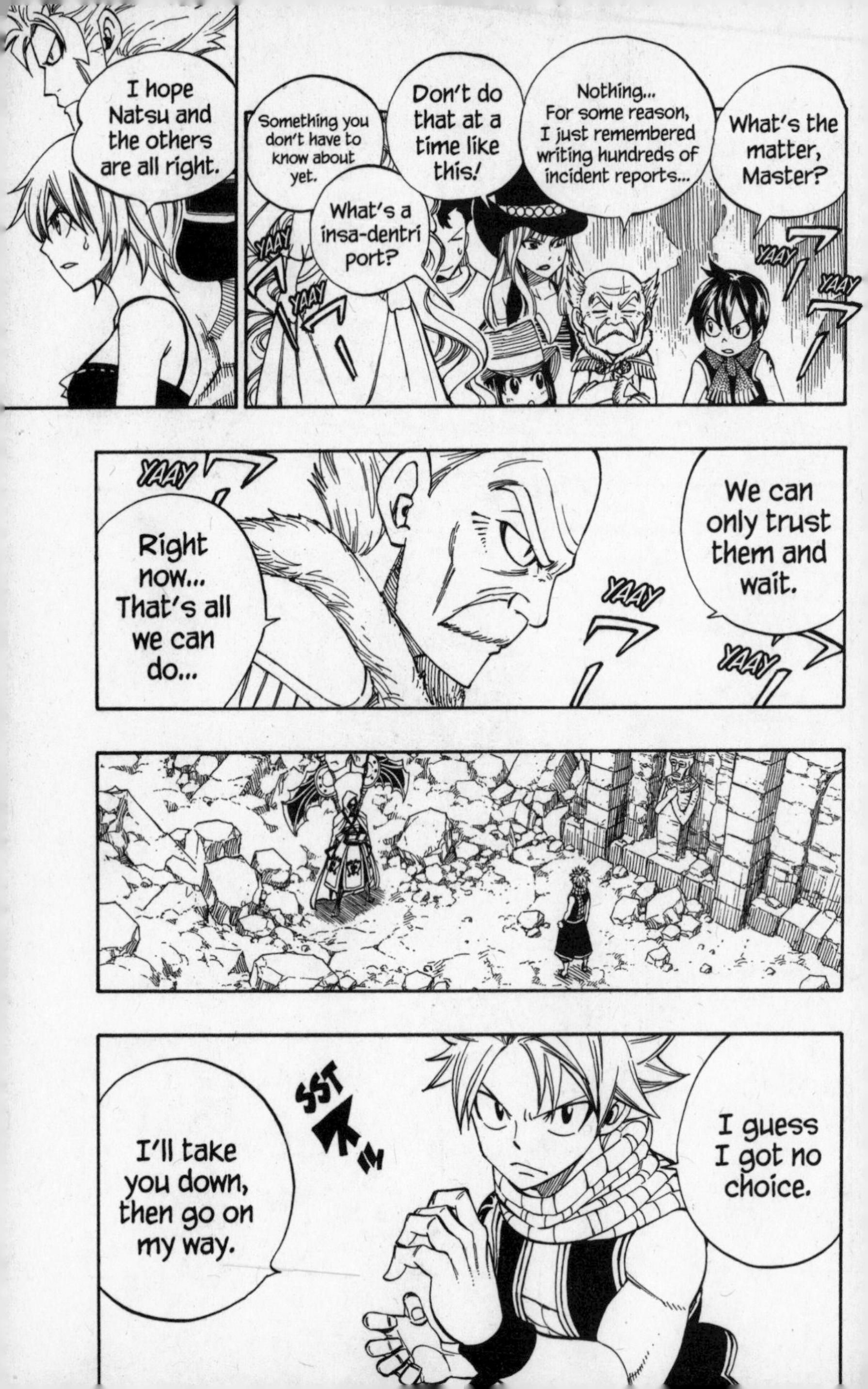
What's the matter, Master?
YAAY
YAAY
Nothing... For some reason, I just remembered writing hundreds of incident reports...
Don't do that at a time like this!
Something you don't have to know about yet.
What's a insa-dentri port?
YAAY
YAAY
I hope Natsu and the others are all right.
We can only trust them and wait.
YAAY
YAAY
YAAY
Right now... That's all we can do...
I guess I got no choice.
SST
I'll take you down, then go on my way.

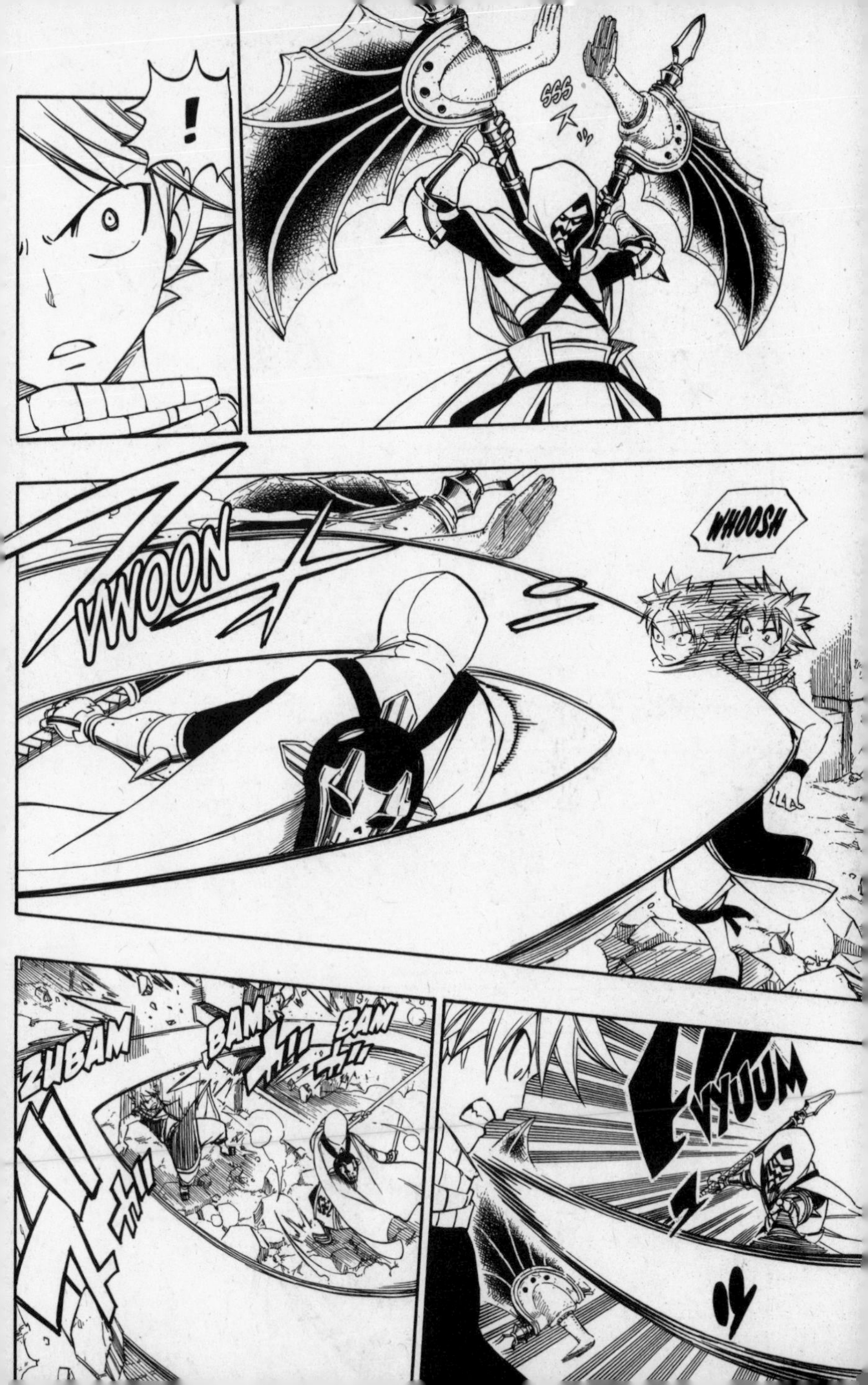
SSS
!
WHOOSH
VWOON
VYUUM
ZUBAM
BAM
BAM

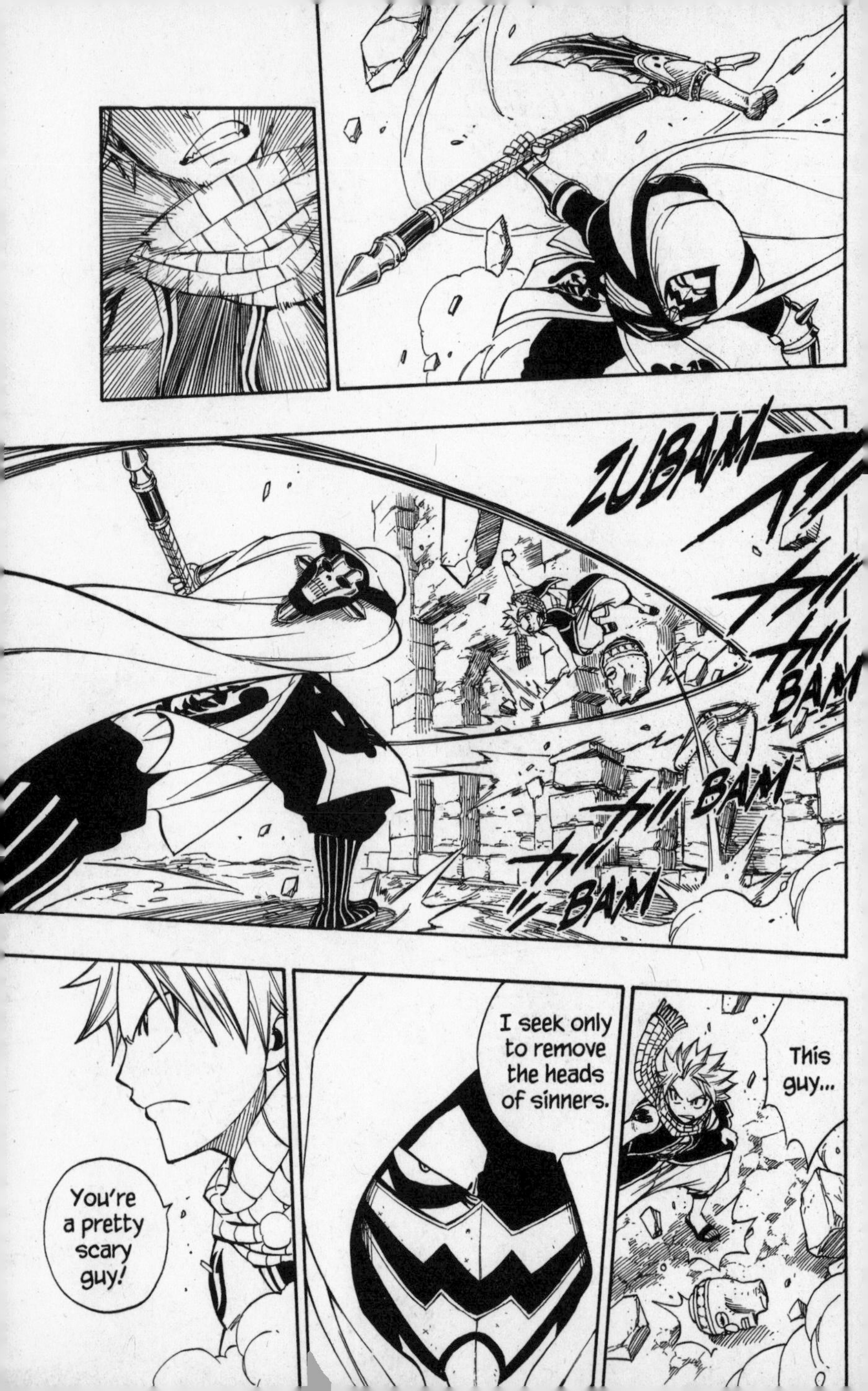
ZUBAM
BAM
BAM
BAM
This guy...
I seek only to remove the heads of sinners.
You're a pretty scary guy!

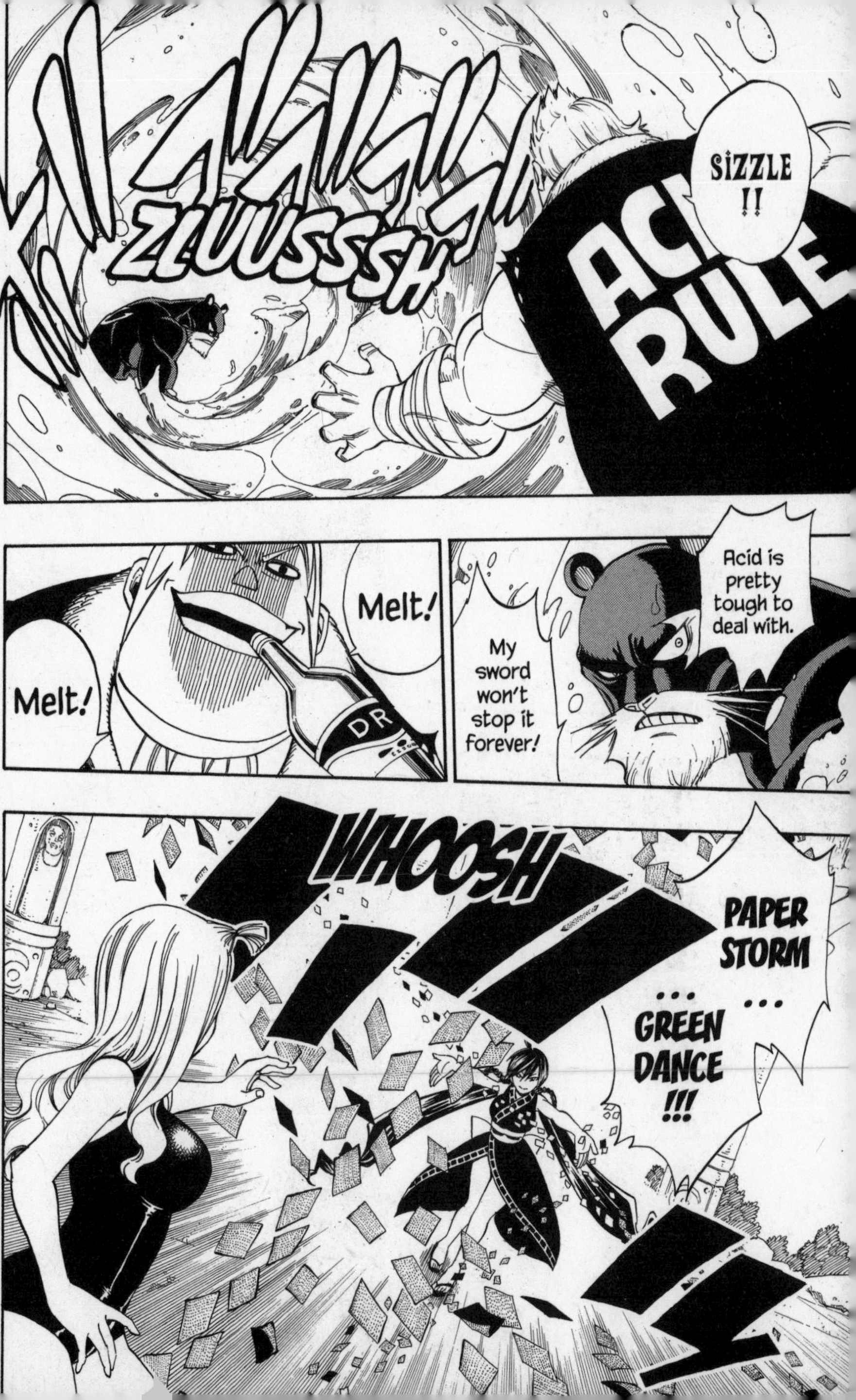
SIZZLE!!
ZLUUSSSH
Acid is pretty tough to deal with.
My sword won't stop it forever!
Melt!
Melt!
PAPER STORM ... ... GREEN DANCE!!!
WHOOSH

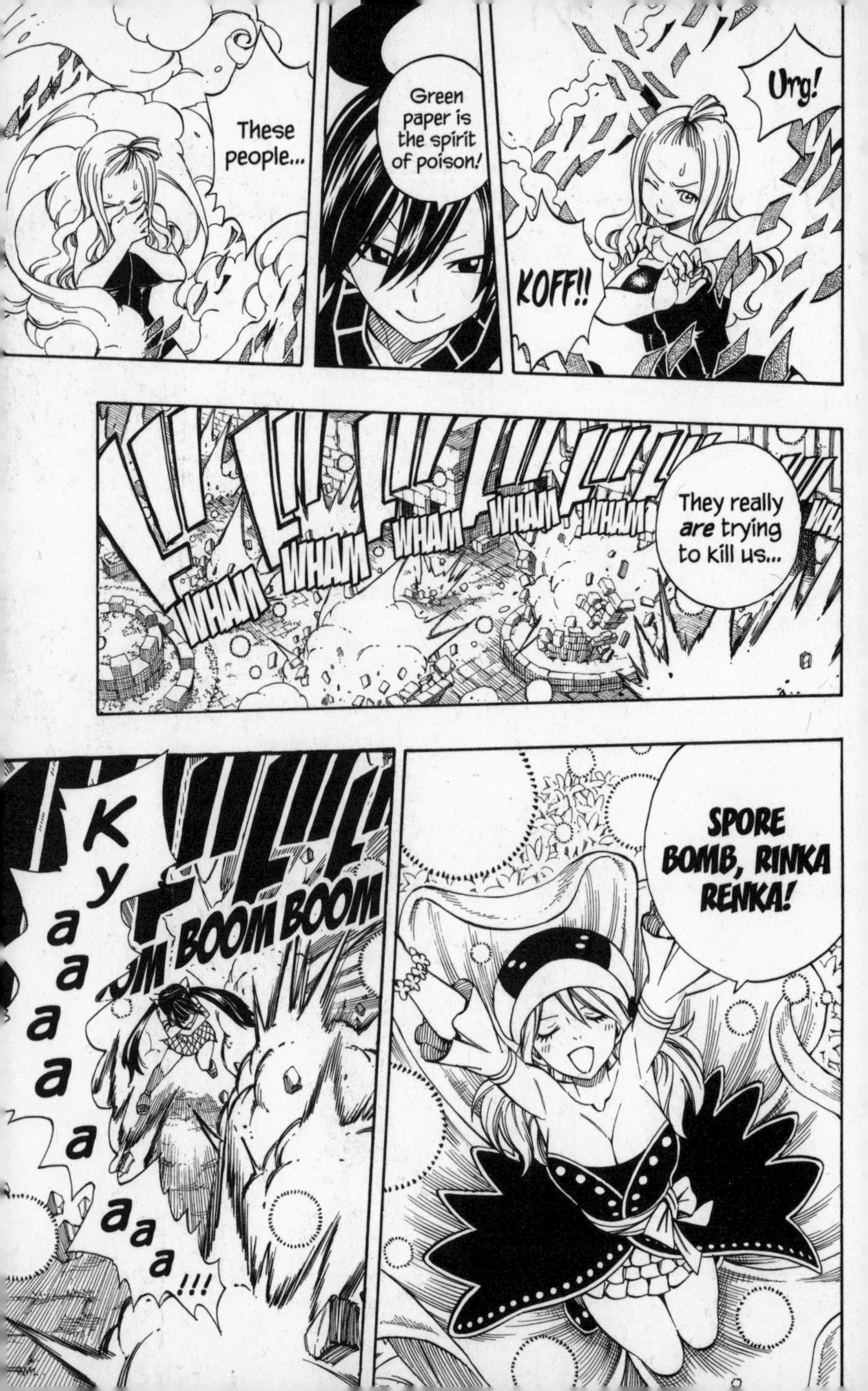
Urg!
KOFF!!
Green paper is the spirit of poison!
These people...
They really *are* trying to kill us...
WHAM WHAM WHAM WHAM WHAM WHAM
SPORE BOMB, RINKA RENKA!
BOOM BOOM
Kyaaaaaaaa!!!

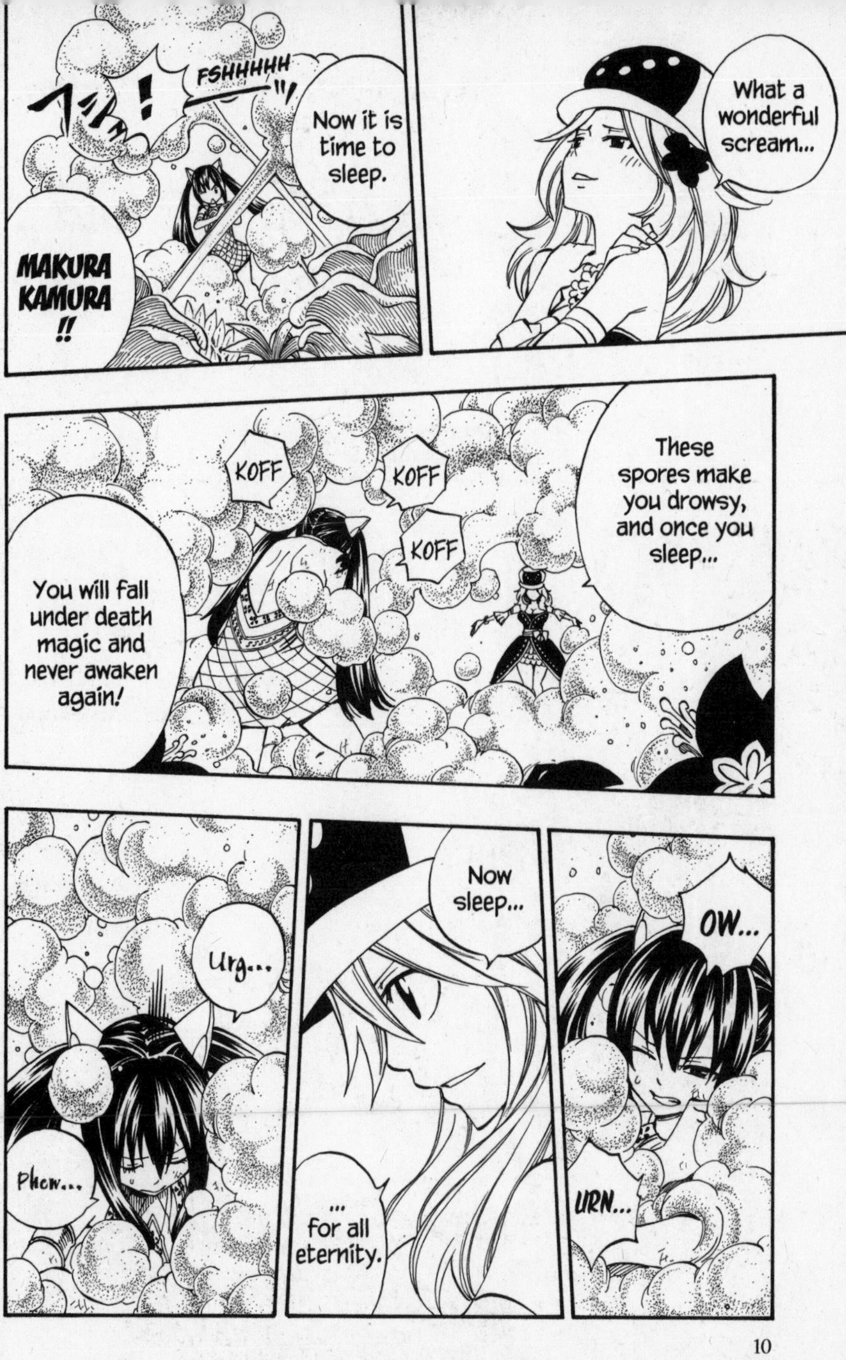
What a wonderful scream...
FSHHHHH
Now it is time to sleep.
MAKURA KAMURA !!
These spores make you drowsy, and once you sleep...
KOFF
KOFF
KOFF
You will fall under death magic and never awaken again!
OW...
URN...
Now sleep...
... for all eternity.
Urg...
Phew...

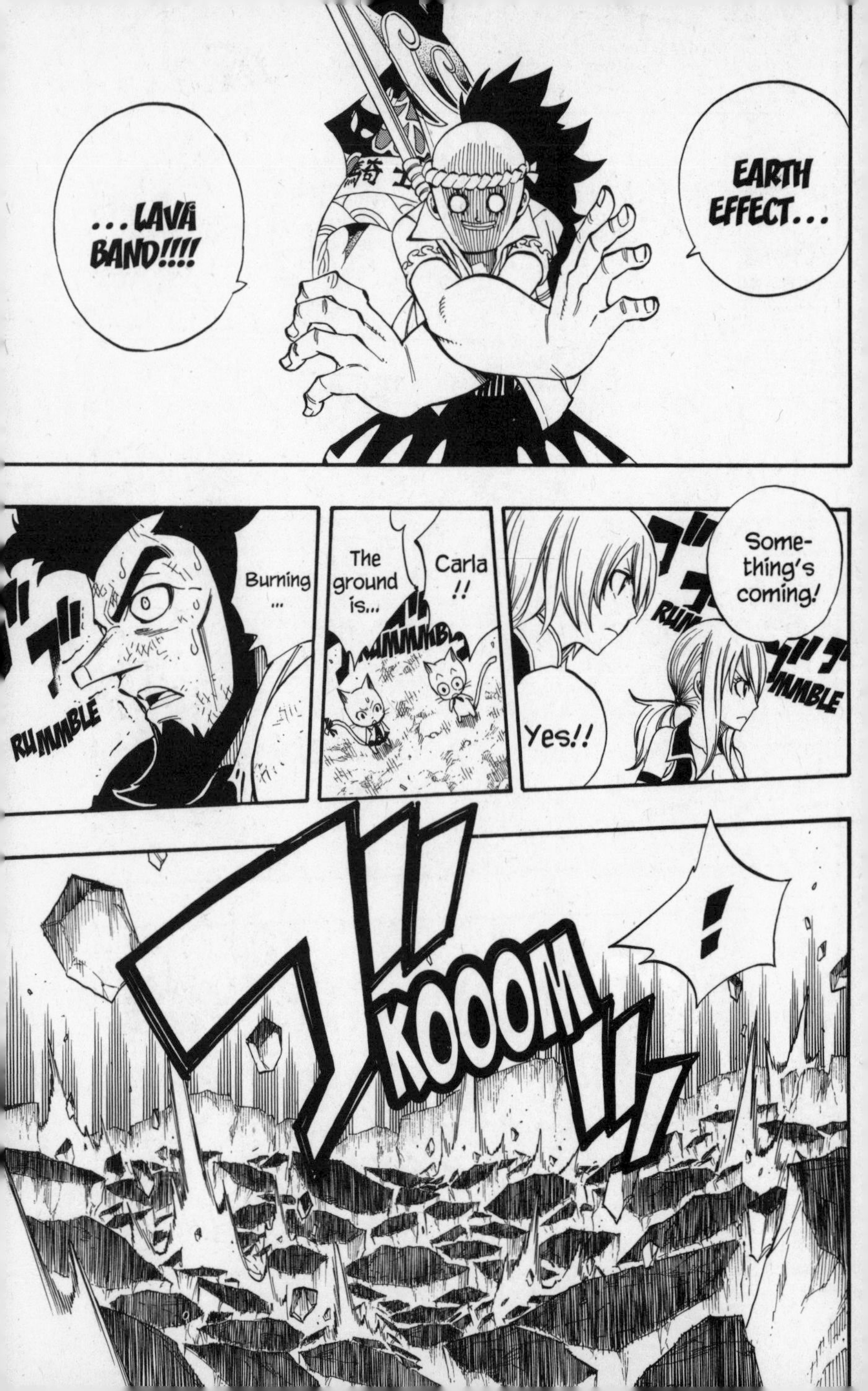
EARTH EFFECT...
...LAVA BAND!!!!
Some-thing's coming!
RUMMBLE
RUMMBLE
Yes!!
Carla!!
The ground is...
RUMMMBLE
Burning...
RUMMBLE
!
KOOOM

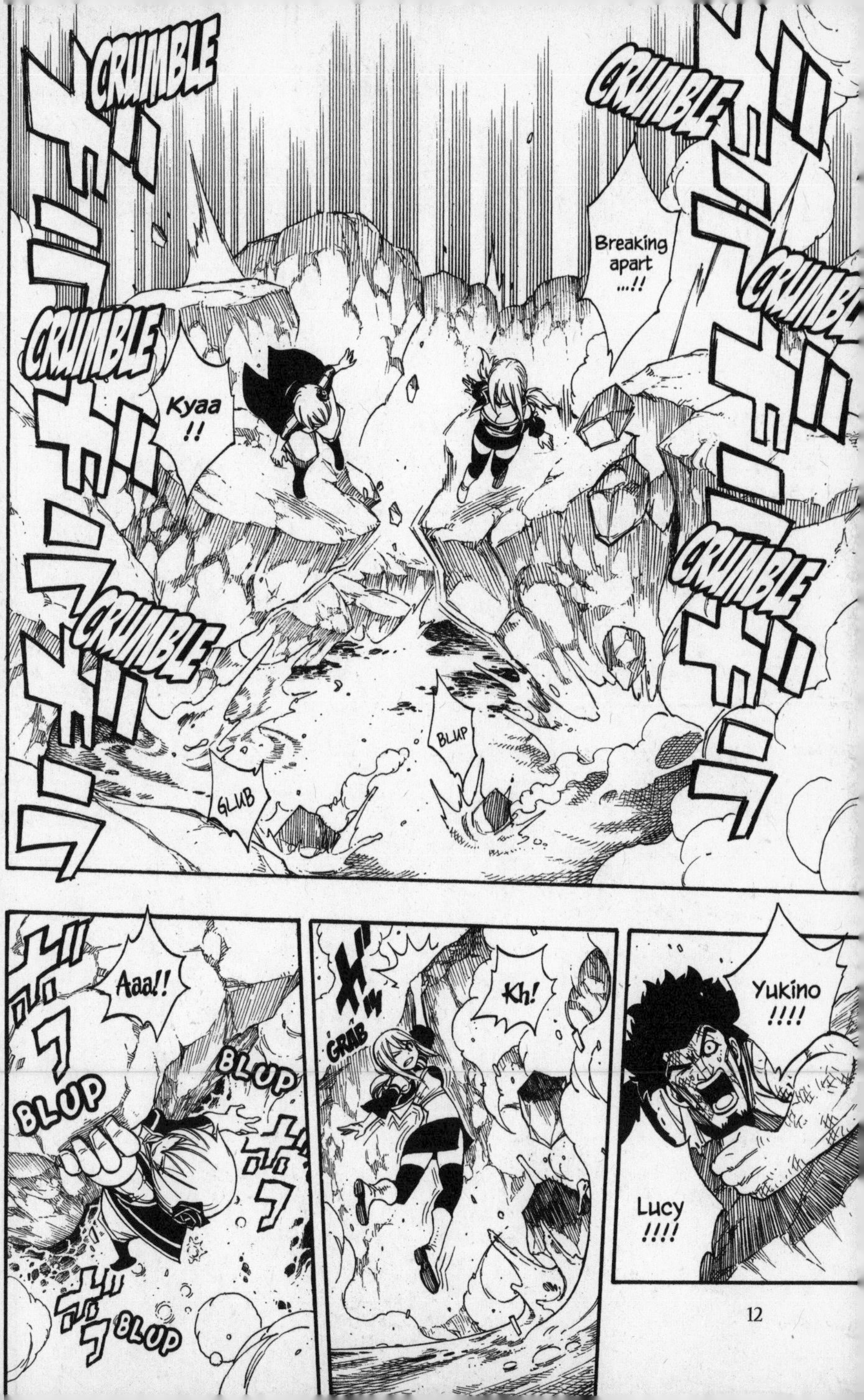
CRUMBLE
Breaking apart ...!!
CRUMBLE
CRUMBLE
Kyaa !!
CRUMBLE
CRUMBLE
CRUMBLE
BLUP
GLUB
Yukino !!!!
Lucy !!!!
Kh!
GRAB
Aaa!!
BLUP
BLUP
BLUP

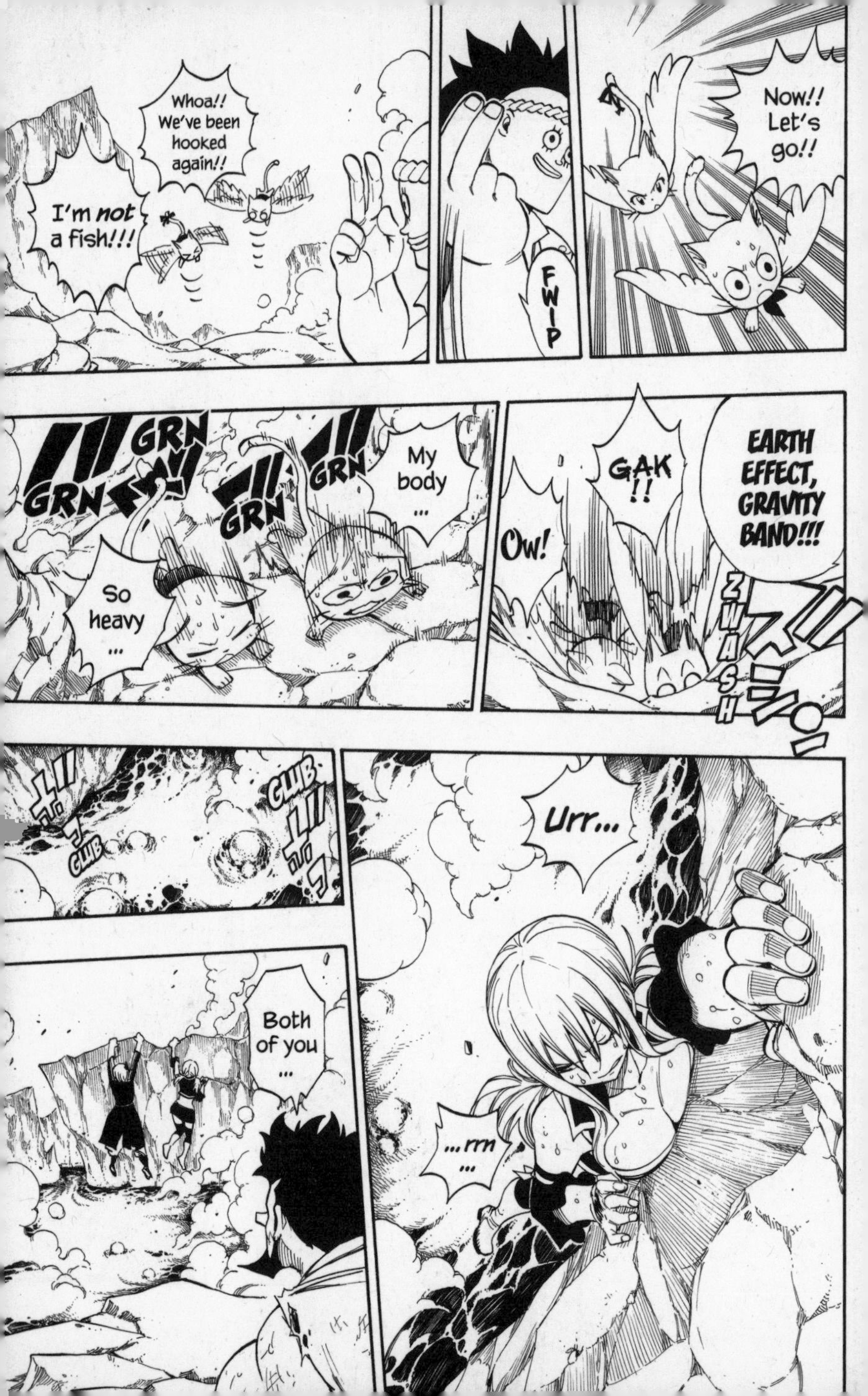
Now!! Let's go!!
FWIP
Whoa!! We've been hooked again!!
I'm *not* a fish!!!
EARTH EFFECT, GRAVITY BAND!!!
ZWASH
GAK!!
Ow!
My body ...
GRN
GRN
GRN
GRN
So heavy ...
Urr...
...rrn ...
GLUB
GLUB
Both of you ...

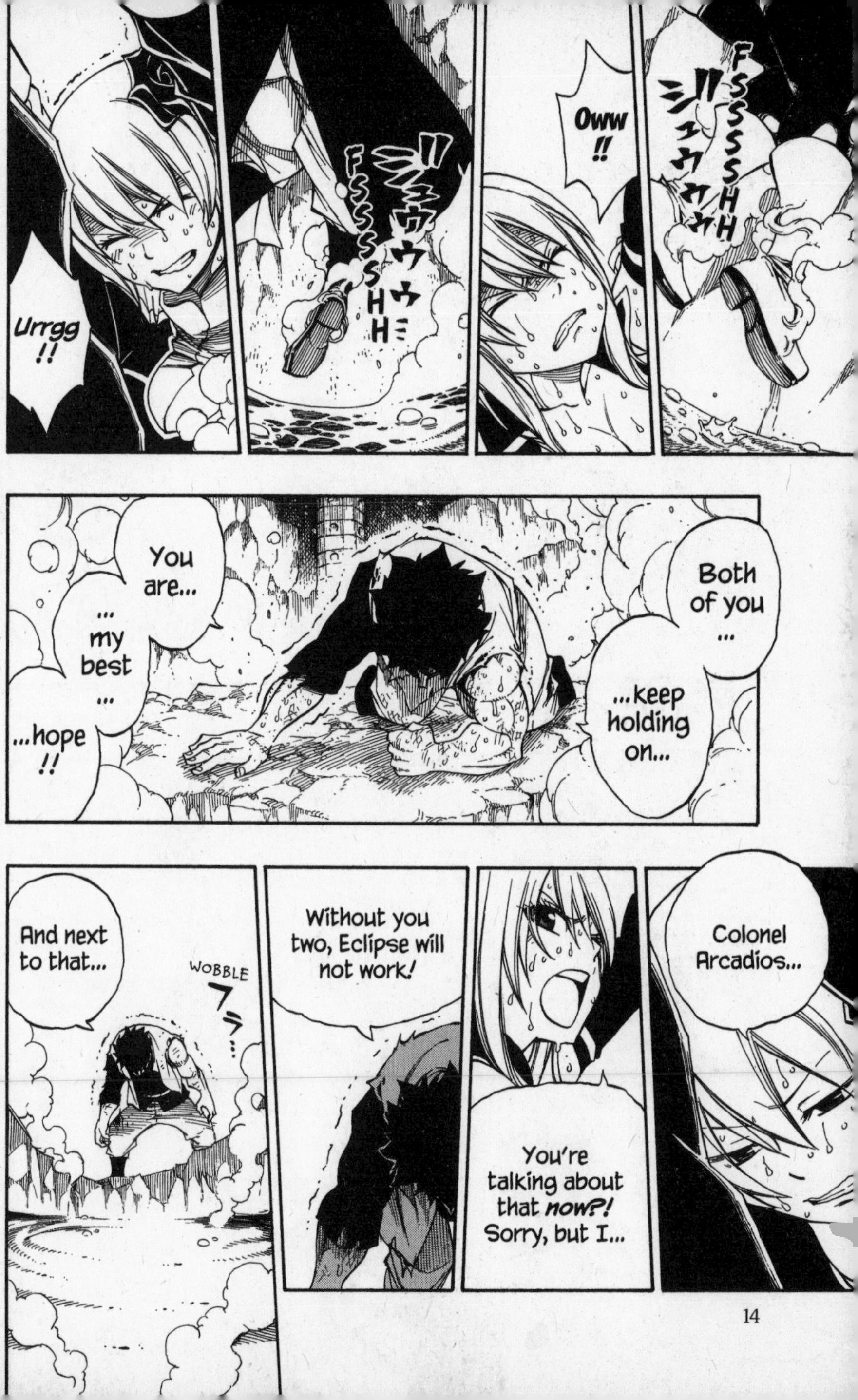

FSSSSHH
シュウウウ!!
Oww !!
FSSSSHH
ジュウウウ!!
Urrgg !!
Both of you ...
...keep holding on...
You are...
... my best ...
...hope !!
Colonel Arcadios...
You're talking about that *now?!* Sorry, but I...
Without you two, Eclipse will not work!
And next to that...
WOBBLE
フラ...

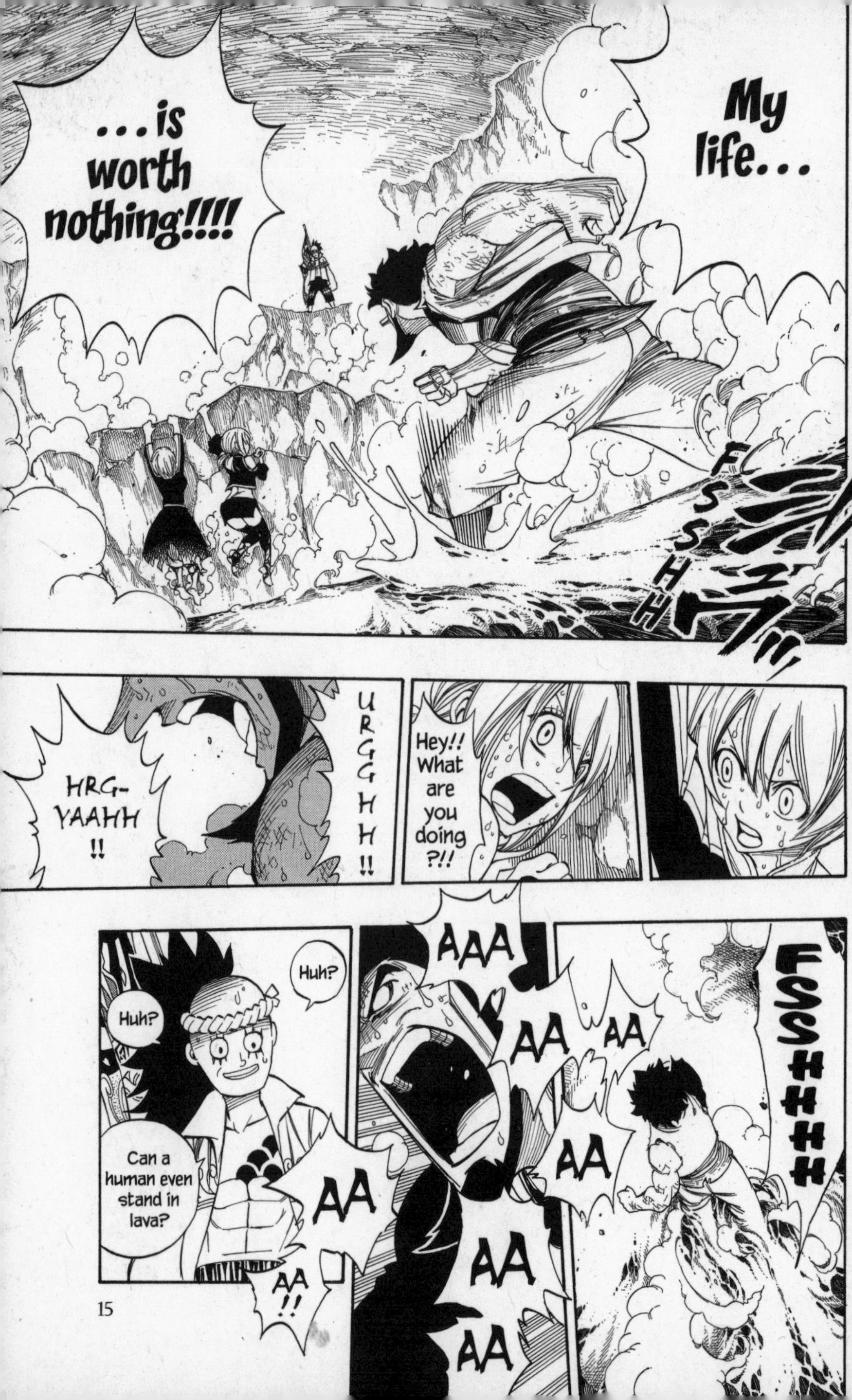
My life...
...is worth nothing!!!!
FSSHH
URGGHH!!
HRG-YAAHH!!
Hey!! What are you doing?!!
FSSHHHHH
AAA
AA
AA
AA
AA
AA
AA
AA!!
Huh?
Huh?
Can a human even stand in lava?

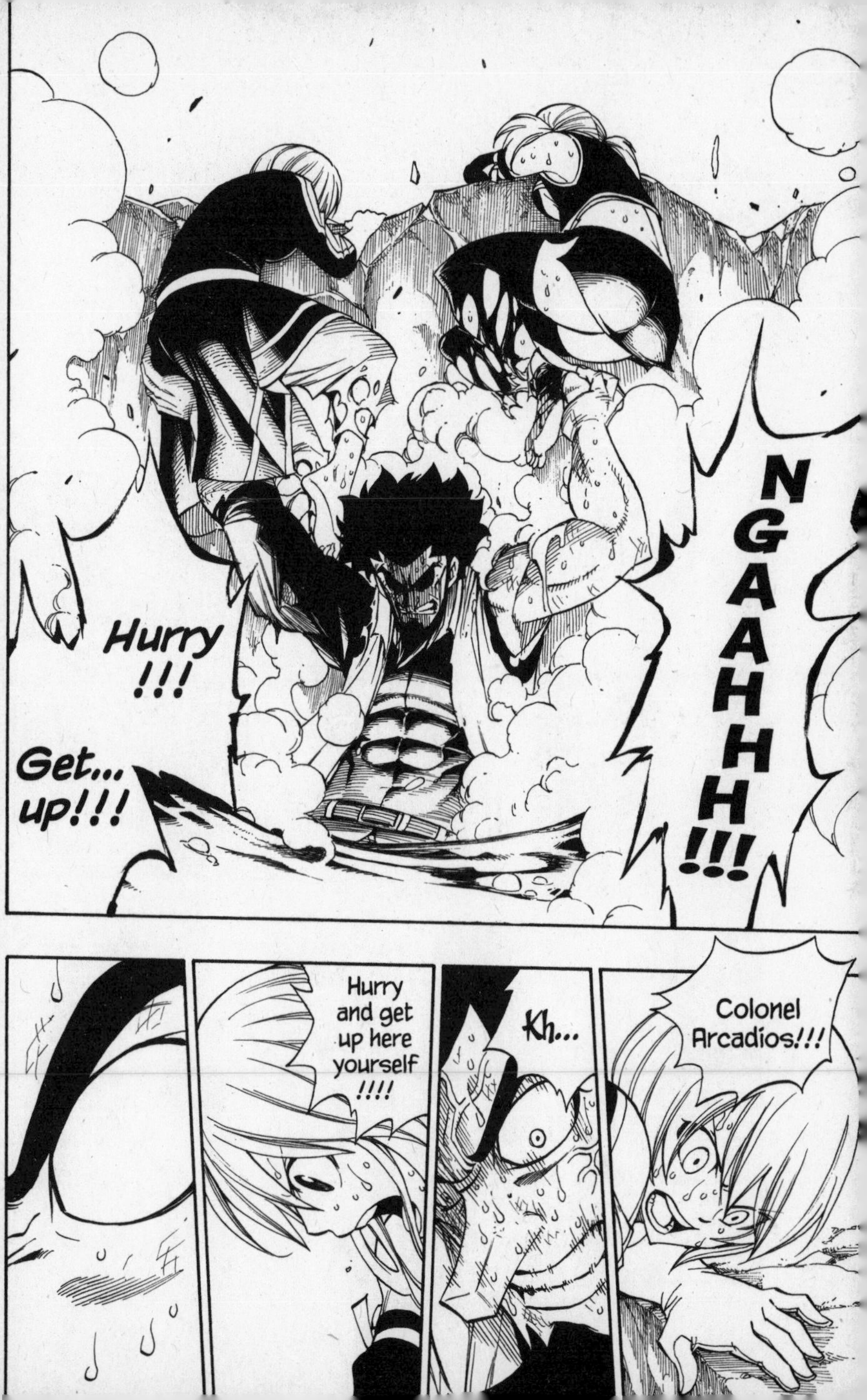
NGAAHHH!!!
Hurry!!!
Get... up!!!
Colonel Arcadios!!!
Kh...
Hurry and get up here yourself!!!!

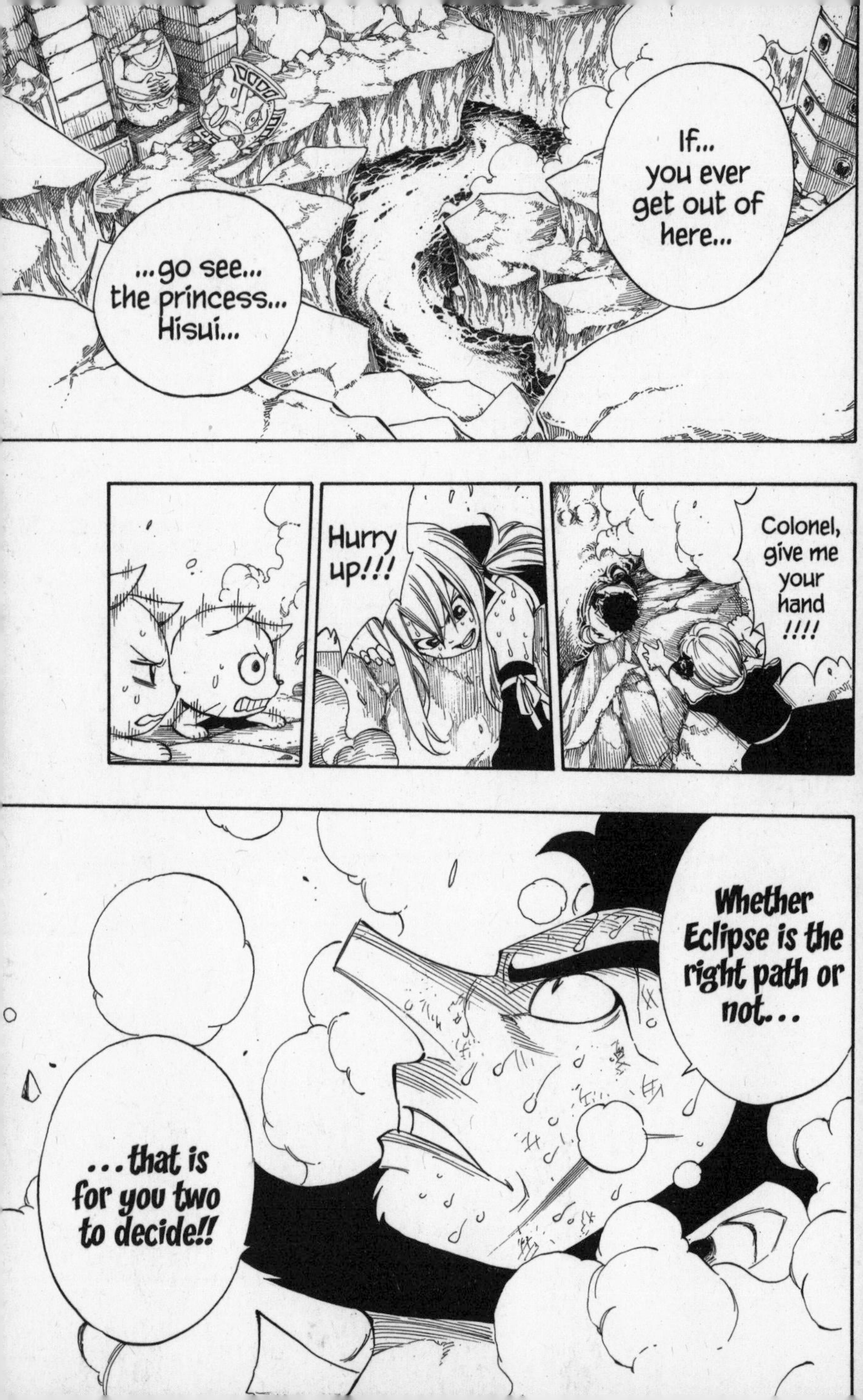
If... you ever get out of here...
...go see... the princess... Hisui...
Colonel, give me your hand!!!!
Hurry up!!!
Whether Eclipse is the right path or not...
...that is for you two to decide!!

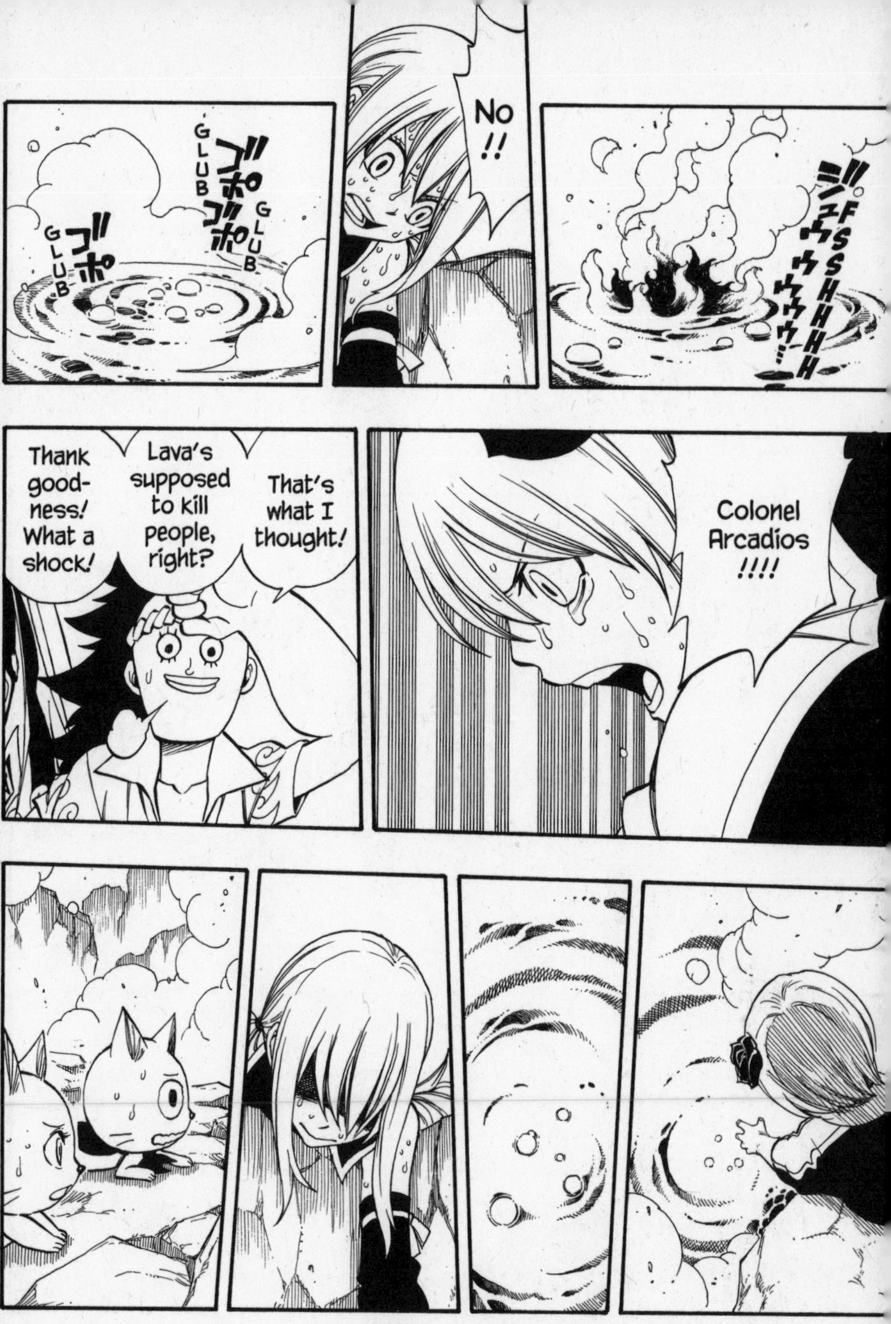
FSSHHHH
ジュウウウウウ
No!!
GLUB GLUB
ゴポゴポ
GLUB
ゴポ
Colonel Arcadios!!!!
That's what I thought!
Lava's supposed to kill people, right?
Thank goodness! What a shock!

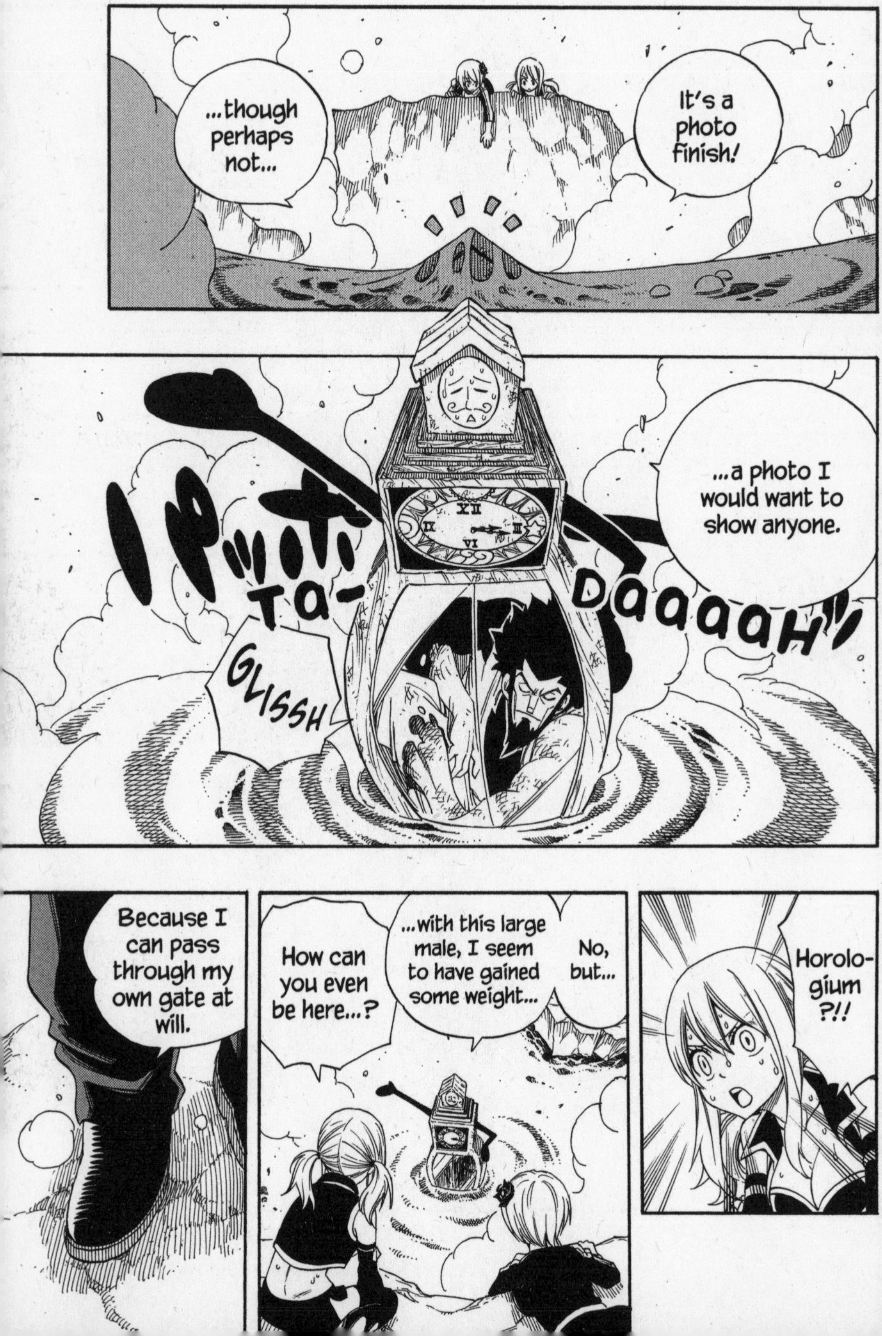

It's a photo finish!
...though perhaps not...
...a photo I would want to show anyone.
TA-DAAAAH!!
GLISSH
Horolo-gium ?!!
No, but...
...with this large male, I seem to have gained some weight...
How can you even be here...?
Because I can pass through my own gate at will.

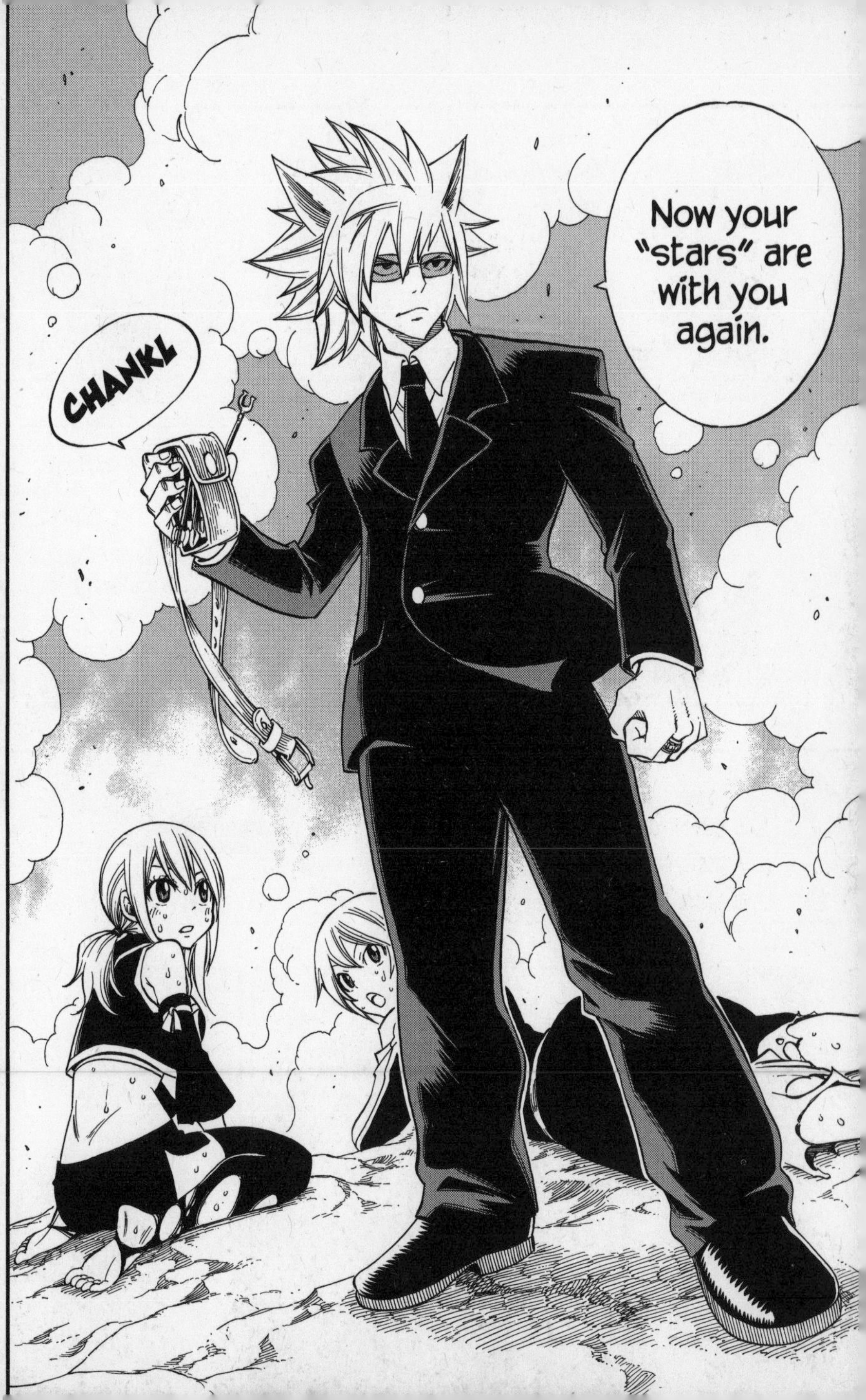
Now your "stars" are with you again.
CHANK!

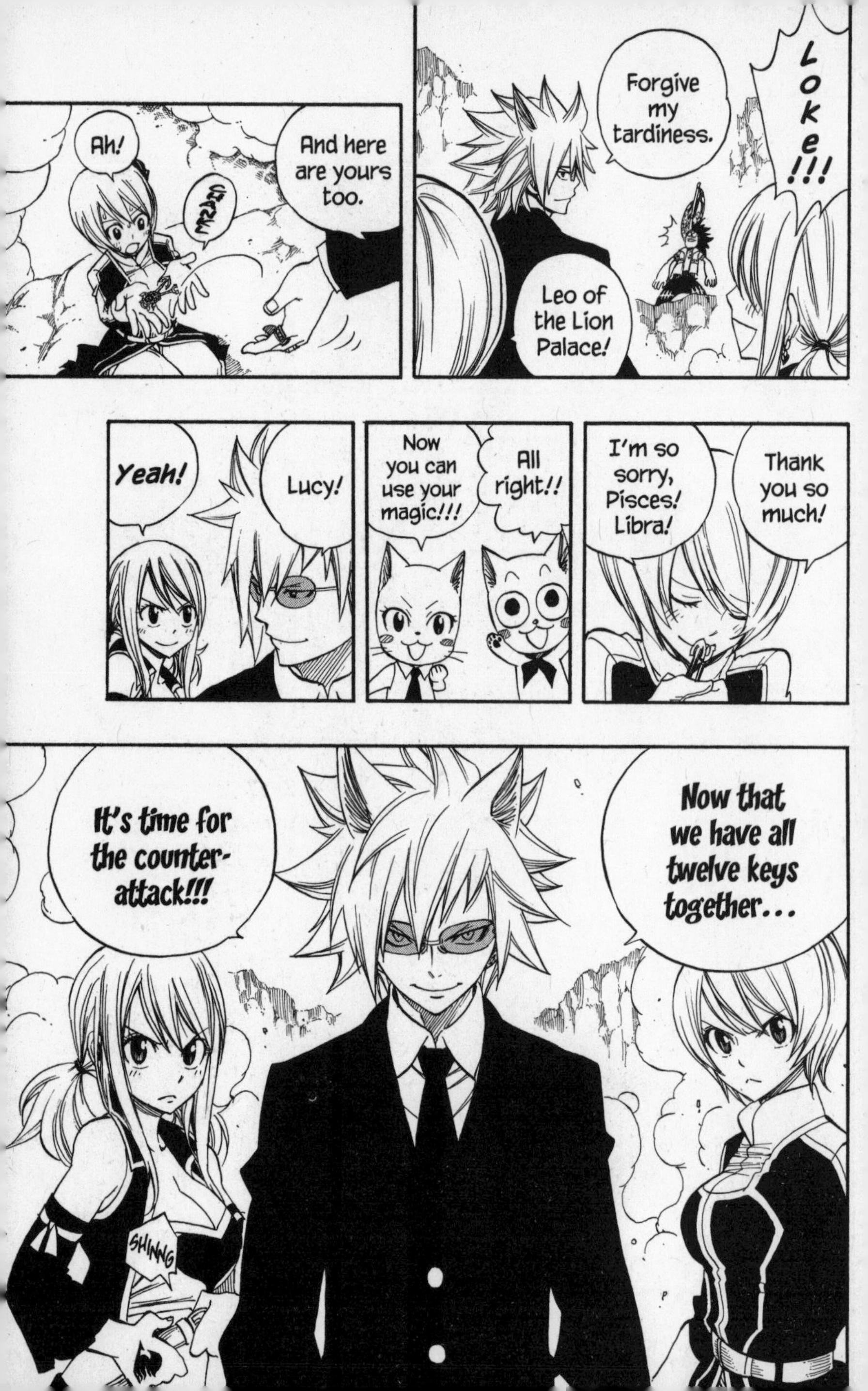
Loke!!!
Forgive my tardiness.
Leo of the Lion Palace!
And here are yours too.
Ah!
Thank you so much!
I'm so sorry, Pisces! Libra!
All right!!
Now you can use your magic!!!
Lucy!
Yeah!
Now that we have all twelve keys together...
It's time for the counter-attack!!!
SHINNG

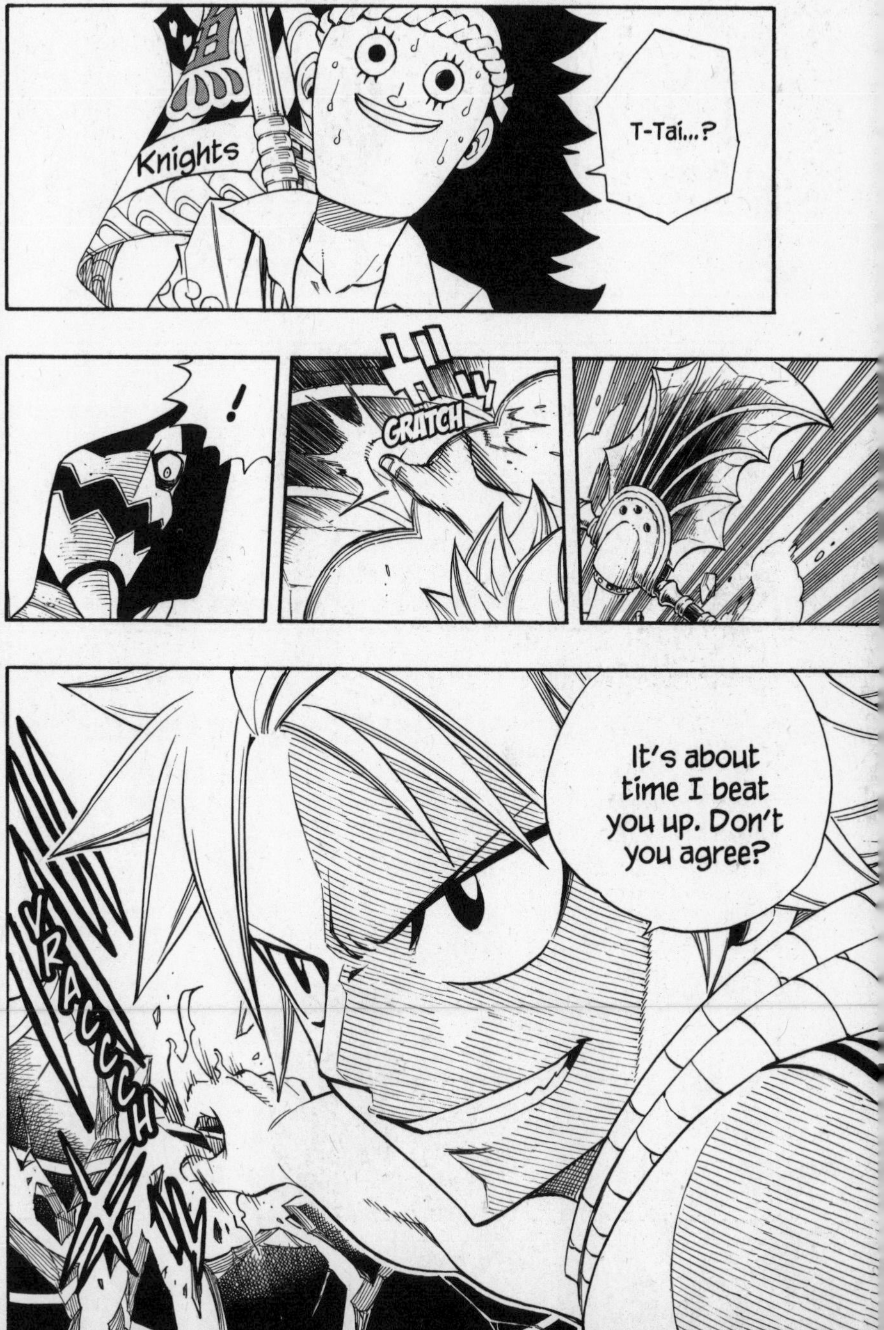
T-Tai...?
Knights
GRATCH
!
It's about time I beat you up. Don't you agree?
VRAUCCH

FAIRY TAIL

フェアリーテイル

Chapter 310: The Place Where We Are

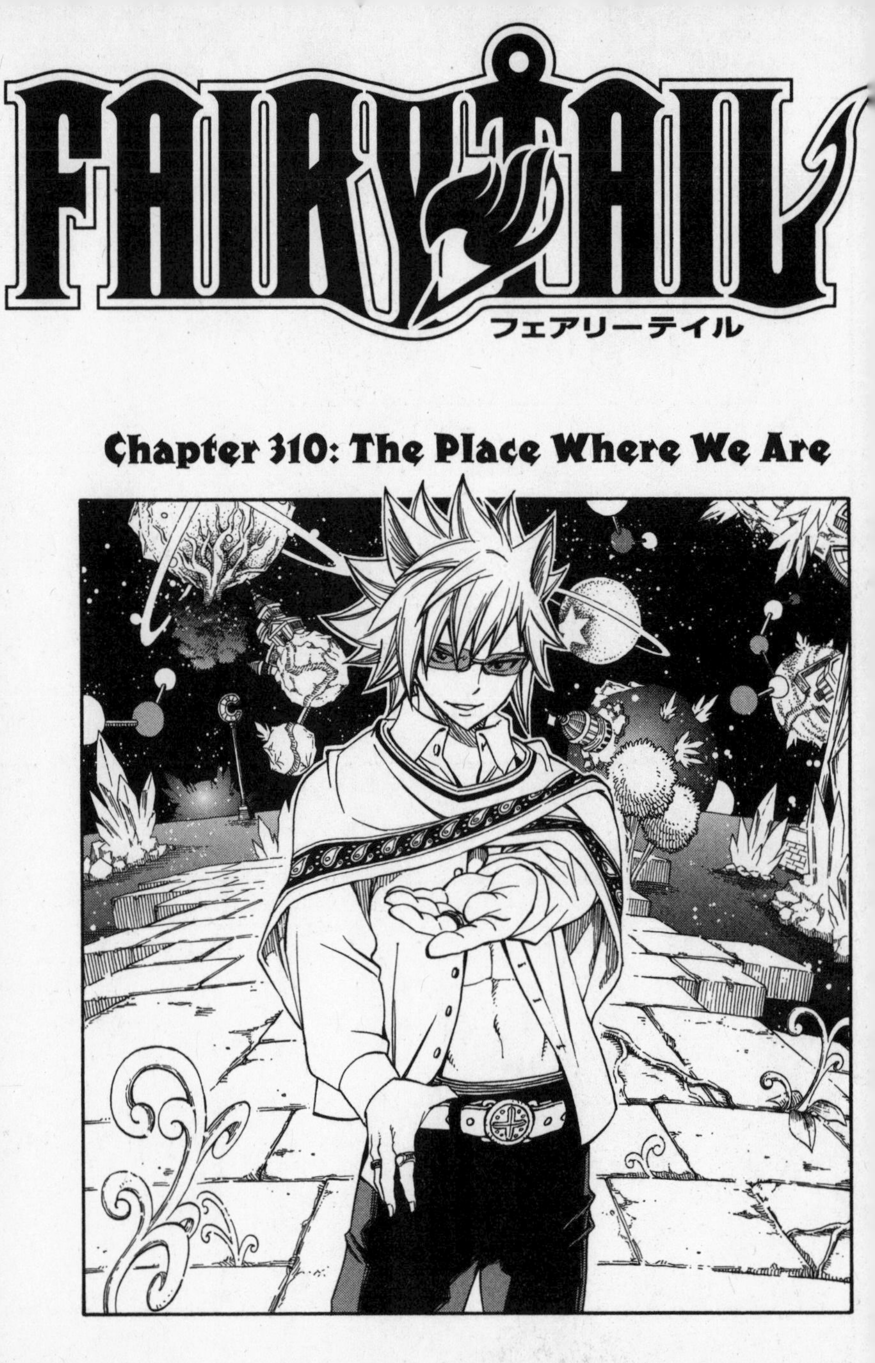

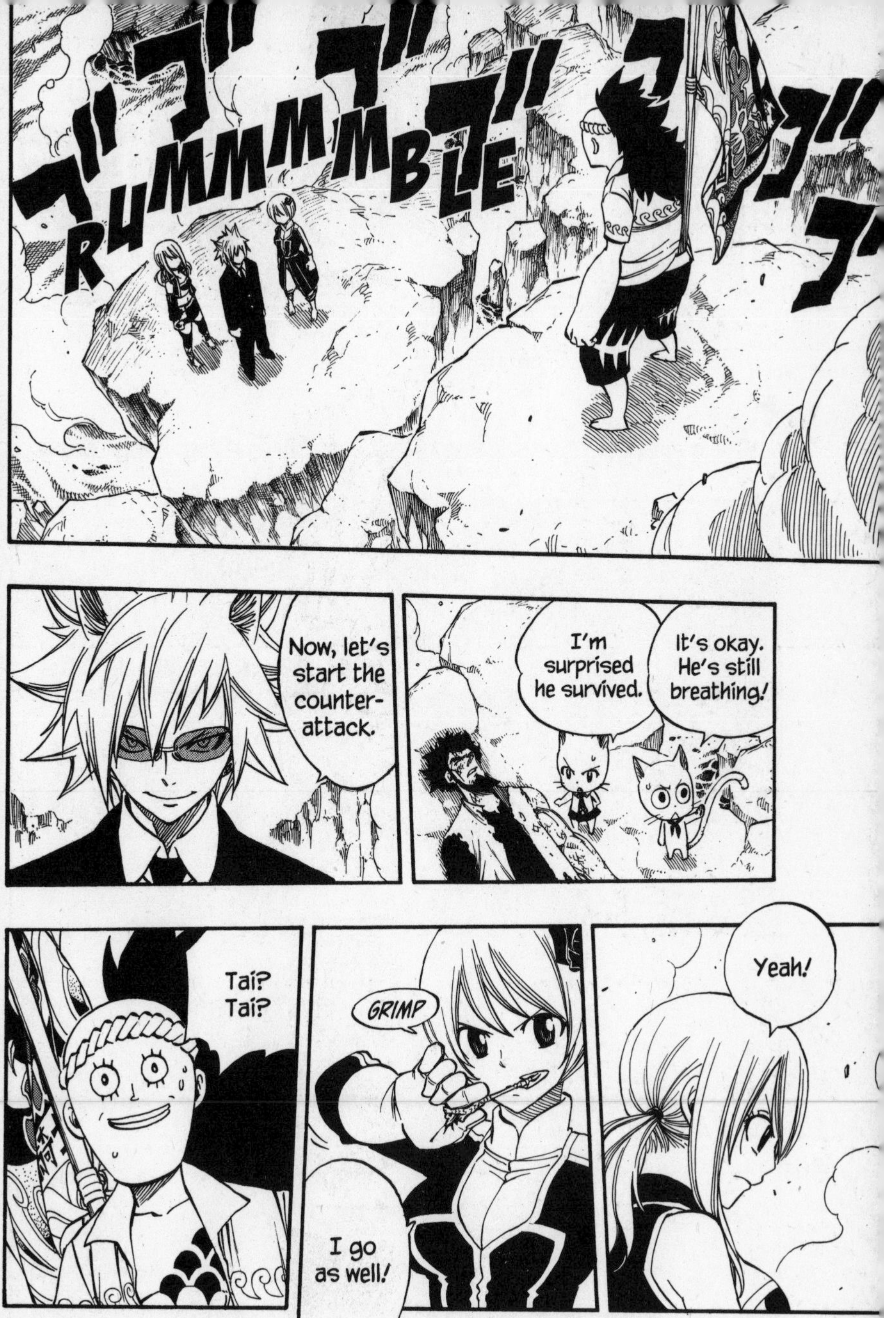
RUMMMMMBLE
It's okay. He's still breathing!
I'm surprised he survived.
Now, let's start the counter-attack.
Yeah!
GRIMP
I go as well!
Tai? Tai?

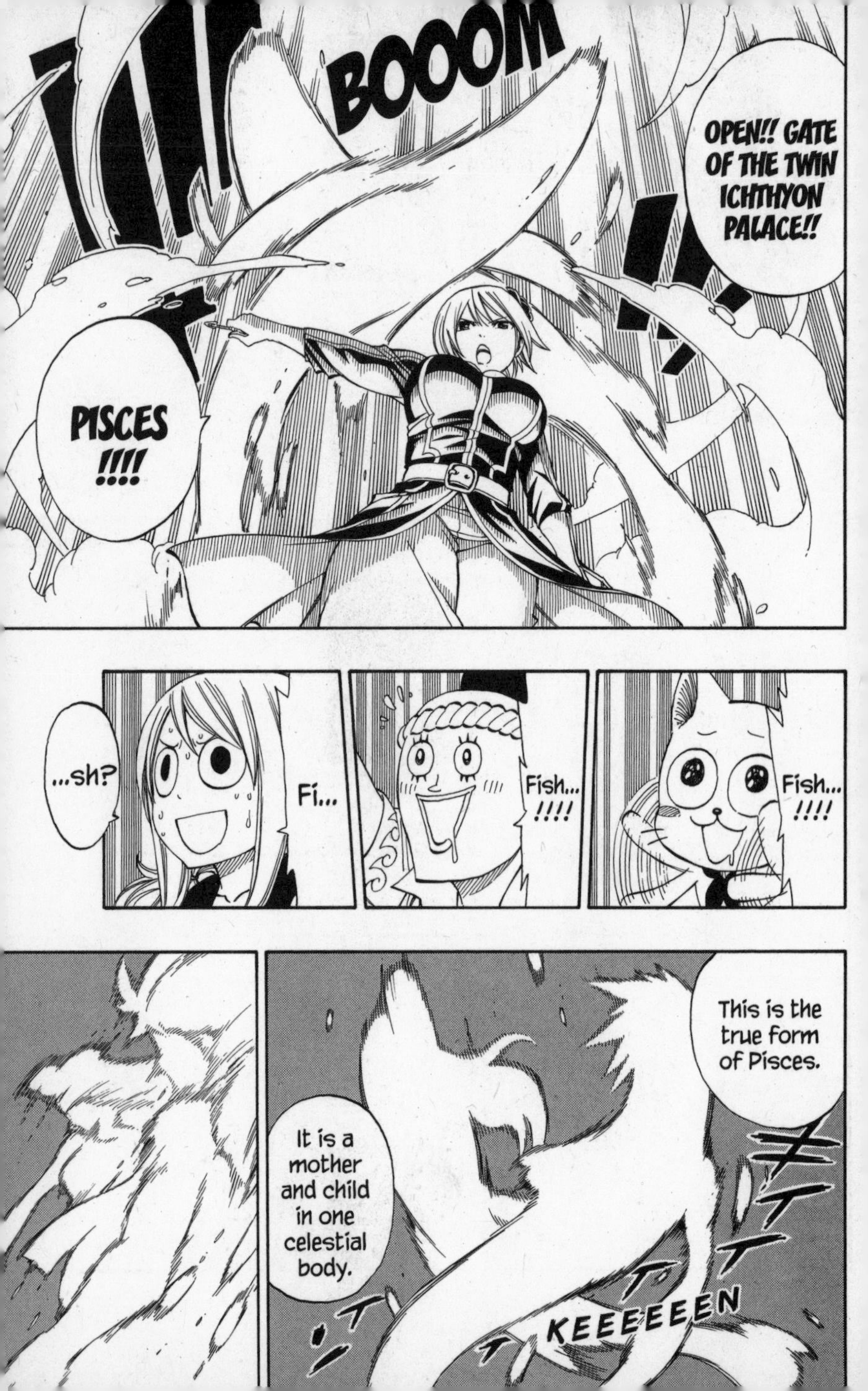
BOOOM
OPEN!! GATE OF THE TWIN ICHTHYON PALACE!!
PISCES !!!!
Fish... !!!!
Fish... !!!!
Fi...
...sh?
This is the true form of Pisces.
It is a mother and child in one celestial body.
KEEEEEEN

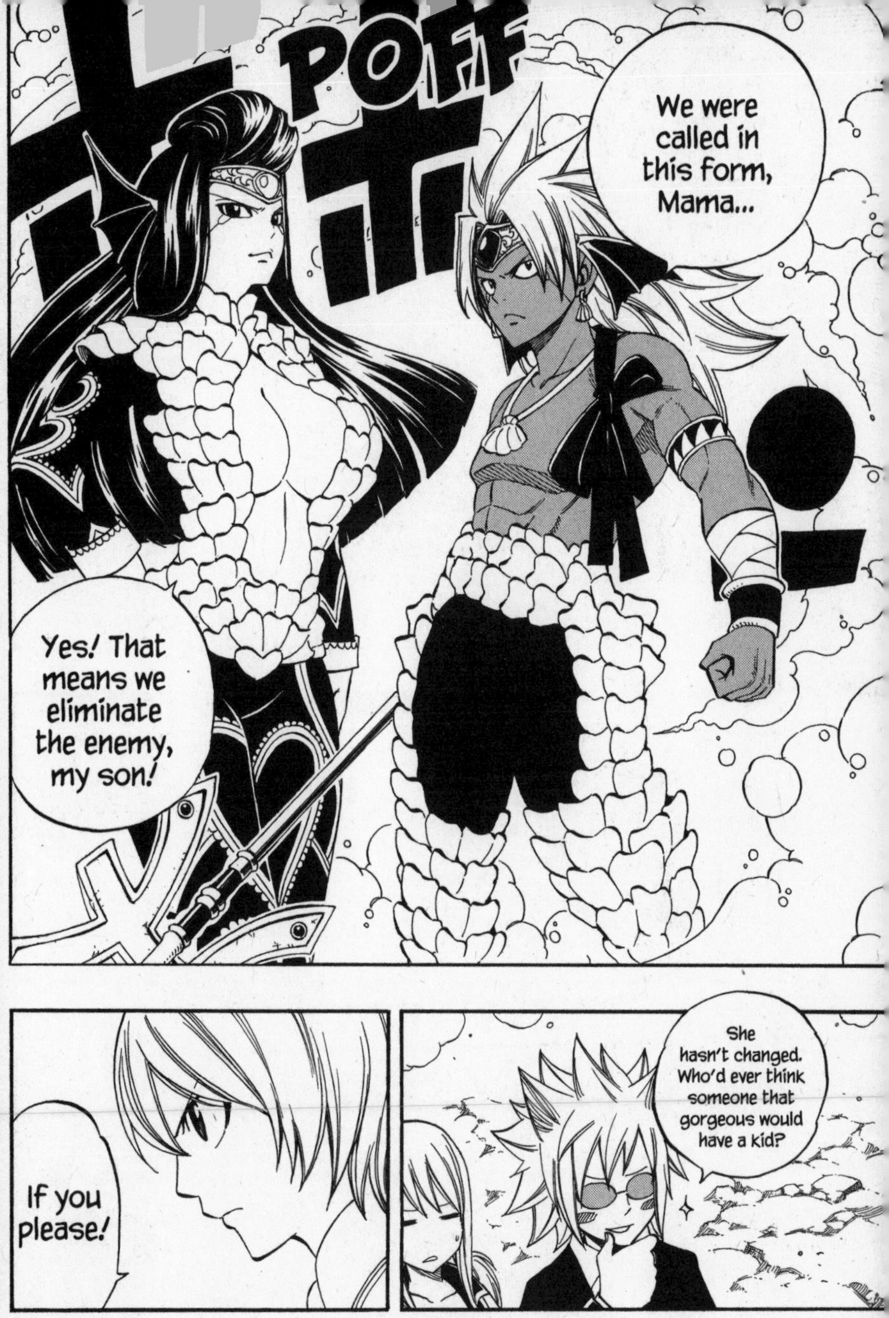
POFF
We were called in this form, Mama...
Yes! That means we eliminate the enemy, my son!
She hasn't changed. Who'd ever think someone that gorgeous would have a kid?
If you please!

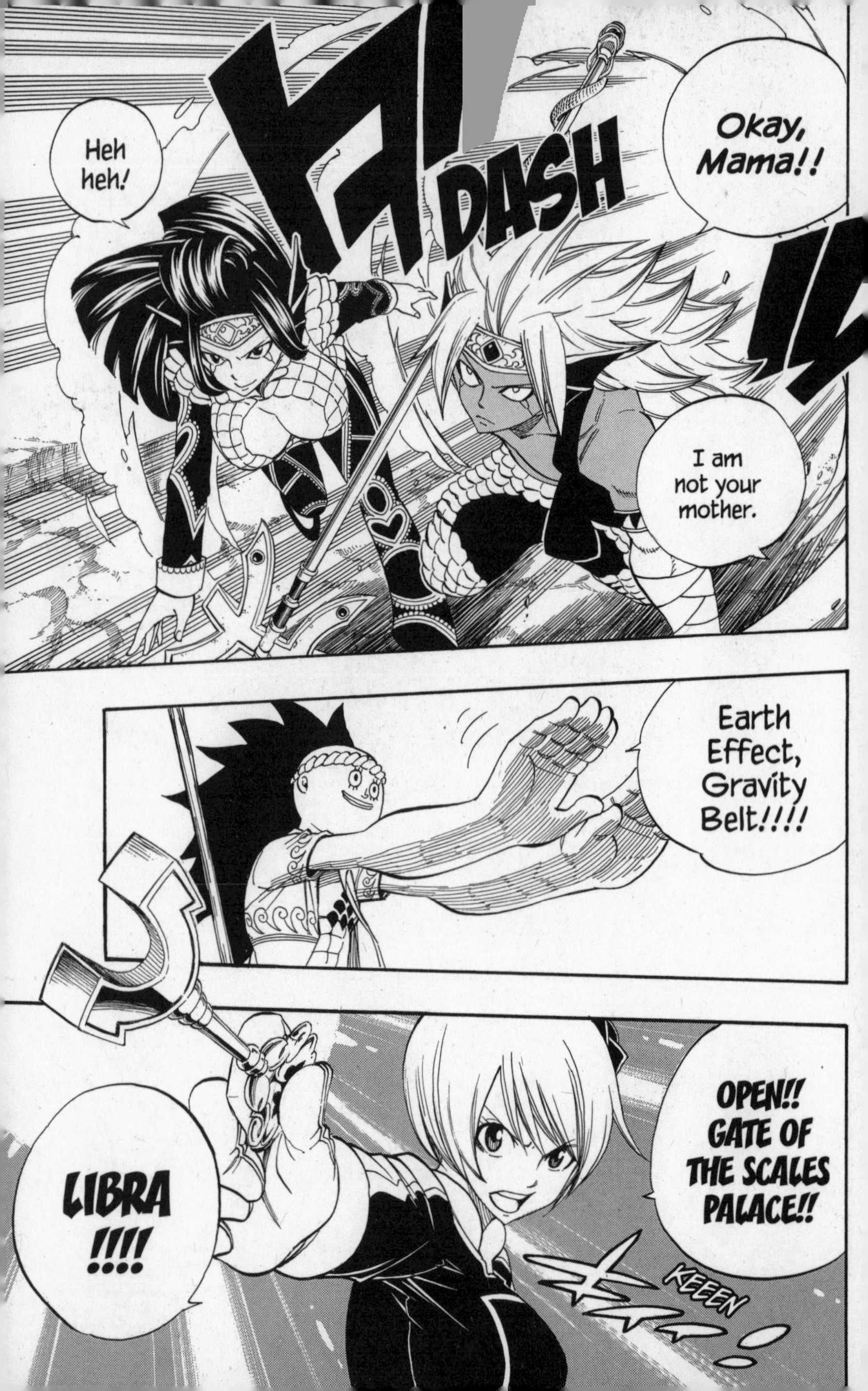
Okay, Mama!!
DASH
Heh heh!
I am not your mother.
Earth Effect, Gravity Belt!!!!
OPEN!! GATE OF THE SCALES PALACE!!
KEEEN
LIBRA!!!!

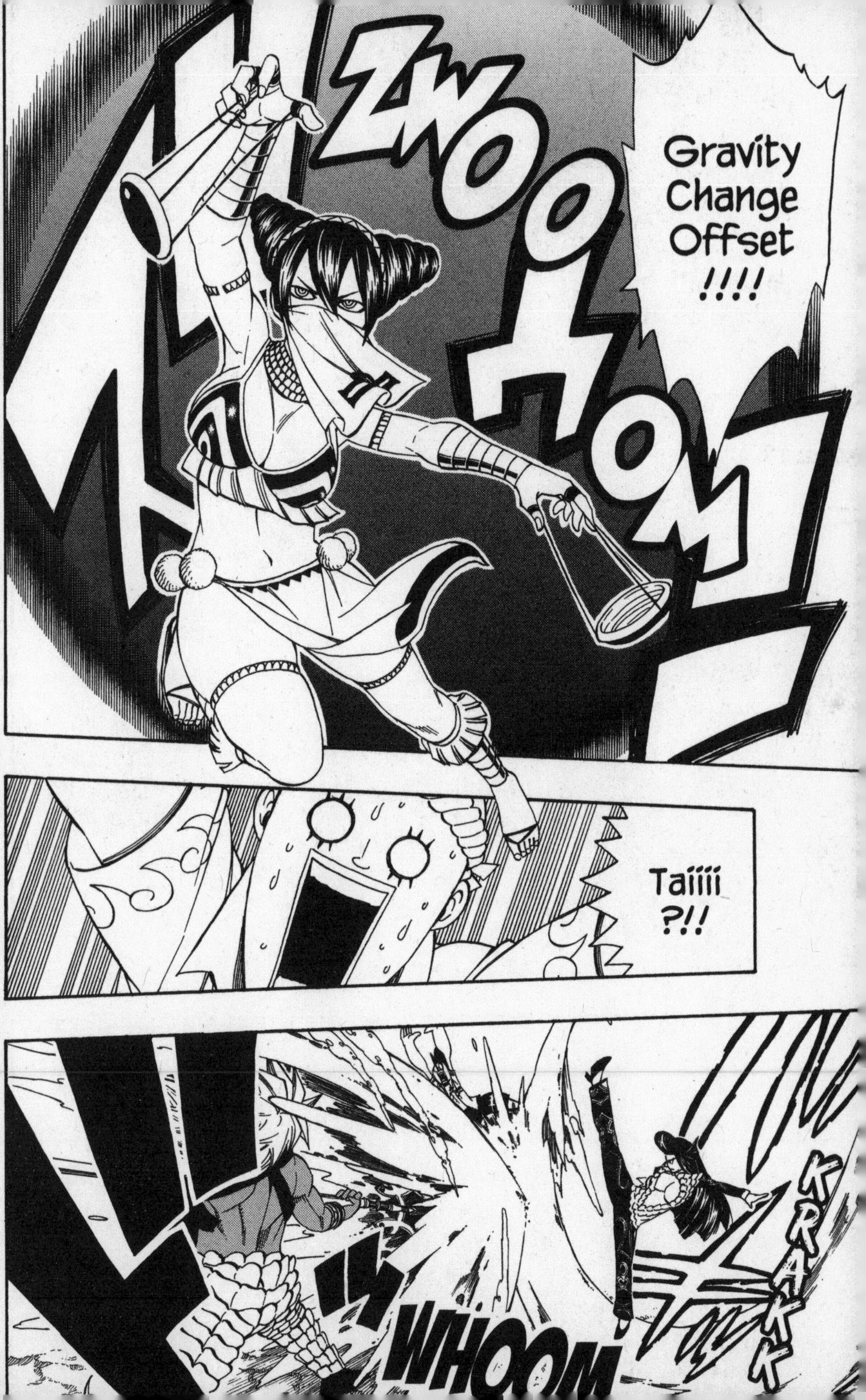
ZWOOOOM
Gravity Change Offset !!!!
Taiiii ?!!
KRAKK
WHOOM

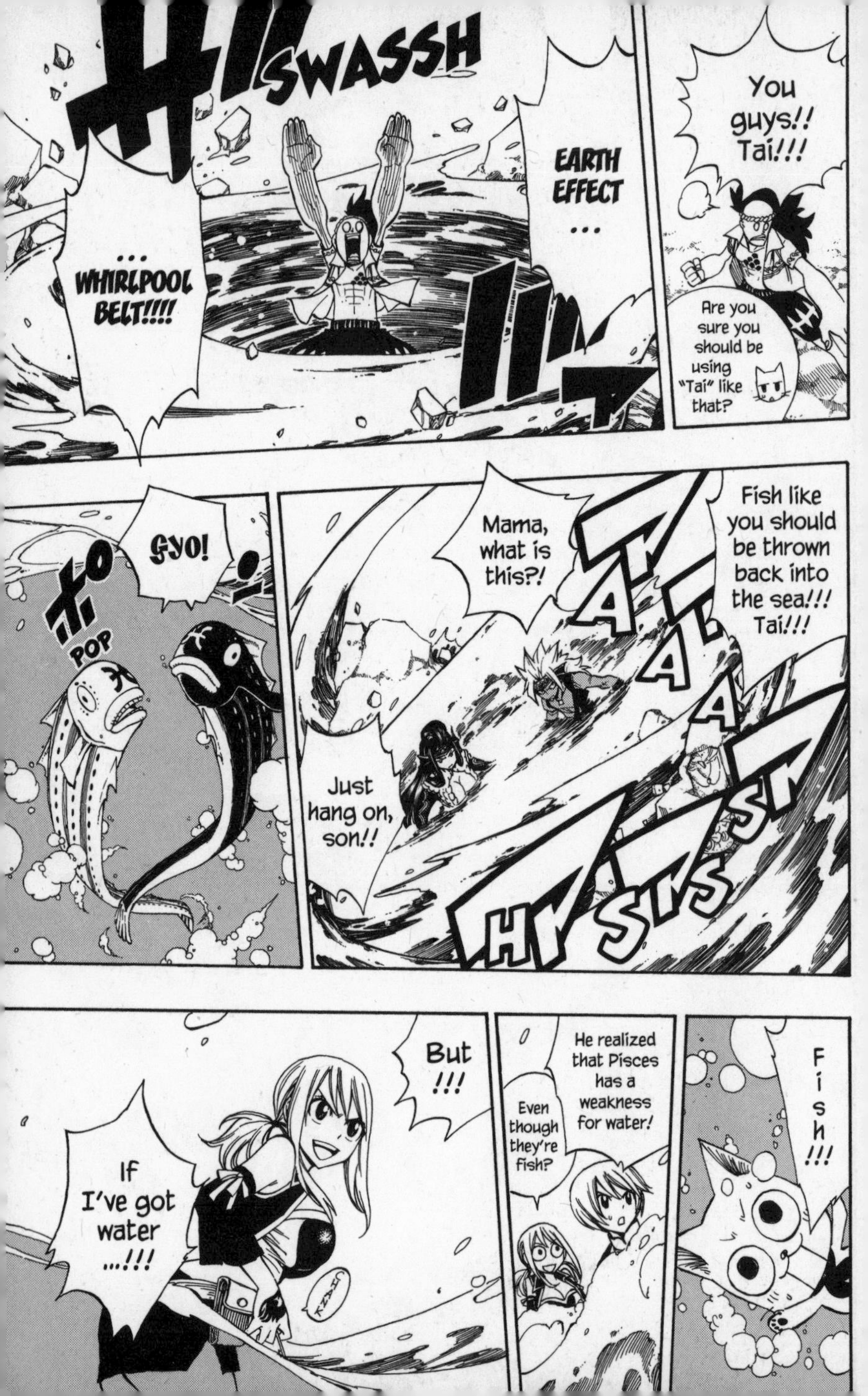
You guys!! Tai!!!
Are you sure you should be using "Tai" like that?
EARTH EFFECT ...
SWASSH
... WHIRLPOOL BELT!!!!
Fish like you should be thrown back into the sea!!! Tai!!!
Mama, what is this?!
Just hang on, son!!
GYO!
POP
Fish!!!
He realized that Pisces has a weakness for water!
Even though they're fish?
But !!!
If I've got water ...!!!

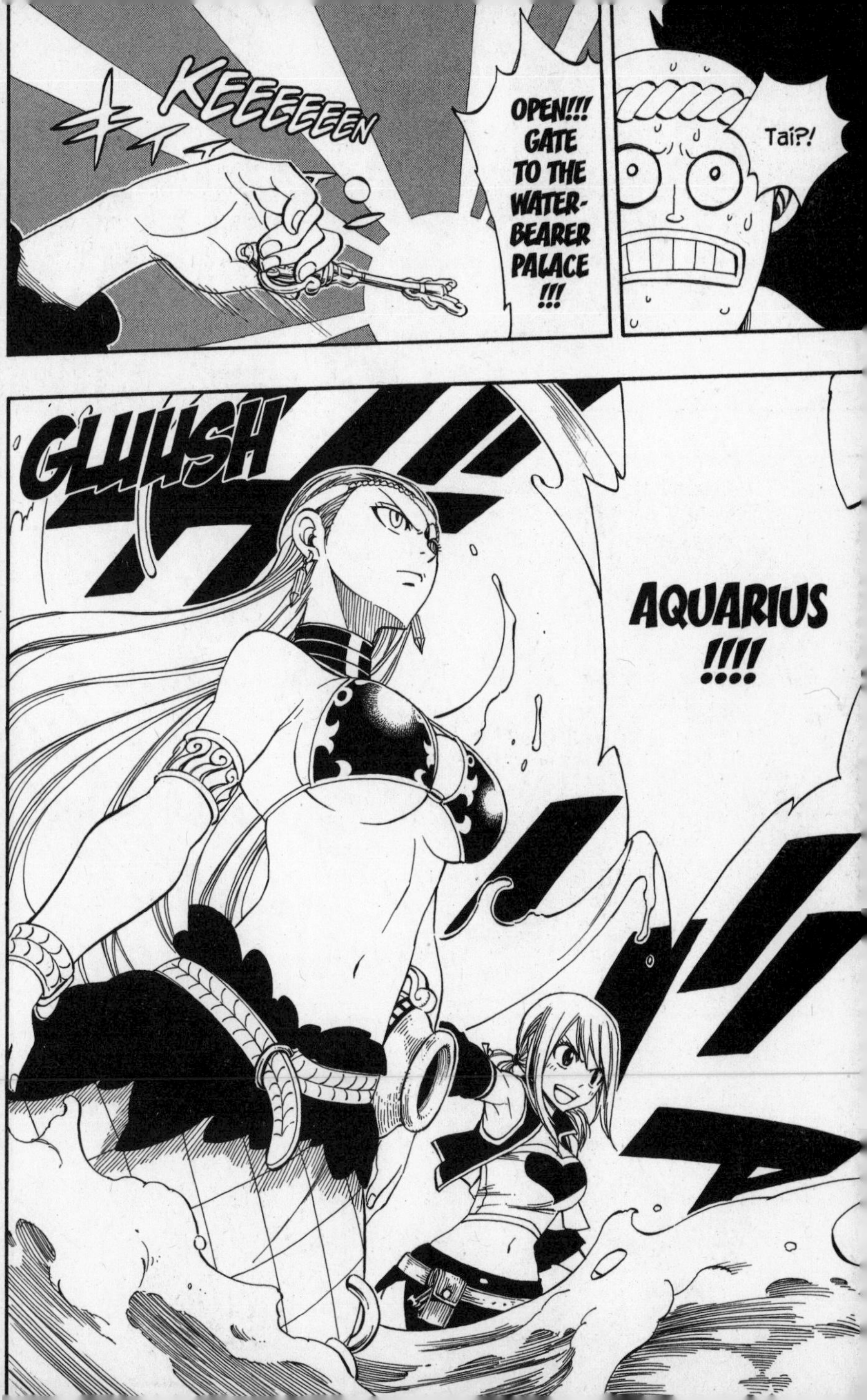

Tai?!
OPEN!!! GATE TO THE WATER-BEARER PALACE !!!
KEEEEEEEN
AQUARIUS !!!!
GLUUSH

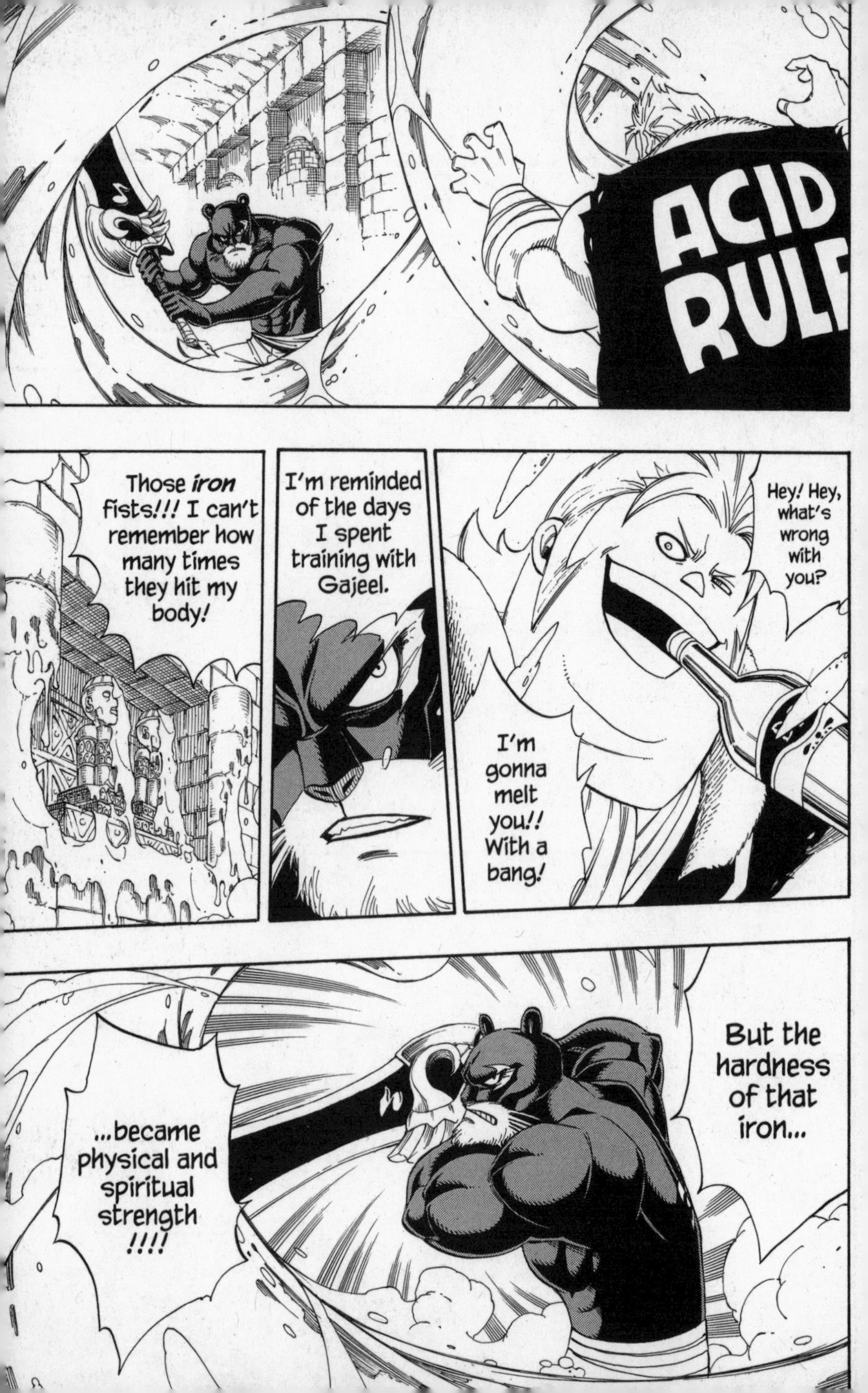
ACID
RULE
Hey! Hey, what's wrong with you?
I'm gonna melt you!! With a bang!
I'm reminded of the days I spent training with Gajeel.
Those *iron* fists!!! I can't remember how many times they hit my body!
But the hardness of that iron...
...became physical and spiritual strength !!!!

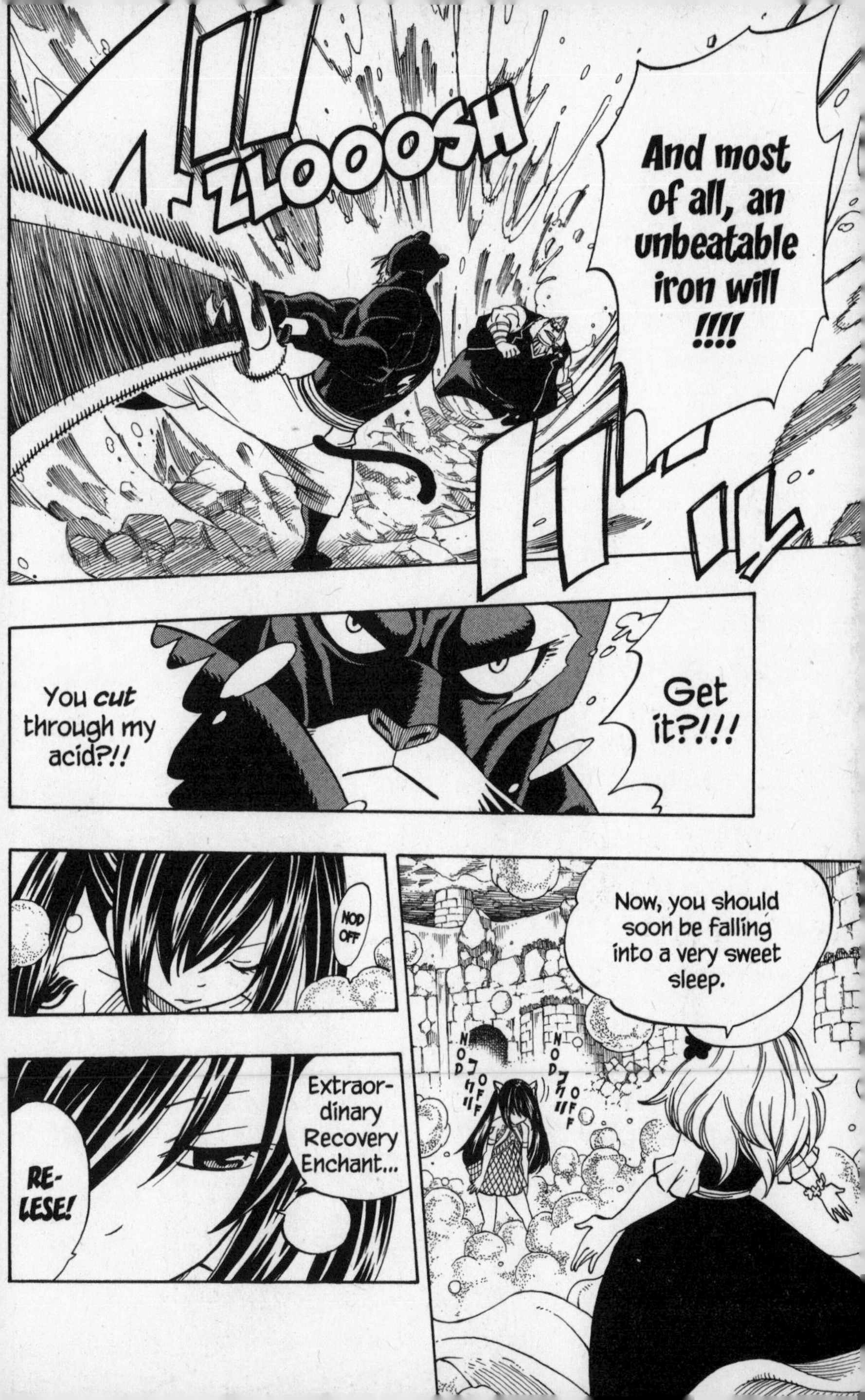
And most of all, an unbeatable iron will !!!!
ZLOOOSH
Get it?!!!
You *cut* through my acid?!!
Now, you should soon be falling into a very sweet sleep.
NOD OFF
NOD OFF
NOD OFF
Extraordinary Recovery Enchant...
RE-LESE!

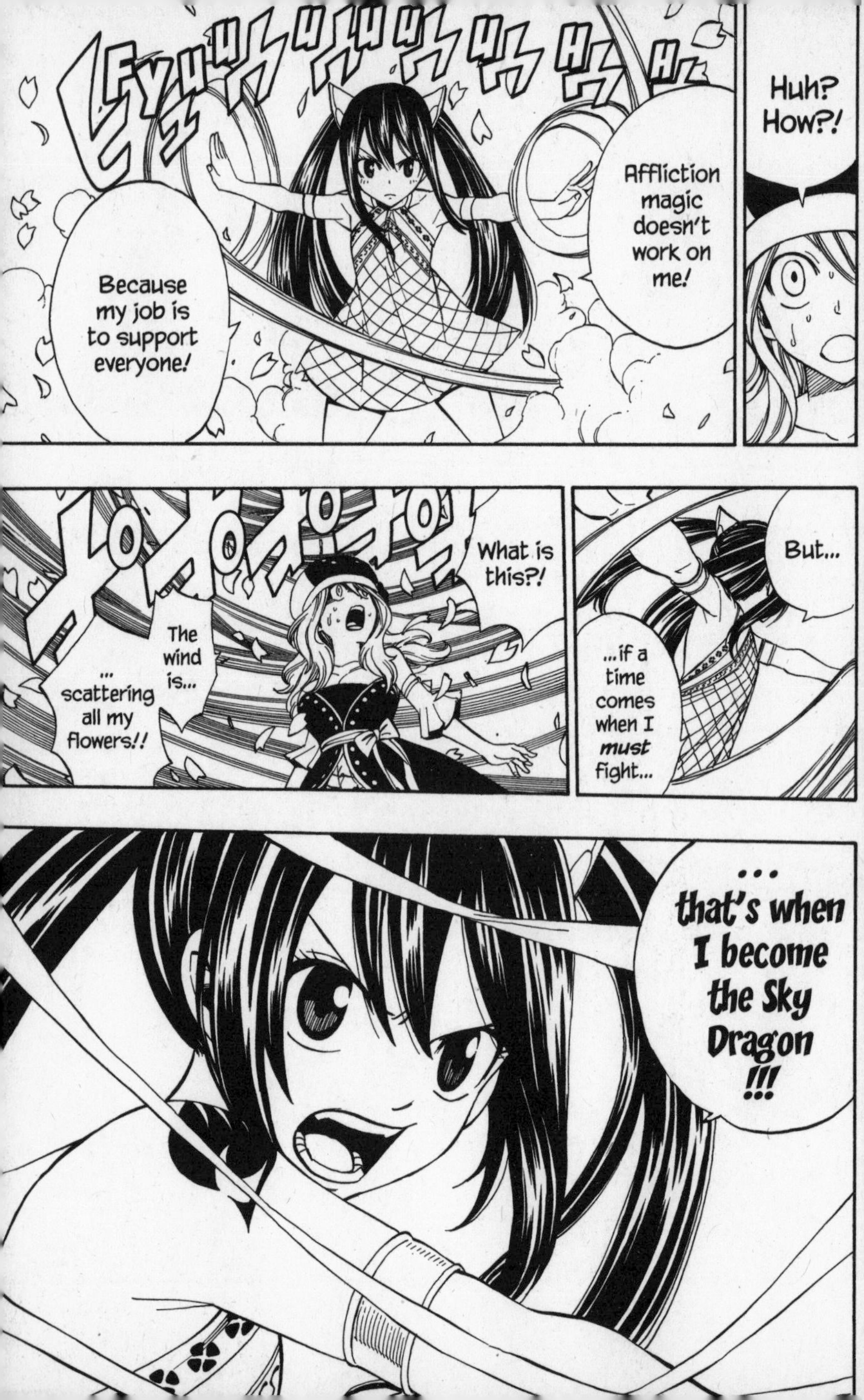
Huh? How?!
Affliction magic doesn't work on me!
Because my job is to support everyone!
But...
...if a time comes when I *must* fight...
What is this?!
The wind is...
...scattering all my flowers!!
...that's when I become the Sky Dragon!!!

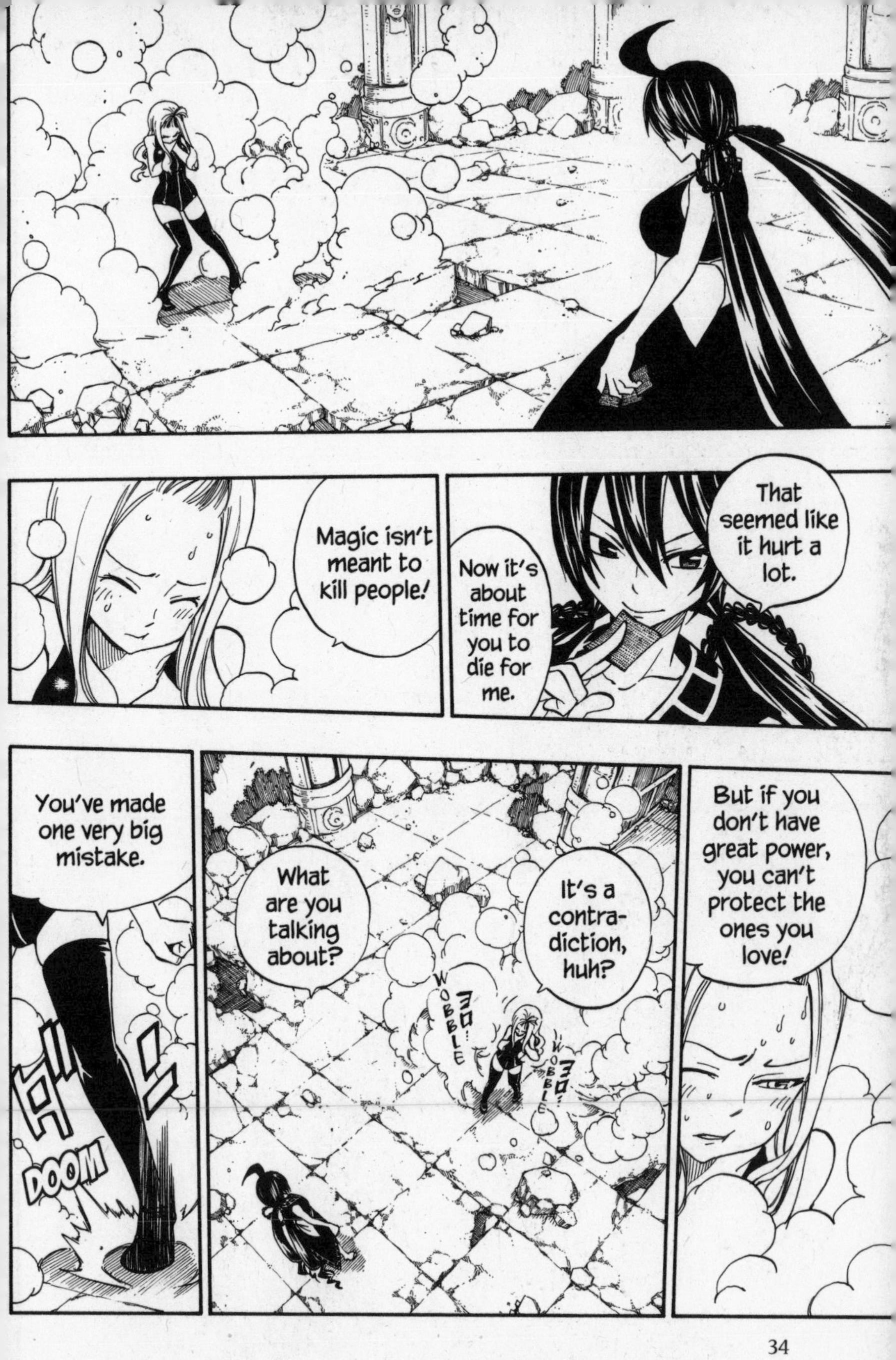
That seemed like it hurt a lot.
Now it's about time for you to die for me.
Magic isn't meant to kill people!
But if you don't have great power, you can't protect the ones you love!
It's a contradiction, huh?
What are you talking about?
WOBBLE
WOBBLE
You've made one very big mistake.
DOOM

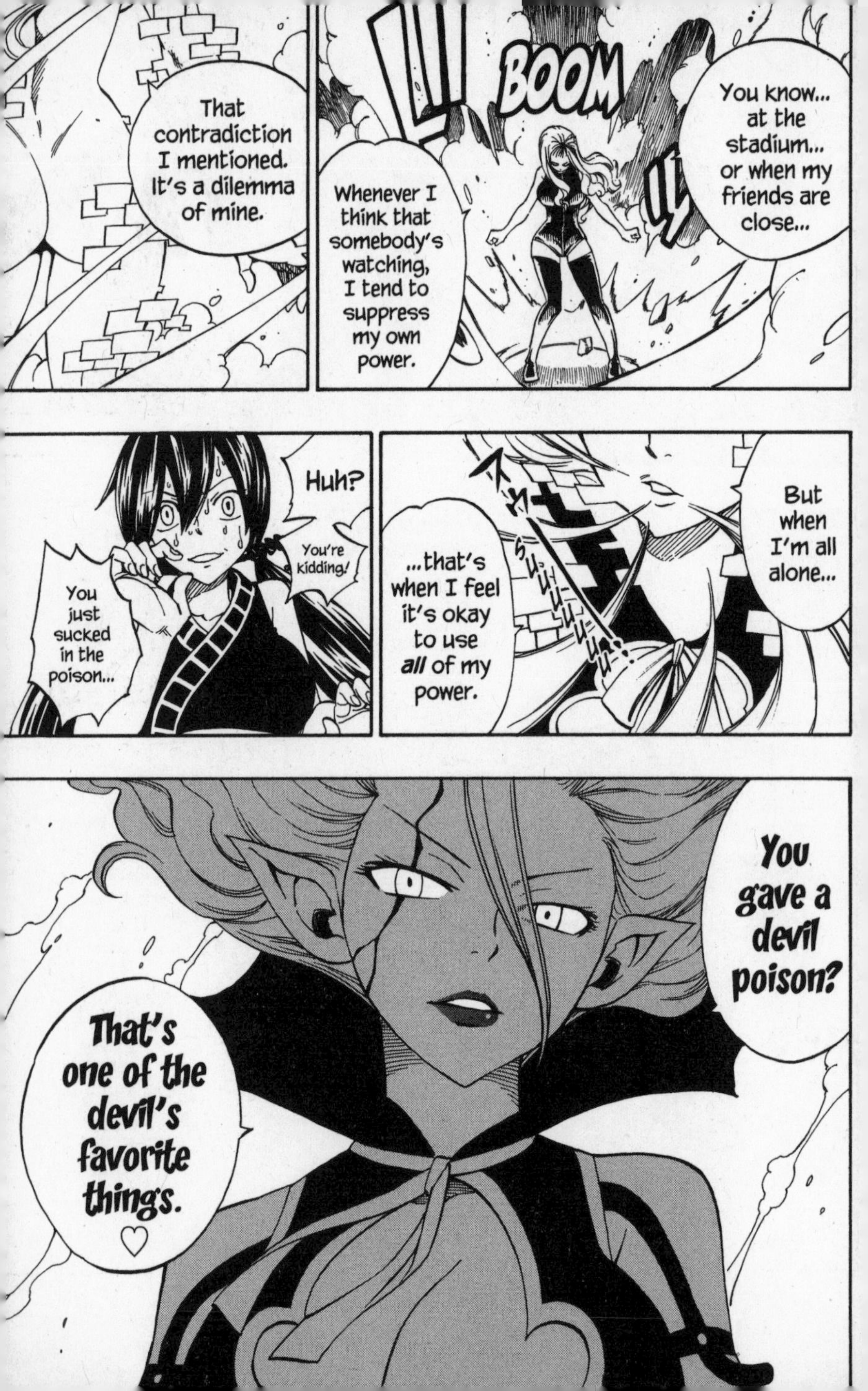
You know... at the stadium... or when my friends are close...
BOOM
Whenever I think that somebody's watching, I tend to suppress my own power.
That contradiction I mentioned. It's a dilemma of mine.
But when I'm all alone...
...that's when I feel it's okay to use *all* of my power.
Huh?
You're kidding!
You just sucked in the poison...
You gave a devil poison?
That's one of the devil's favorite things. ♡

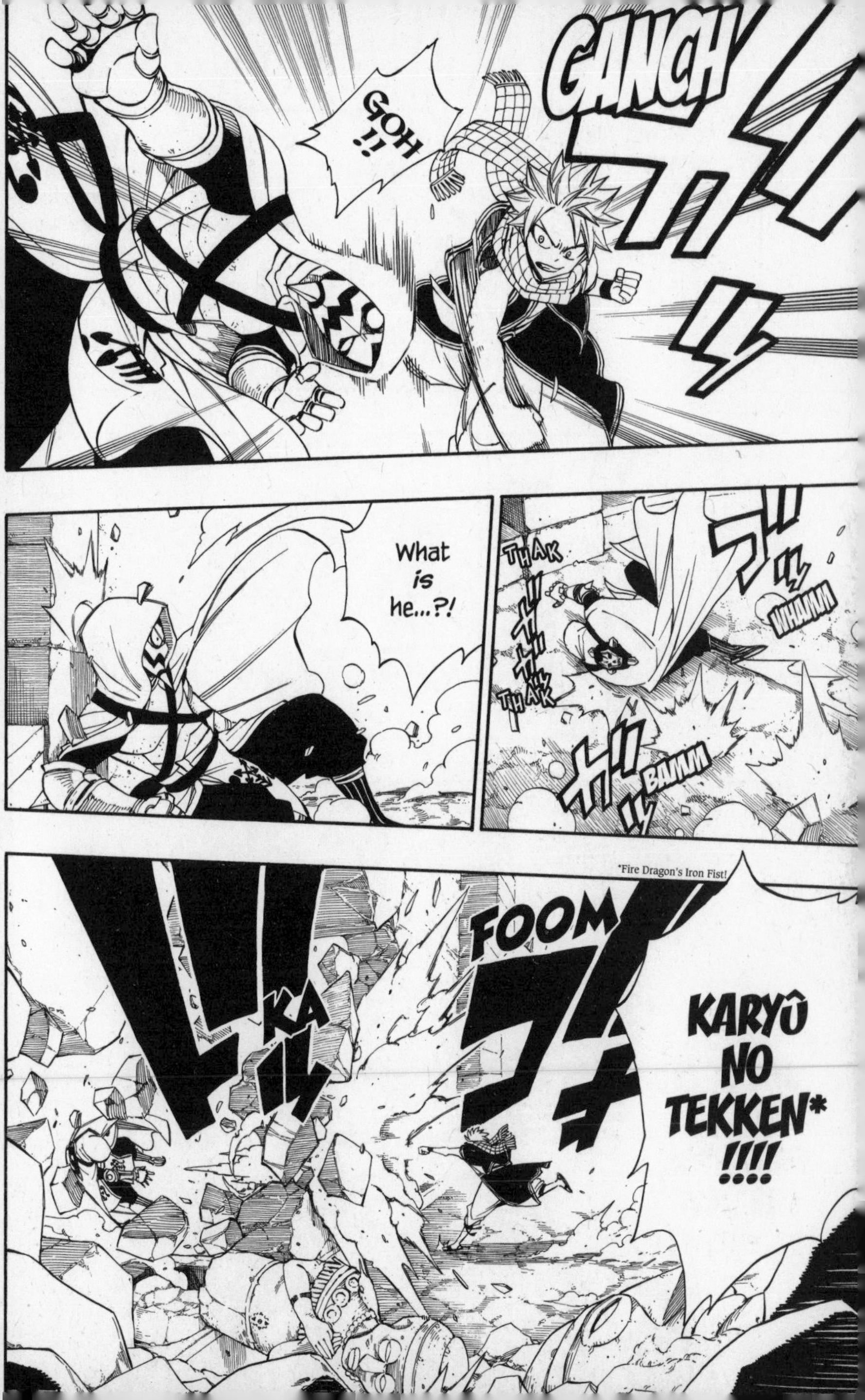
GANCH
GOH!!
WHAMM
THAK
THAK
BAMM
What is he...?!
KARYÛ NO TEKKEN*!!!!
FOOM
KA
*Fire Dragon's Iron Fist!

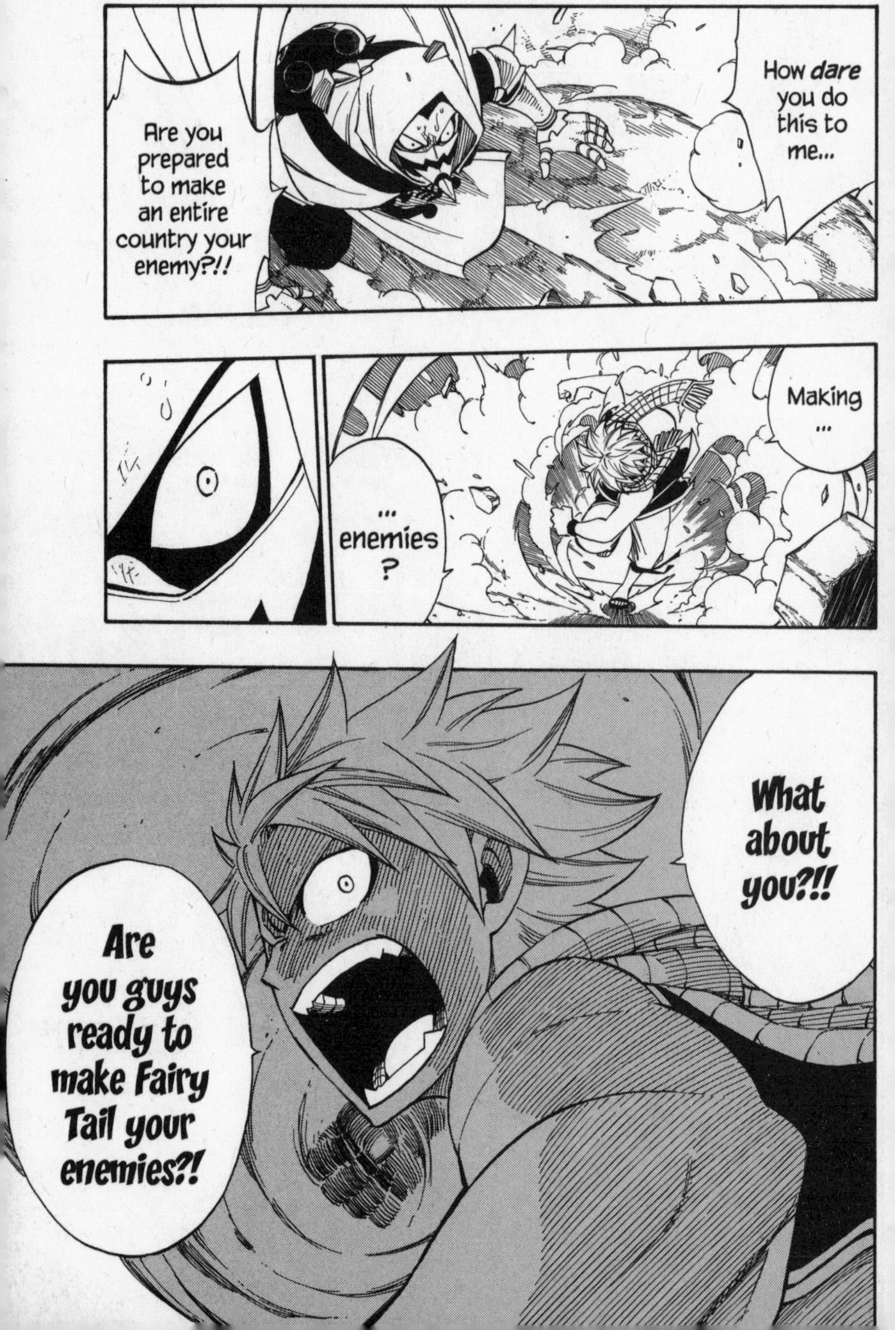
How *dare* you do this to me...
Are you prepared to make an entire country your enemy?!!
Making ...
... enemies ?
What about you?!!
Are you guys ready to make Fairy Tail your enemies?!

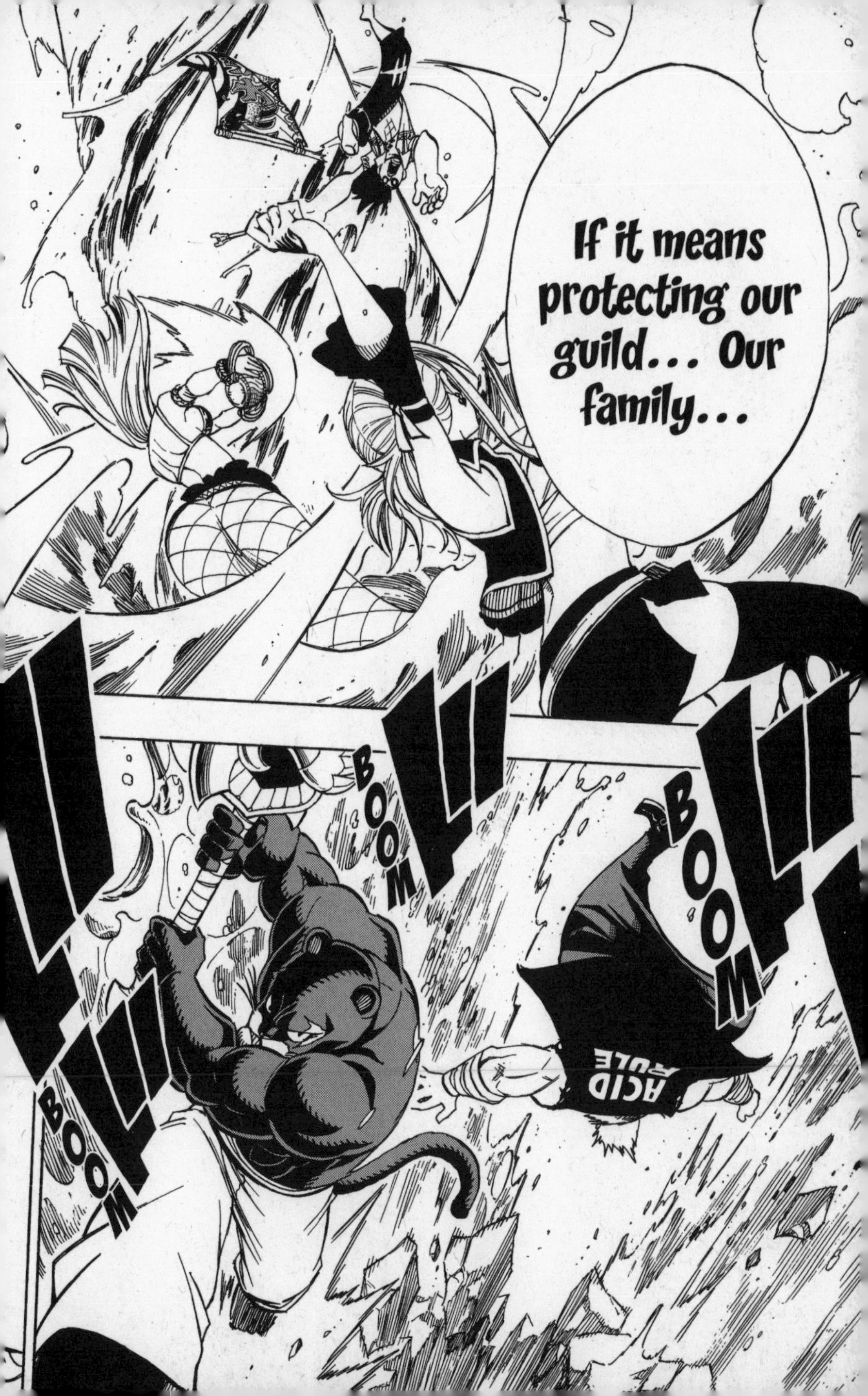
If it means protecting our guild... Our family...
BOOM
BOOM
BOOM

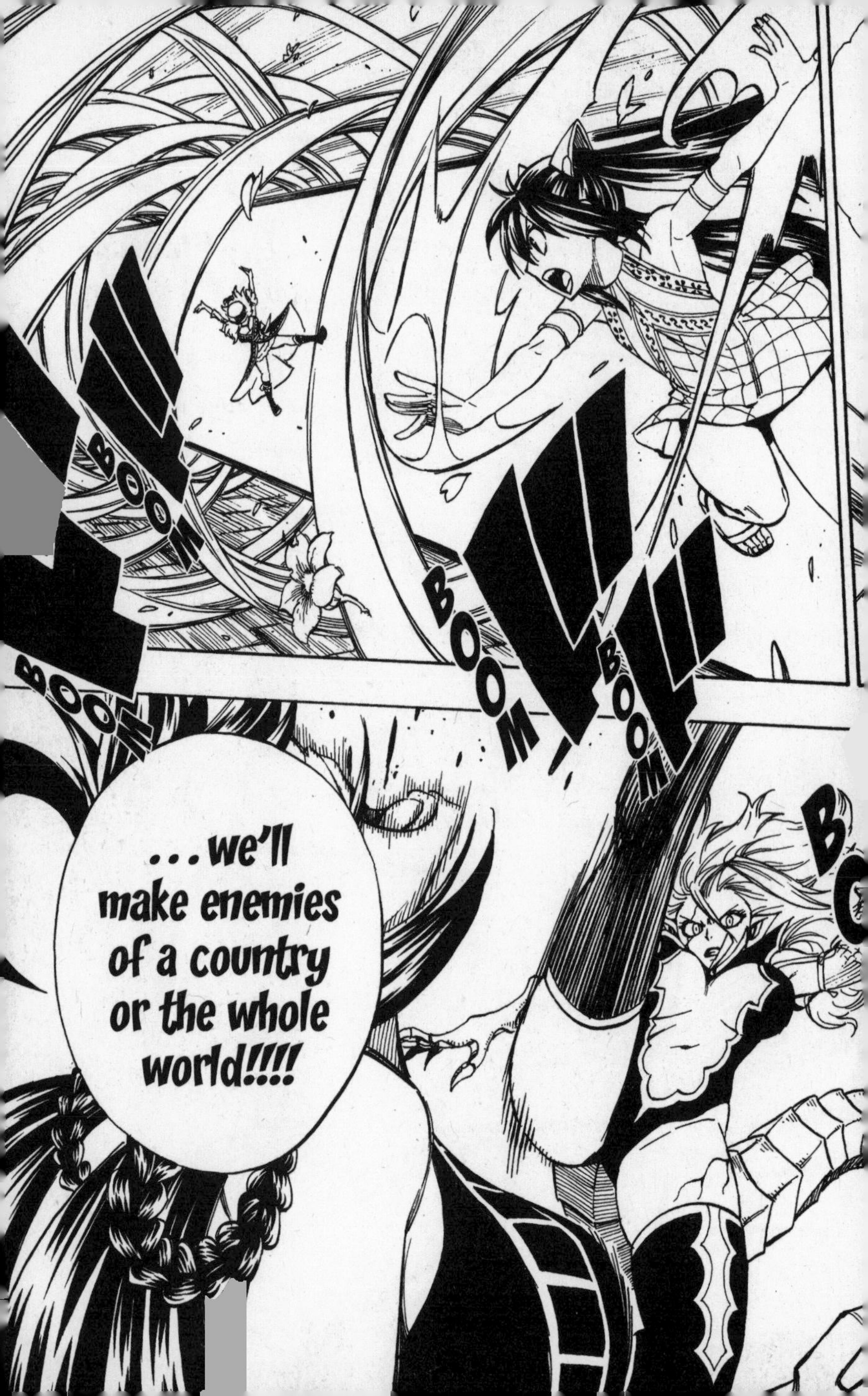
BOOM
BOOM
BOOM
BOOM
BOOM
...we'll make enemies of a country or the whole world!!!!

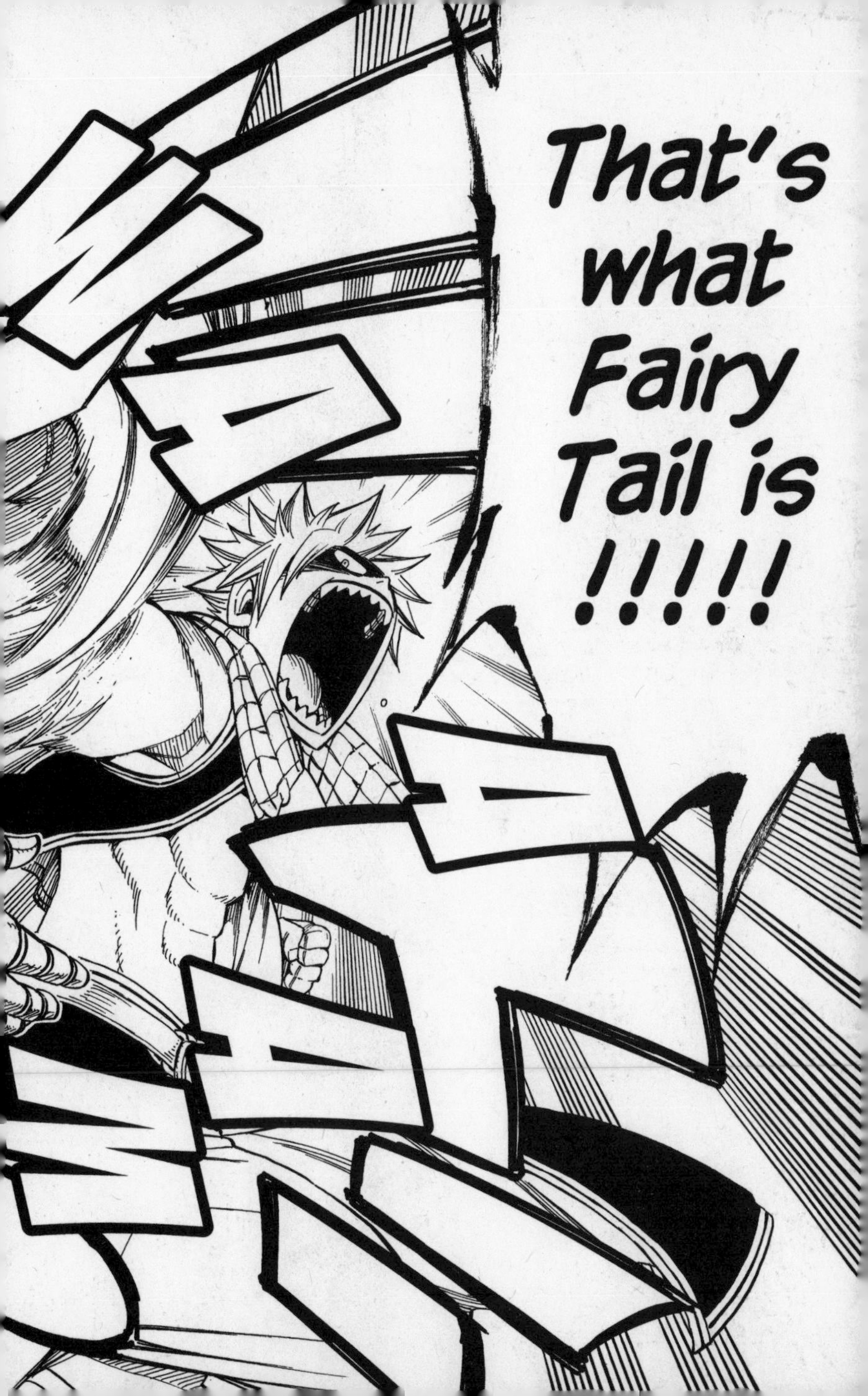
That's what Fairy Tail is !!!!!

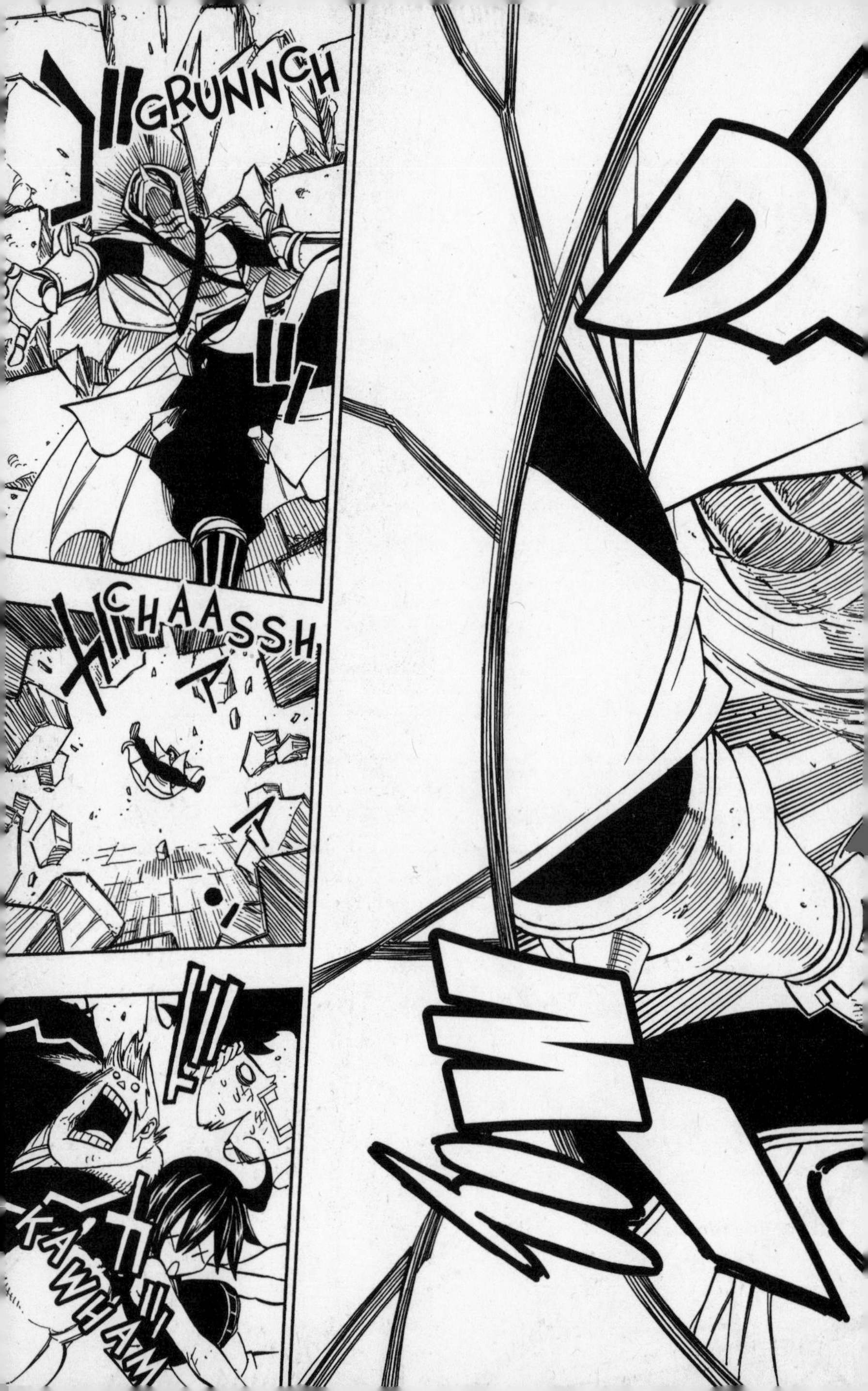
GRUNNCH
CHAASSH
KAWHAM

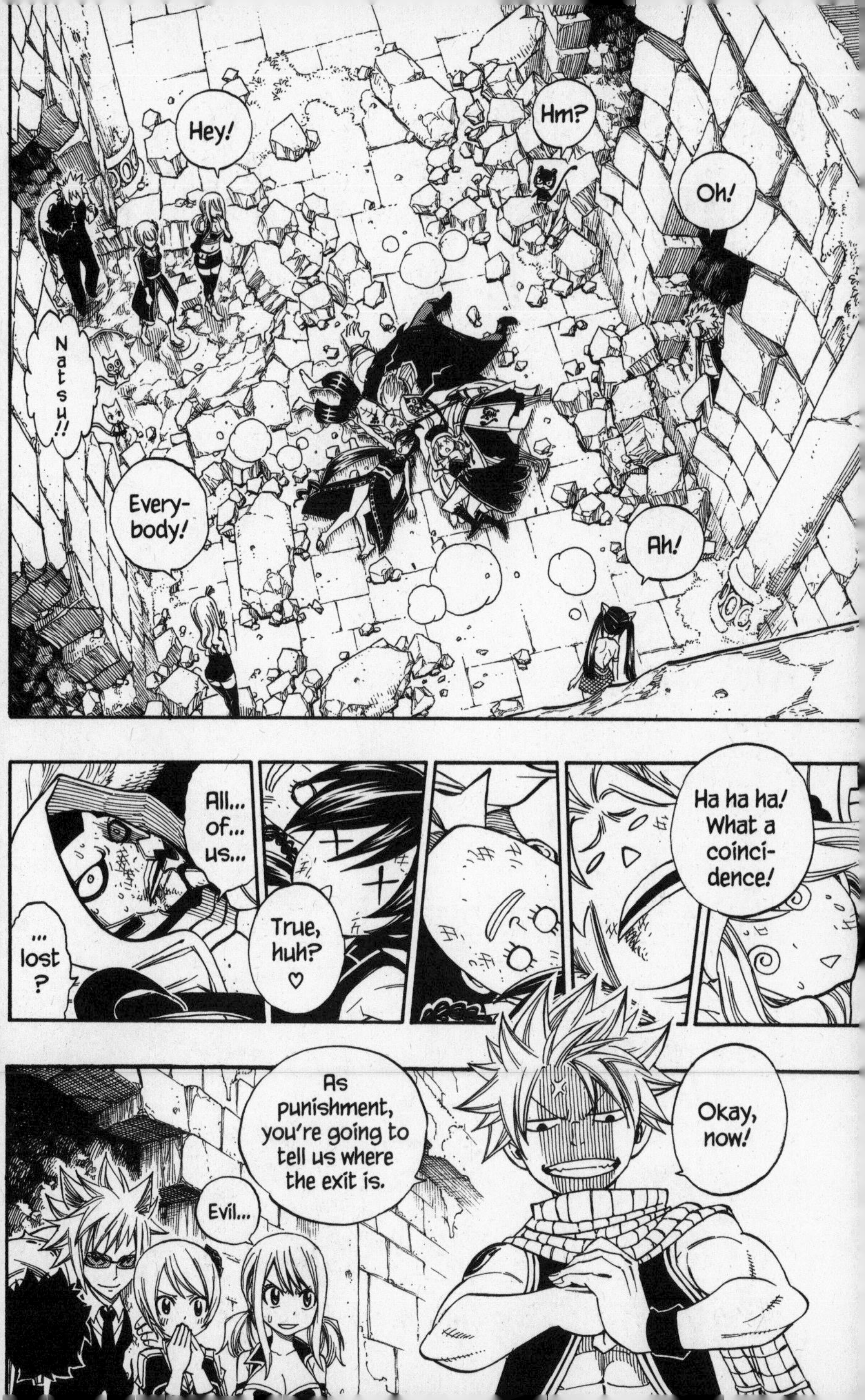

Oh!
Hm?
Hey!
Natsu!!
Ah!
Every-body!
Ha ha ha! What a coinci-dence!
True, huh? ♡
All... of... us...
... lost ?
Okay, now!
As punishment, you're going to tell us where the exit is.
Evil...

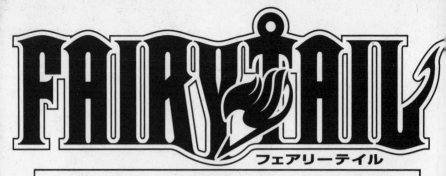

Grand Magic Games Final Day Interim Results

		Members left	
		Leader	Normal
1. Fairy Tail	50P	● x1	○ x4
2. Saber Tooth	49P	● x1	○ x3
2. Lamia Scale	49P	● x1	○ x2
4. Mermaid Heel	43P	● x1	○ x1

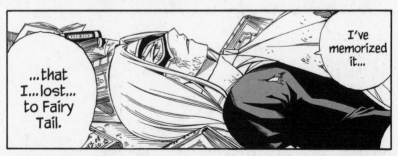

I've memorized it...

...that I...lost... to Fairy Tail.

Chapter 311: The Land of Until Tomorrow

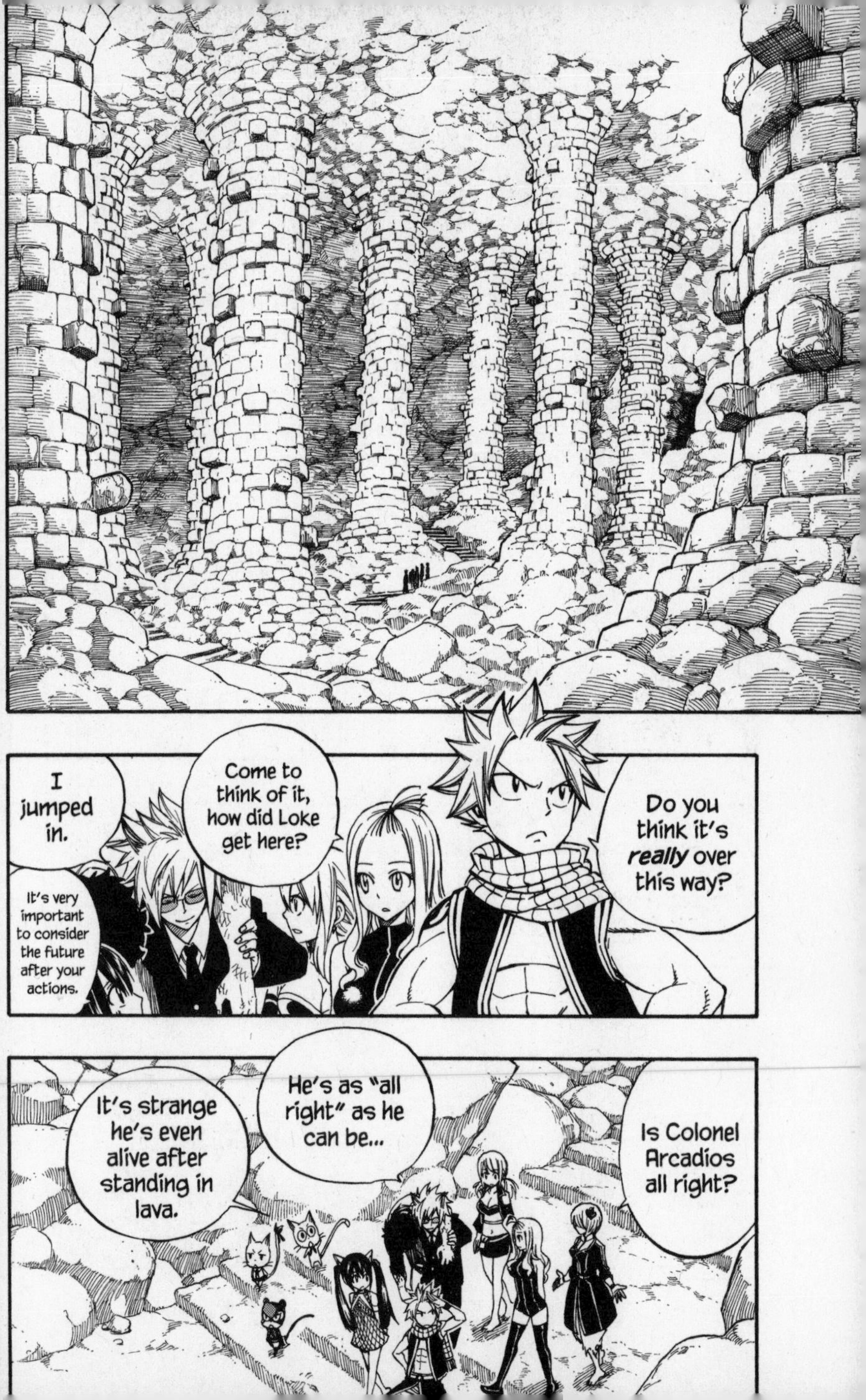
Do you think it's *really* over this way?
Come to think of it, how did Loke get here?
I jumped in.
It's very important to consider the future after your actions.
Is Colonel Arcadios all right?
He's as "all right" as he can be...
It's strange he's even alive after standing in lava.

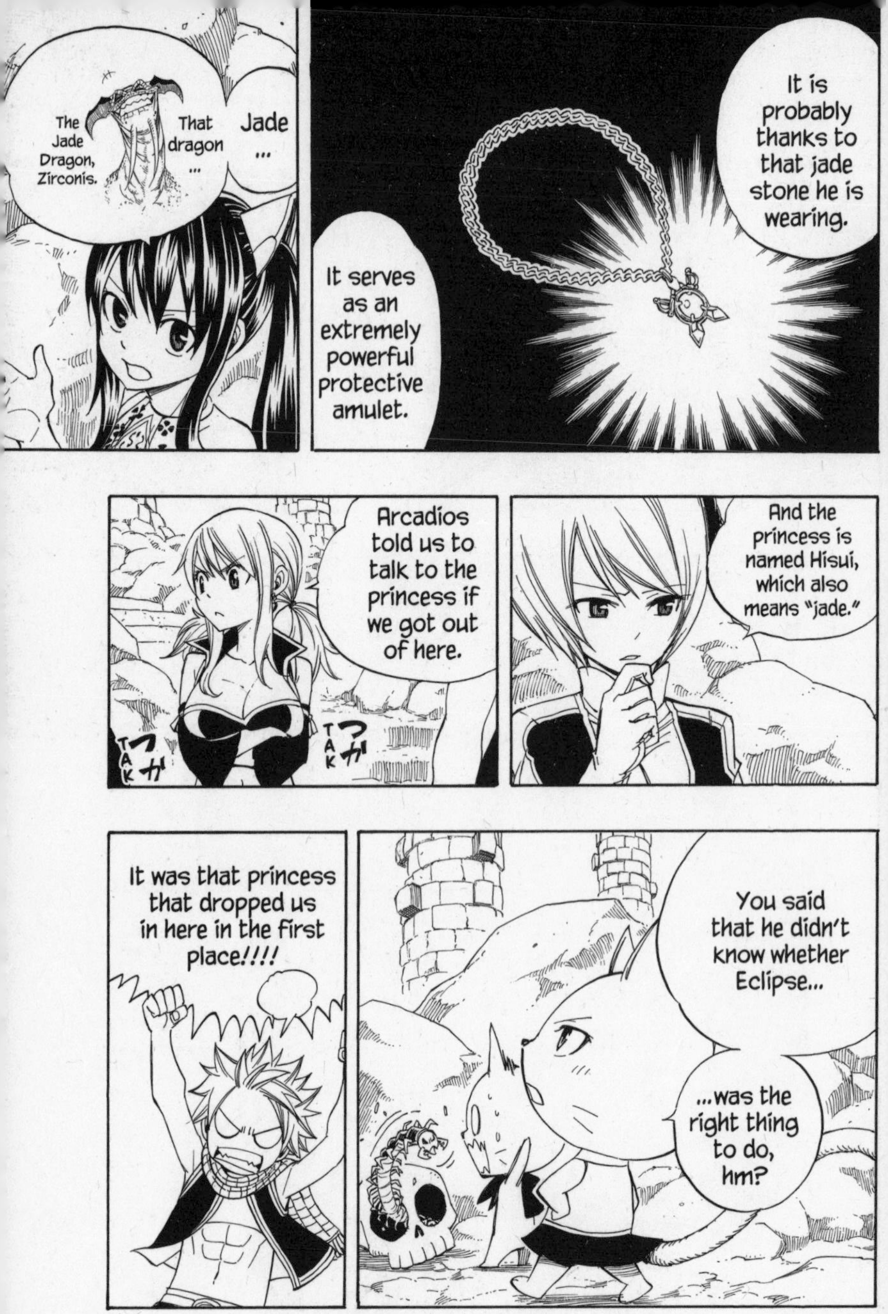
It is probably thanks to that jade stone he is wearing.
It serves as an extremely powerful protective amulet.
Jade ...
That dragon ...
The Jade Dragon, Zirconis.
And the princess is named Hisui, which also means "jade."
Arcadios told us to talk to the princess if we got out of here.
TAK
TAK
You said that he didn't know whether Eclipse...
...was the right thing to do, hm?
It was that princess that dropped us in here in the first place!!!!

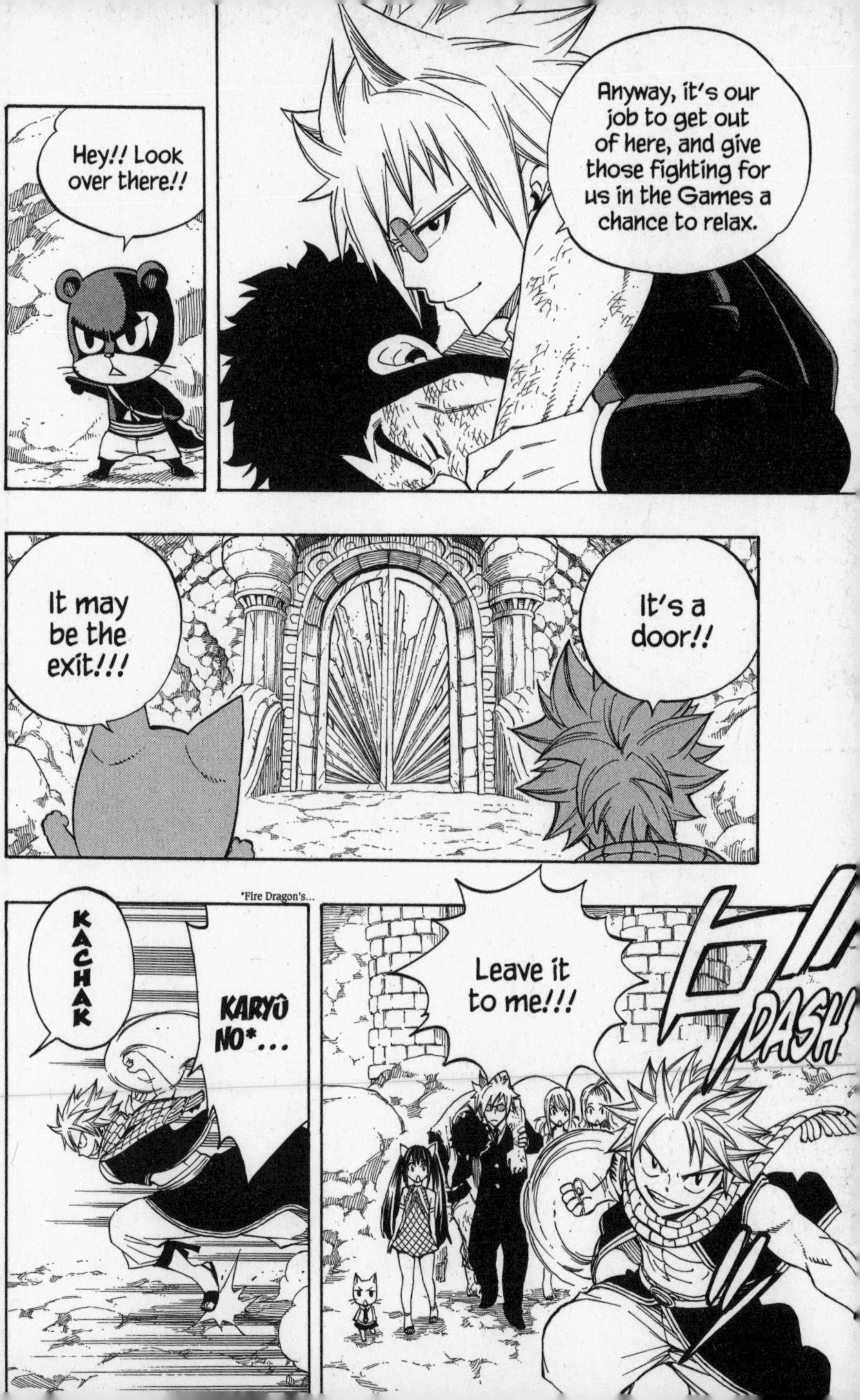
Anyway, it's our job to get out of here, and give those fighting for us in the Games a chance to relax.
Hey!! Look over there!!
It's a door!!
It may be the exit!!!
Leave it to me!!!
DASH
KACHAK
KARYÛ NO*...
*Fire Dragon's...

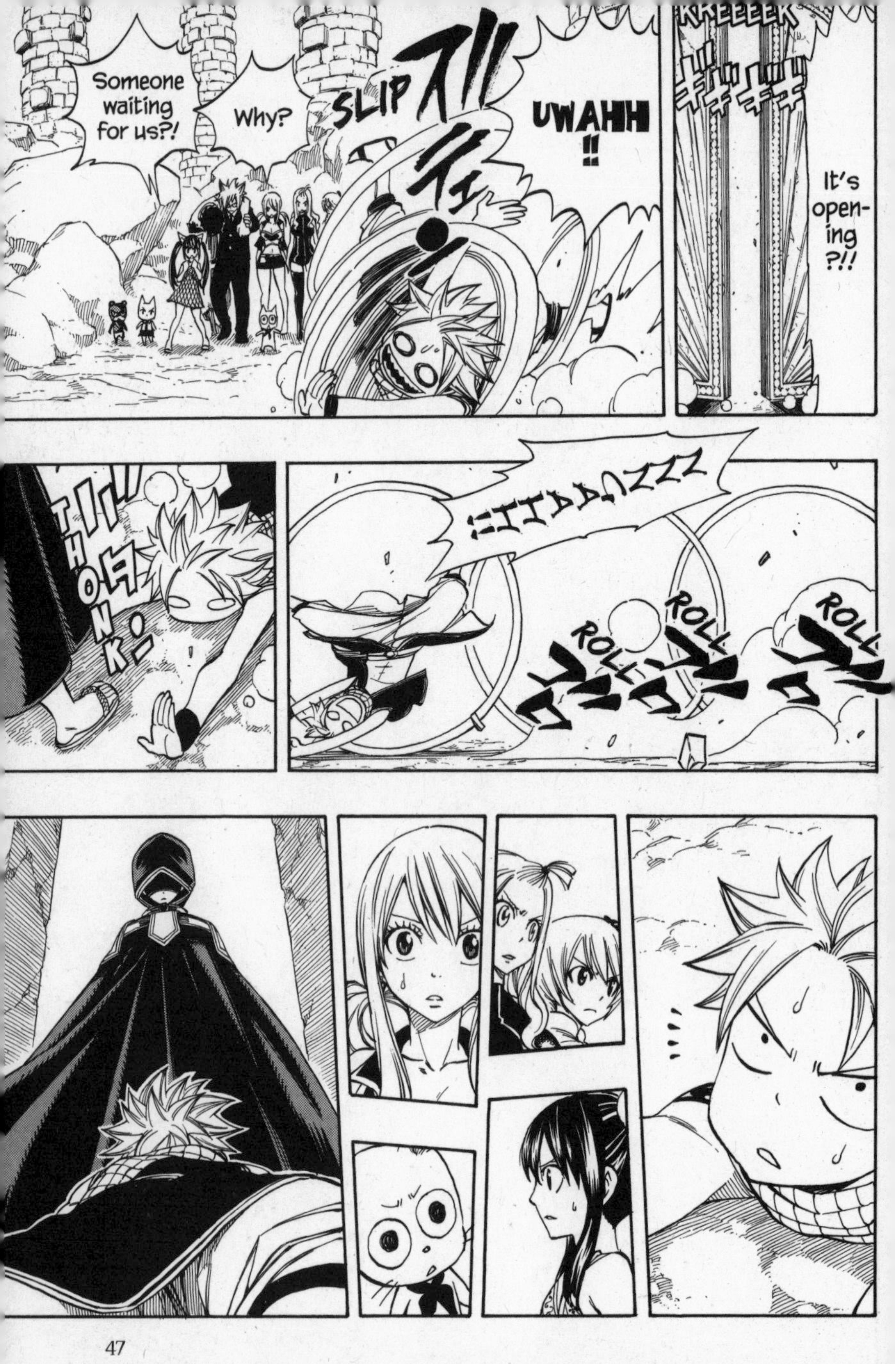
KREEEEK
It's opening?!!
UWAHH!!
SLIP
Why?
Someone waiting for us?!
ROLL
ROLL
ROLL
THONK!

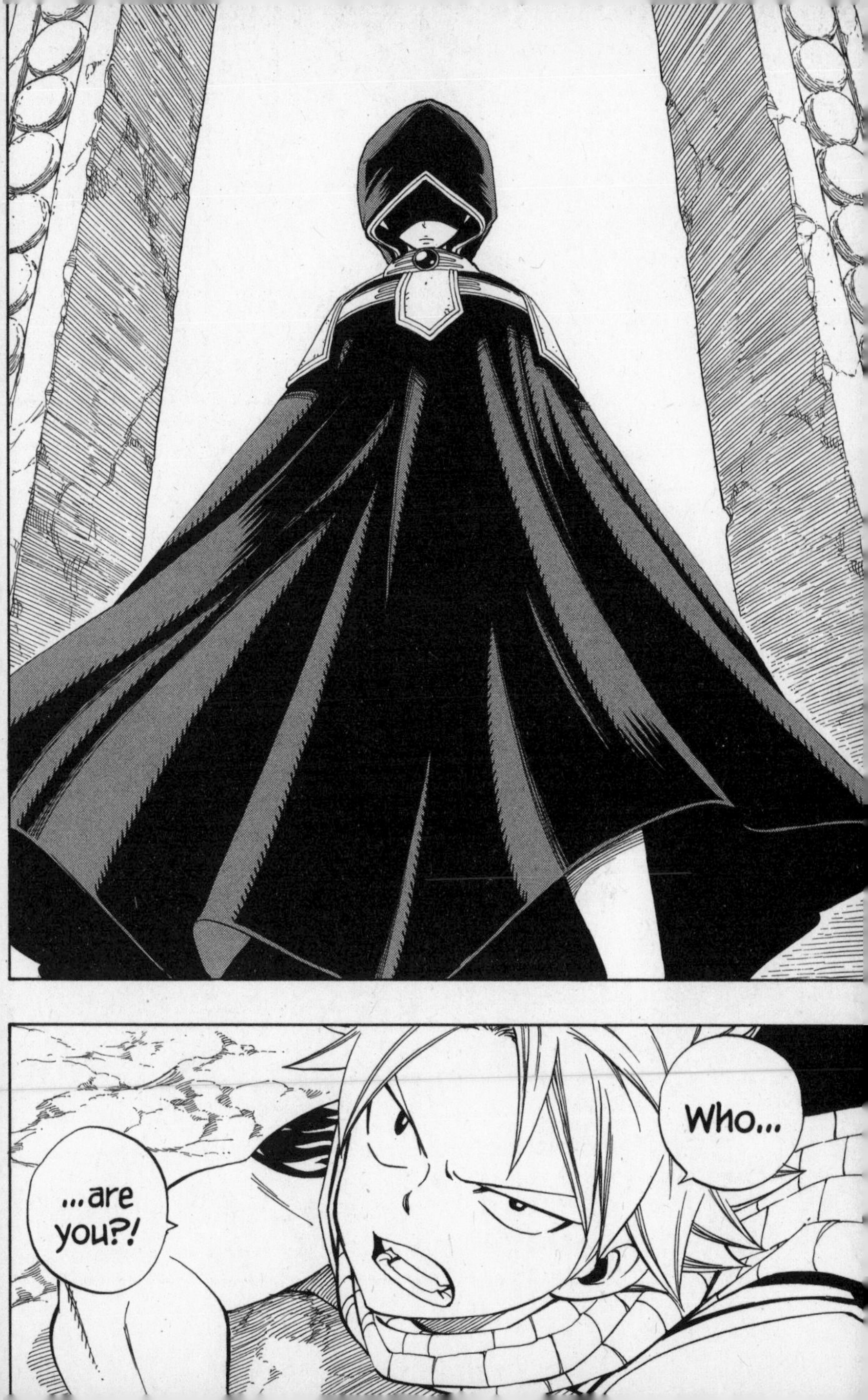
Who...
...are you?!

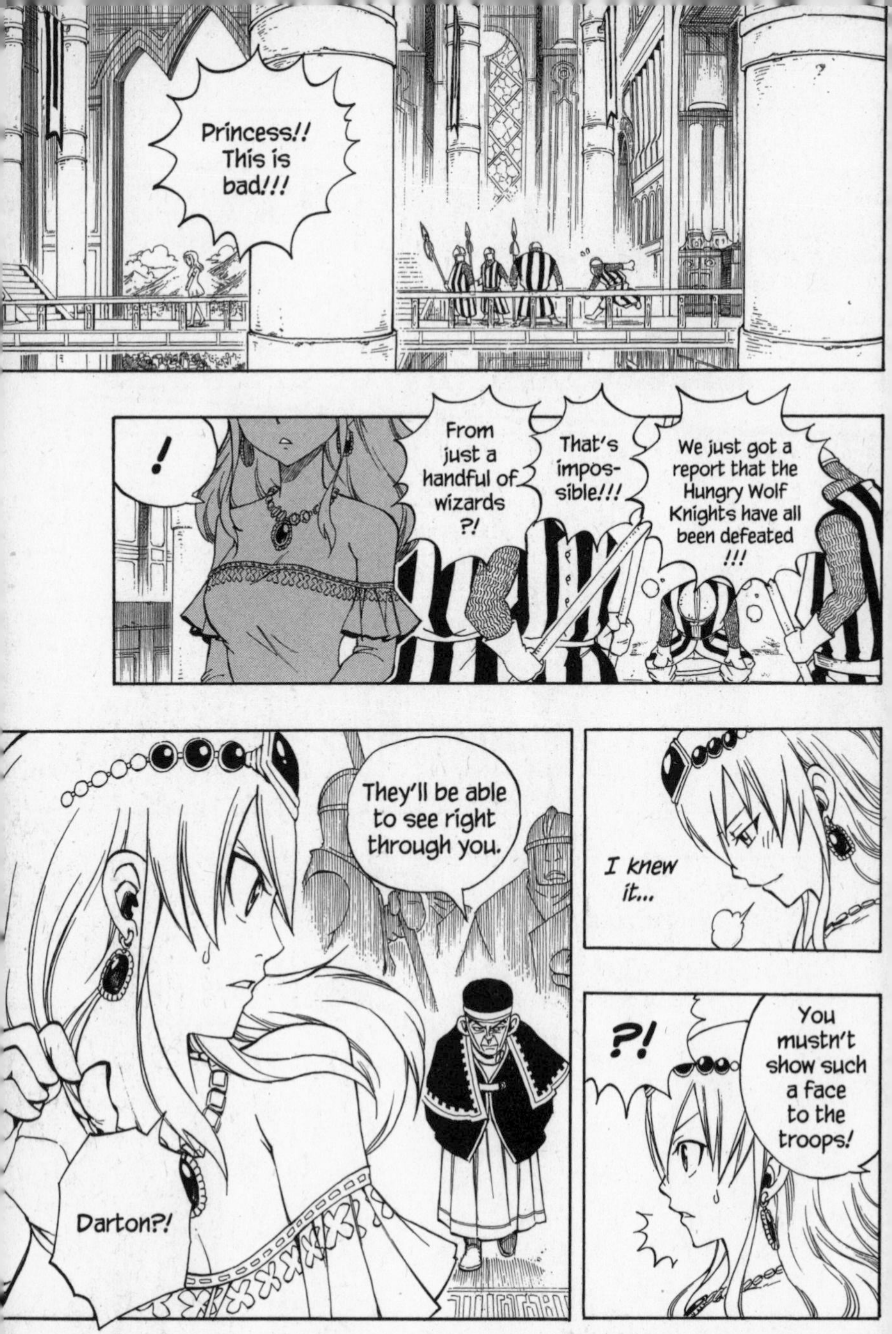
Princess!! This is bad!!!
We just got a report that the Hungry Wolf Knights have all been defeated!!!
That's impos-sible!!!
From just a handful of wizards?!
!
I knew it...
You mustn't show such a face to the troops!
?!
They'll be able to see right through you.
Darton?!

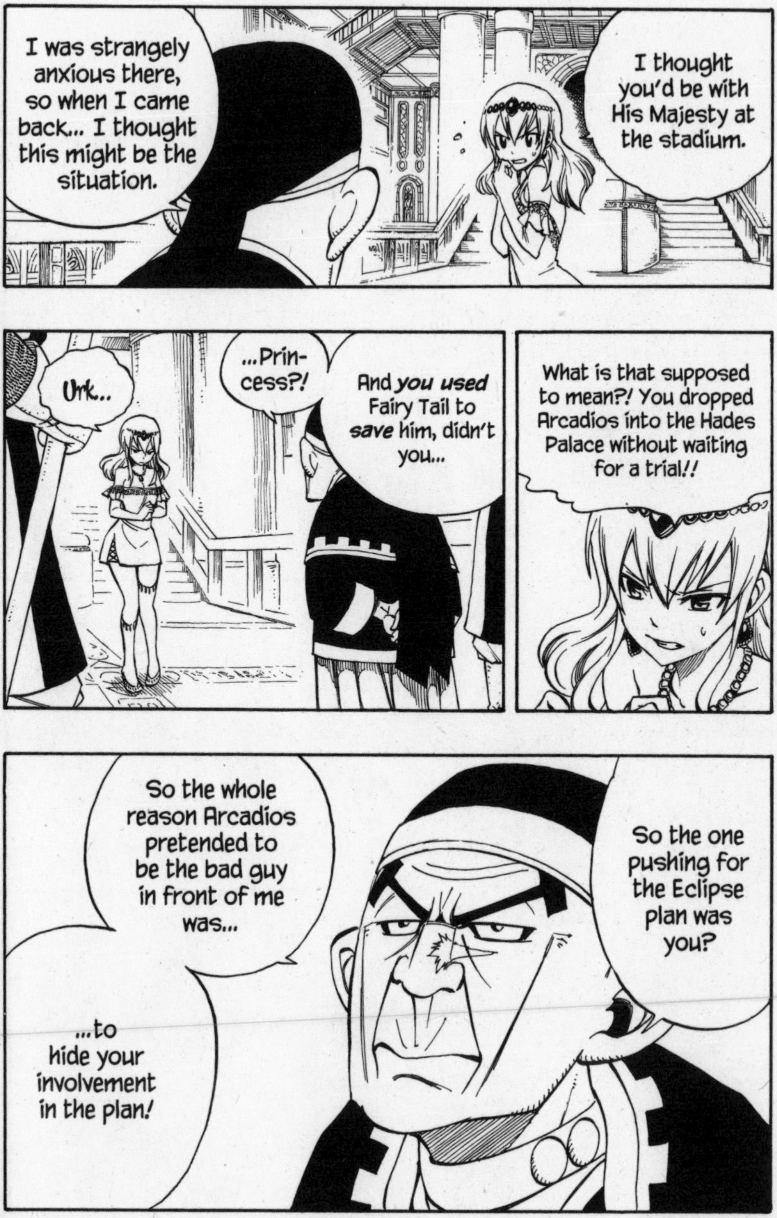
I thought you'd be with His Majesty at the stadium.
I was strangely anxious there, so when I came back... I thought this might be the situation.
What is that supposed to mean?! You dropped Arcadios into the Hades Palace without waiting for a trial!!
And *you used* Fairy Tail to *save* him, didn't you...
...Prin-cess?!
Urk...
So the one pushing for the Eclipse plan was you?
So the whole reason Arcadios pretended to be the bad guy in front of me was...
...to hide your involvement in the plan!

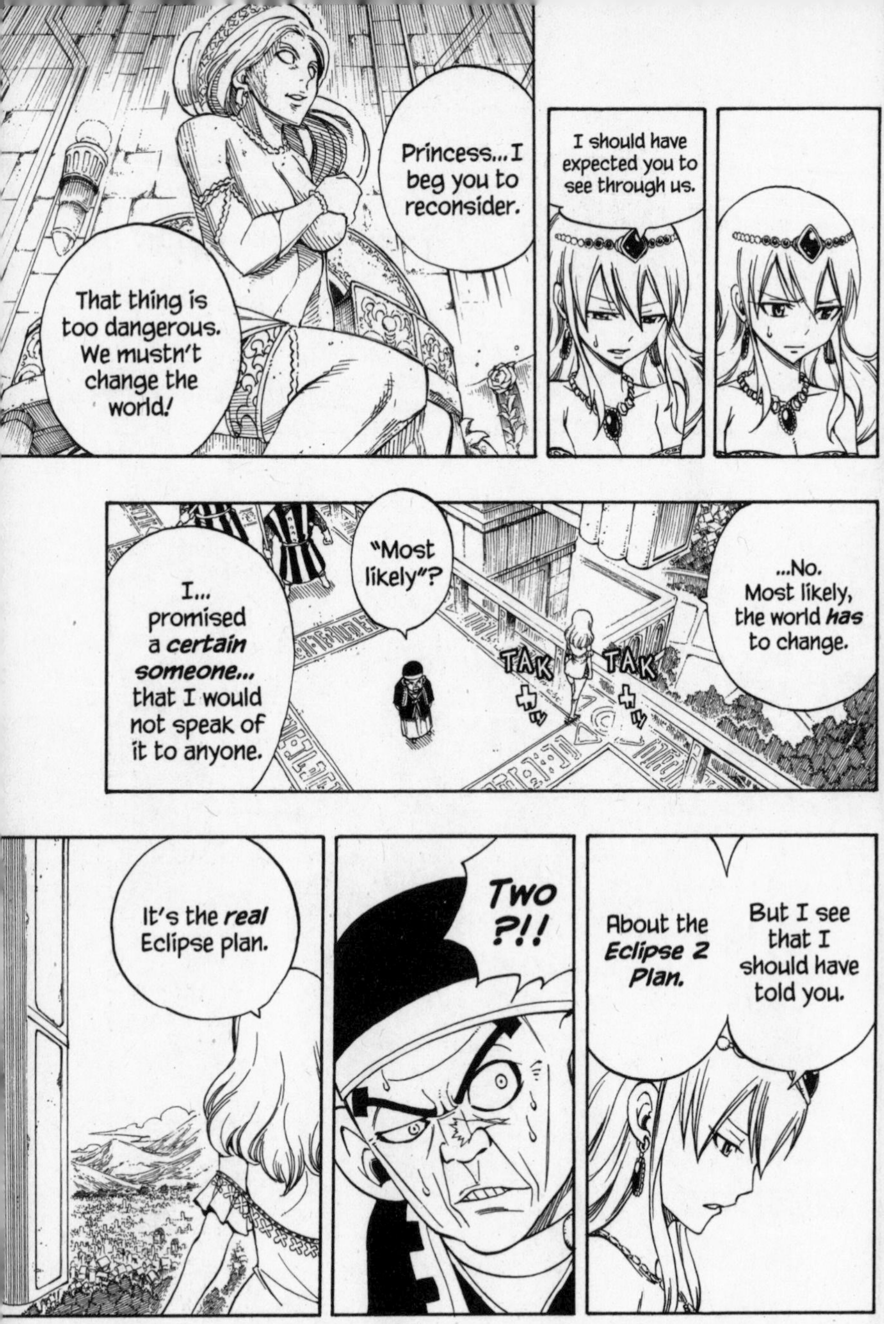
I should have expected you to see through us.
Princess...I beg you to reconsider.
That thing is too dangerous. We mustn't change the world!
...No. Most likely, the world has to change.
TAK
TAK
"Most likely"?
I... promised a certain someone... that I would not speak of it to anyone.
But I see that I should have told you.
About the Eclipse 2 Plan.
Two?!!
It's the real Eclipse plan.

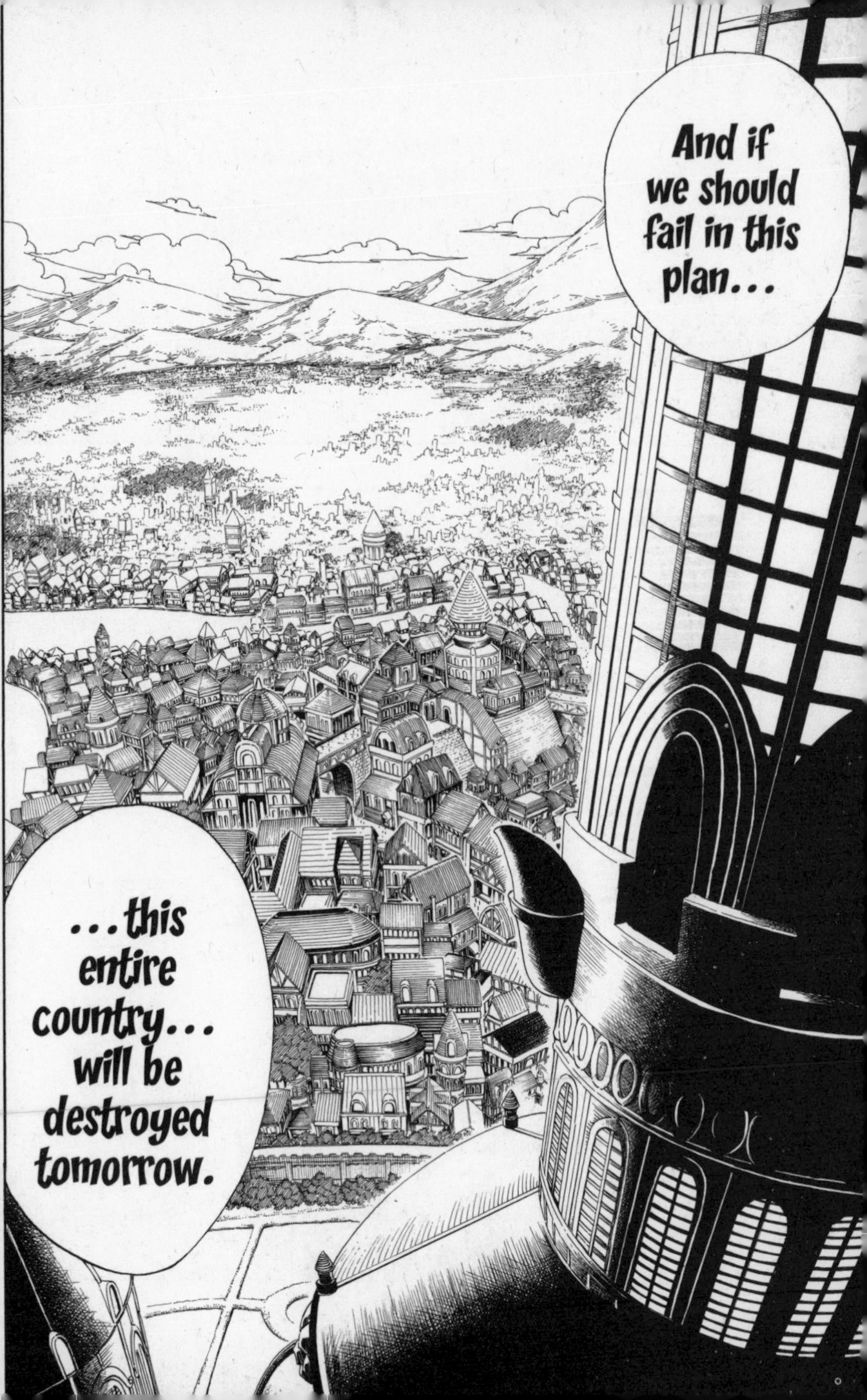
And if we should fail in this plan...
...this entire country... will be destroyed tomorrow.

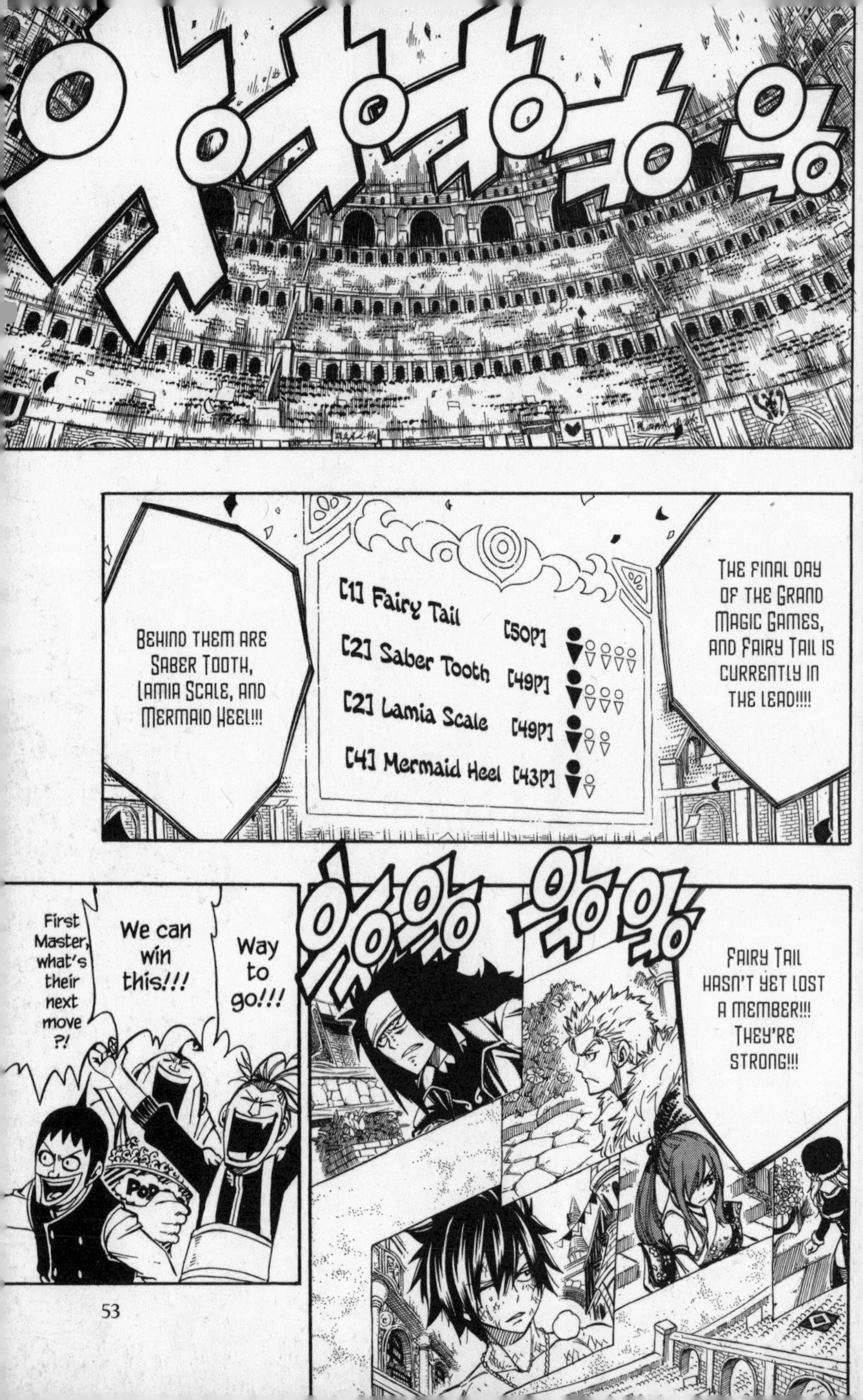
THE FINAL DAY OF THE GRAND MAGIC GAMES, AND FAIRY TAIL IS CURRENTLY IN THE LEAD!!!!
[1] Fairy Tail [50P]
[2] Saber Tooth [49P]
[2] Lamia Scale [49P]
[4] Mermaid Heel [43P]
BEHIND THEM ARE SABER TOOTH, LAMIA SCALE, AND MERMAID HEEL!!!
FAIRY TAIL HASN'T YET LOST A MEMBER!!! THEY'RE STRONG!!!
Way to go!!!
We can win this!!!
First Master, what's their next move ?!
POP

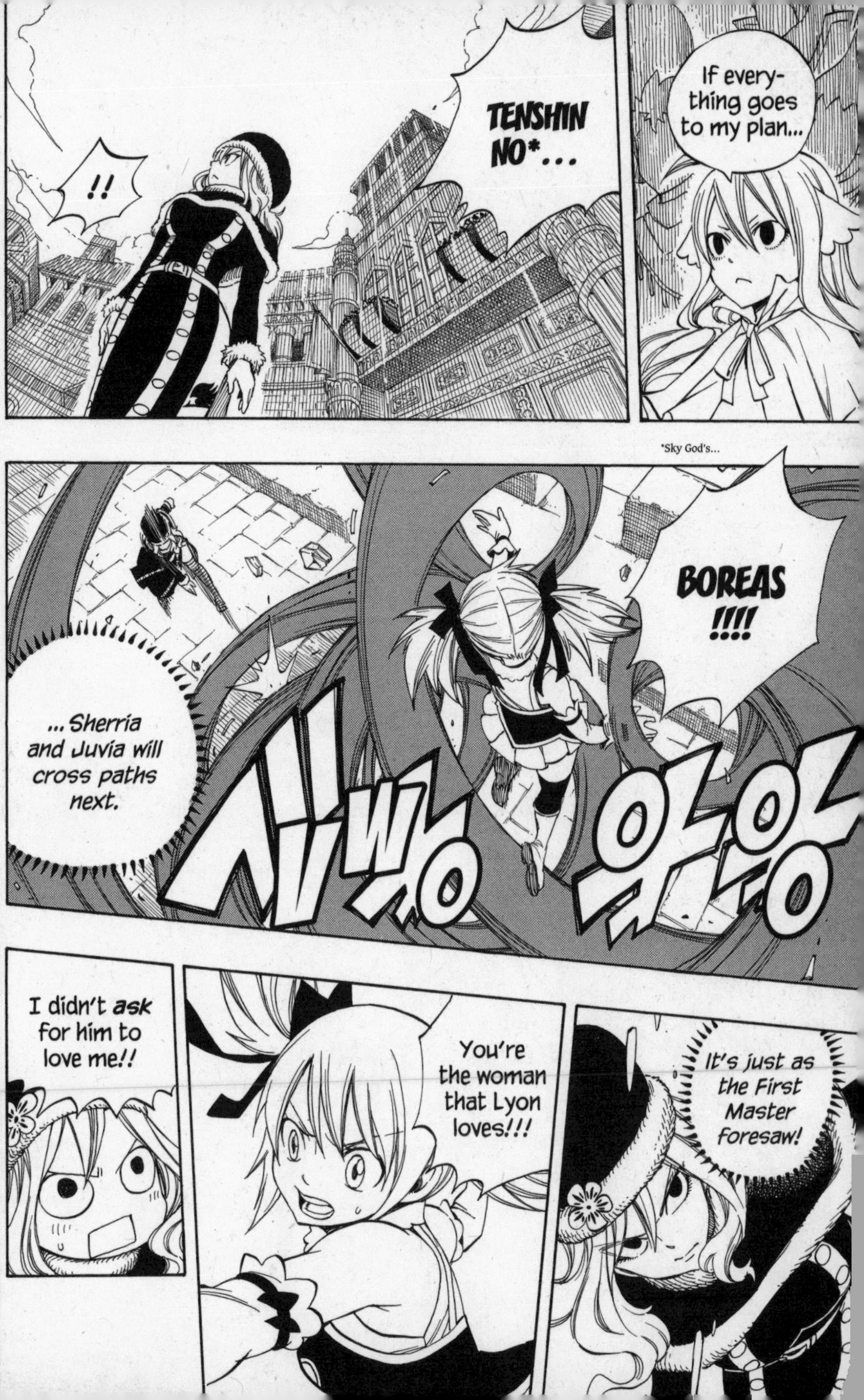
If everything goes to my plan...
TENSHIN NO*...
!!
BOREAS!!!!
...Sherria and Juvia will cross paths next.
It's just as the First Master foresaw!
You're the woman that Lyon loves!!!
I didn't ask for him to love me!!
*Sky God's...

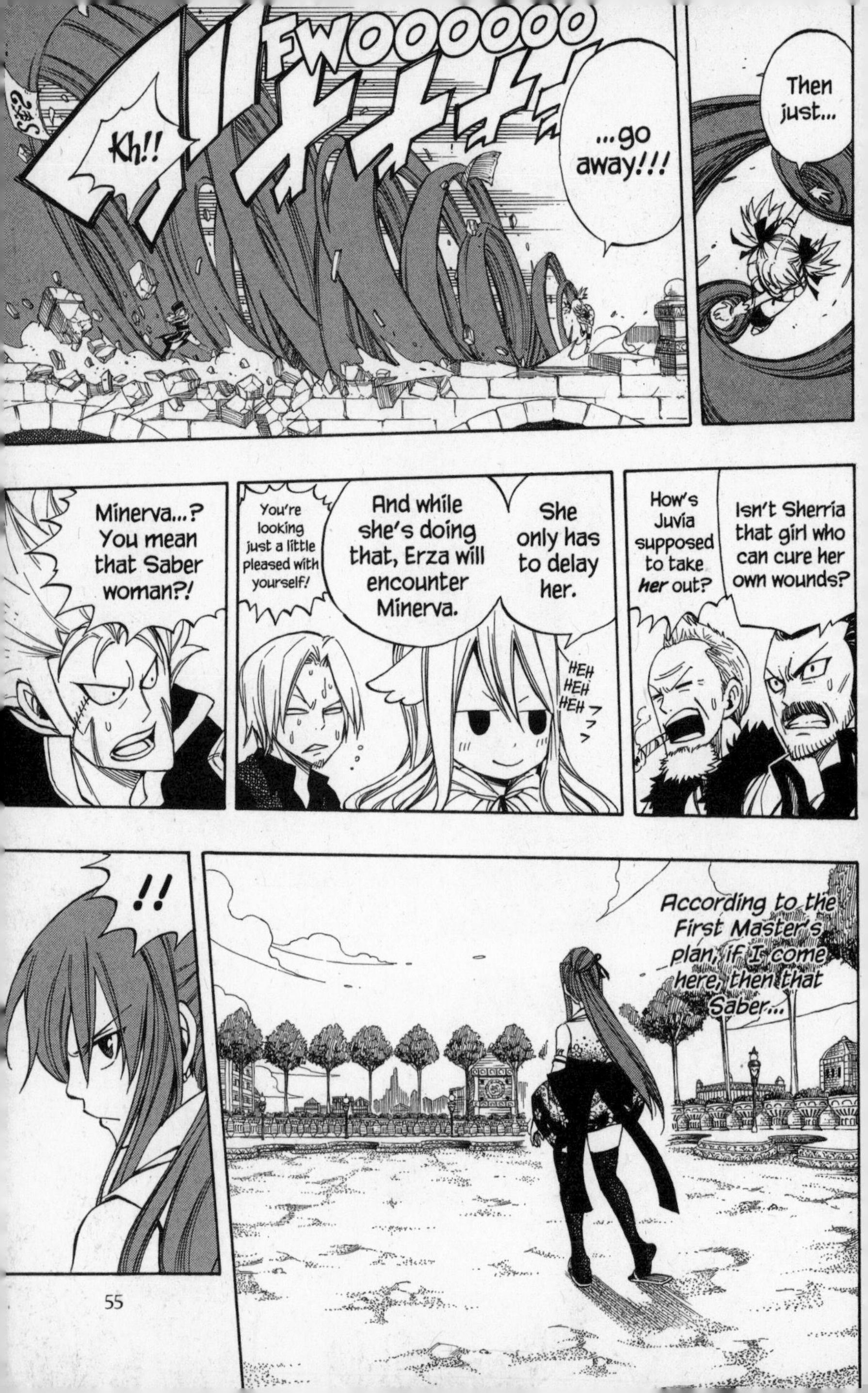
Then just...
...go away!!!
FWOOOOOO
Kh!!
Isn't Sherria that girl who can cure her own wounds?
How's Juvia supposed to take *her* out?
She only has to delay her.
And while she's doing that, Erza will encounter Minerva.
HEH HEH HEH
You're looking just a little pleased with yourself!
Minerva...? You mean that Saber woman?!
According to the First Master's plan, if I come here, then that Saber...
!!

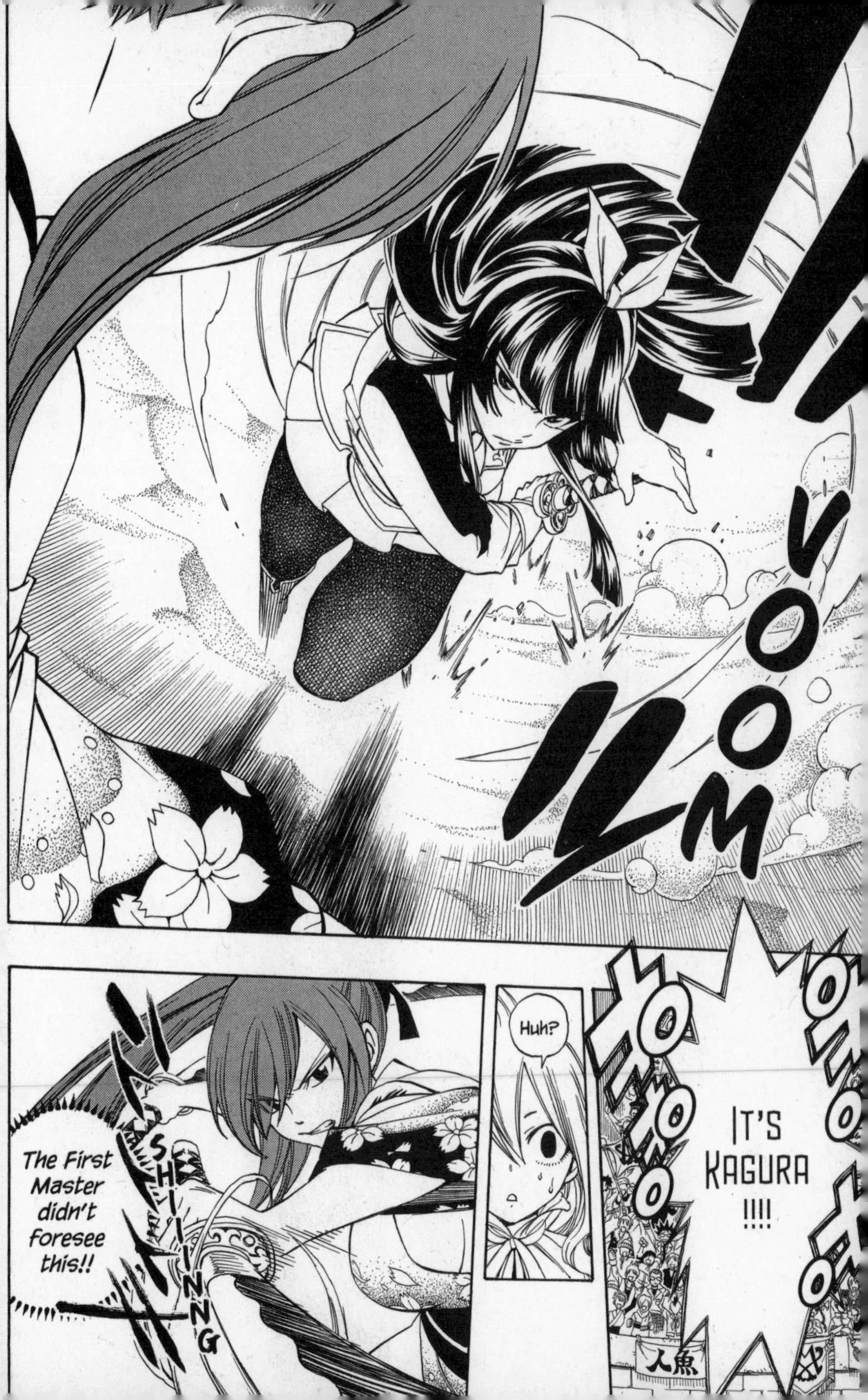
VOOOM
It's Kagura!!!!
Huh?
SHIIIINNG
The First Master didn't foresee this!!
人魚

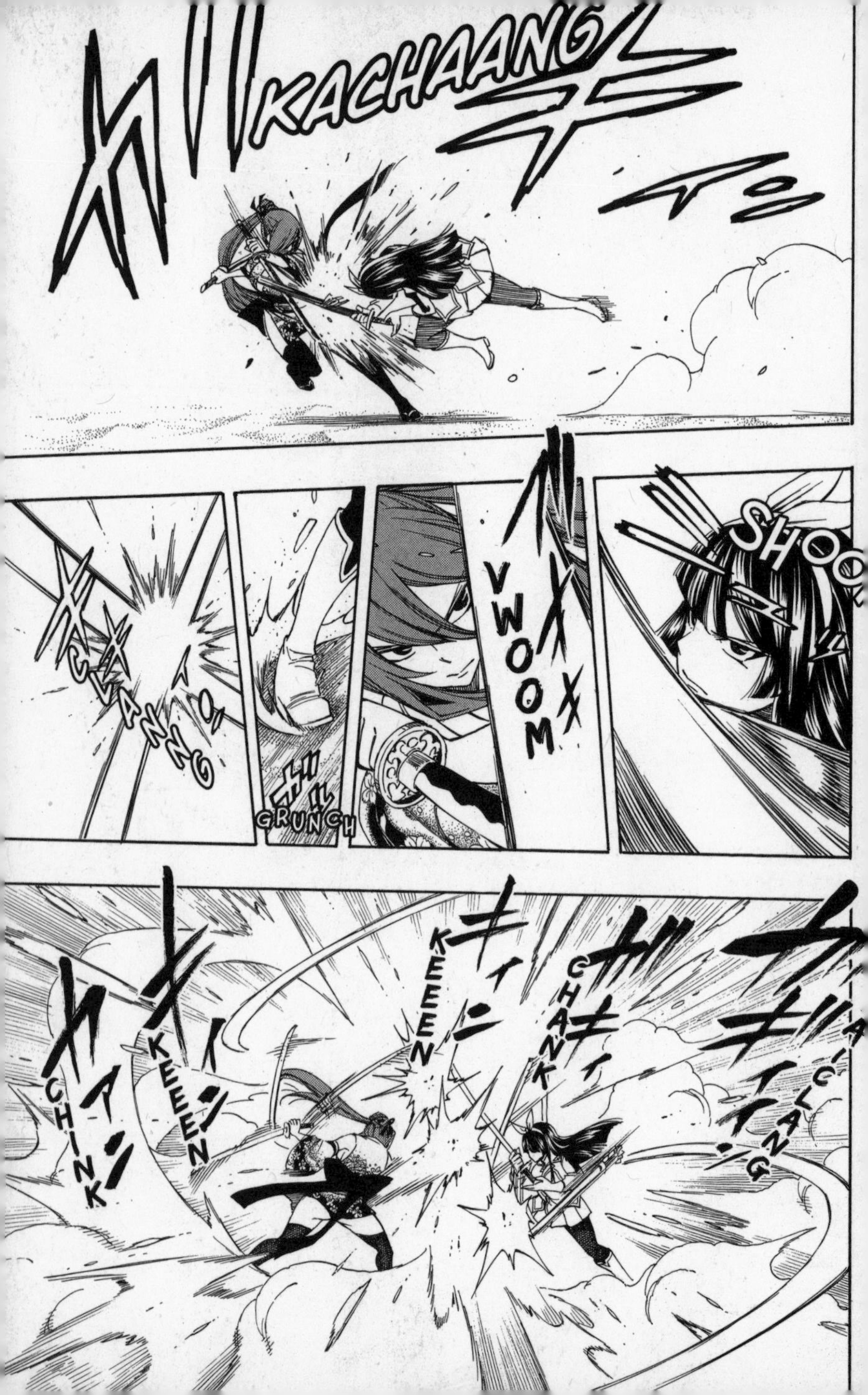
KACHAANG
SHOO
VWOOM
GRUNCH
CLANNG
CLANG
CHANK
KEEEEN
KEEEEN
CHINK

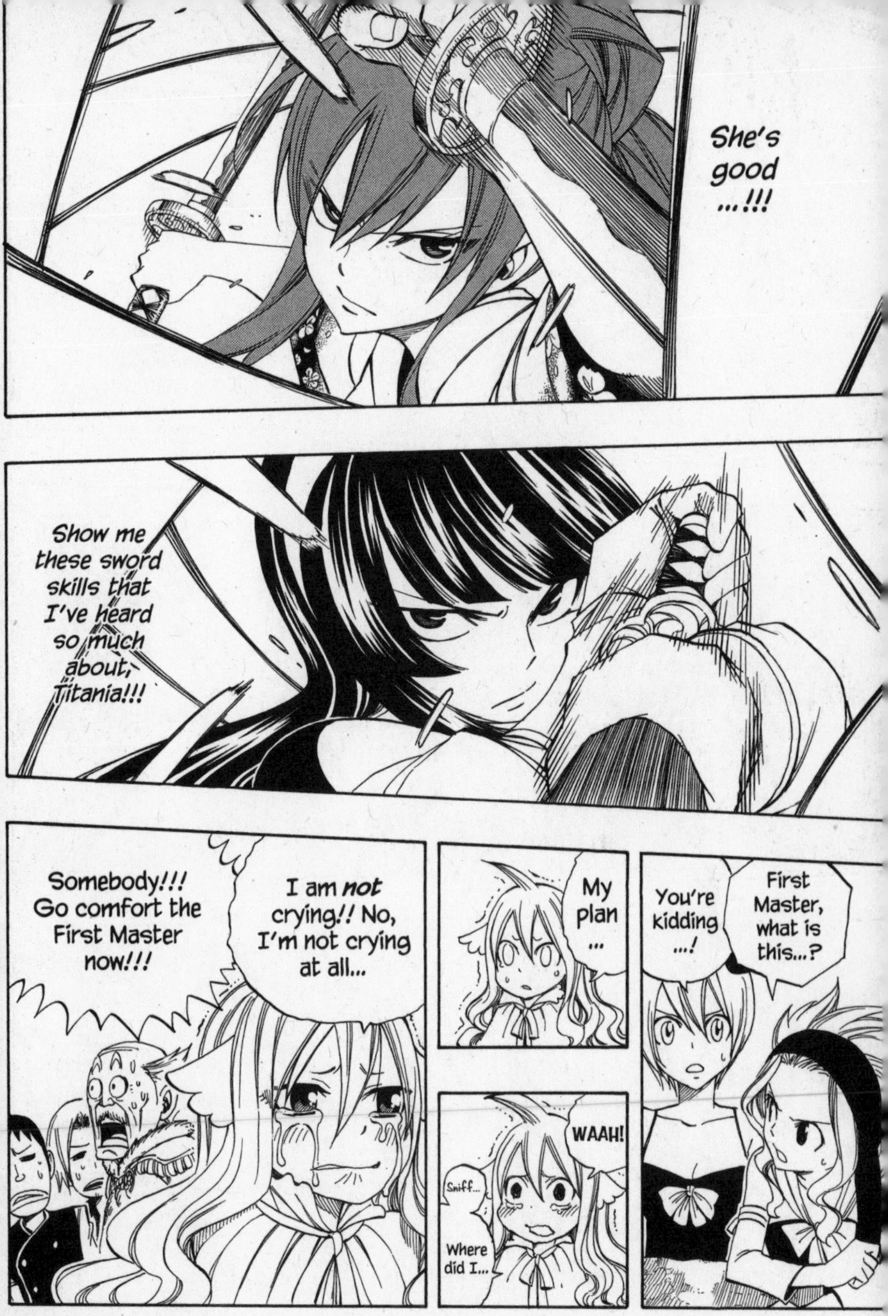
She's good ...!!!
Show me these sword skills that I've heard so much about, Titania!!!
First Master, what is this...?
You're kidding ...!
My plan ...
WAAH!
Sniff...
Where did I...
I am *not* crying!! No, I'm not crying at all...
Somebody!!! Go comfort the First Master now!!!

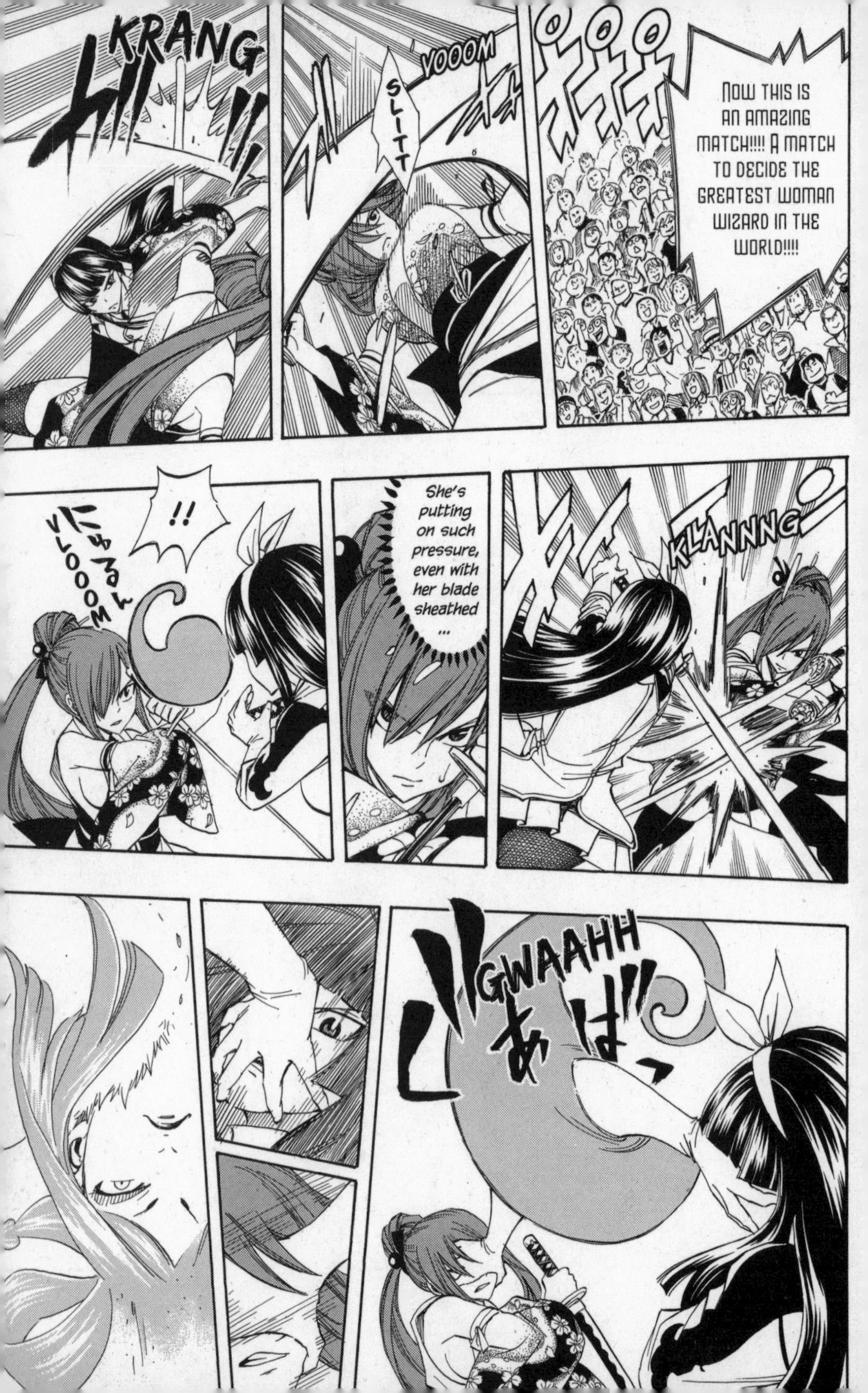
NOW THIS IS AN AMAZING MATCH!!!! A MATCH TO DECIDE THE GREATEST WOMAN WIZARD IN THE WORLD!!!!
VOOOM
SLITT
KRANG
KLANNNG
She's putting on such pressure, even with her blade sheathed ...
!!
にゅるん
VLOOOOM
GWAAHH
あはっ

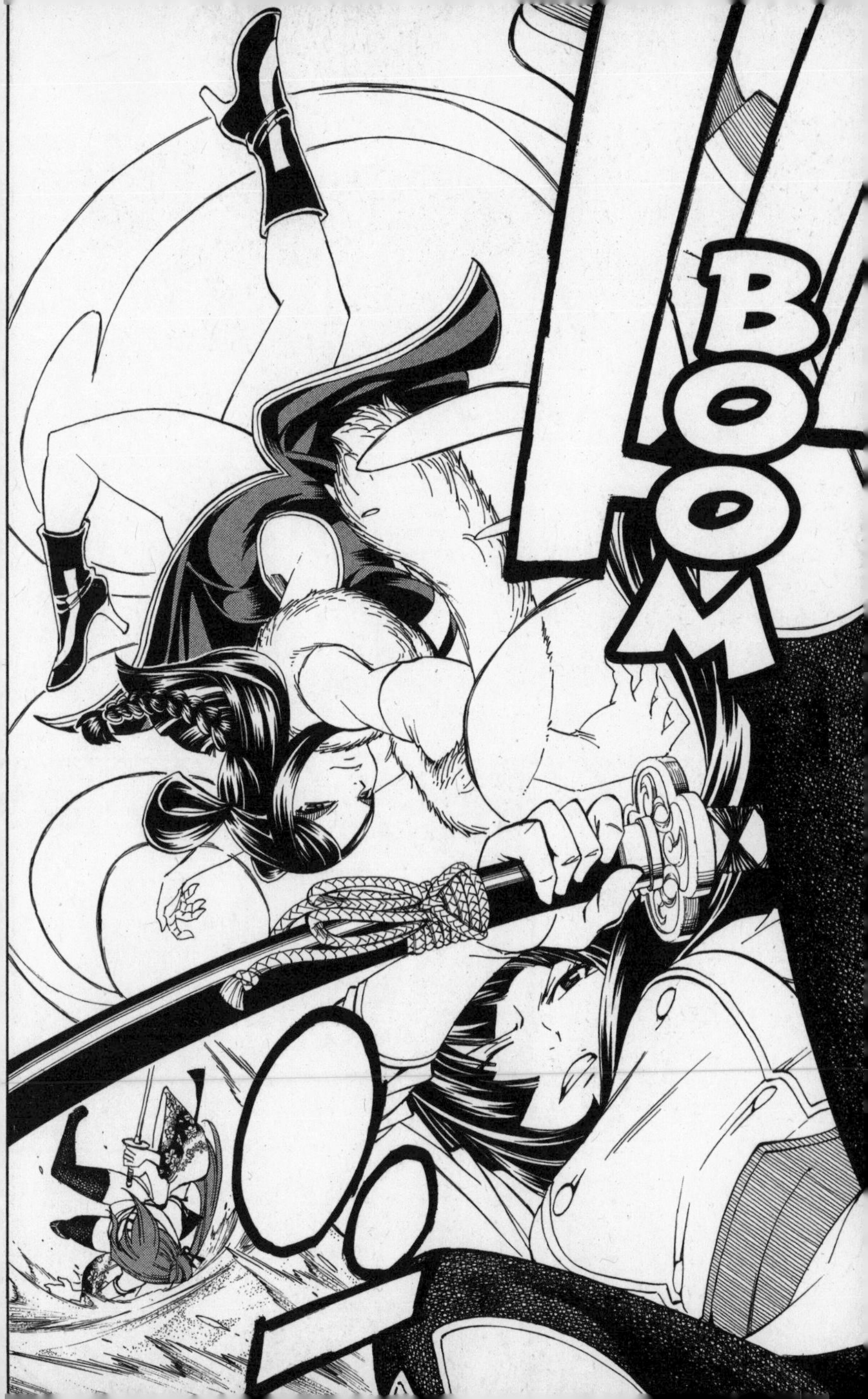
BOOM

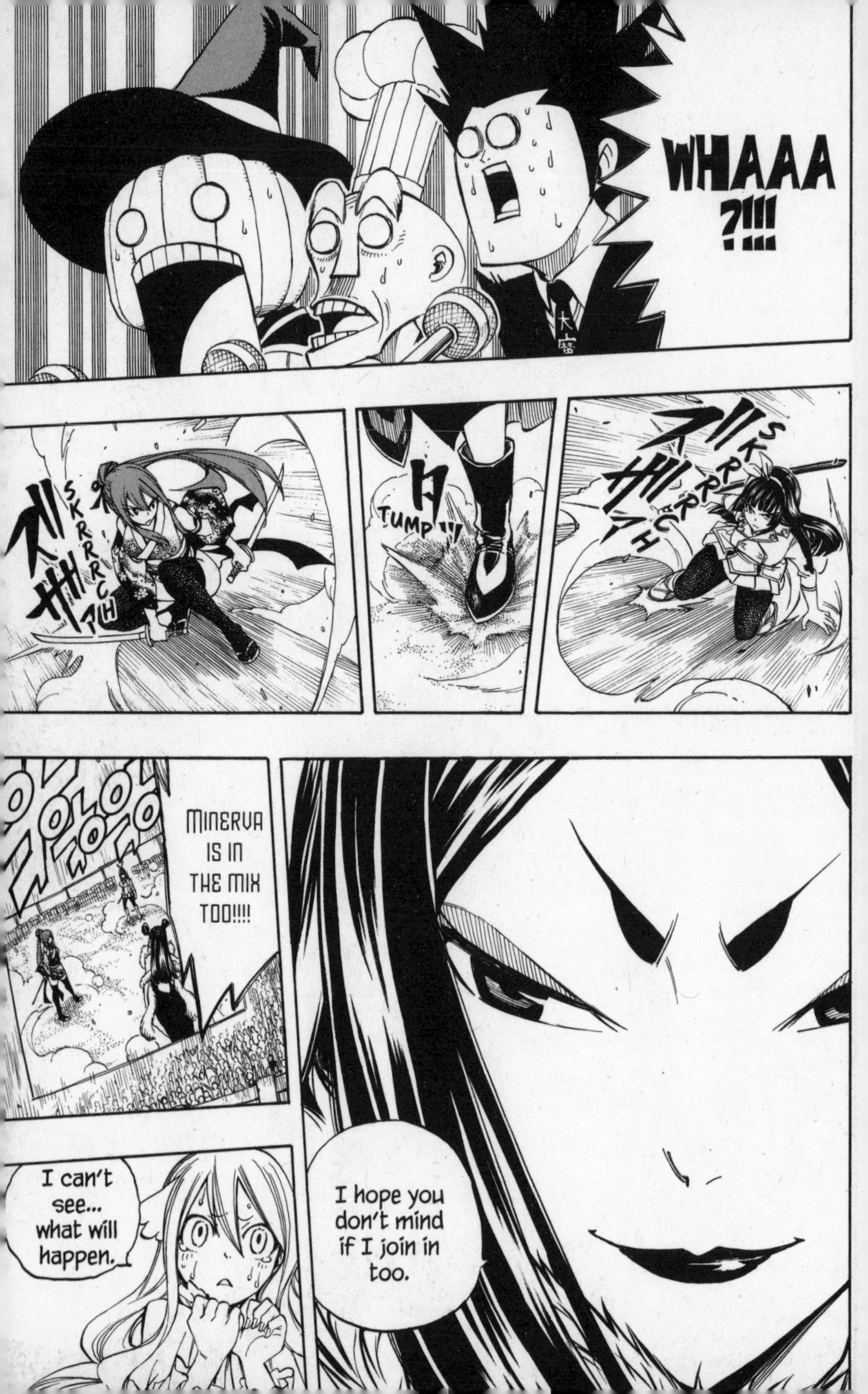
WHAAA ?!!!
SKRRRCH
TUMP!!!
SKRRRCH
I hope you don't mind if I join in too.
MINERVA IS IN THE MIX TOO!!!!
I can't see... what will happen.

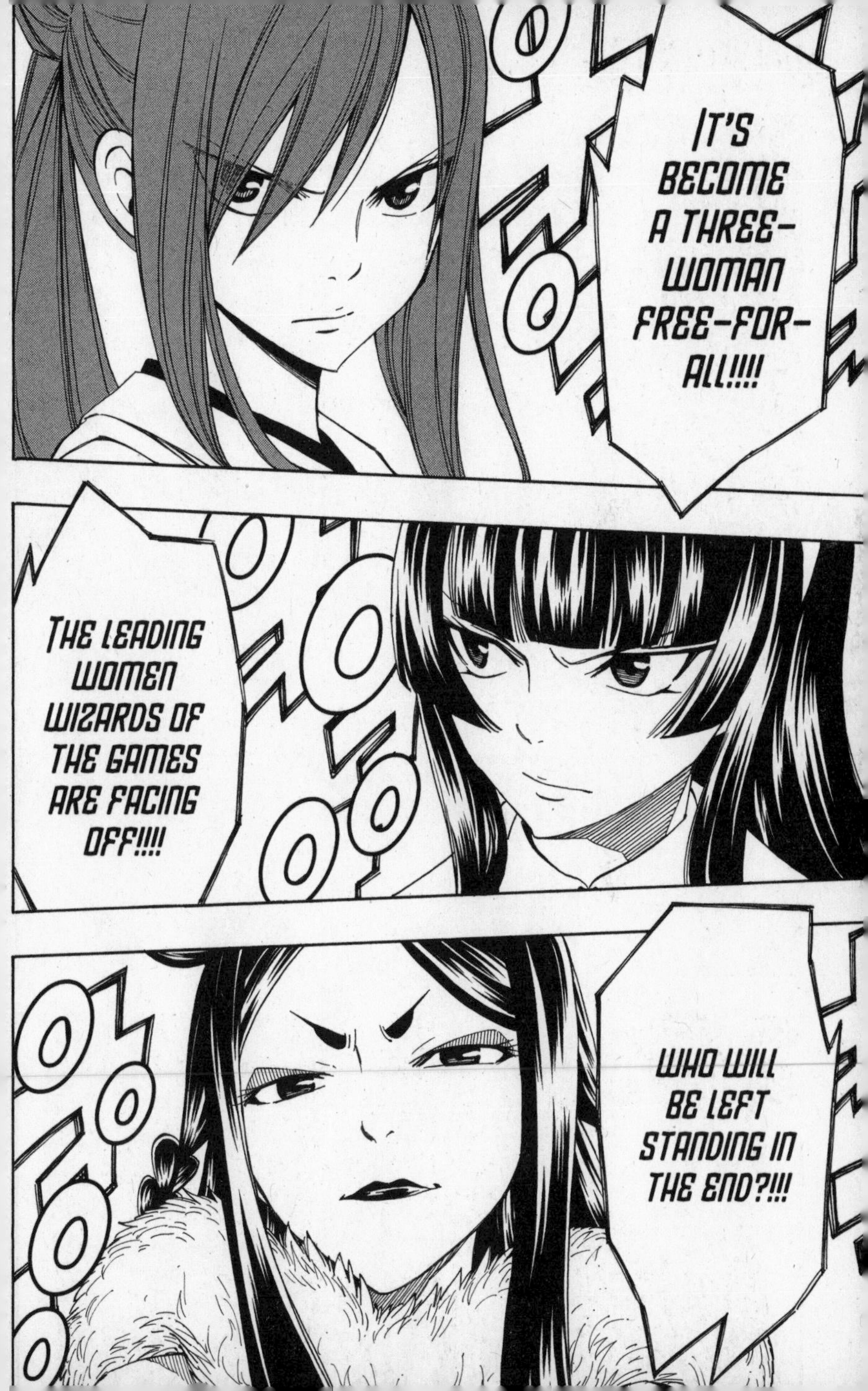
IT'S BECOME A THREE-WOMAN FREE-FOR-ALL!!!!
THE LEADING WOMEN WIZARDS OF THE GAMES ARE FACING OFF!!!!
WHO WILL BE LEFT STANDING IN THE END?!!!

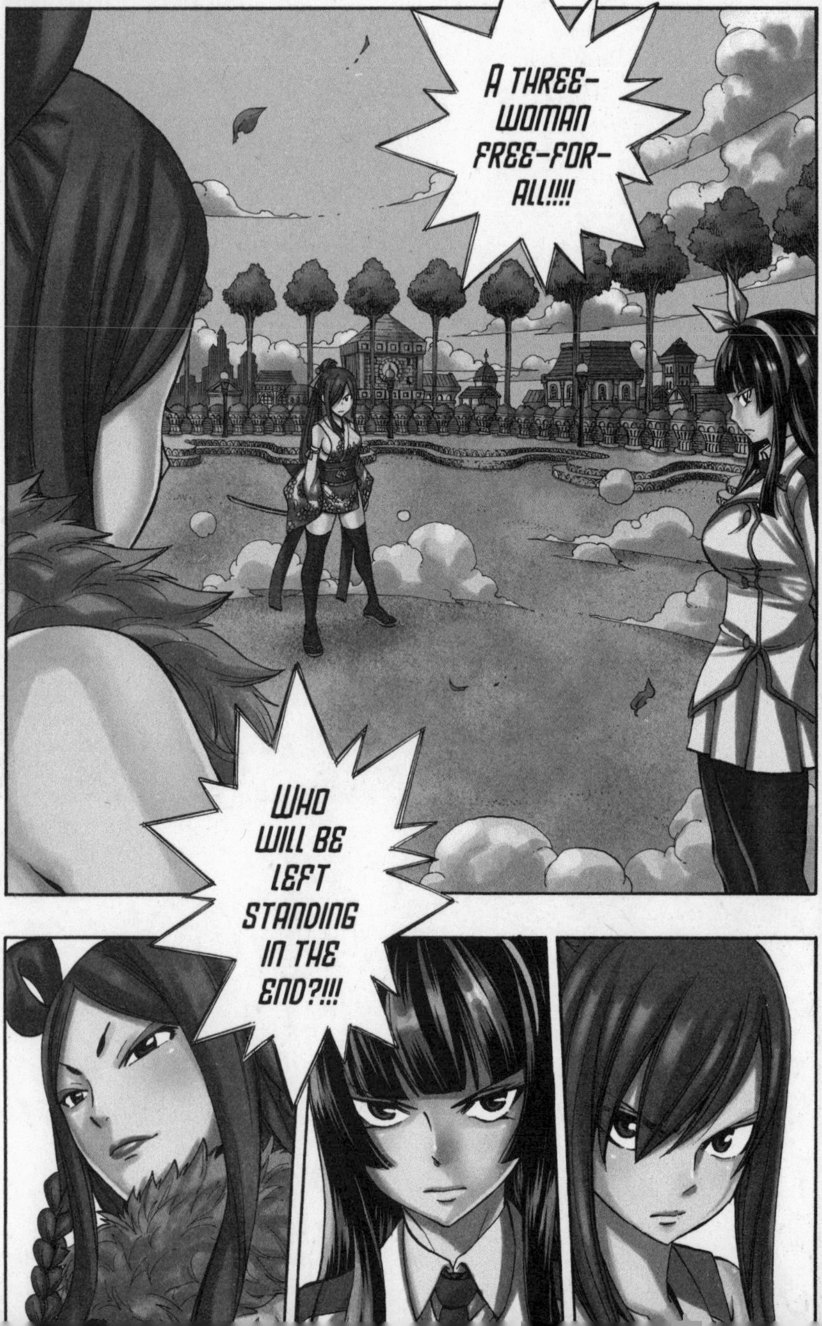
A THREE-WOMAN FREE-FOR-ALL!!!!
WHO WILL BE LEFT STANDING IN THE END?!!!

Chapter 312: Threesomes

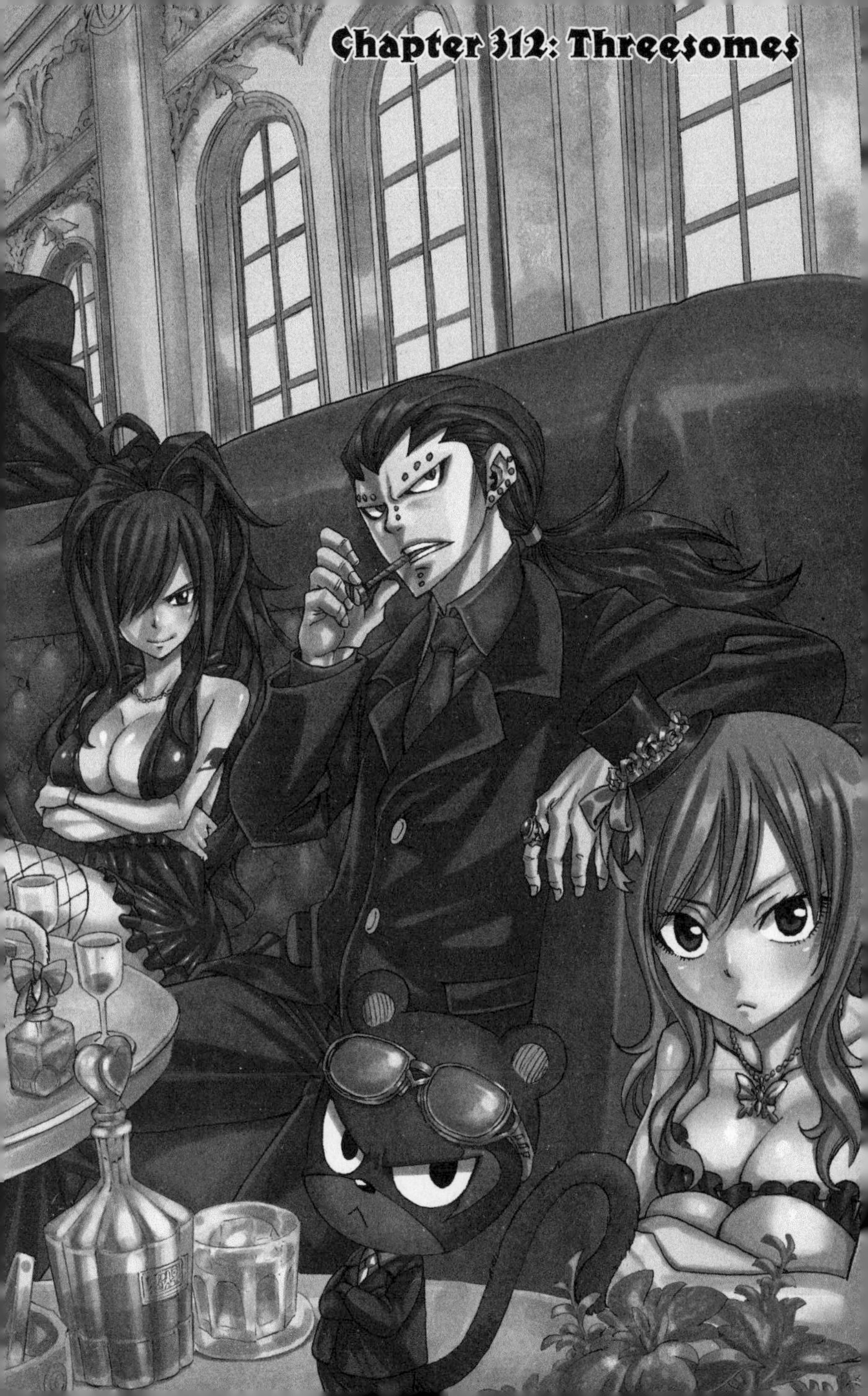

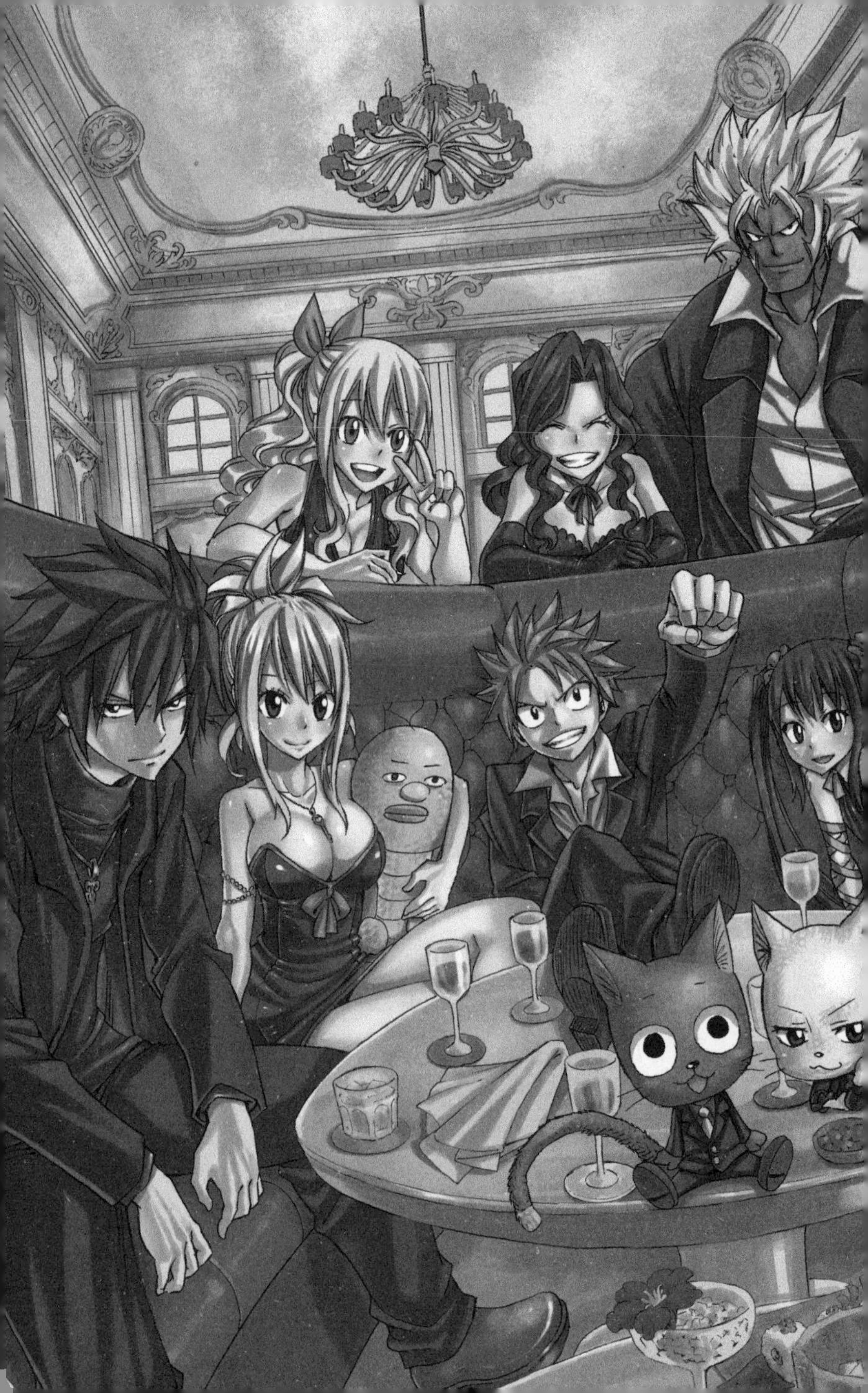

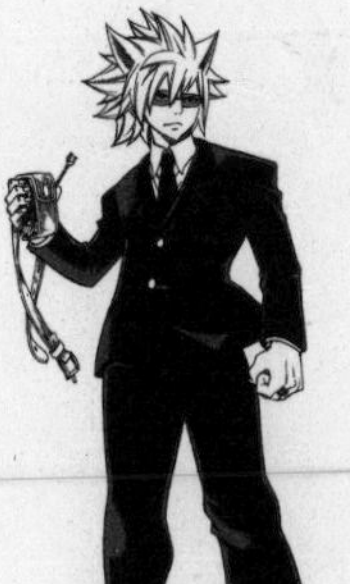

FAIRY TAIL

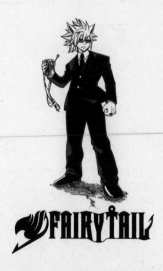

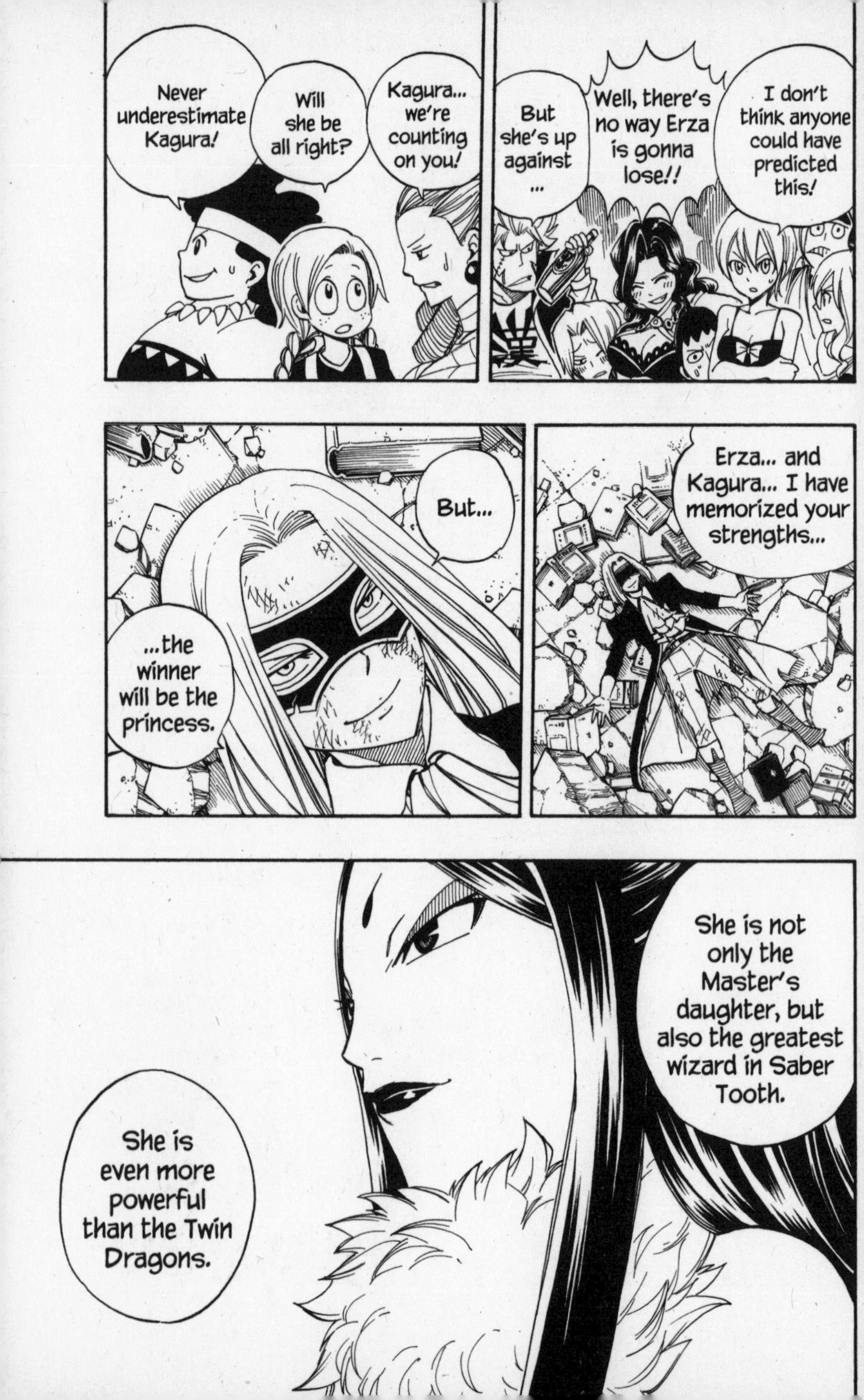
I don't think anyone could have predicted this!
Well, there's no way Erza is gonna lose!!
But she's up against ...
Kagura... we're counting on you!
Will she be all right?
Never underestimate Kagura!
Erza... and Kagura... I have memorized your strengths...
But...
...the winner will be the princess.
She is not only the Master's daughter, but also the greatest wizard in Saber Tooth.
She is even more powerful than the Twin Dragons.

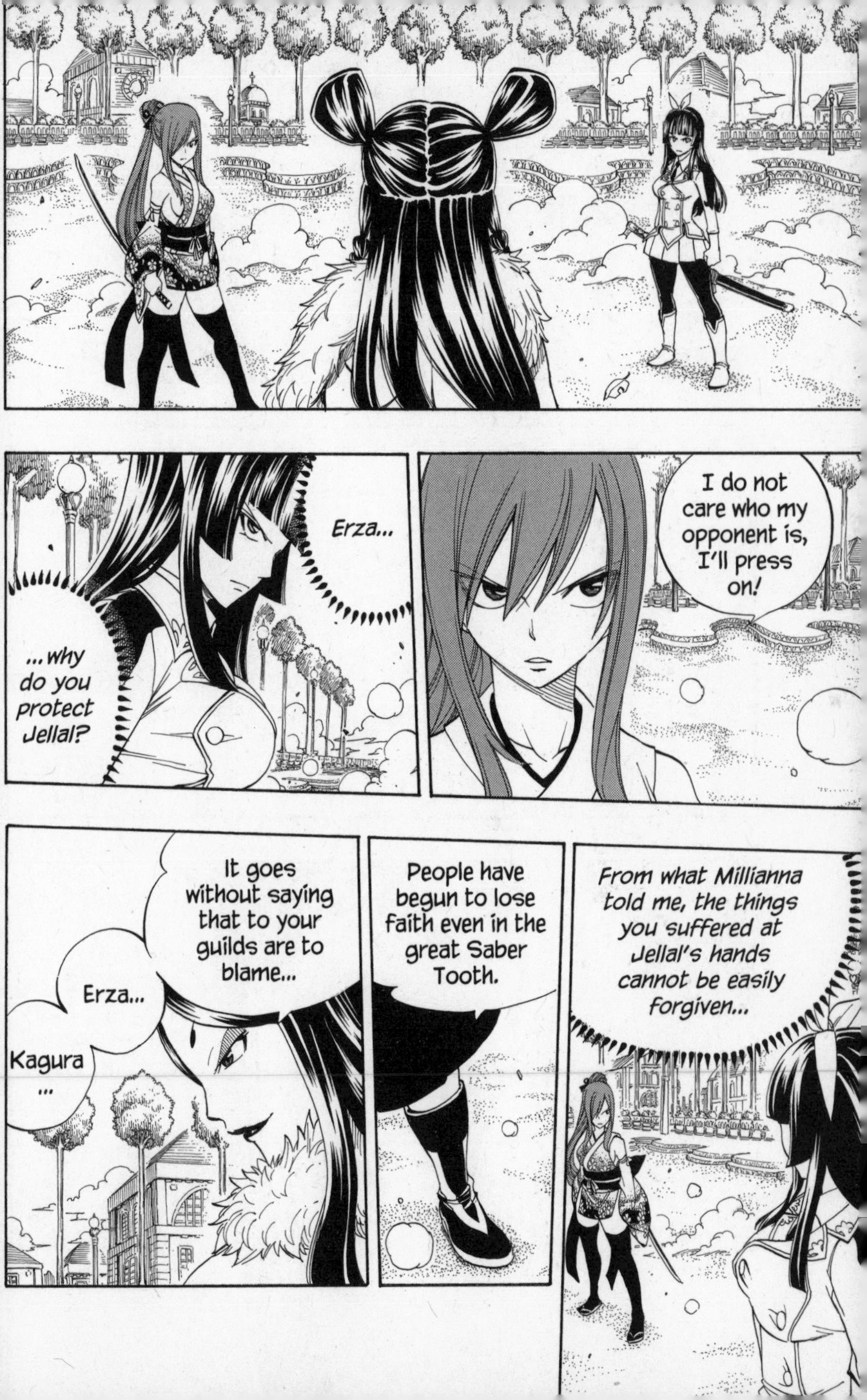
I do not care who my opponent is, I'll press on!
Erza...
...why do you protect Jellal?
From what Millianna told me, the things you suffered at Jellal's hands cannot be easily forgiven...
People have begun to lose faith even in the great Saber Tooth.
It goes without saying that to your guilds are to blame...
Erza...
Kagura ...

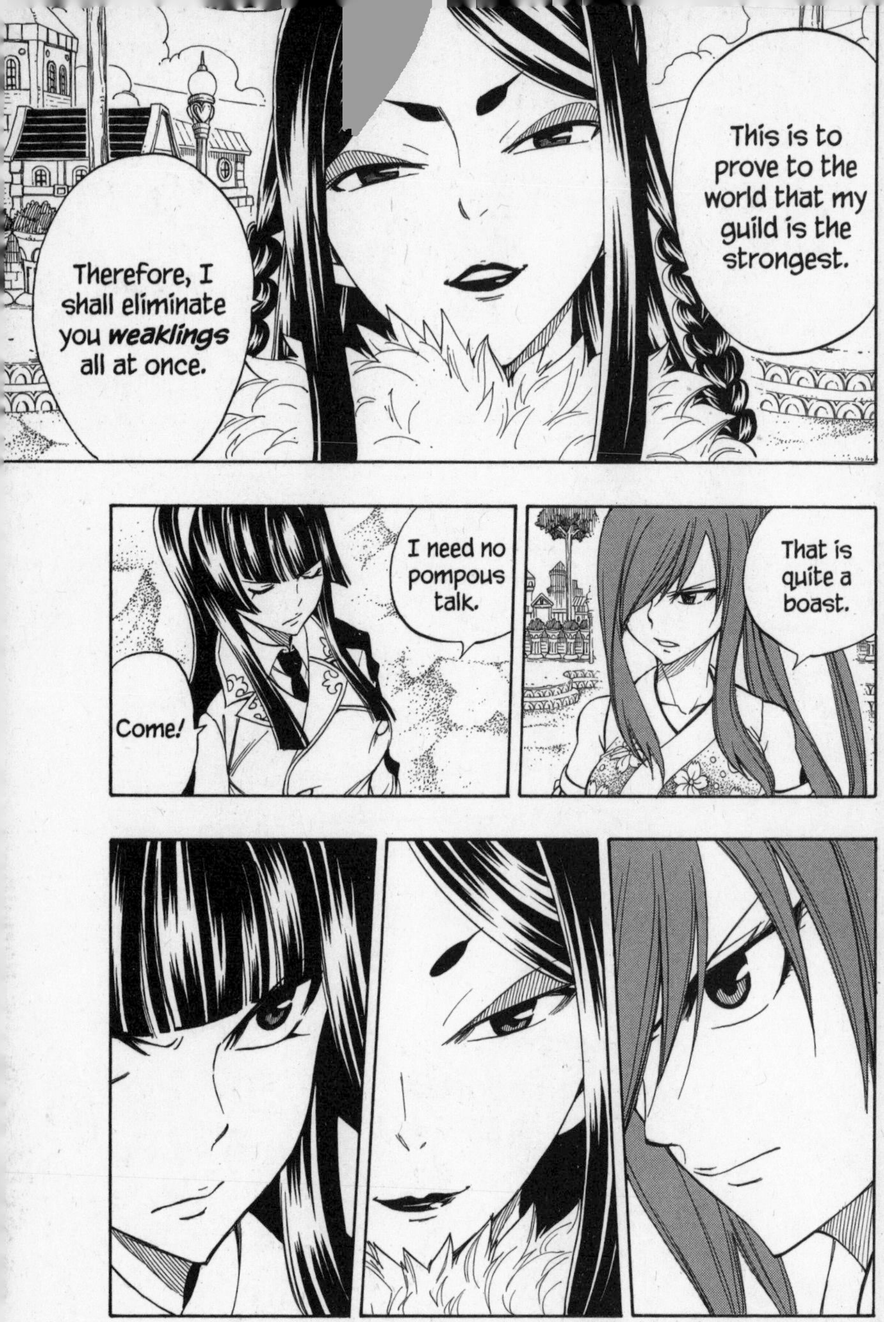
This is to prove to the world that my guild is the strongest.
Therefore, I shall eliminate you *weaklings* all at once.
That is quite a boast.
I need no pompous talk.
Come!

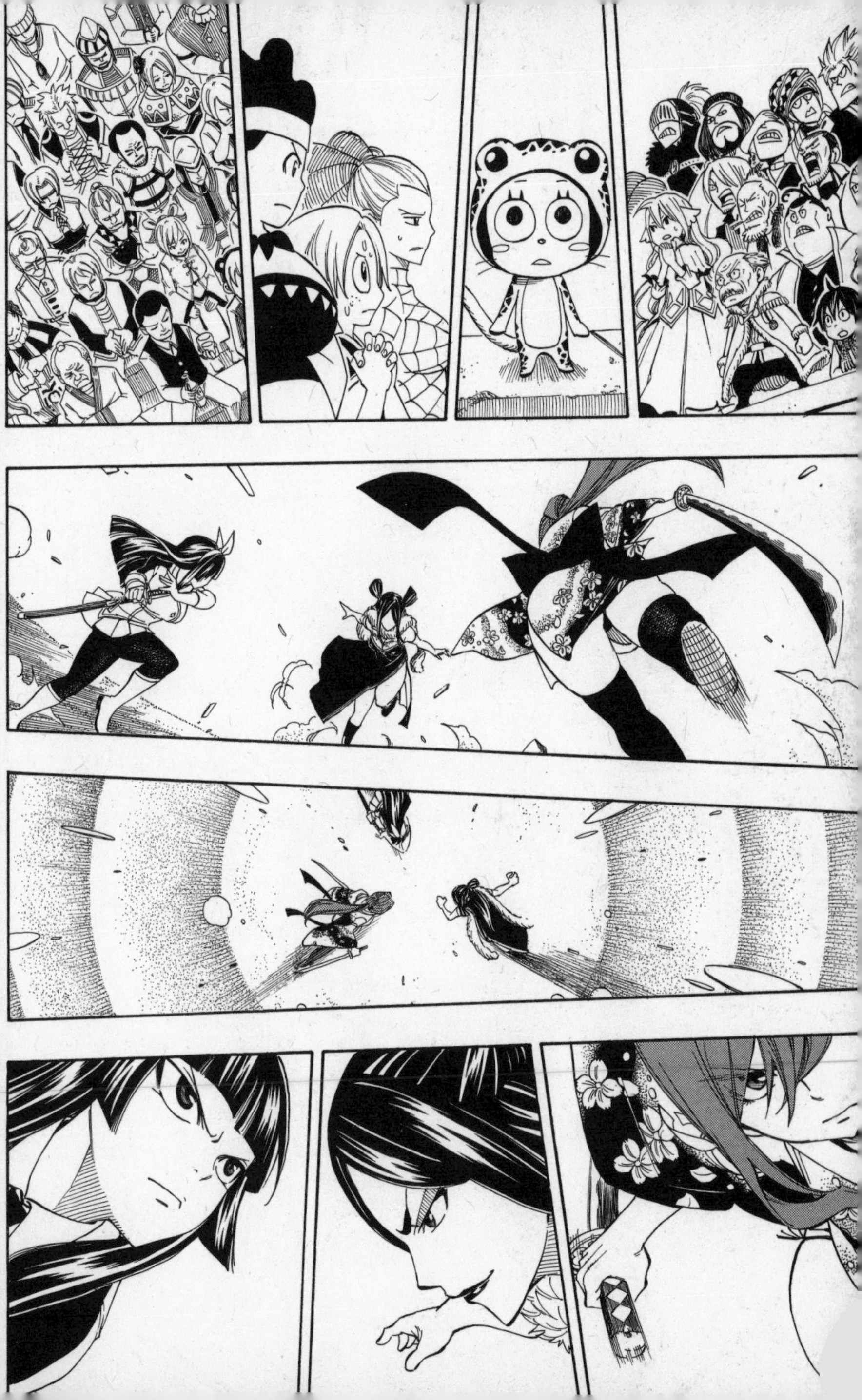

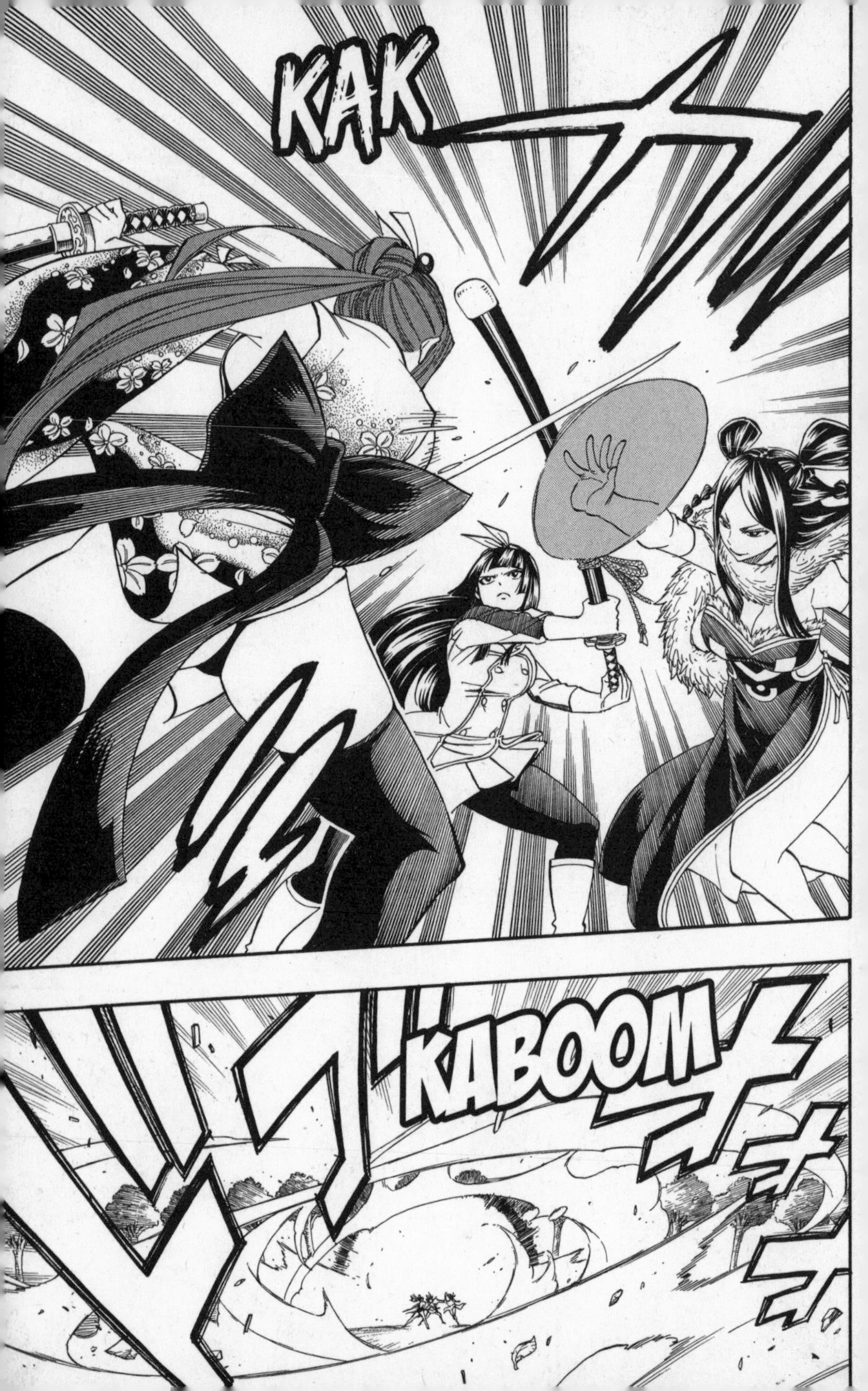
KAK
KABOOM

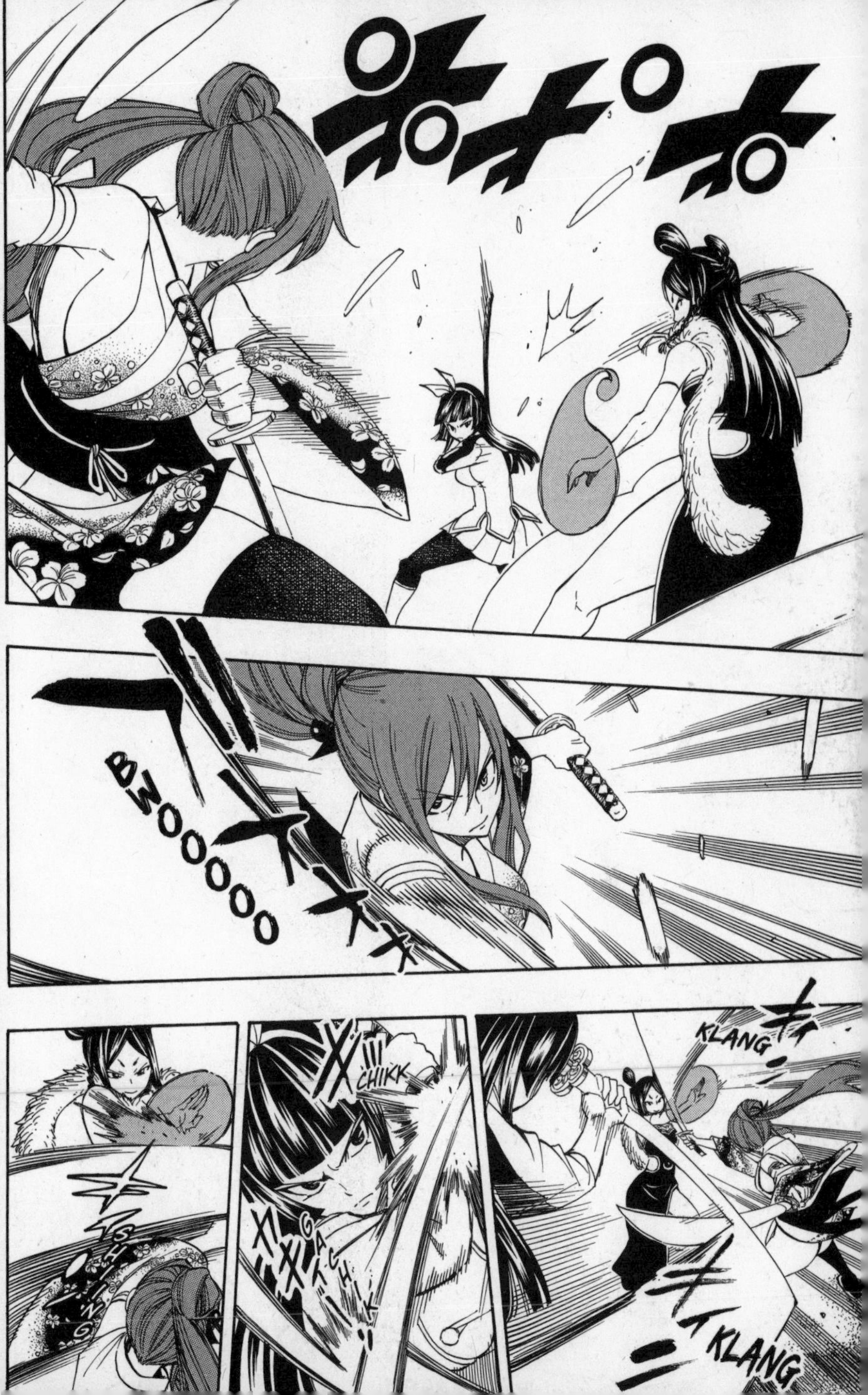
BWOOOOOO
KLANG
KLANG
CHIKK
GACHIK!
SHIING

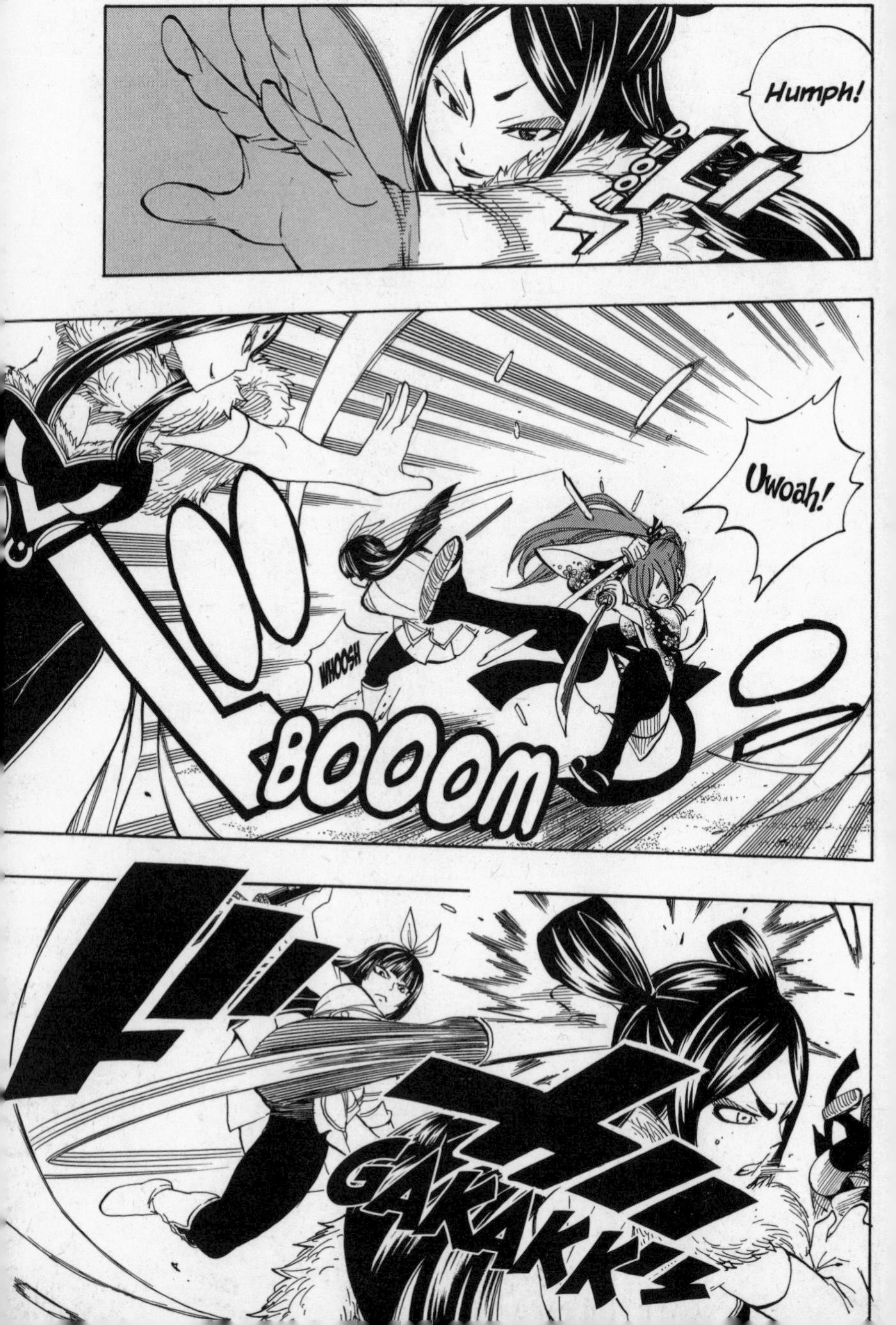
Humph!
DWOOM
Uwoah!
WHOOSH
BOOOM
GAKAKK

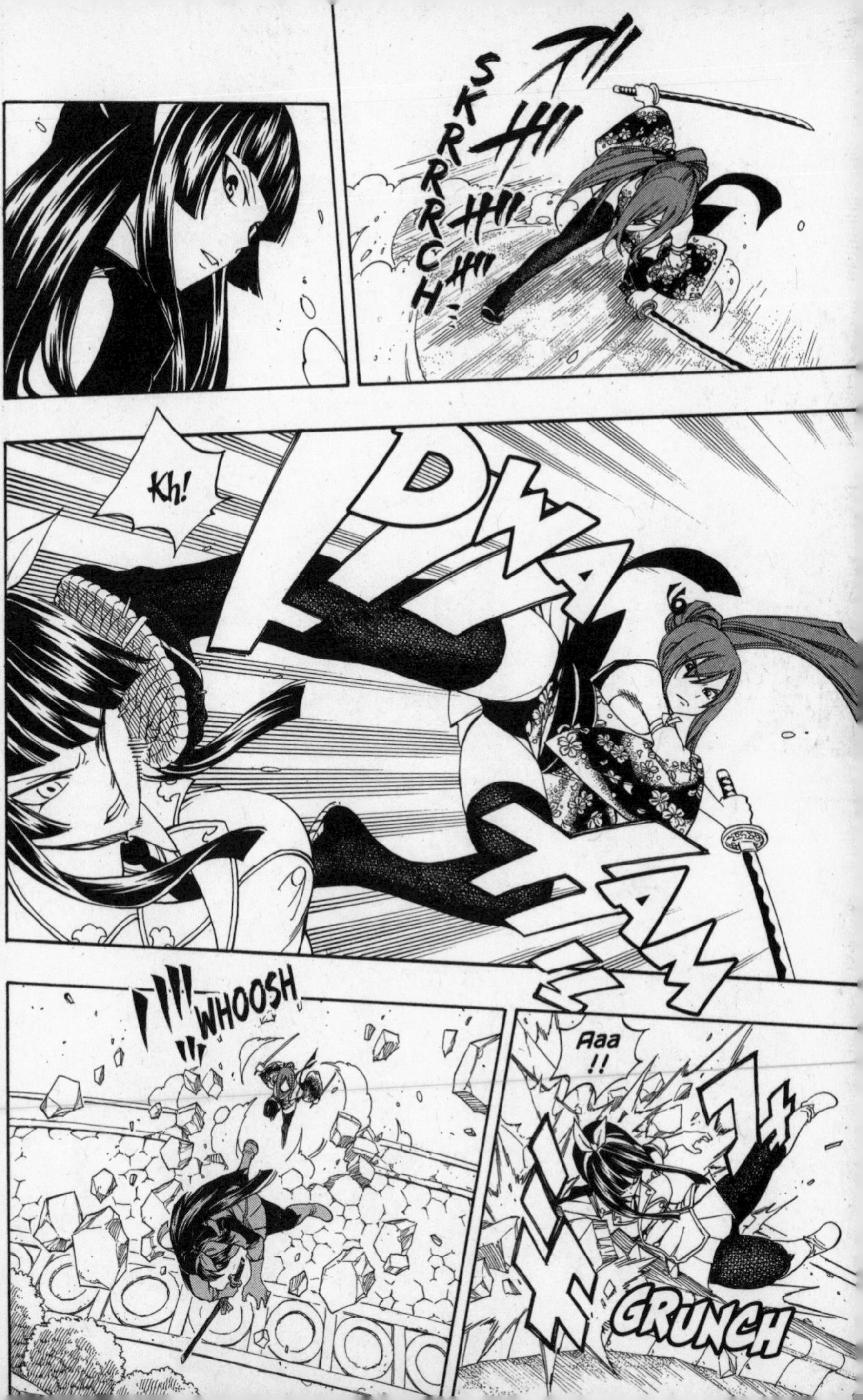
SKRRRRCH
SHHHH
Kh!
DWAM
WHAM!
Aaa !!
GRUNCH
WHOOSH

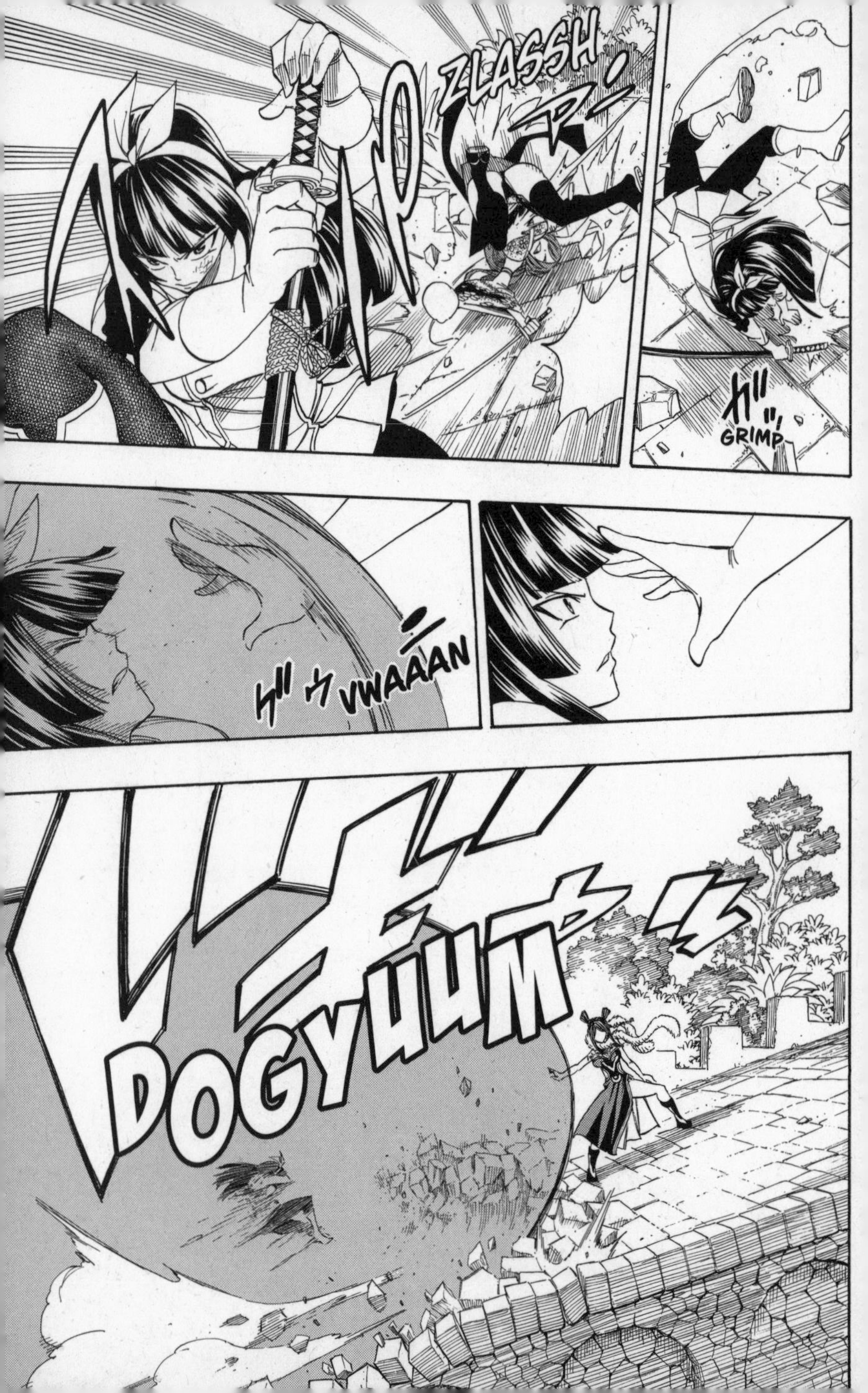
GRIMP
ZLASSH
VWAAAN
DOGYUUM

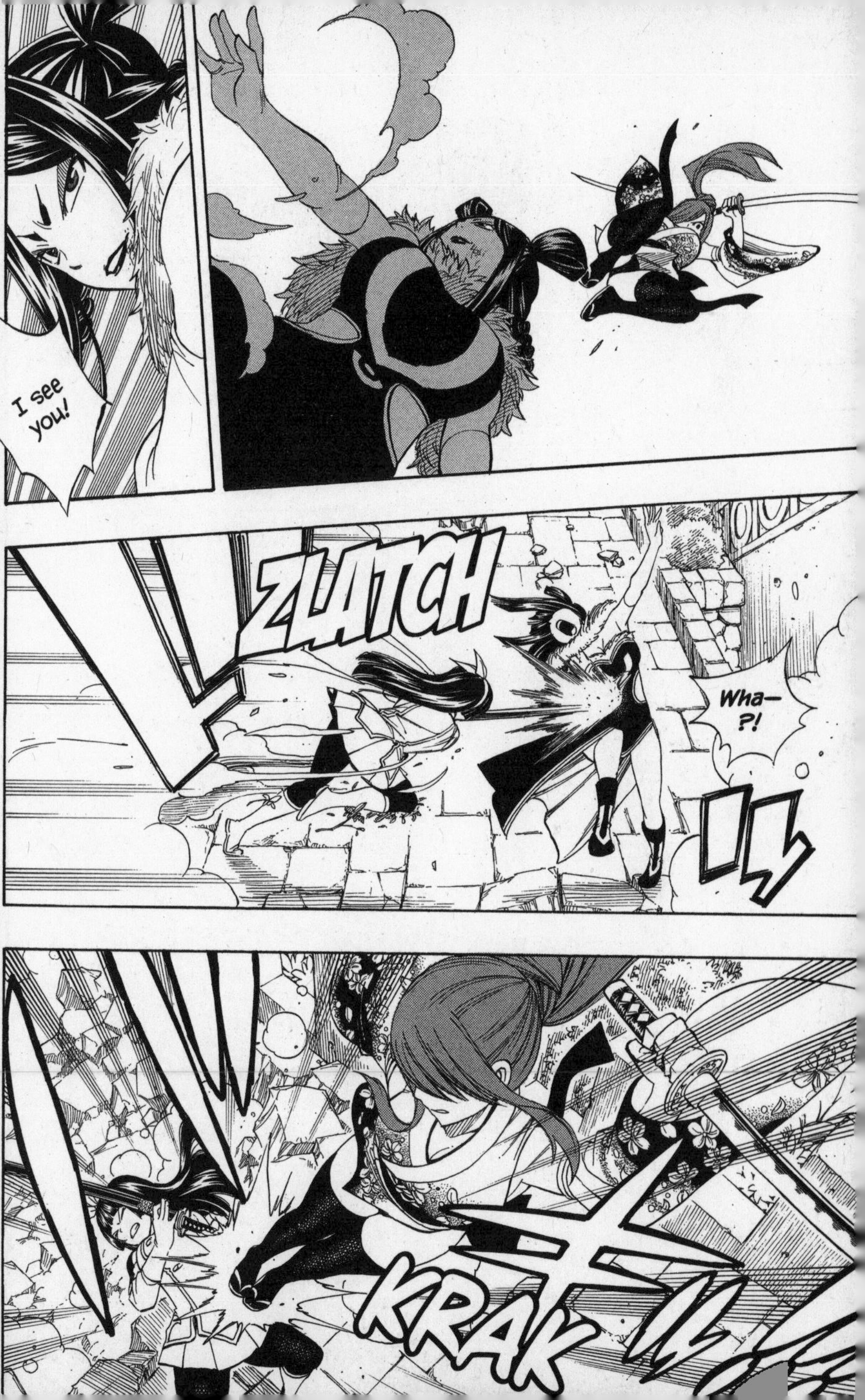
I see you!
ZLATCH
Wha—?!
KRAK

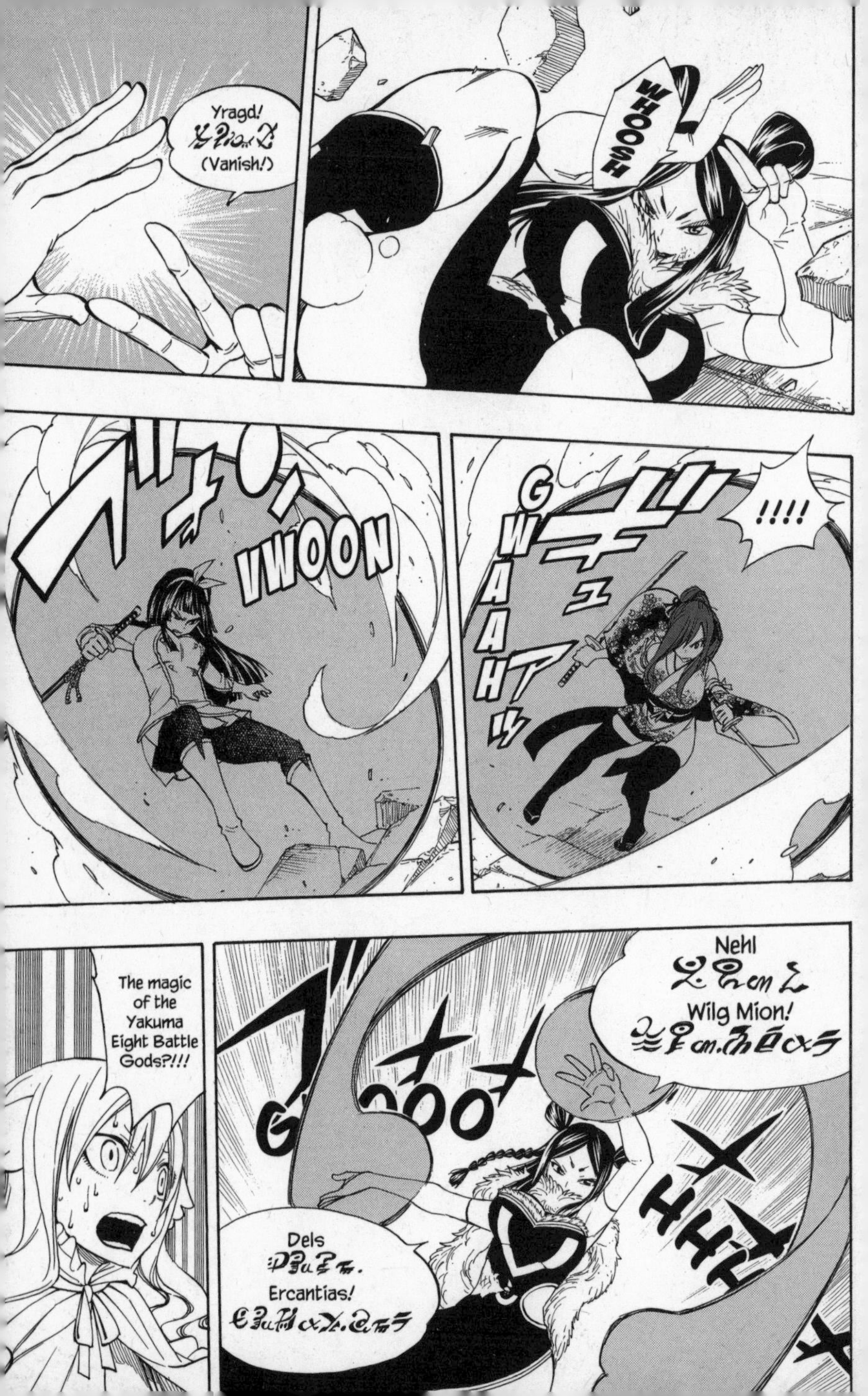
WHOOSH
Yragd!
(Vanish!)
GWAAAH
!!!!
VWOON
Nehl
Wilg Mion!
Dels
Ercantias!
The magic of the Yakuma Eight Battle Gods?!!!

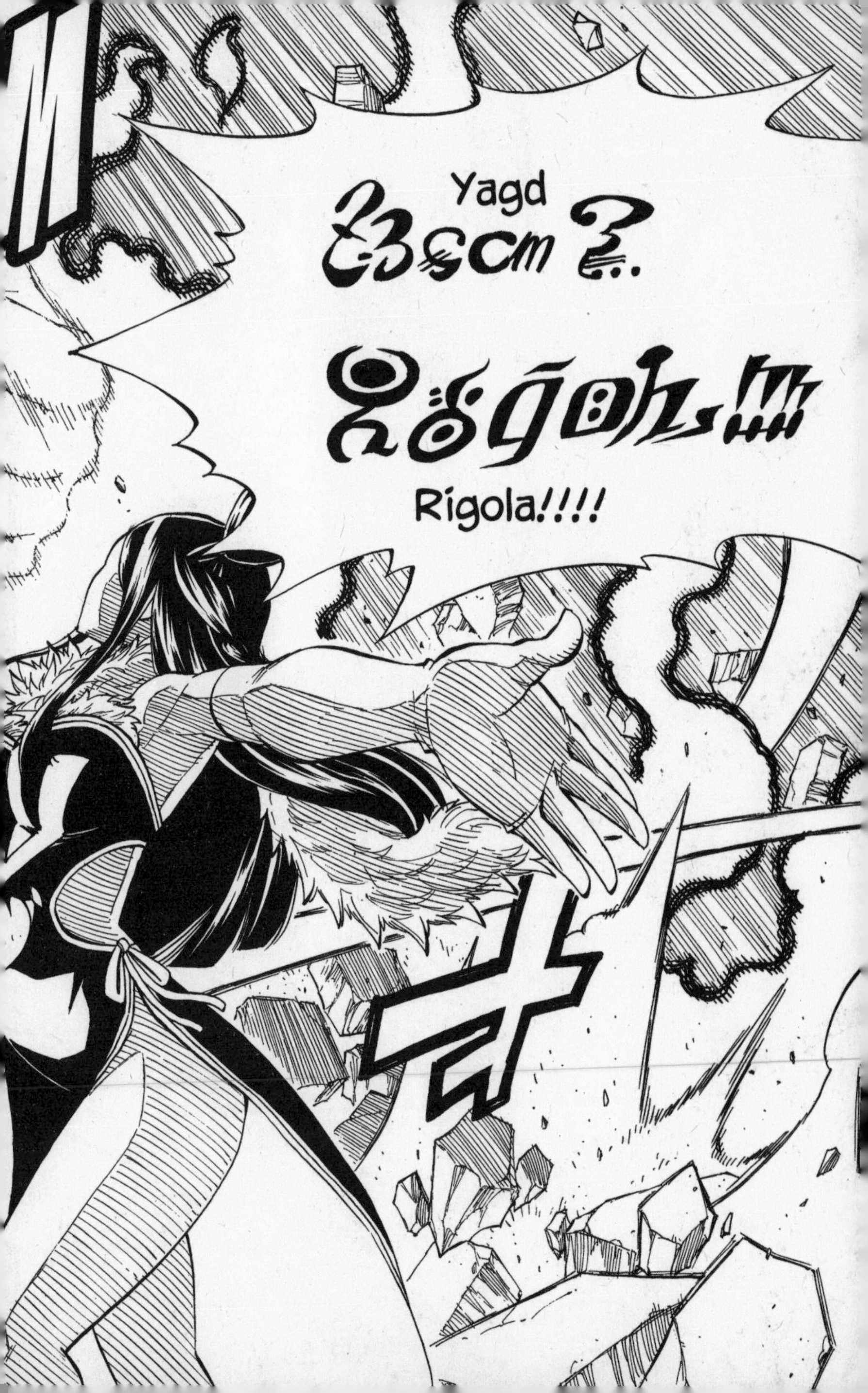
Yagd
Rigola!!!!

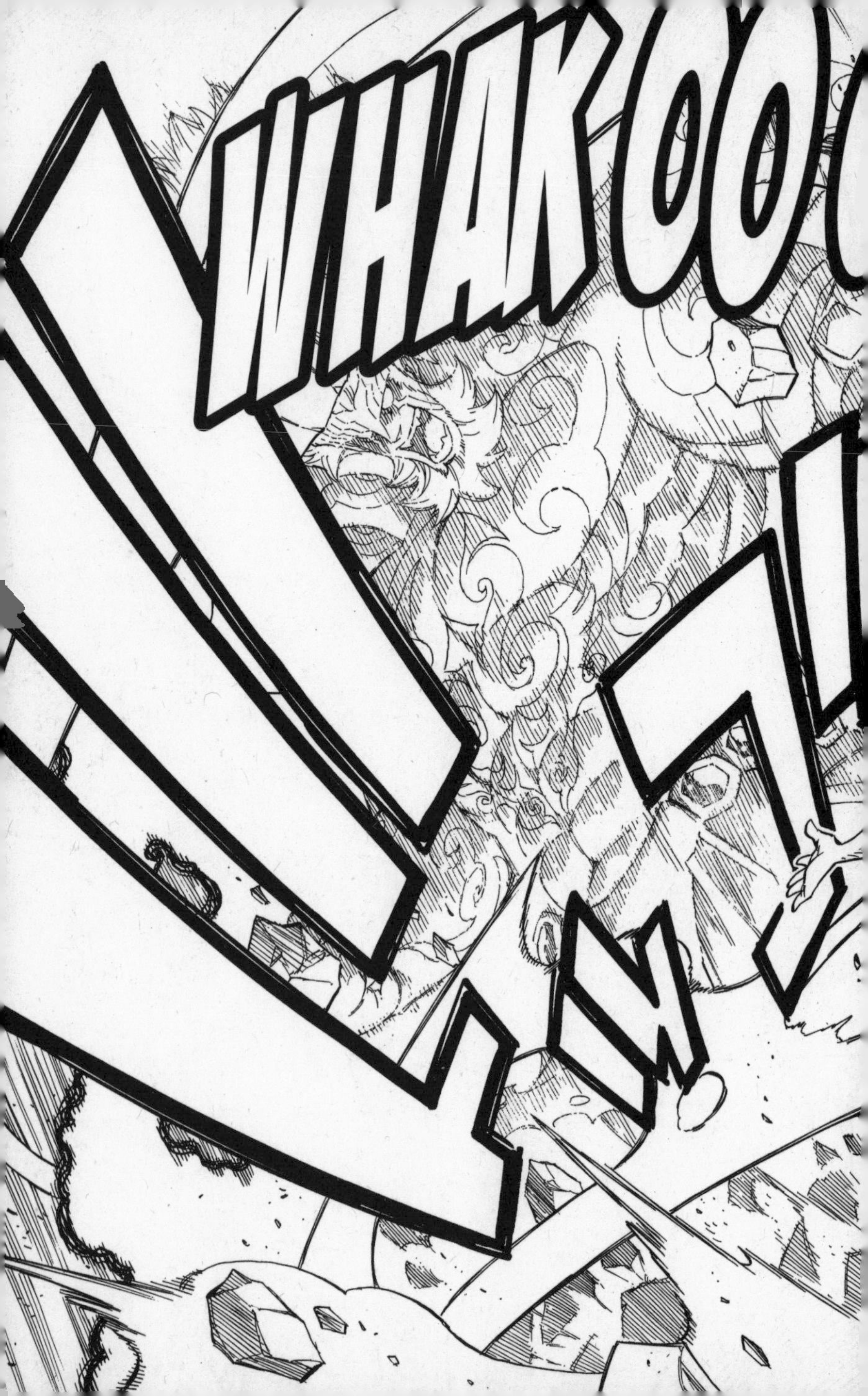
WHAKOO

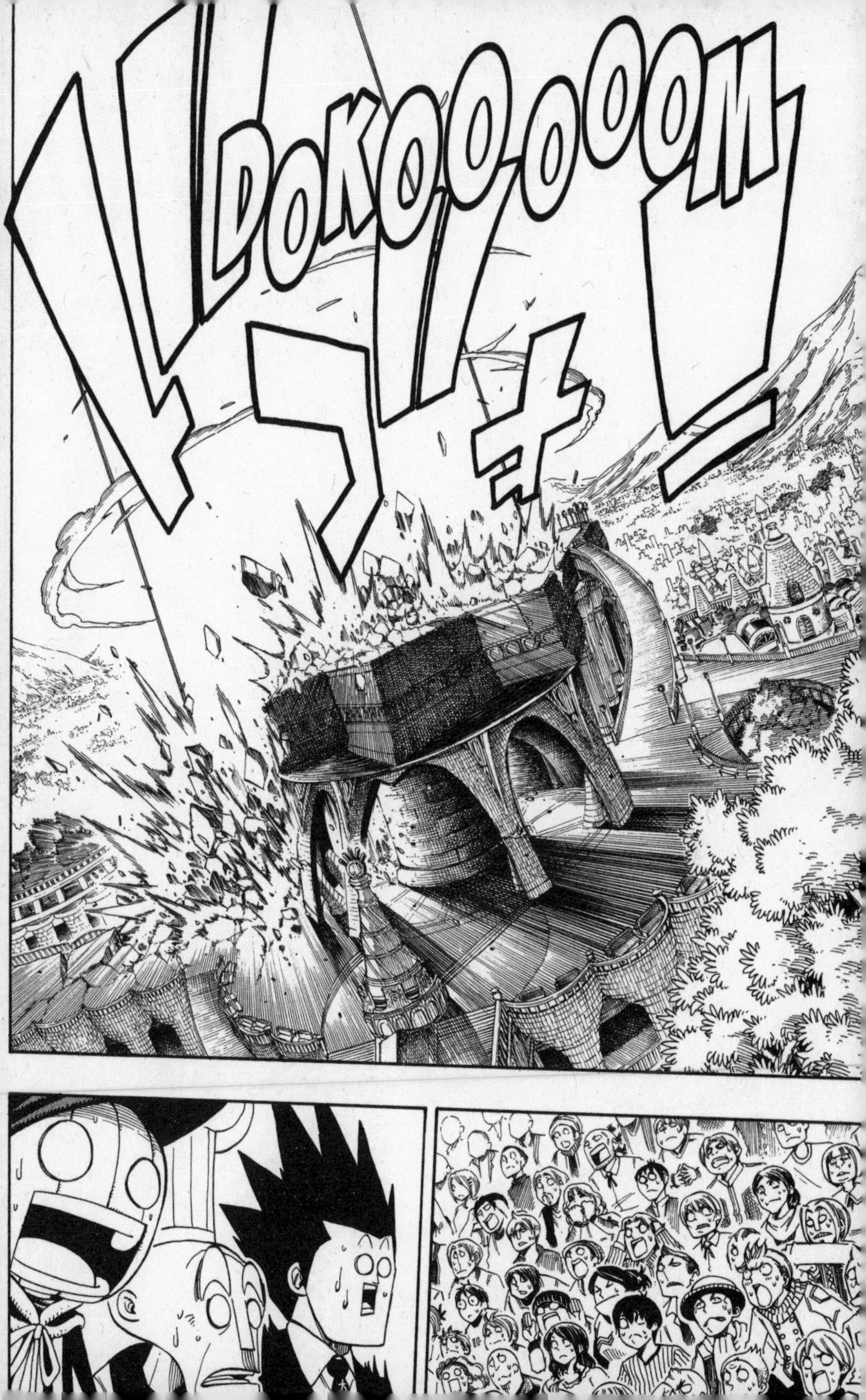
DOKOOOOOM

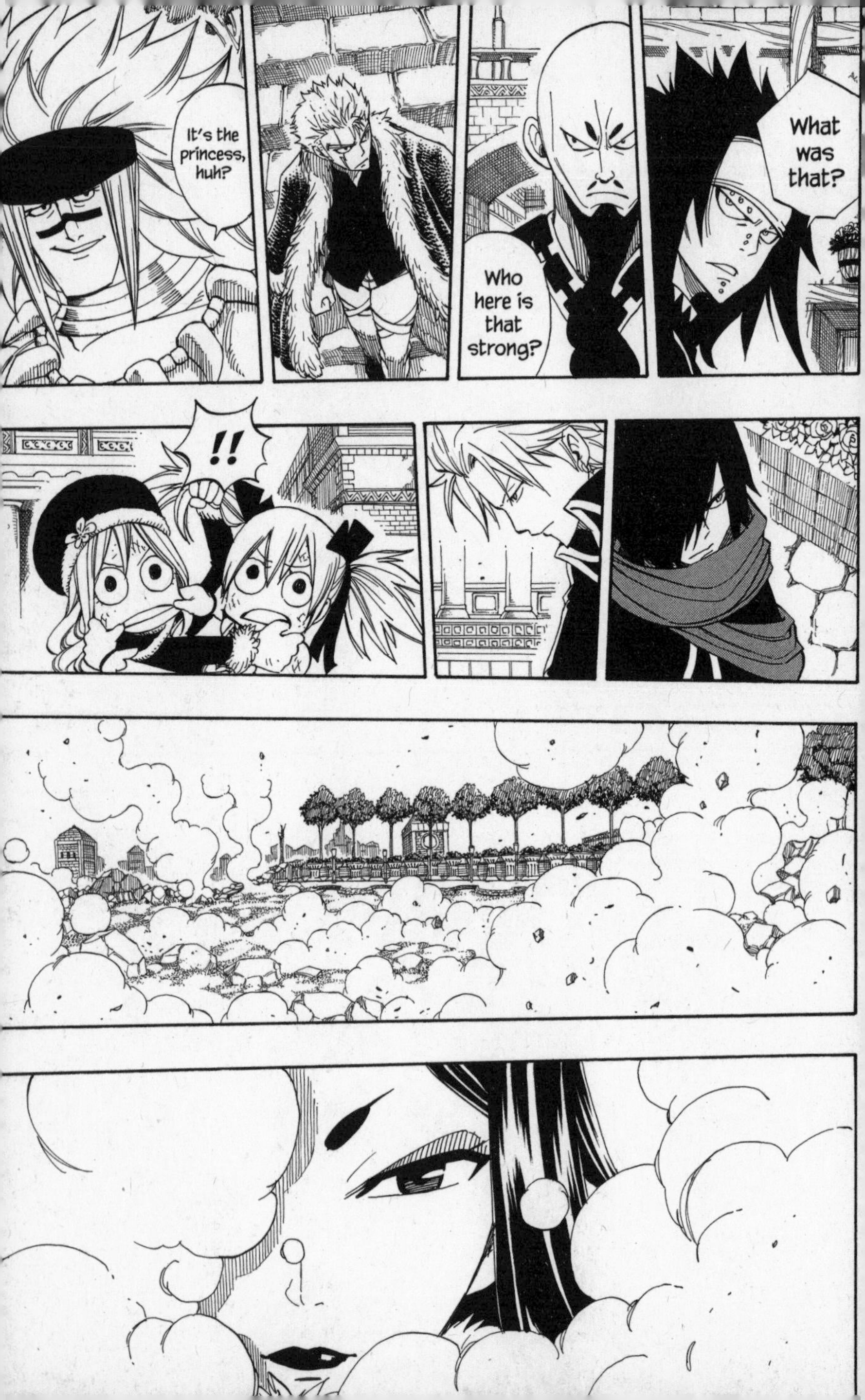
What was that?
Who here is that strong?
It's the princess, huh?
!!

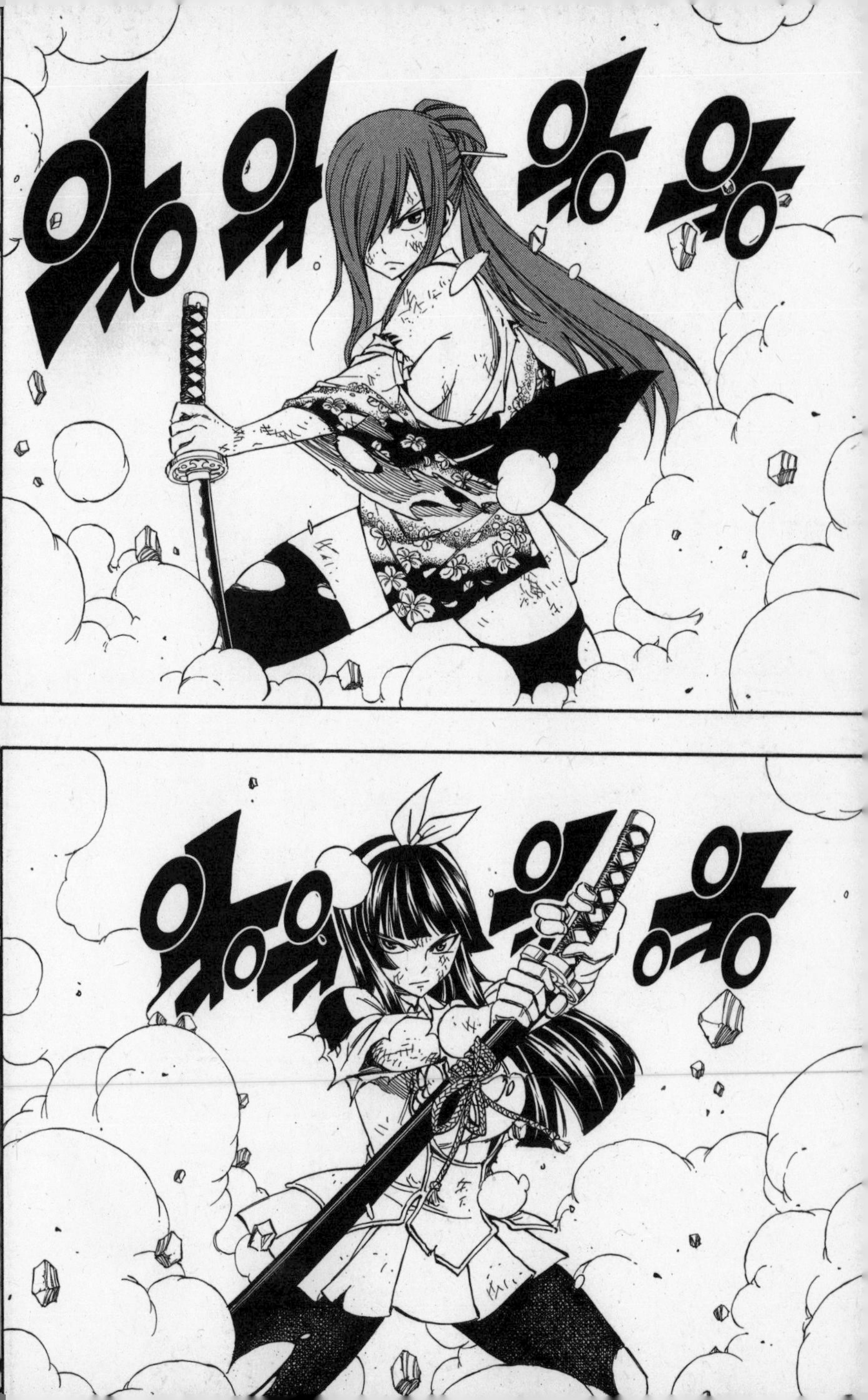

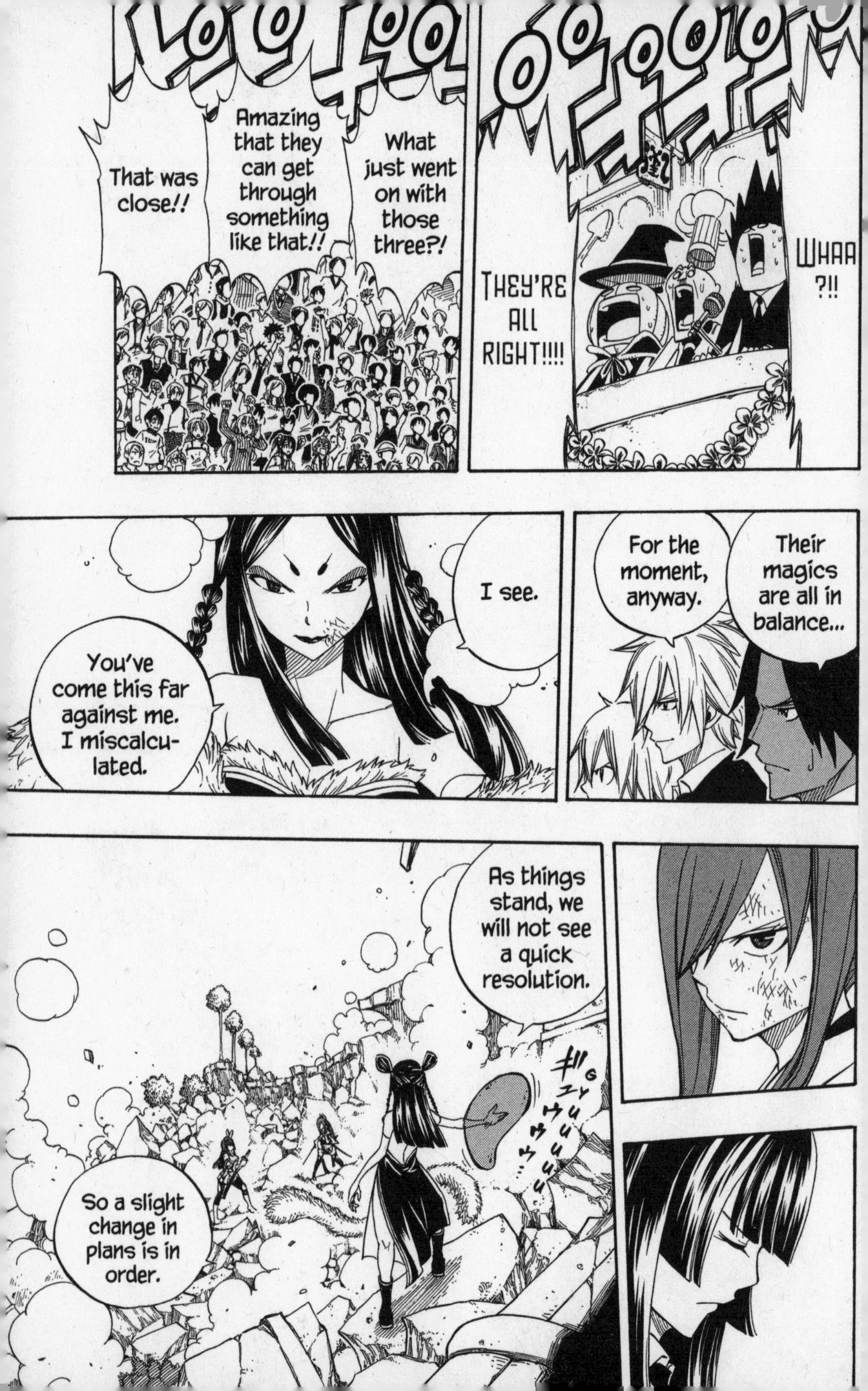
WHAA ?!!
THEY'RE ALL RIGHT!!!!
What just went on with those three?!
Amazing that they can get through something like that!!
That was close!!
Their magics are all in balance...
For the moment, anyway.
I see.
You've come this far against me. I miscalculated.
As things stand, we will not see a quick resolution.
So a slight change in plans is in order.

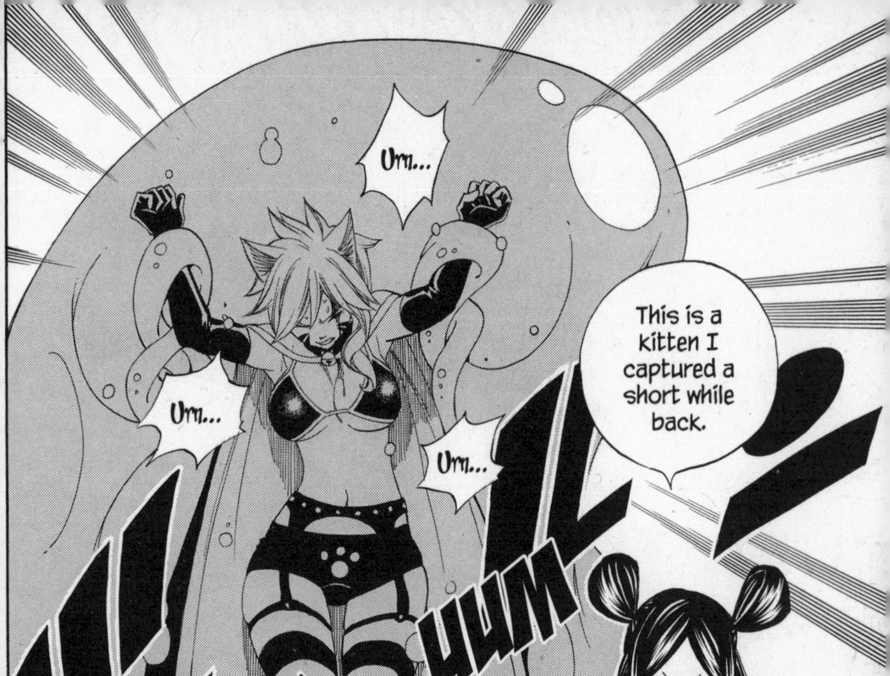
Um...
This is a kitten I captured a short while back.
Um...
Um...
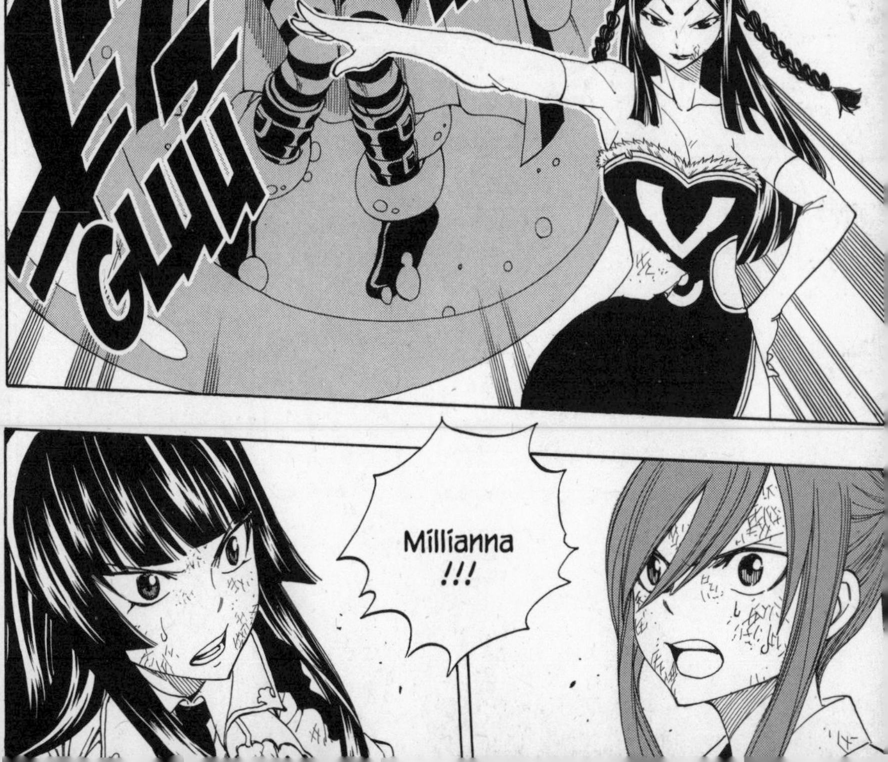
Millianna !!!

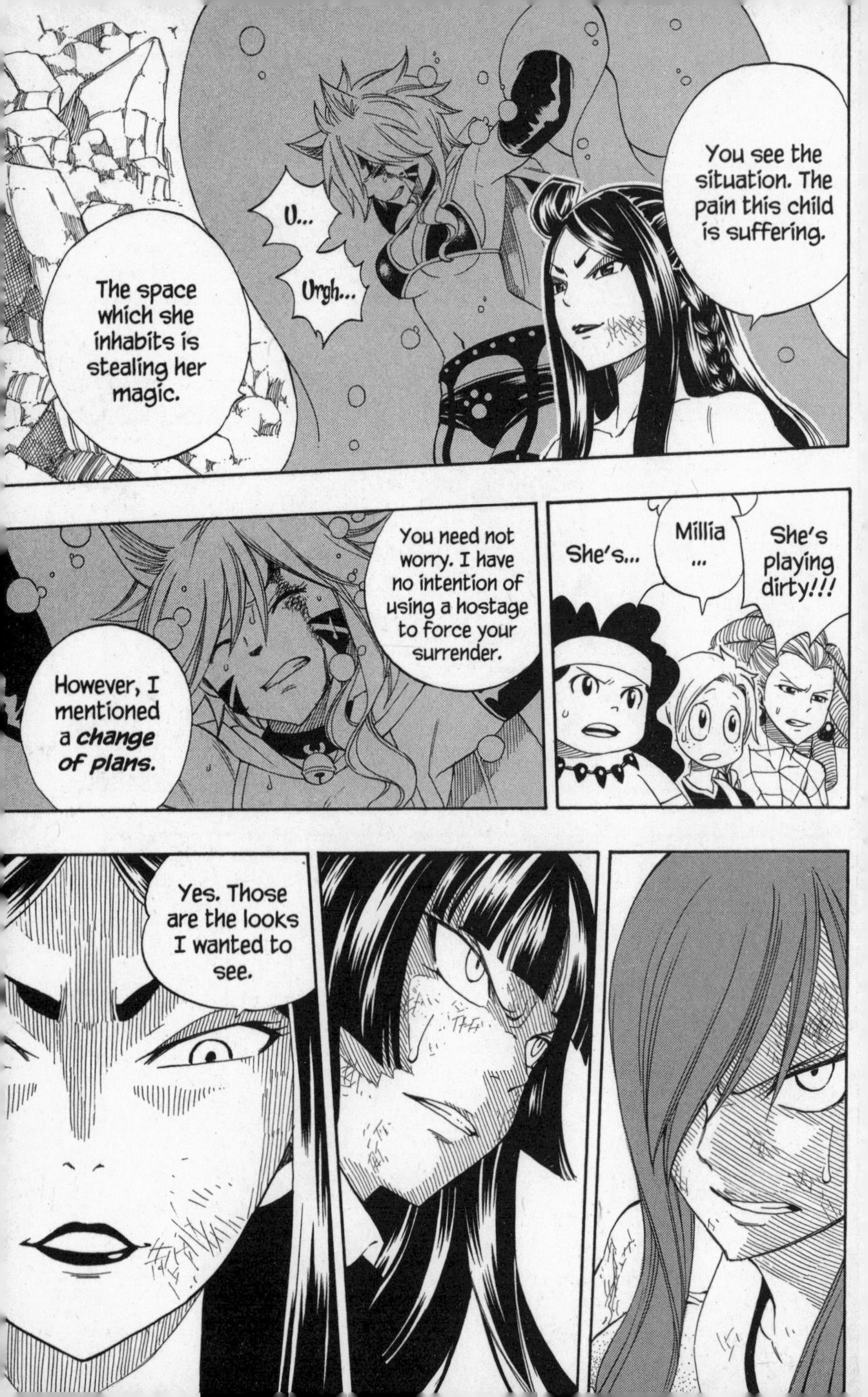
You see the situation. The pain this child is suffering.
U...
Urgh...
The space which she inhabits is stealing her magic.
She's playing dirty!!!
Millia ...
She's...
You need not worry. I have no intention of using a hostage to force your surrender.
However, I mentioned a *change of plans.*
Yes. Those are the looks I wanted to see.

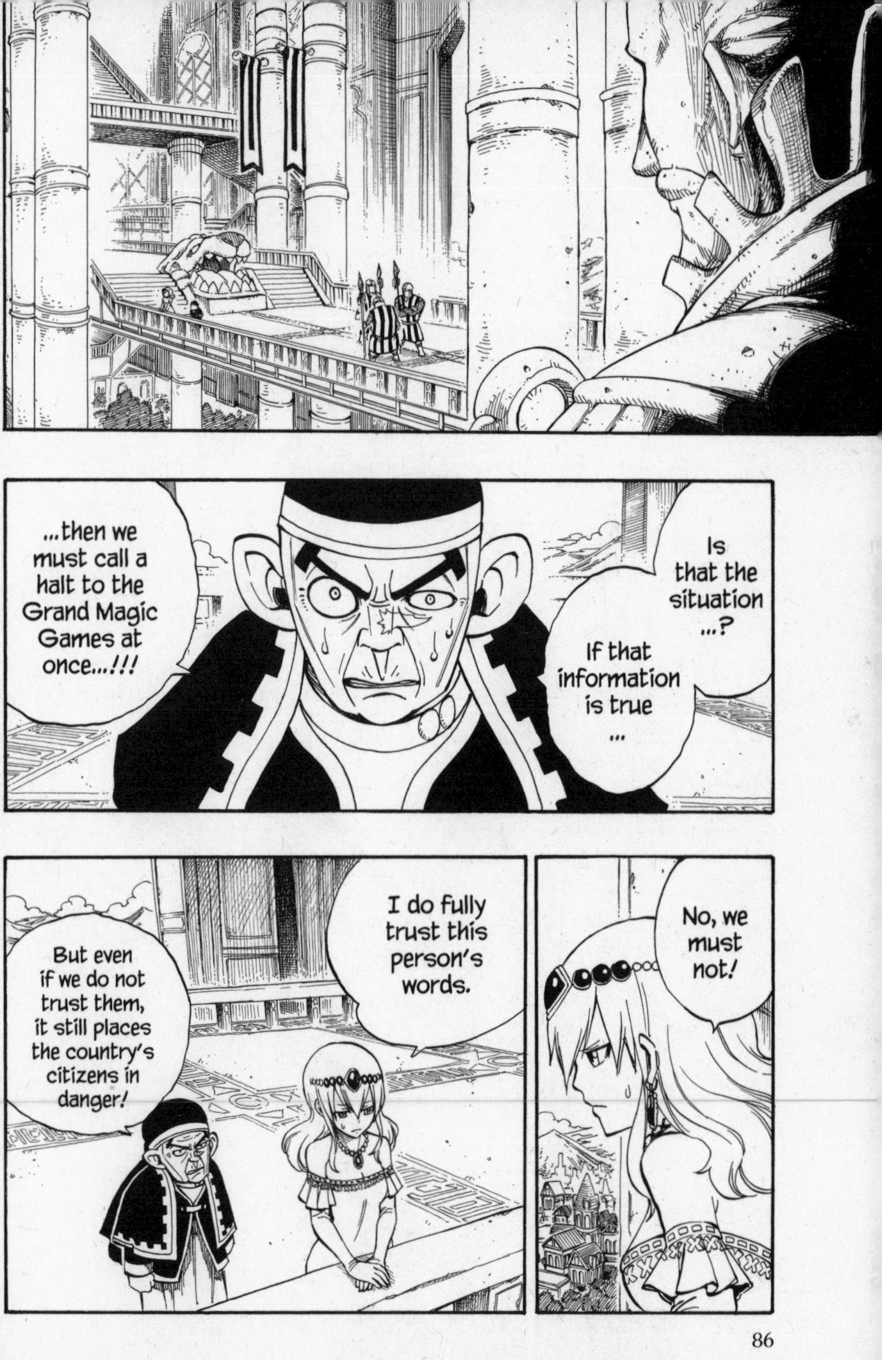
If that information is true ...
Is that the situation ...?
...then we must call a halt to the Grand Magic Games at once...!!!
No, we must not!
I do fully trust this person's words.
But even if we do not trust them, it still places the country's citizens in danger!

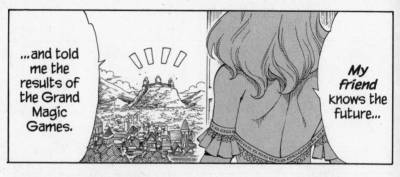

My friend knows the future...
...and told me the results of the Grand Magic Games.
?
I've heard a certain guild will win in an impossible manner.
An impossible manner?
It is such an unusual manner, that I've decided that if that result comes true, then I will believe the other things my friend told me.
You're saying the future of this country depends on the results of the Games?
The result my friend spoke of was so unusual.
Until now, I never thought that it could possibly come to pass.

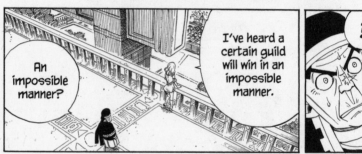

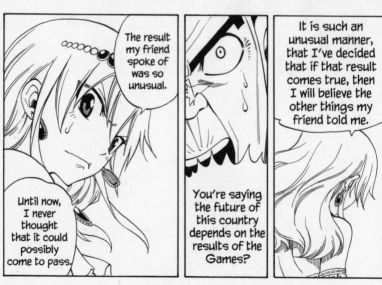

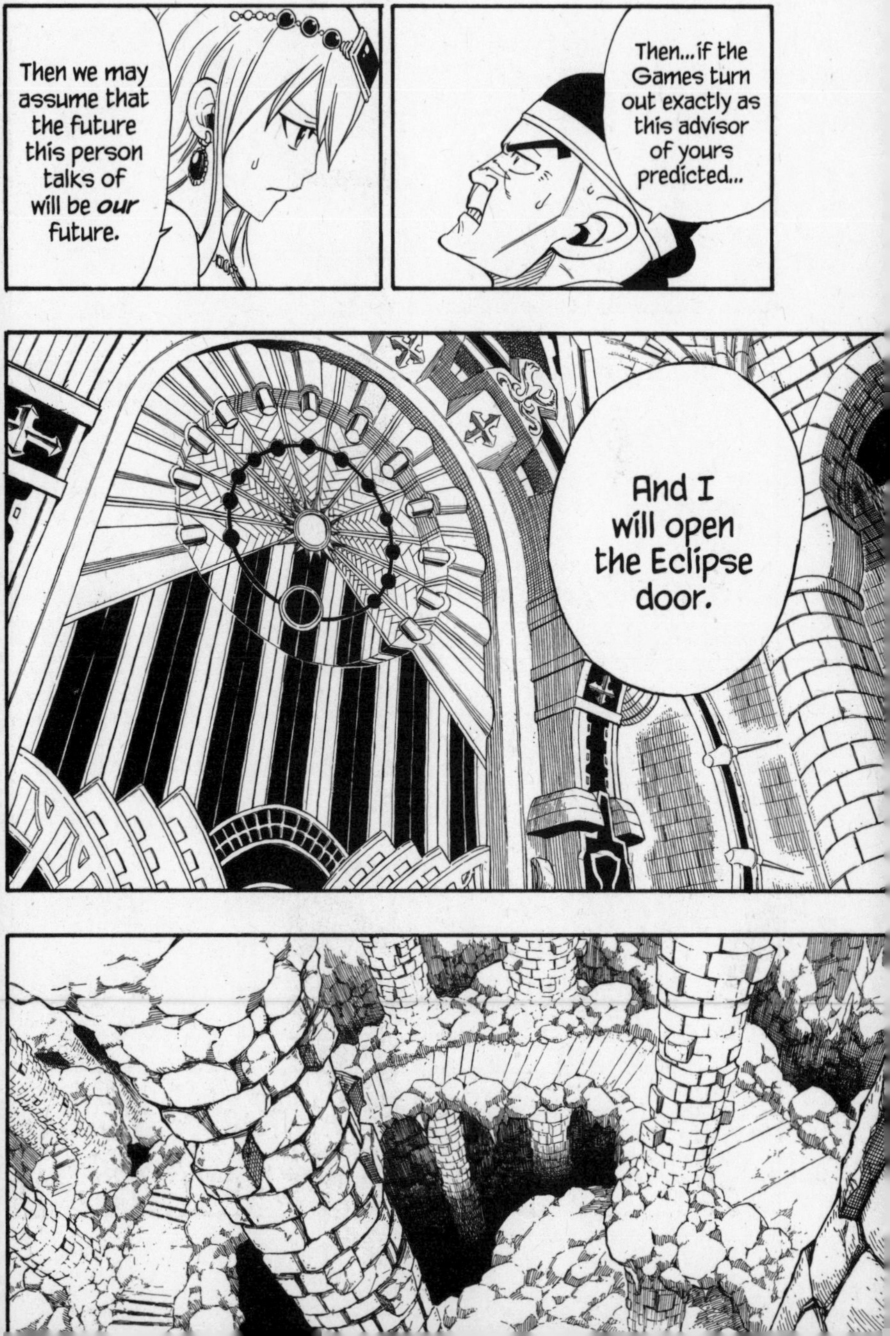
Then...if the Games turn out exactly as this advisor of yours predicted...
Then we may assume that the future this person talks of will be *our* future.
And I will open the Eclipse door.

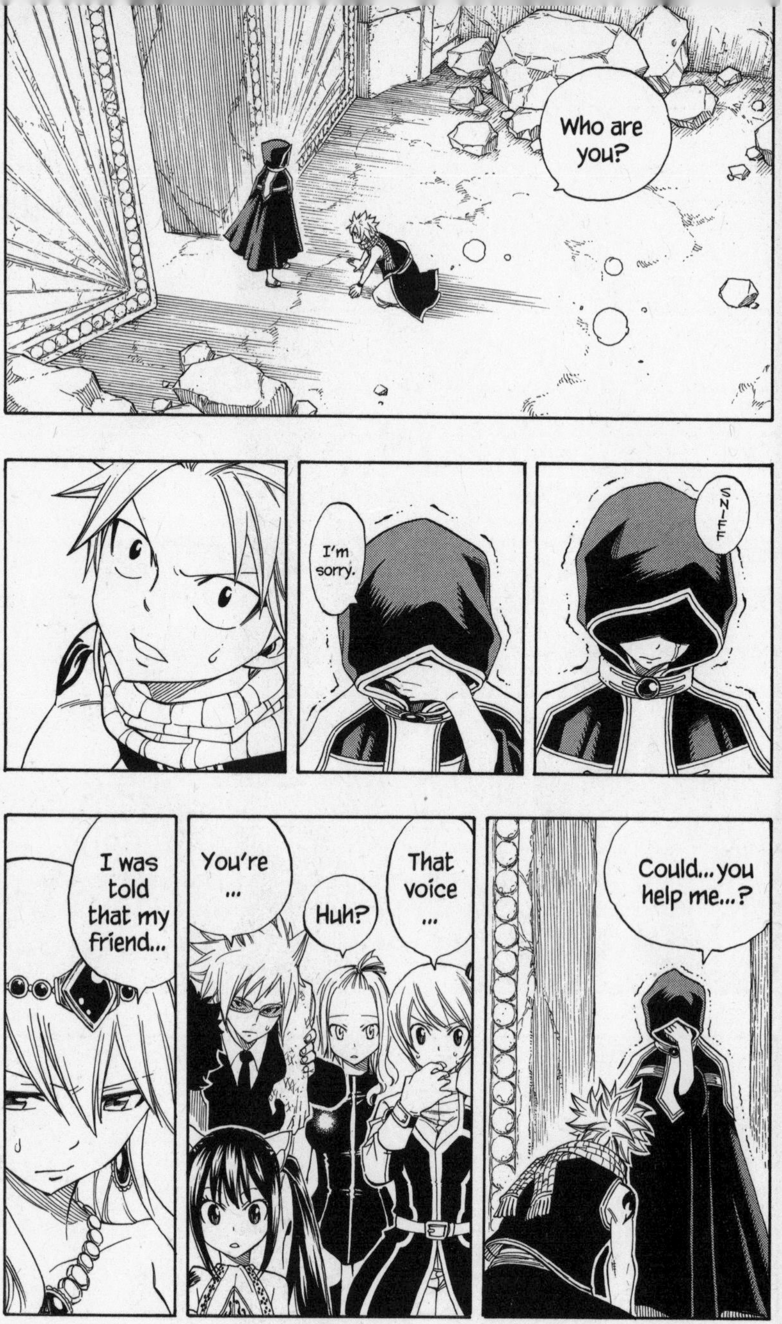
Who are you?
SNIFF
I'm sorry.
Could...you help me...?
That voice ...
Huh?
You're ...
I was told that my friend...

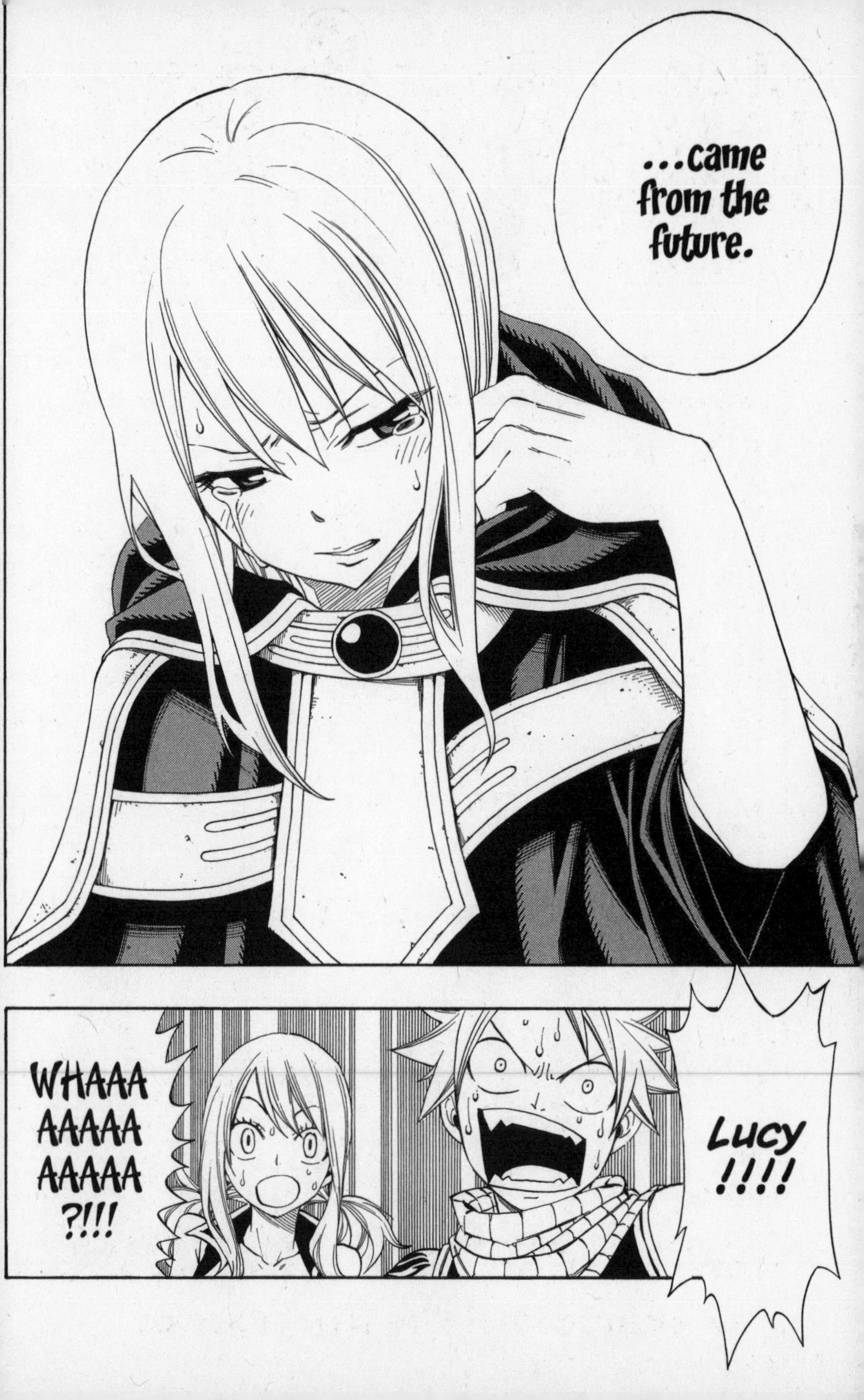
...came from the future.
Lucy!!!!
WHAAAAAAAAAAAAA?!!!

FAIRY TAIL

フェアリーテイル

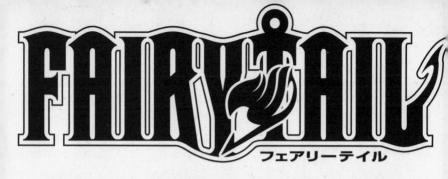

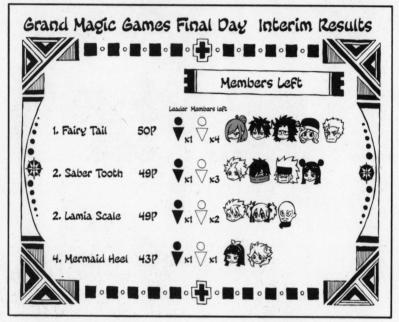

Grand Magic Games Final Day Interim Results

Members Left

		Leader	Members left
1. Fairy Tail	50P	x1	x4
2. Saber Tooth	49P	x1	x3
2. Lamia Scale	49P	x1	x2
4. Mermaid Heel	43P	x1	x1

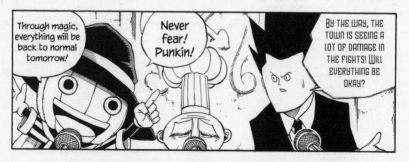

BY THE WAY, THE TOWN IS SEEING A LOT OF DAMAGE IN THE FIGHTS! WILL EVERYTHING BE OKAY?
Never fear! Punkin!
Through magic, everything will be back to normal tomorrow!

Chapter 313: The King's Script

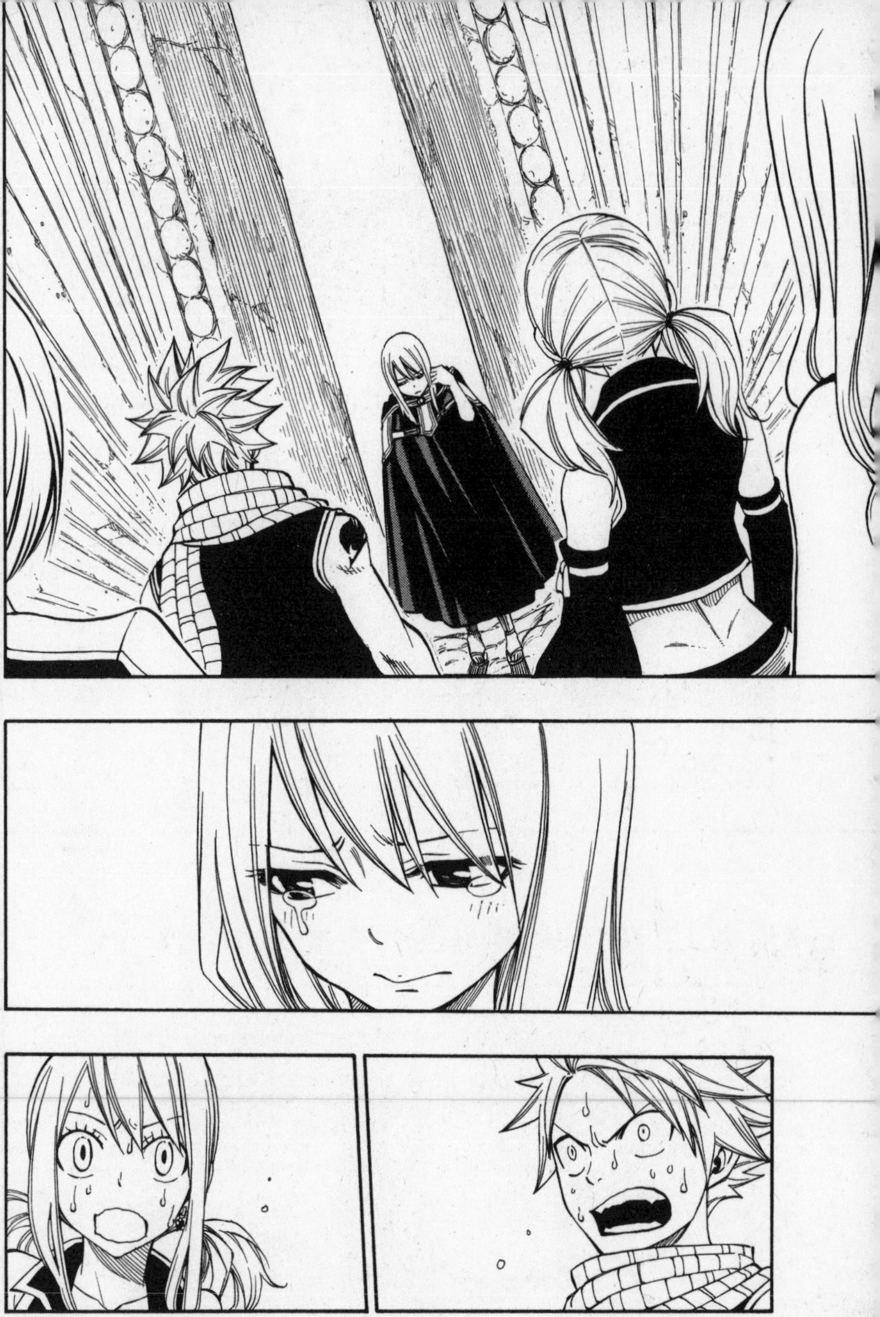

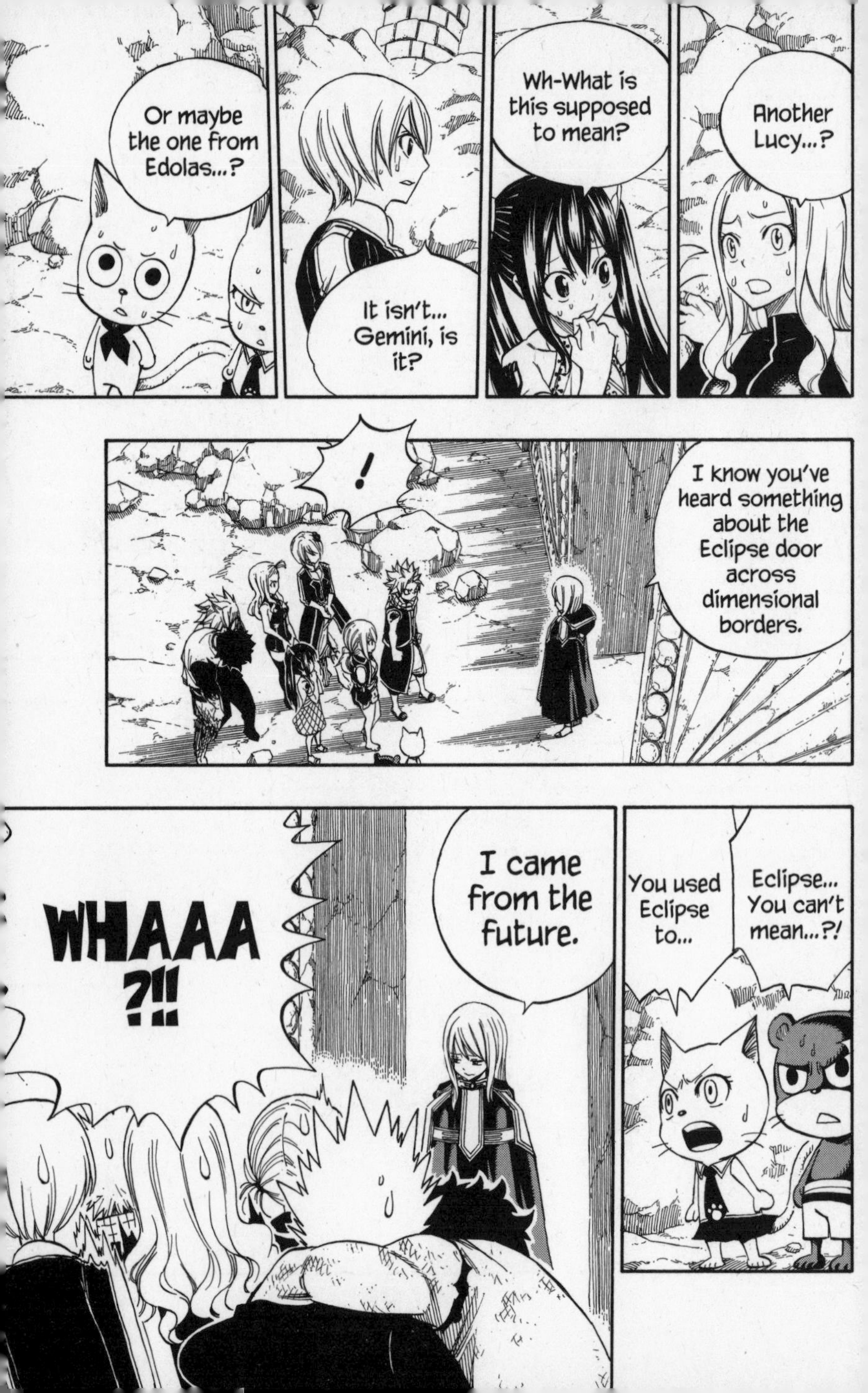
Another Lucy...?
Wh-What is this supposed to mean?
It isn't... Gemini, is it?
Or maybe the one from Edolas...?
I know you've heard something about the Eclipse door across dimensional borders.
!
Eclipse... You can't mean...?!
You used Eclipse to...
I came from the future.
WHAAA ?!!

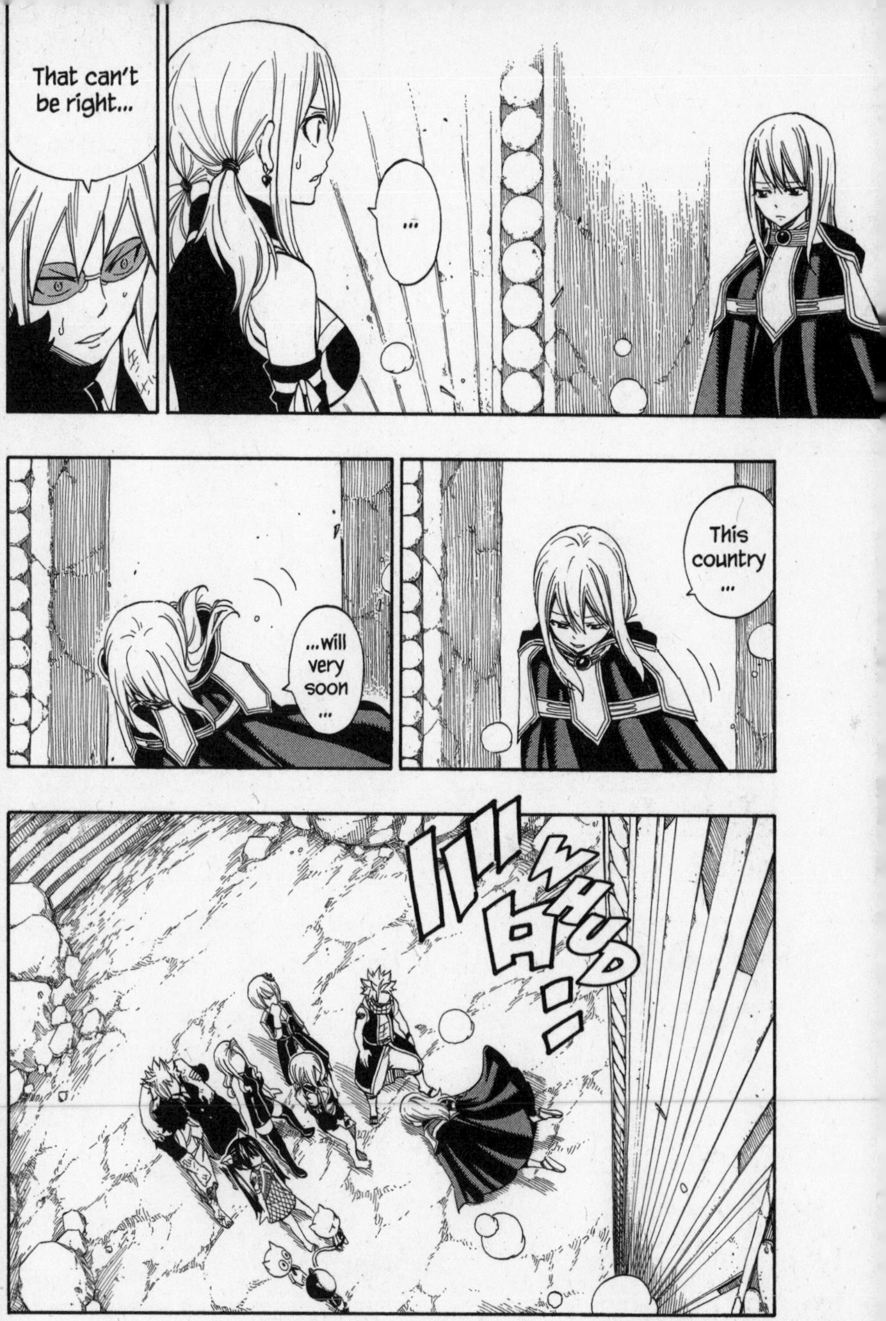
...
That can't be right...
This country ...
...will very soon ...
WHUD

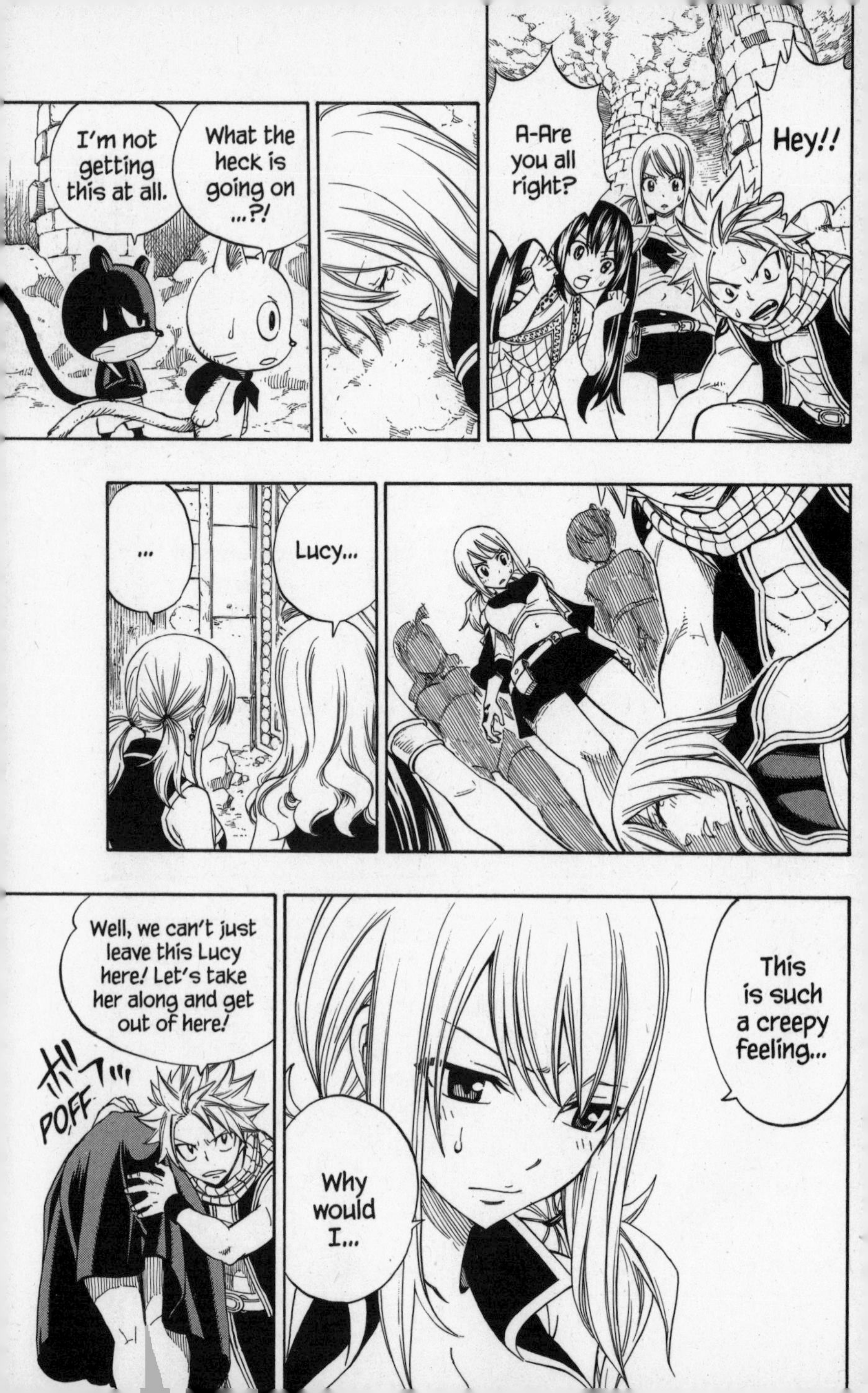
Hey!!
A-Are you all right?
What the heck is going on ...?!
I'm not getting this at all.
Lucy...
...
This is such a creepy feeling...
Why would I...
Well, we can't just leave this Lucy here! Let's take her along and get out of here!
POFF

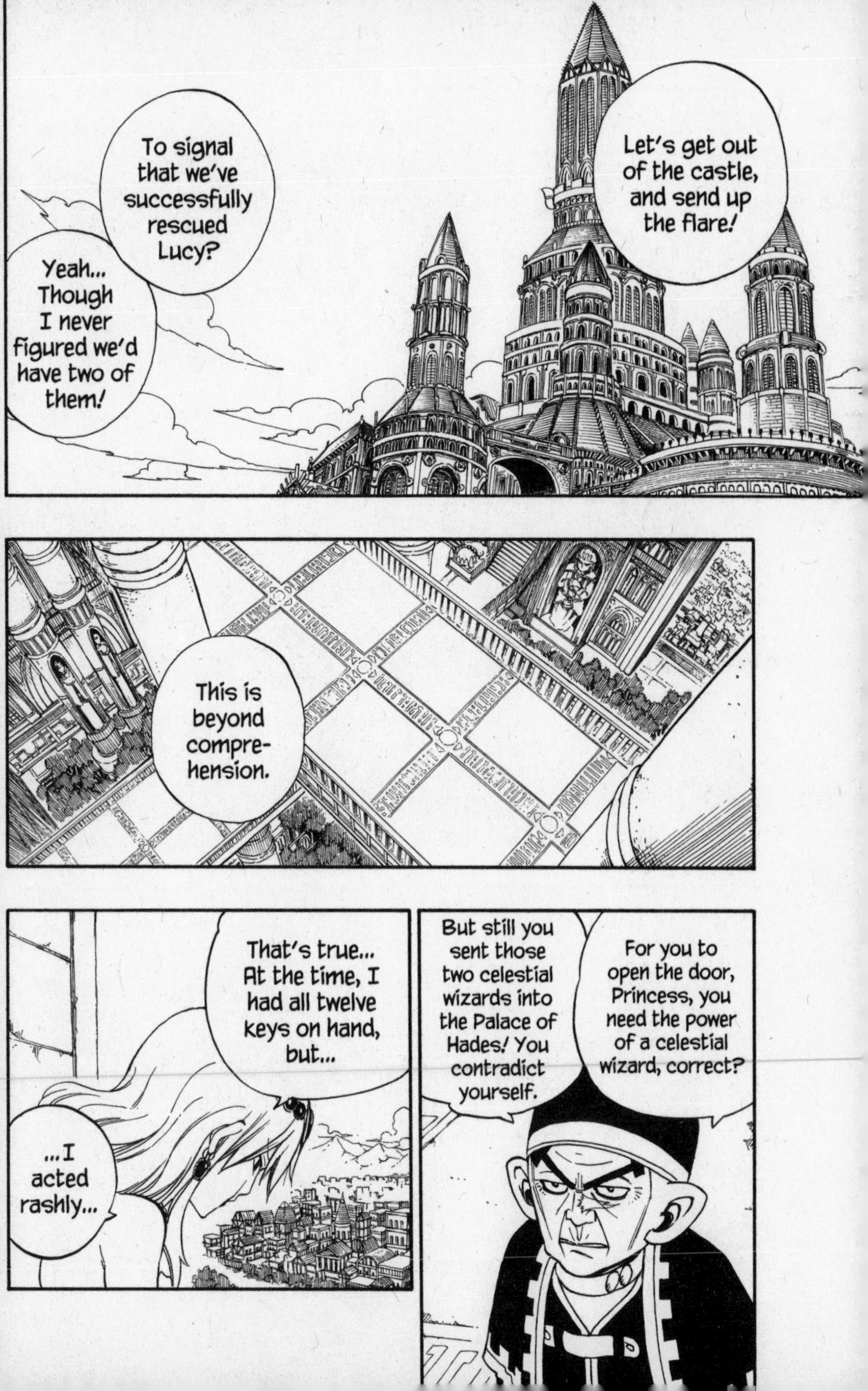
Let's get out of the castle, and send up the flare!
To signal that we've successfully rescued Lucy?
Yeah... Though I never figured we'd have two of them!
This is beyond compre-hension.
For you to open the door, Princess, you need the power of a celestial wizard, correct?
But still you sent those two celestial wizards into the Palace of Hades! You contradict yourself.
That's true... At the time, I had all twelve keys on hand, but...
...I acted rashly...

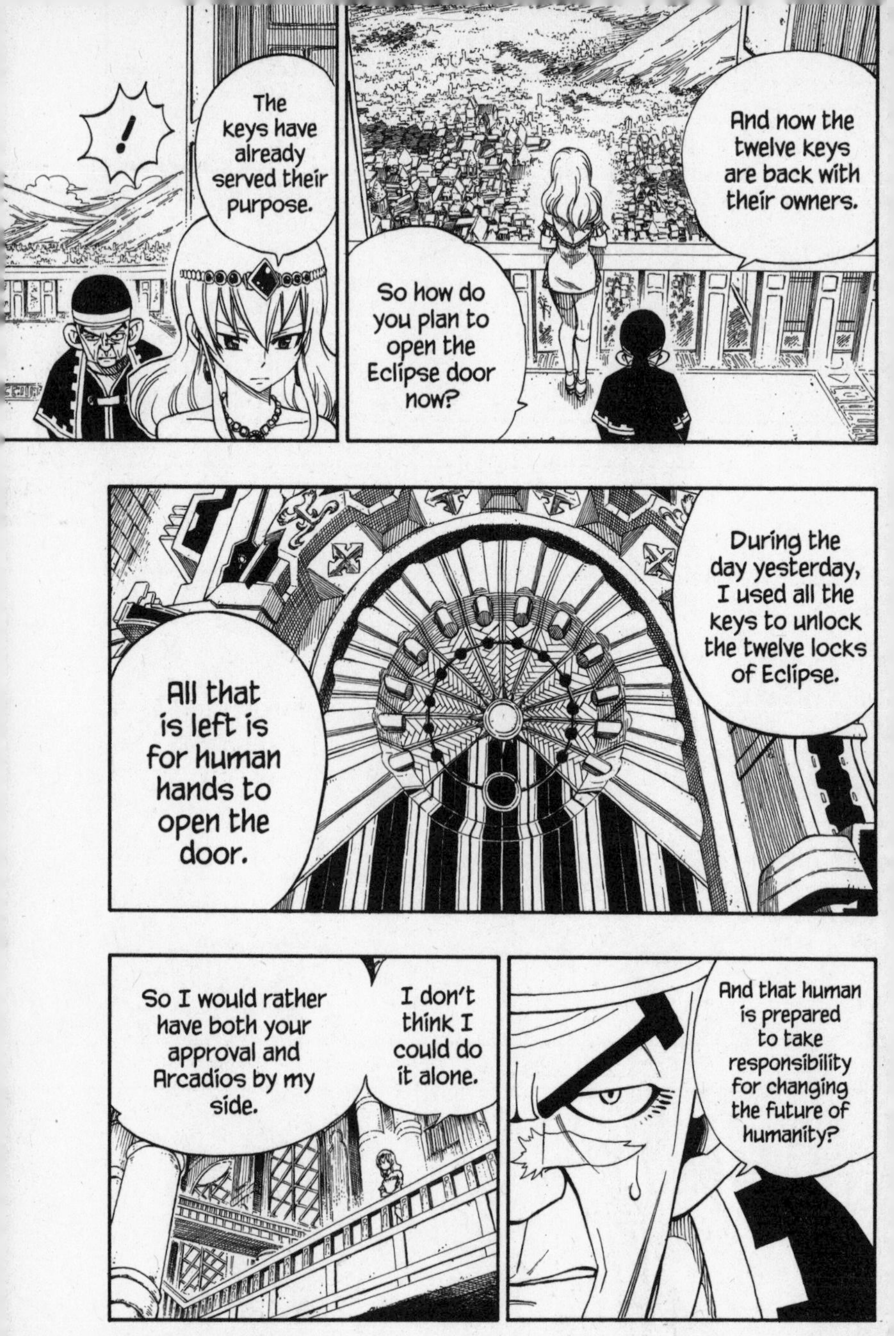
And now the twelve keys are back with their owners.
So how do you plan to open the Eclipse door now?
The keys have already served their purpose.
!
During the day yesterday, I used all the keys to unlock the twelve locks of Eclipse.
All that is left is for human hands to open the door.
And that human is prepared to take responsibility for changing the future of humanity?
I don't think I could do it alone.
So I would rather have both your approval and Arcadios by my side.

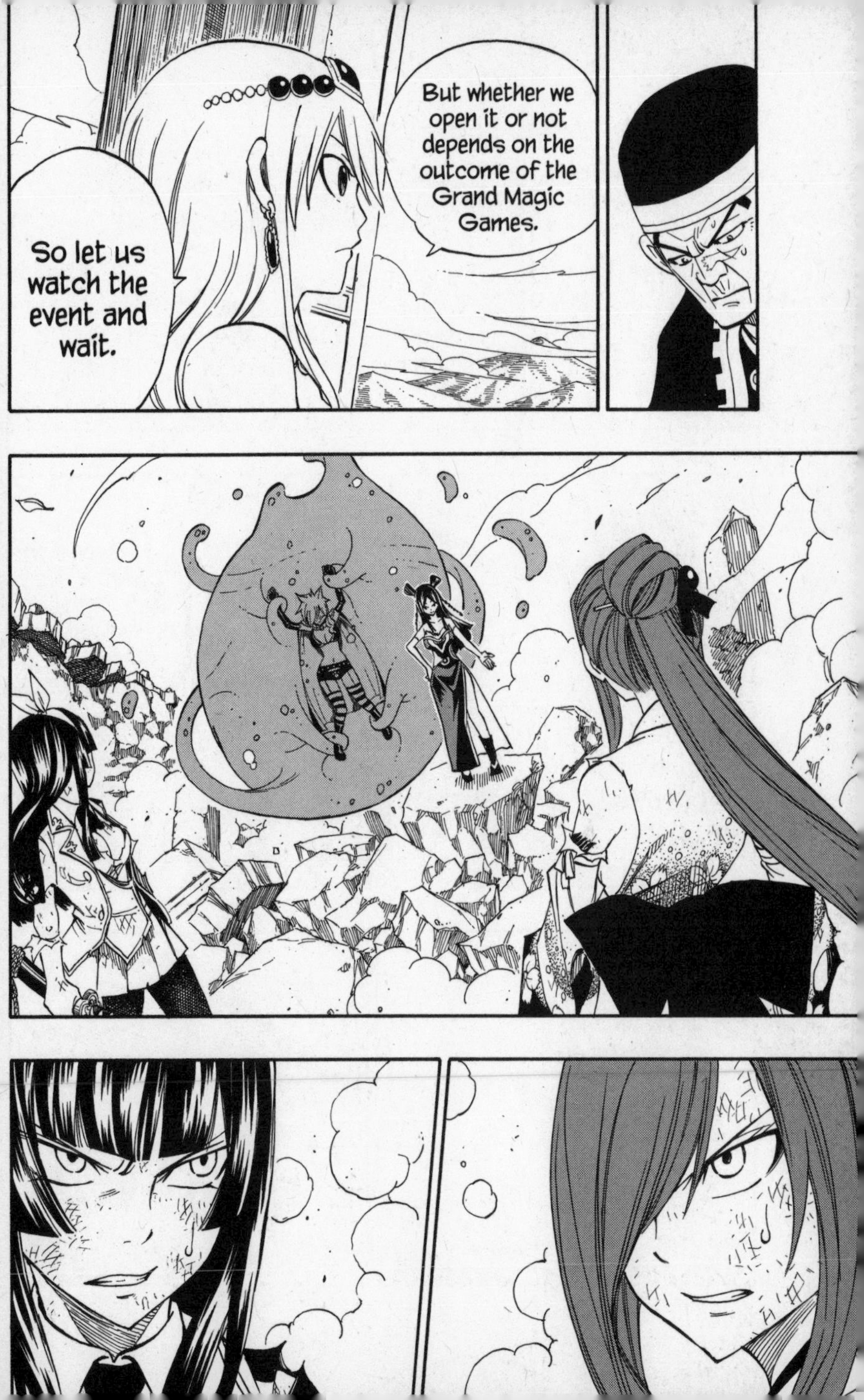
But whether we open it or not depends on the outcome of the Grand Magic Games.
So let us watch the event and wait.

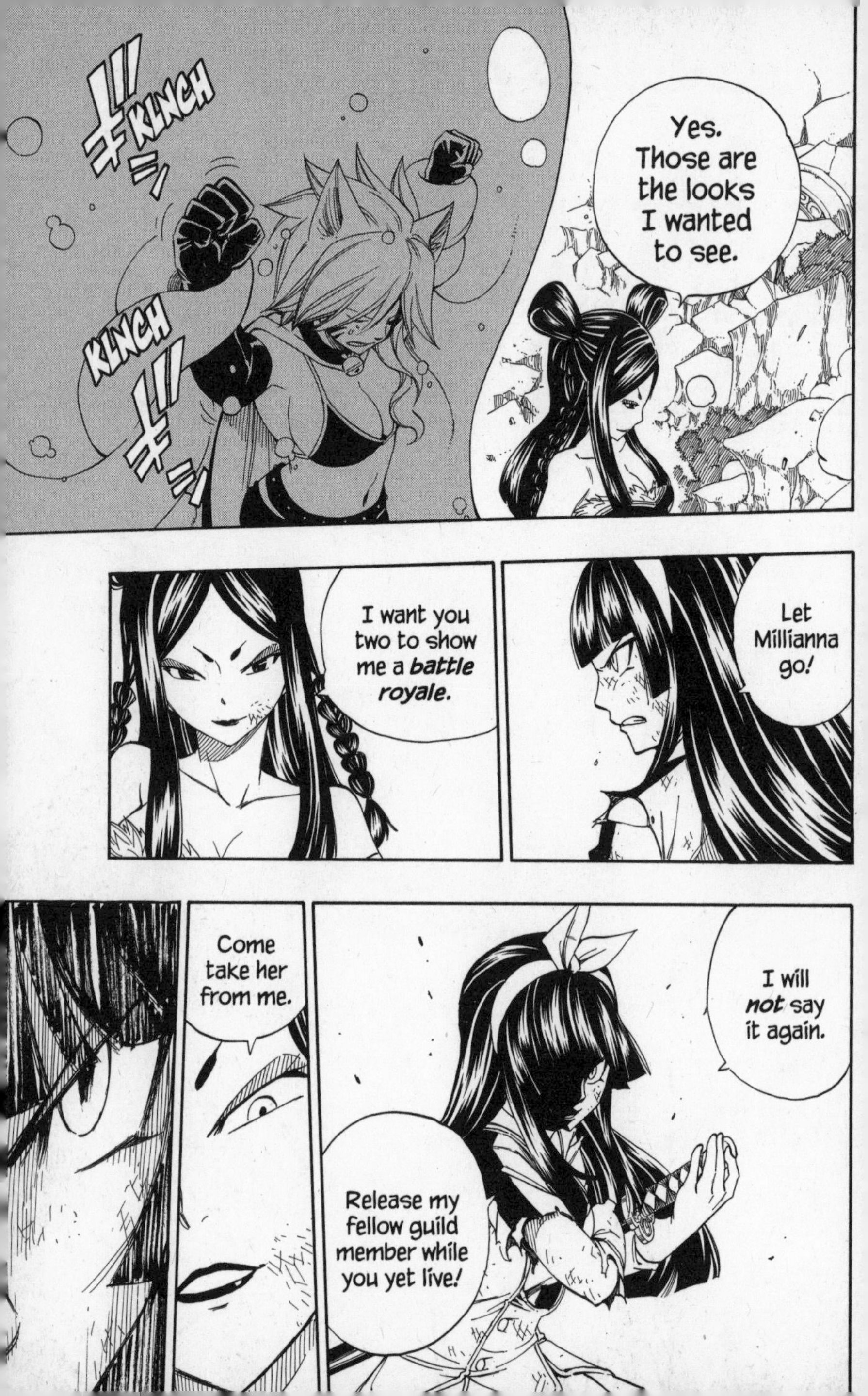
Yes. Those are the looks I wanted to see.
KLINCH
KLINCH
Let Millianna go!
I want you two to show me a *battle royale*.
I will *not* say it again.
Release my fellow guild member while you yet live!
Come take her from me.

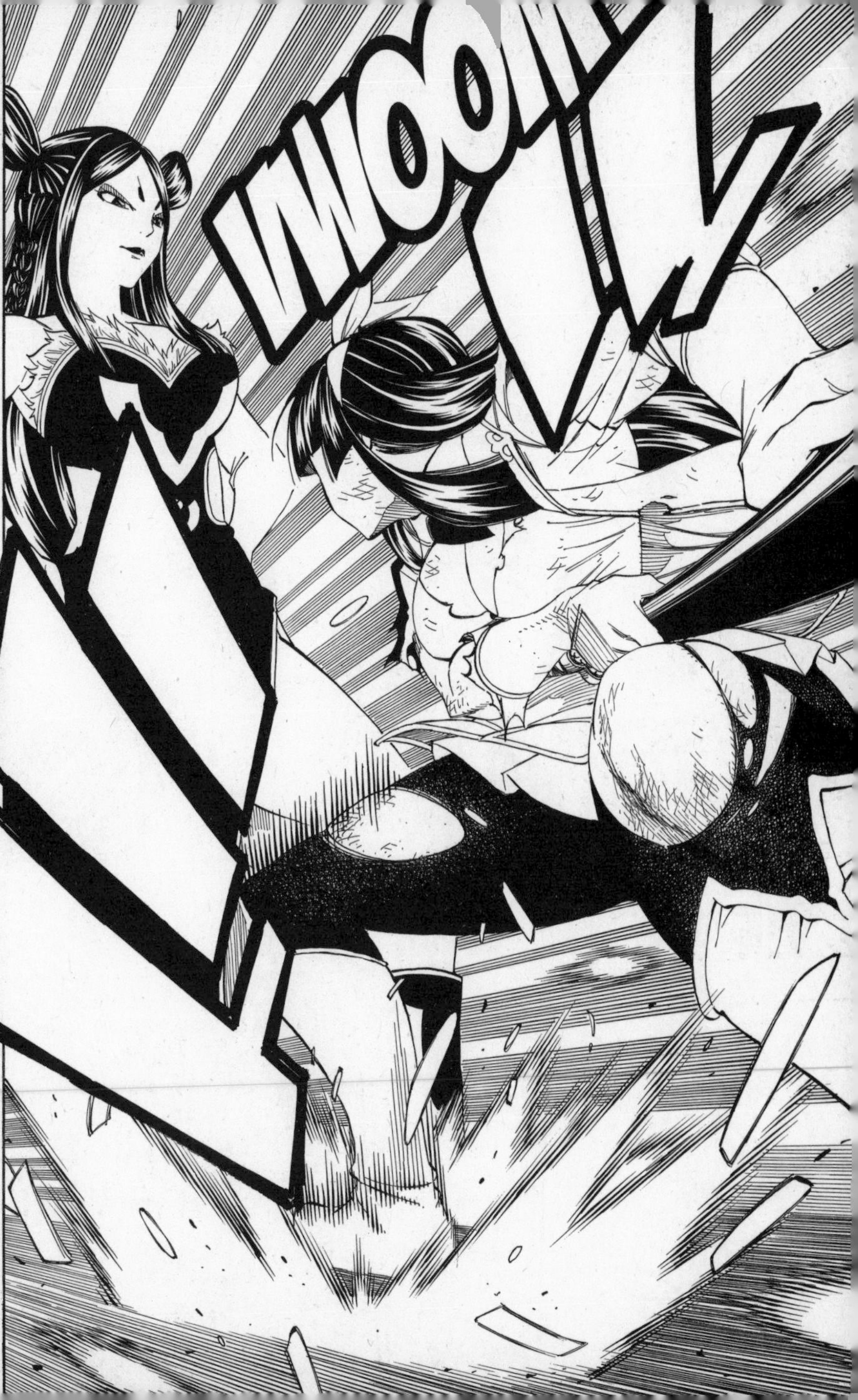
WOOM

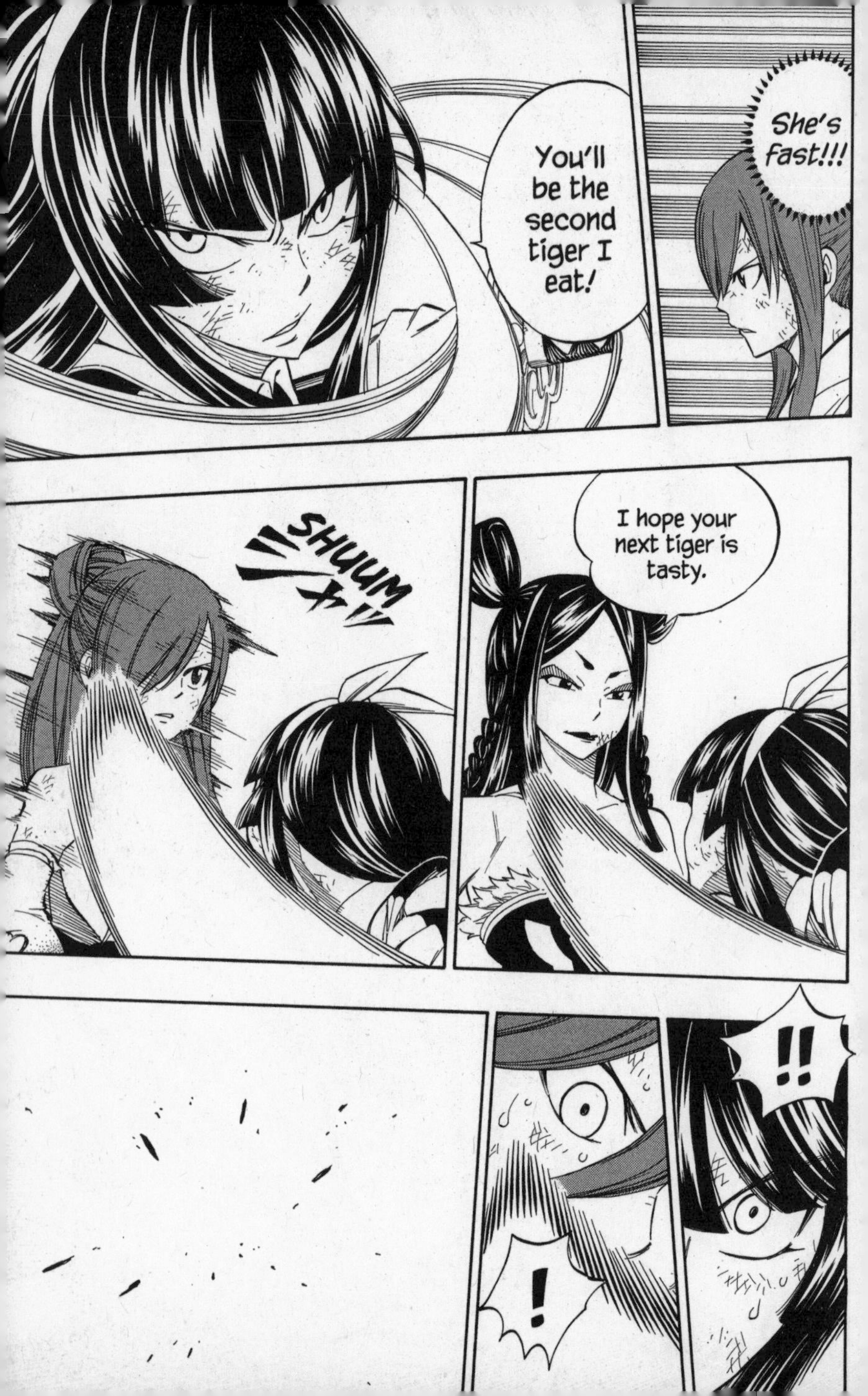
She's fast!!!
You'll be the second tiger I eat!
I hope your next tiger is tasty.
SHUUM
!!
!

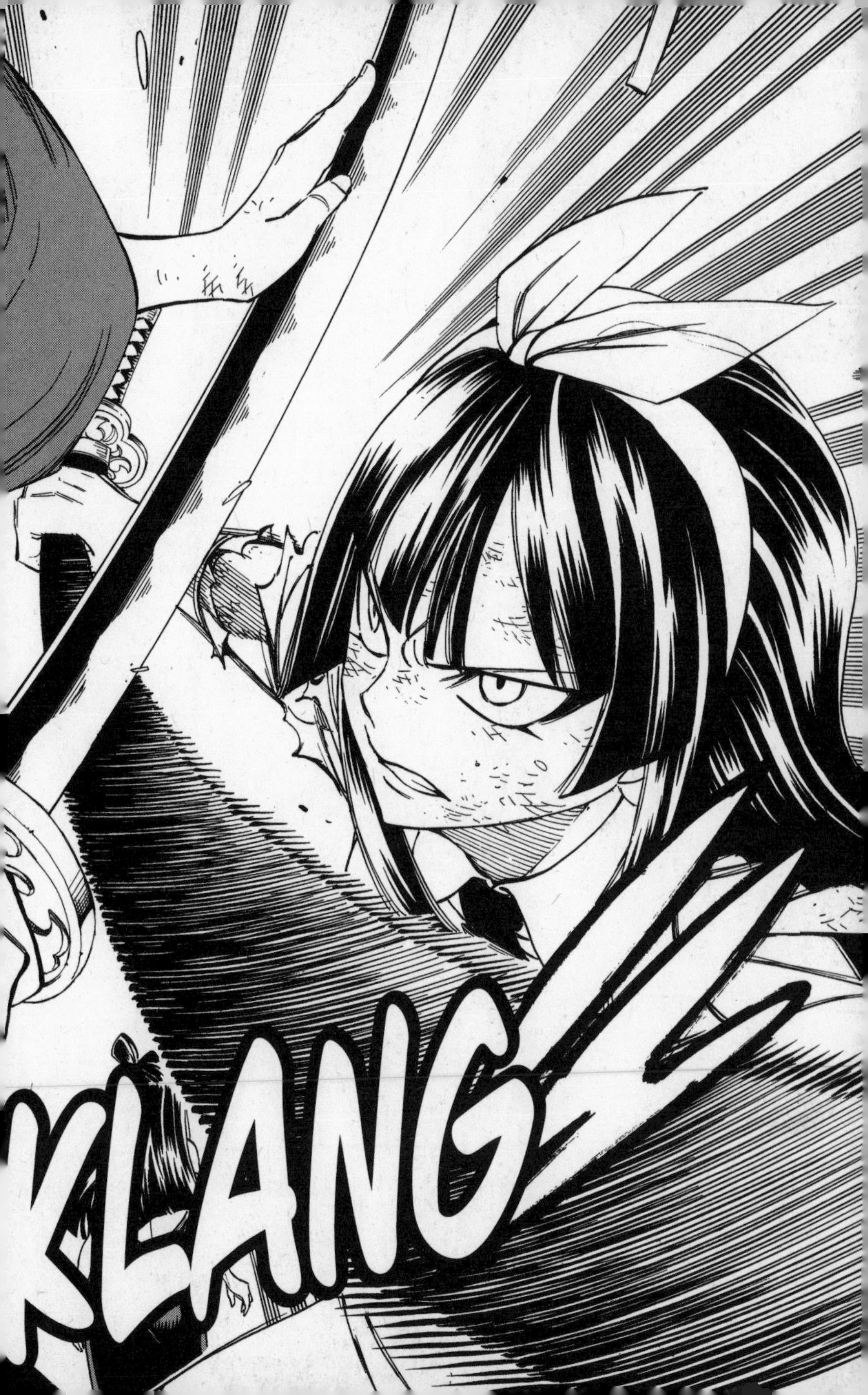
KLANG

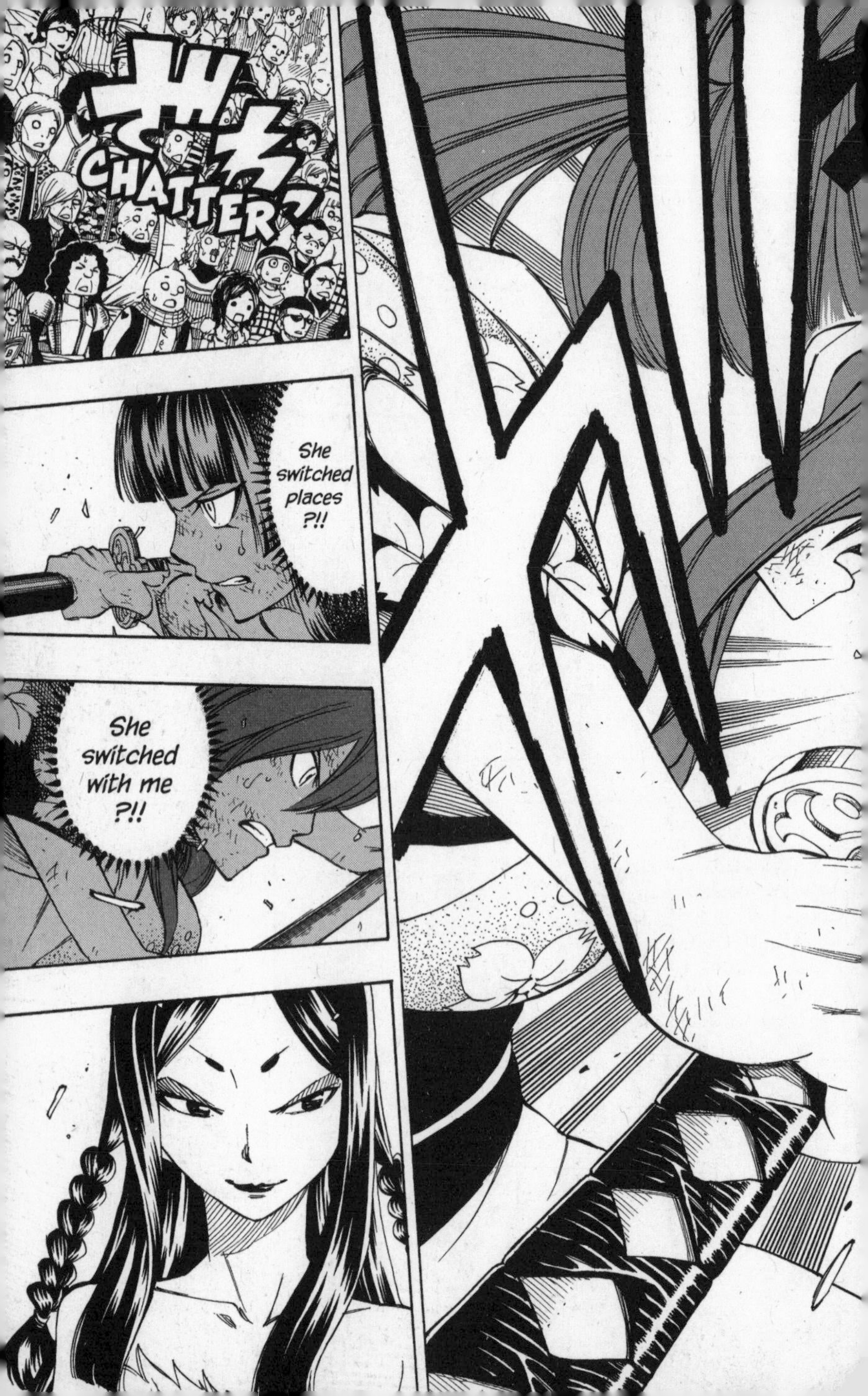
CHATTER
She switched places?!!
She switched with me?!!

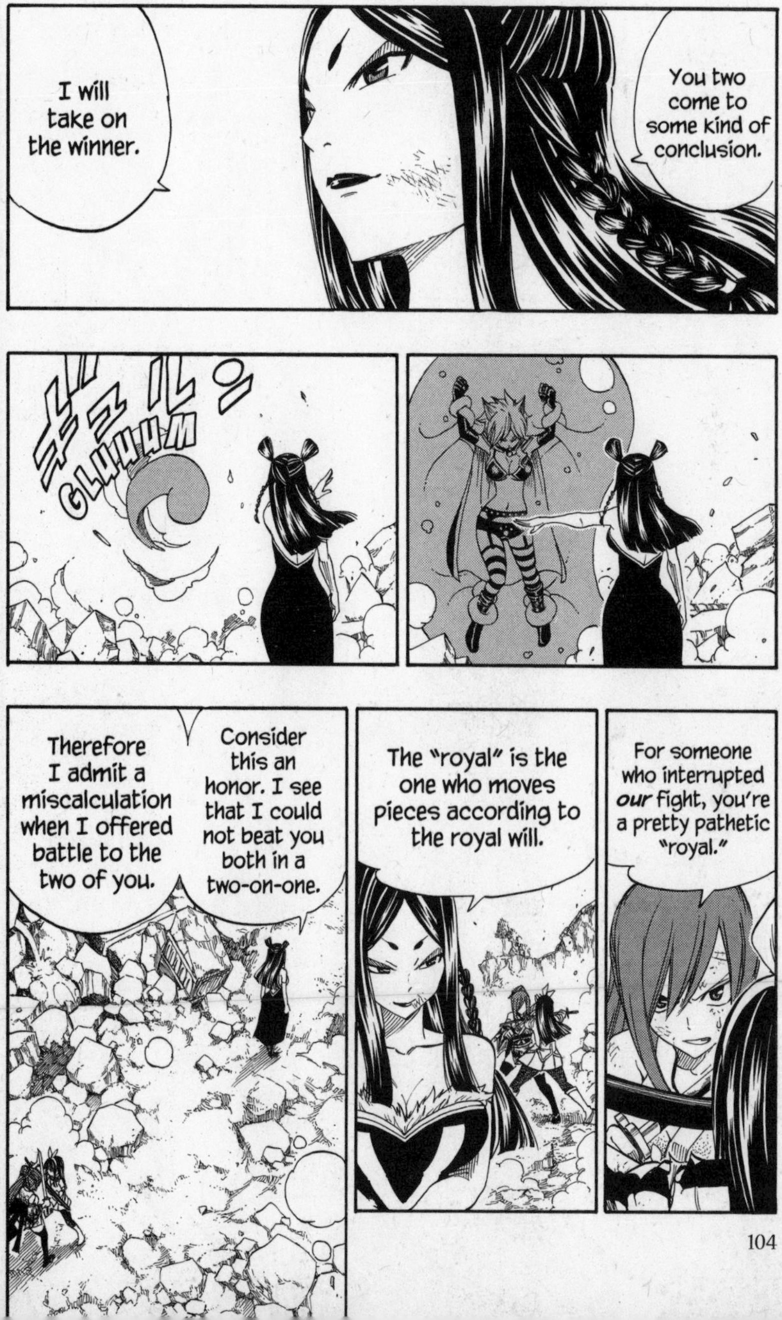
You two come to some kind of conclusion.
I will take on the winner.
GLUUUM
For someone who interrupted *our* fight, you're a pretty pathetic "royal."
The "royal" is the one who moves pieces according to the royal will.
Consider this an honor. I see that I could not beat you both in a two-on-one.
Therefore I admit a miscalculation when I offered battle to the two of you.

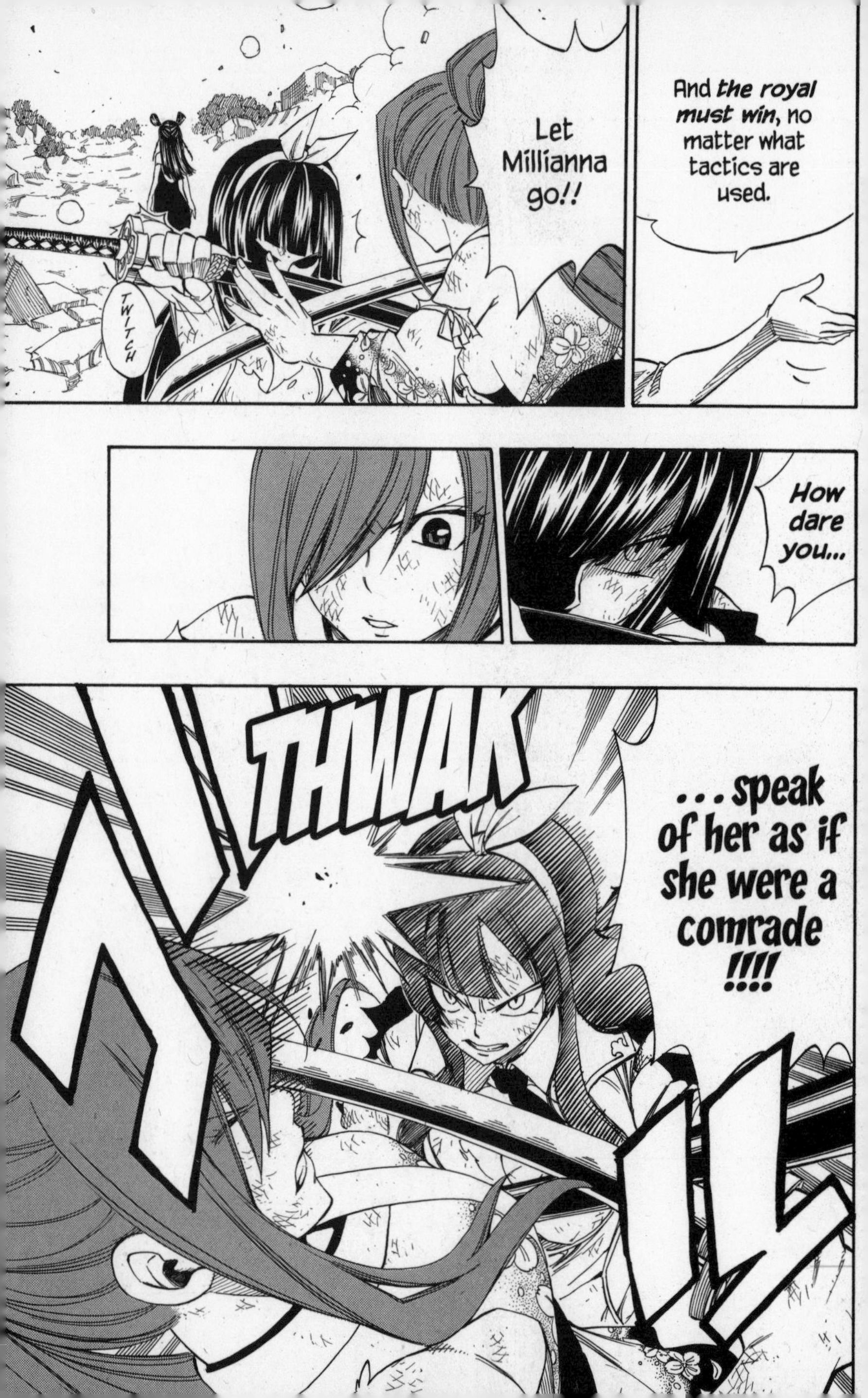

And *the royal must win*, no matter what tactics are used.
Let Millianna go!!
TWITCH
How dare you...
THWAK
...speak of her as if she were a comrade!!!!

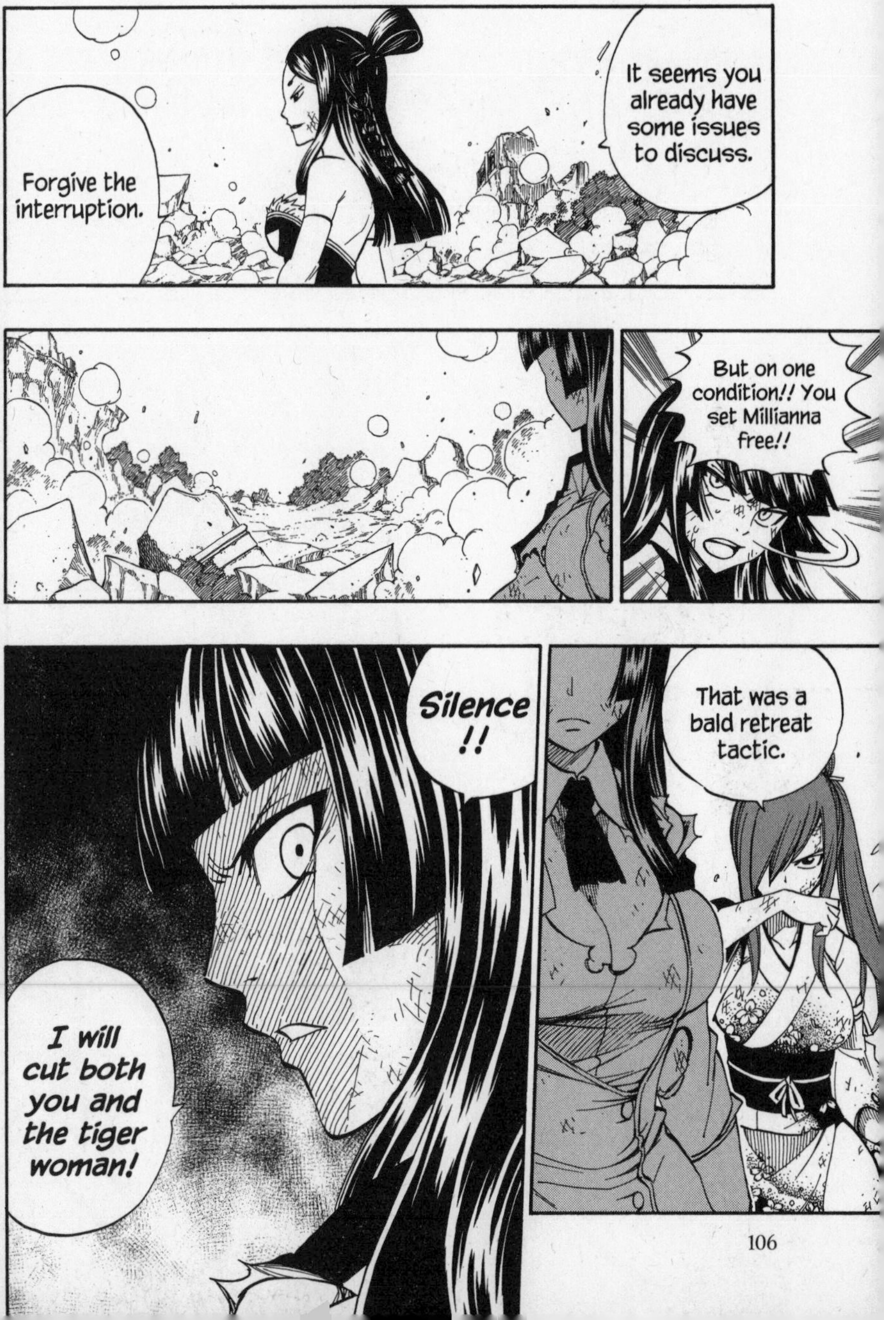
It seems you already have some issues to discuss.
Forgive the interruption.
But on one condition!! You set Millianna free!!
That was a bald retreat tactic.
Silence!!
I will cut both you and the tiger woman!

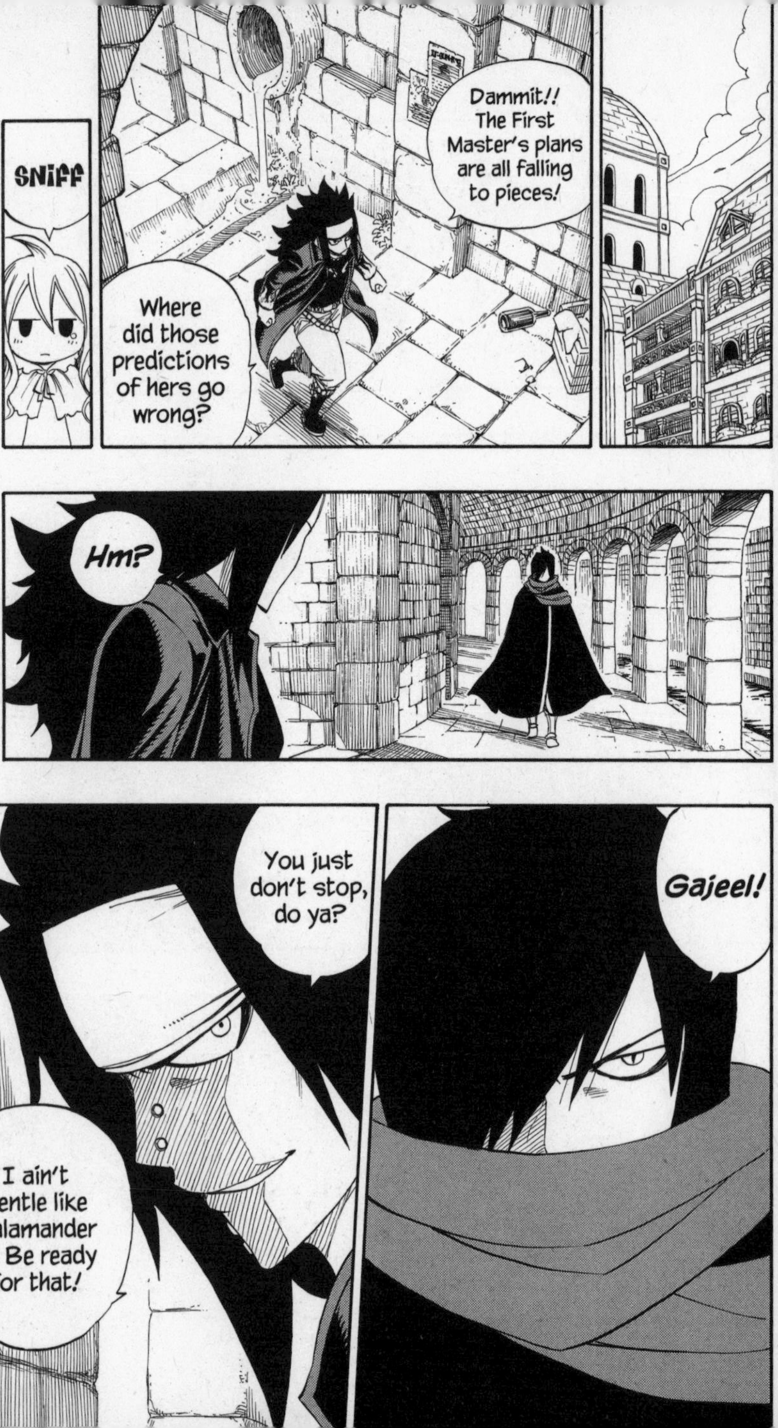
Dammit!! The First Master's plans are all falling to pieces!
Where did those predictions of hers go wrong?
SNIFF
Hm?
Gajeel!
You just don't stop, do ya?
I ain't gentle like Salamander is. Be ready for that!

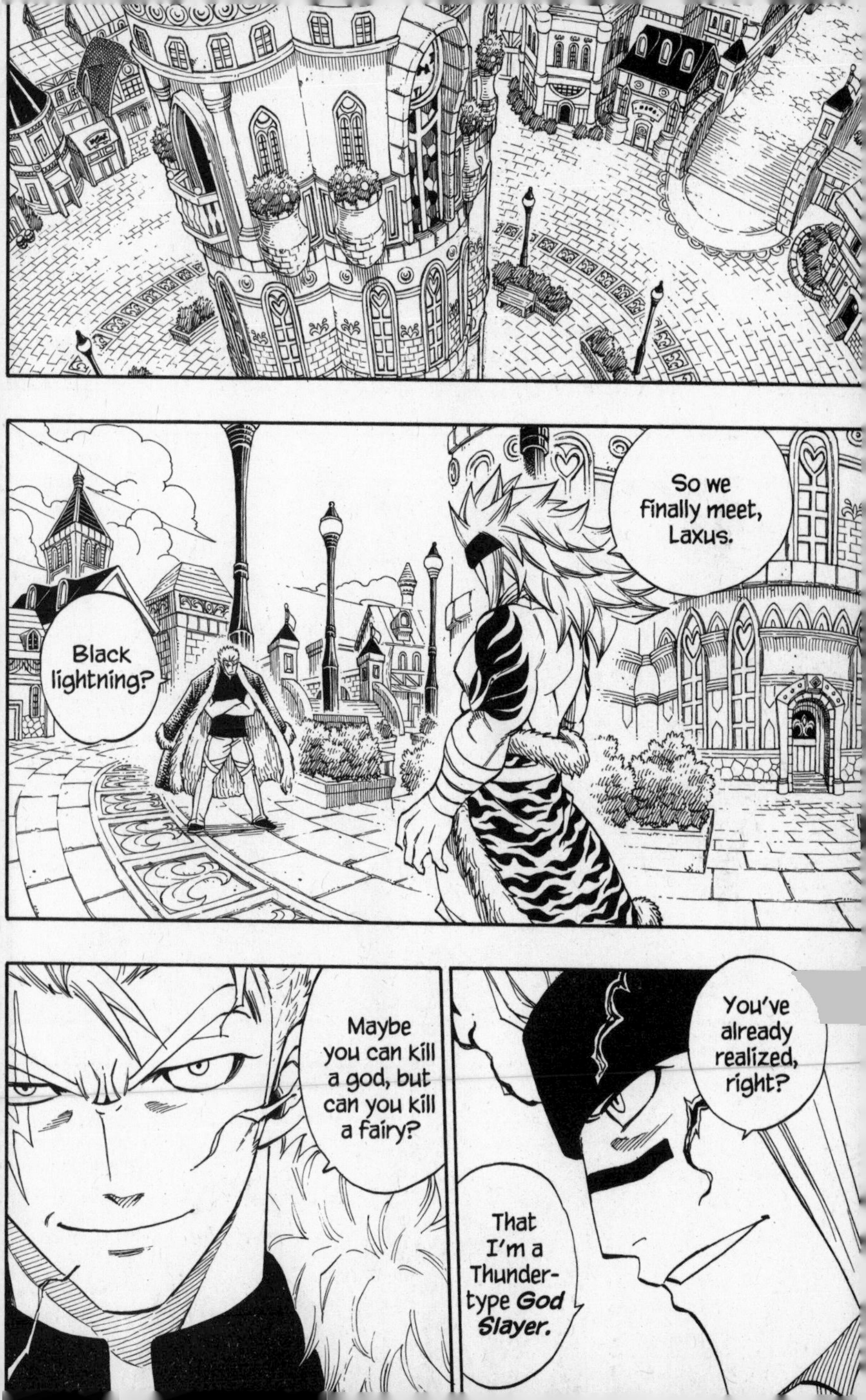
So we finally meet, Laxus.
Black lightning?
You've already realized, right?
That I'm a Thunder-type *God Slayer.*
Maybe you can kill a god, but can you kill a fairy?

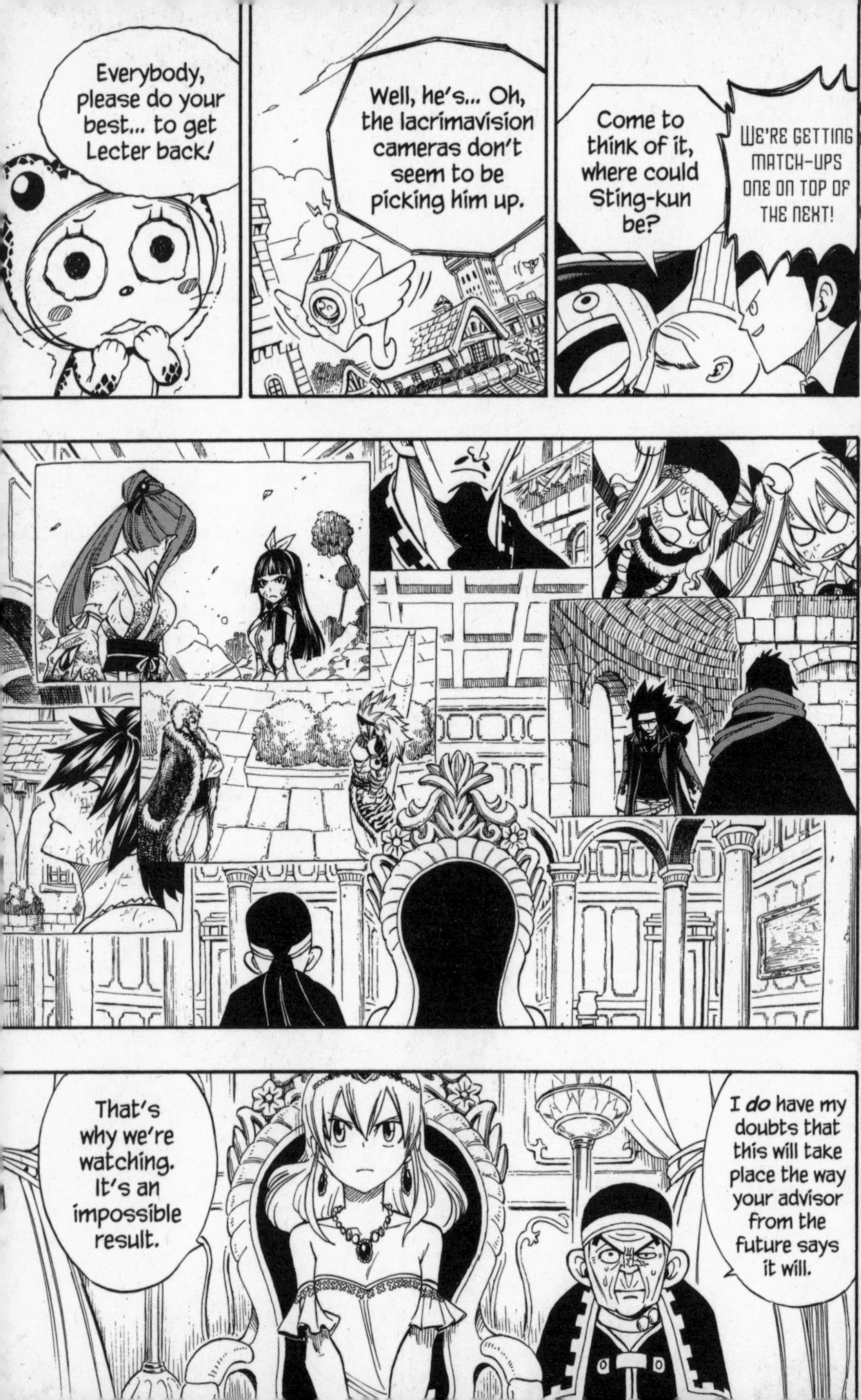

WE'RE GETTING MATCH-UPS ONE ON TOP OF THE NEXT!
Come to think of it, where could Sting-kun be?
Well, he's... Oh, the lacrimavision cameras don't seem to be picking him up.
Everybody, please do your best... to get Lecter back!
I *do* have my doubts that this will take place the way your advisor from the future says it will.
That's why we're watching. It's an impossible result.

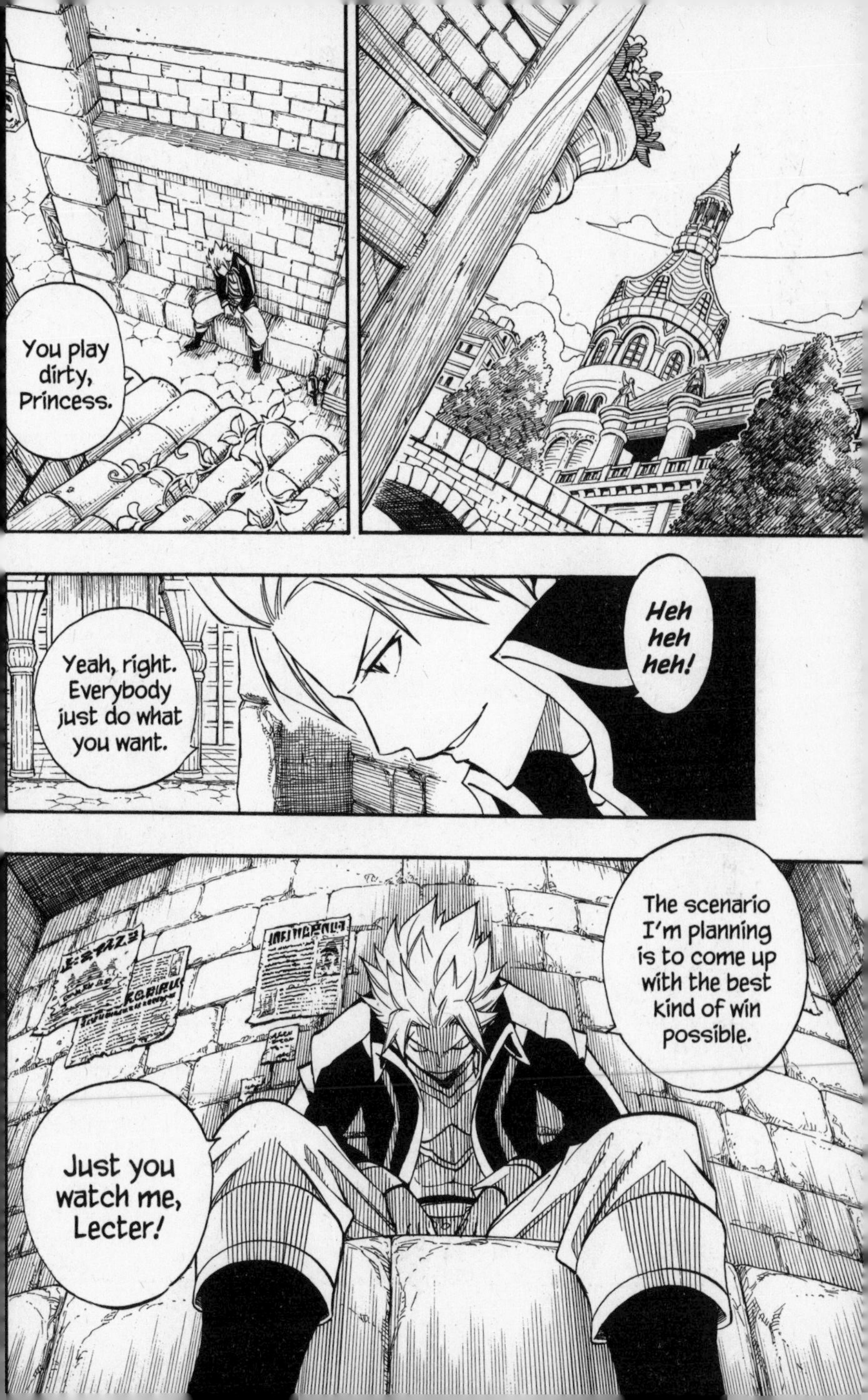
You play dirty, Princess.
Heh heh heh!
Yeah, right. Everybody just do what you want.
The scenario I'm planning is to come up with the best kind of win possible.
Just you watch me, Lecter!

FAIRY TAIL

フェアリーテイル

Chapter 314: Erza vs. Kagura

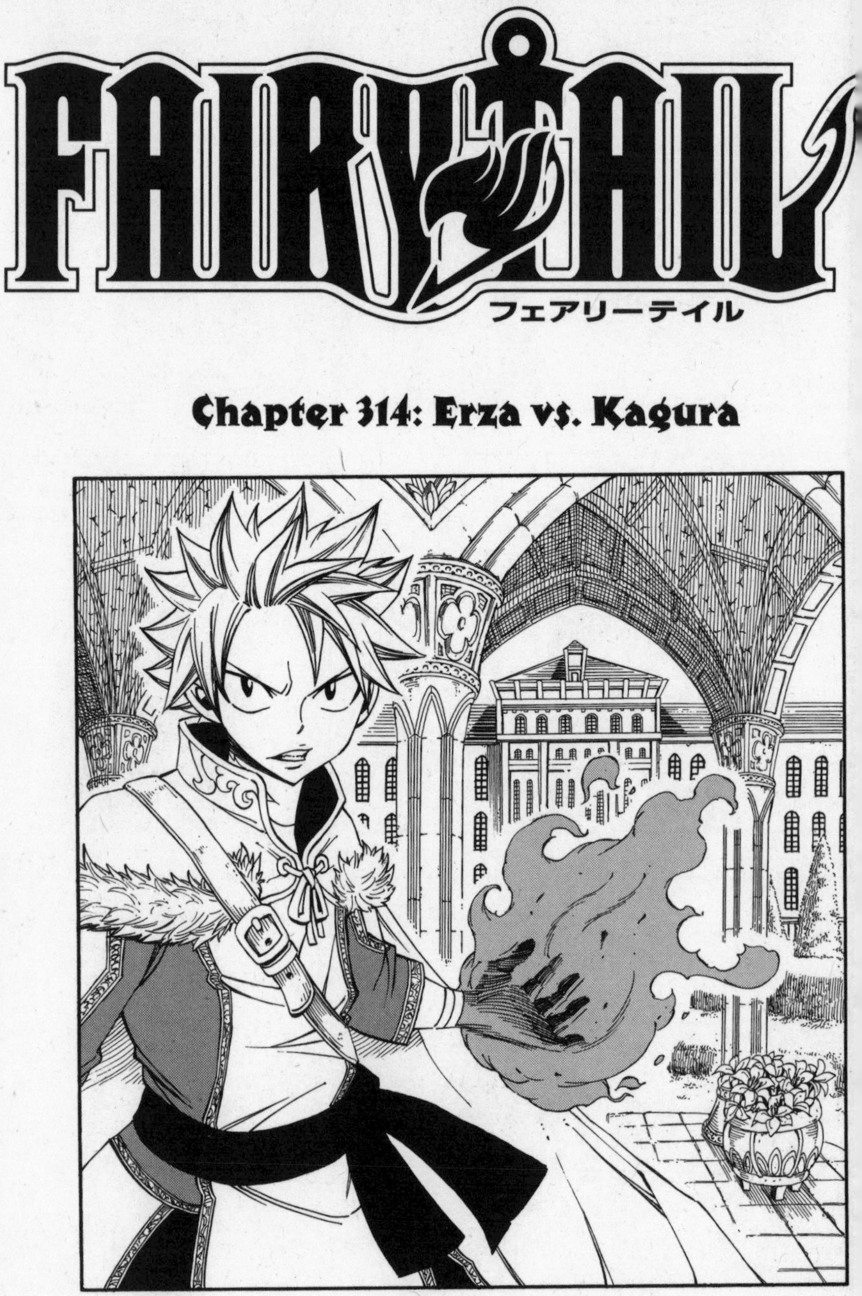

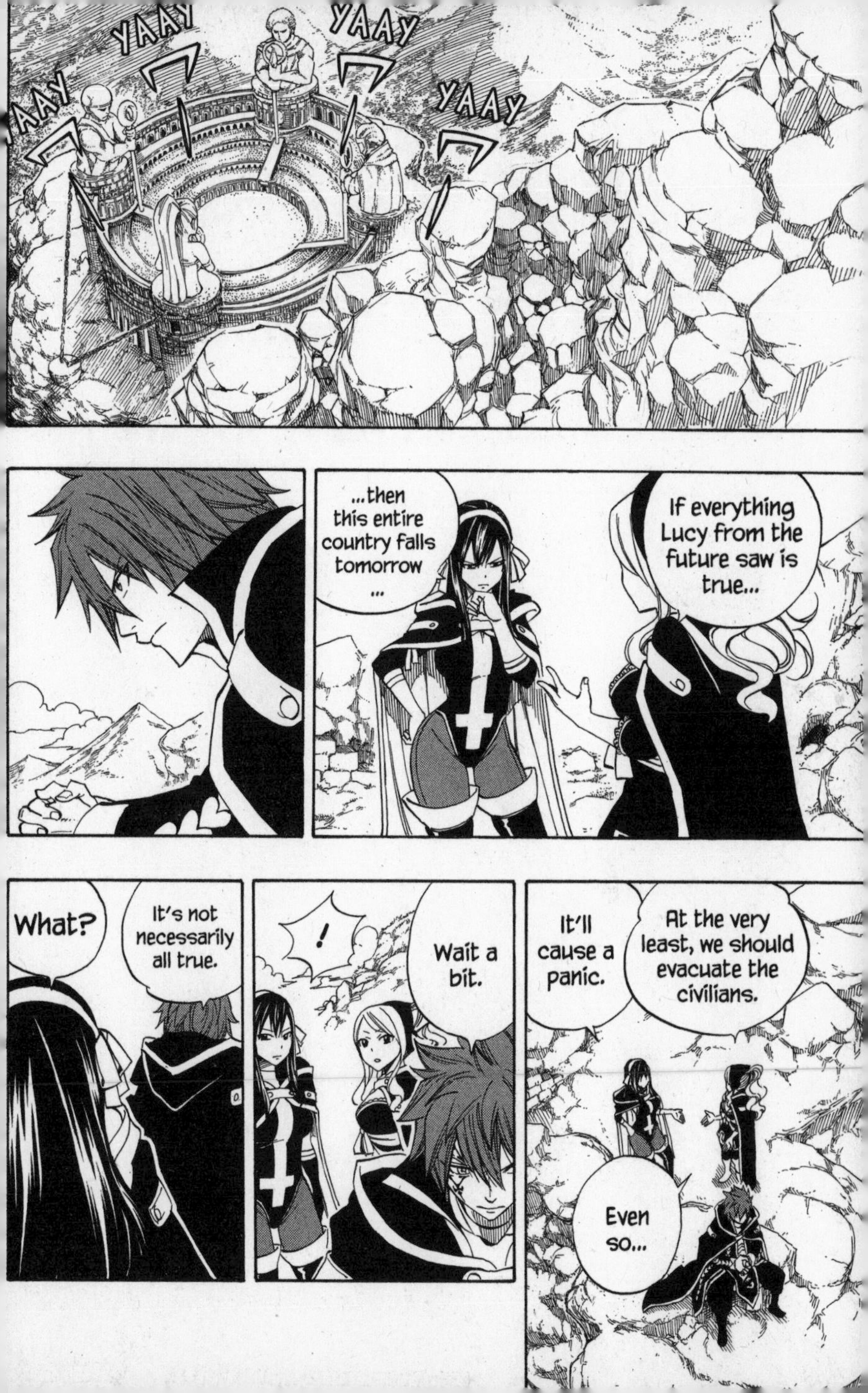
YAAY
YAAY
YAAY
AAAY
If everything Lucy from the future saw is true...
...then this entire country falls tomorrow ...
At the very least, we should evacuate the civilians.
It'll cause a panic.
Even so...
Wait a bit.
!
It's not necessarily all true.
What?

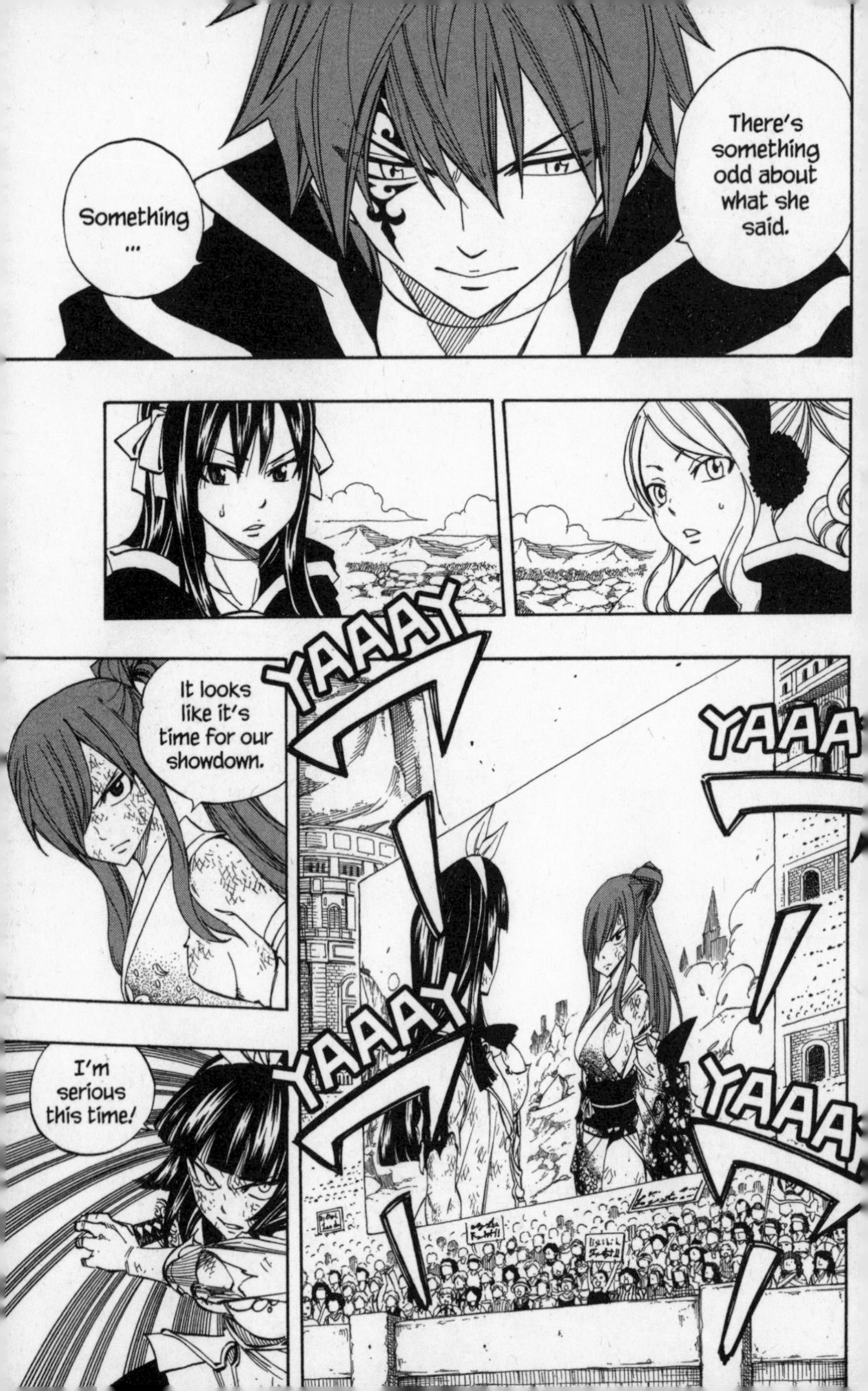
There's something odd about what she said.
Something ...
YAAA
YAAAY
YAAA
YAAAY
It looks like it's time for our showdown.
I'm serious this time!

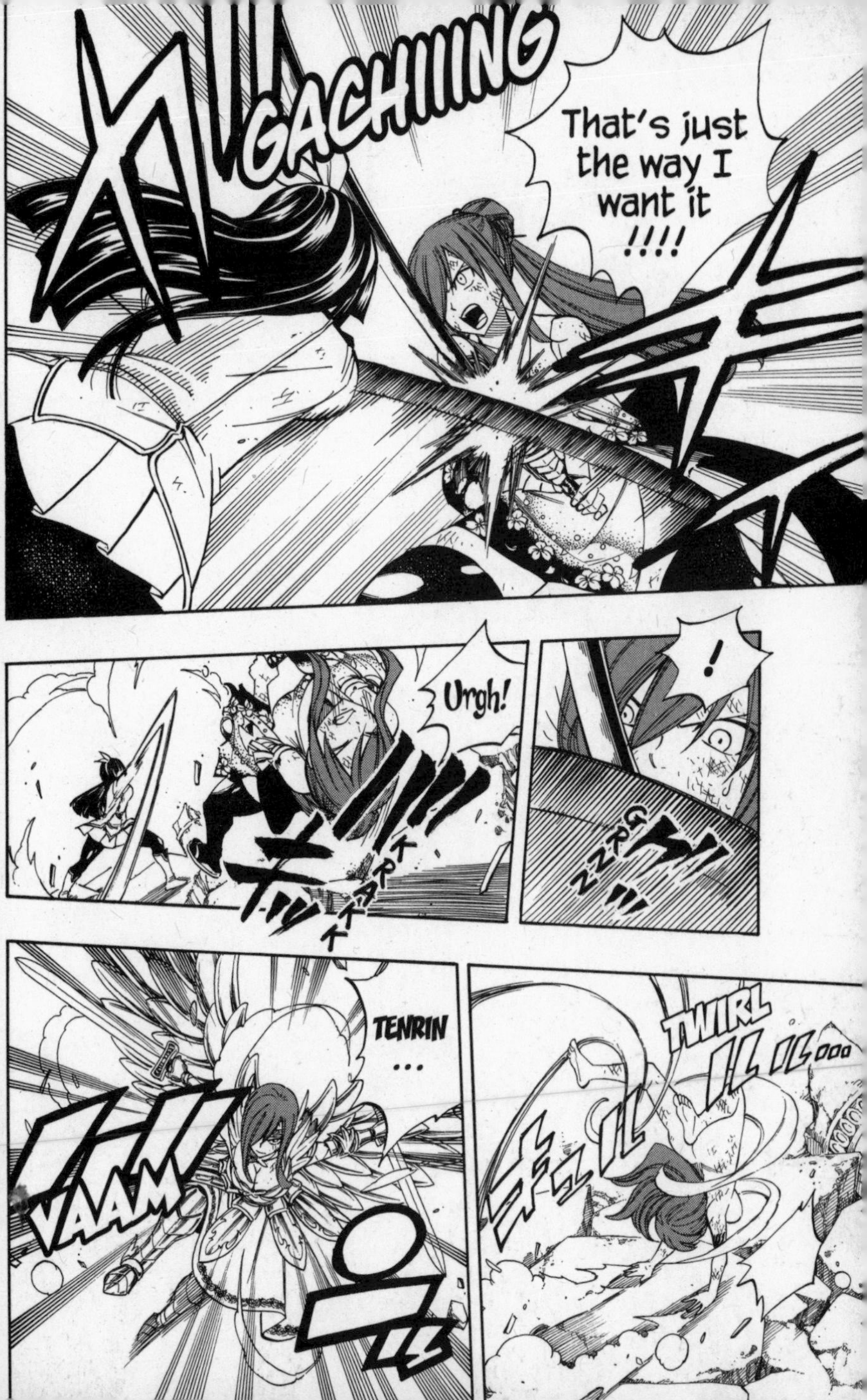
GACHIIIING
That's just the way I want it !!!!
!
ZZRRGH!!
Urgh!
KRAK K
TWIRL
TENRIN ...
VAAM

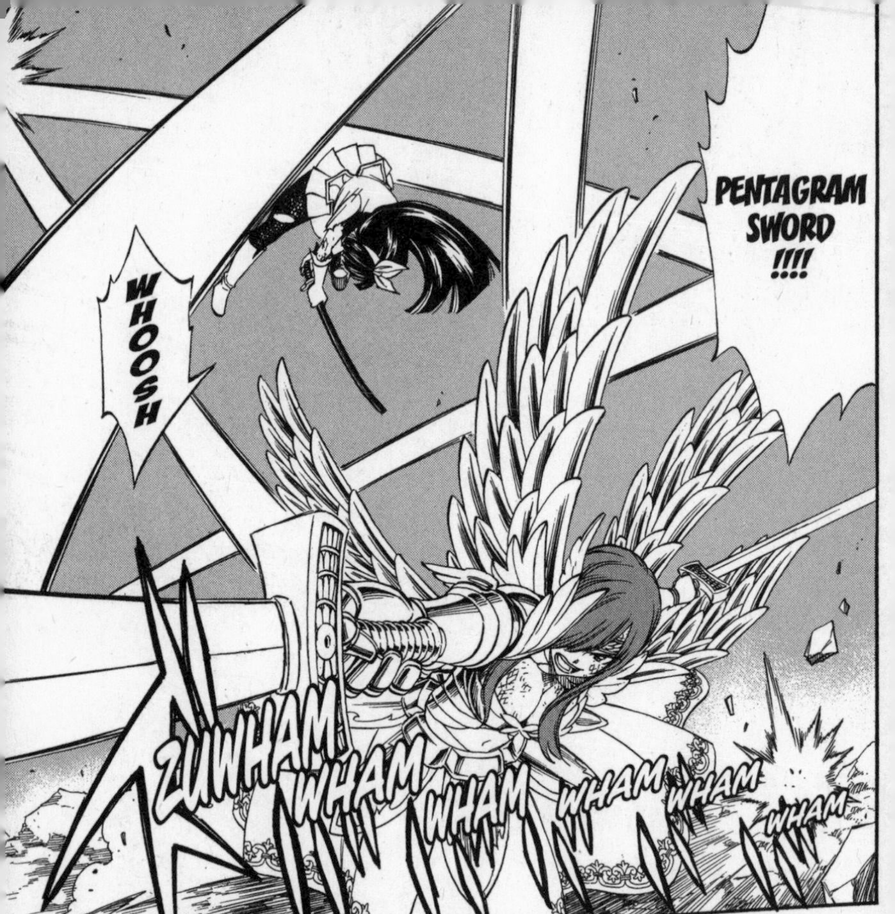
PENTAGRAM SWORD !!!!
WHOOSH
ZUWHAM WHAM WHAM WHAM WHAM WHAM

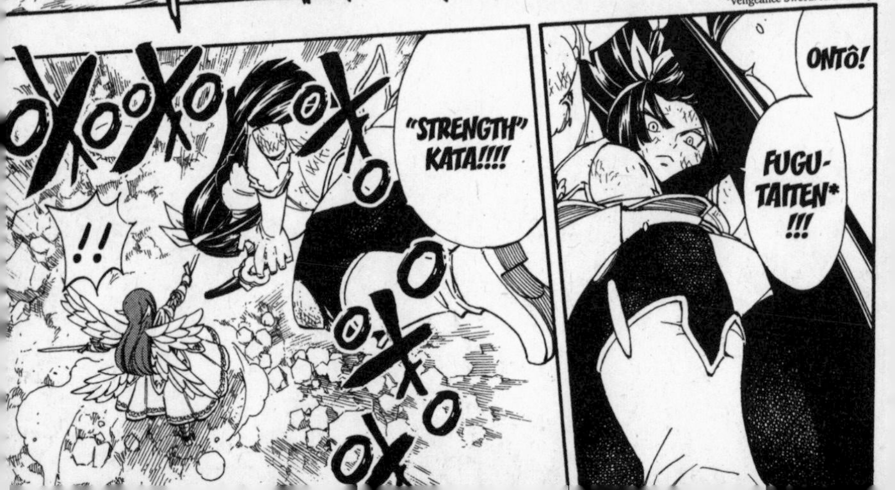
ONTÔ!
FUGU-TAITEN* !!!
"STRENGTH" KATA!!!!
!!

*Vengeance Sword: Archenemy

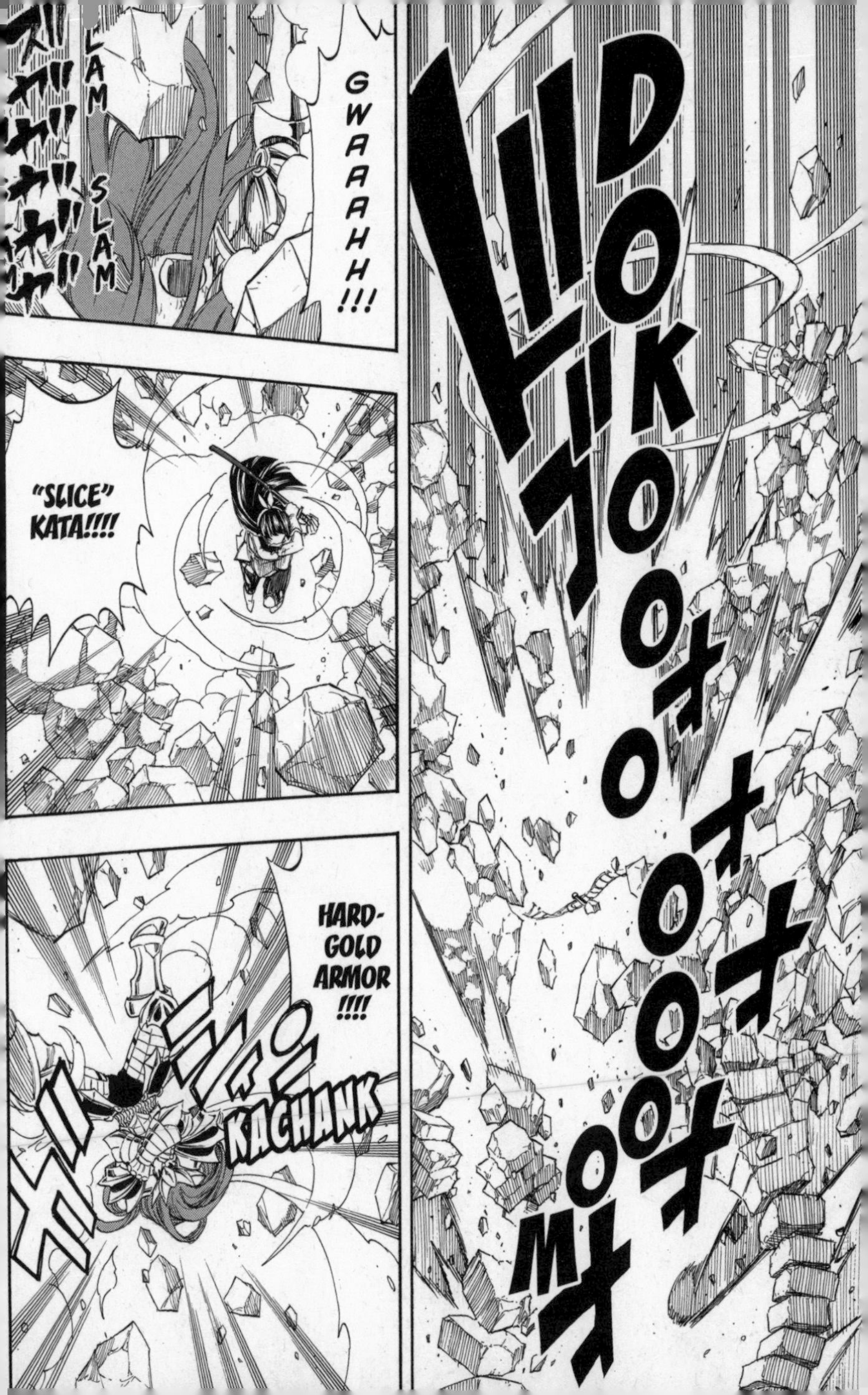
DOKOOOOOM
GWAAAAHH!!!
SLAM SLAM
"SLICE" KATA!!!!
HARD-GOLD ARMOR!!!!
KACHANK

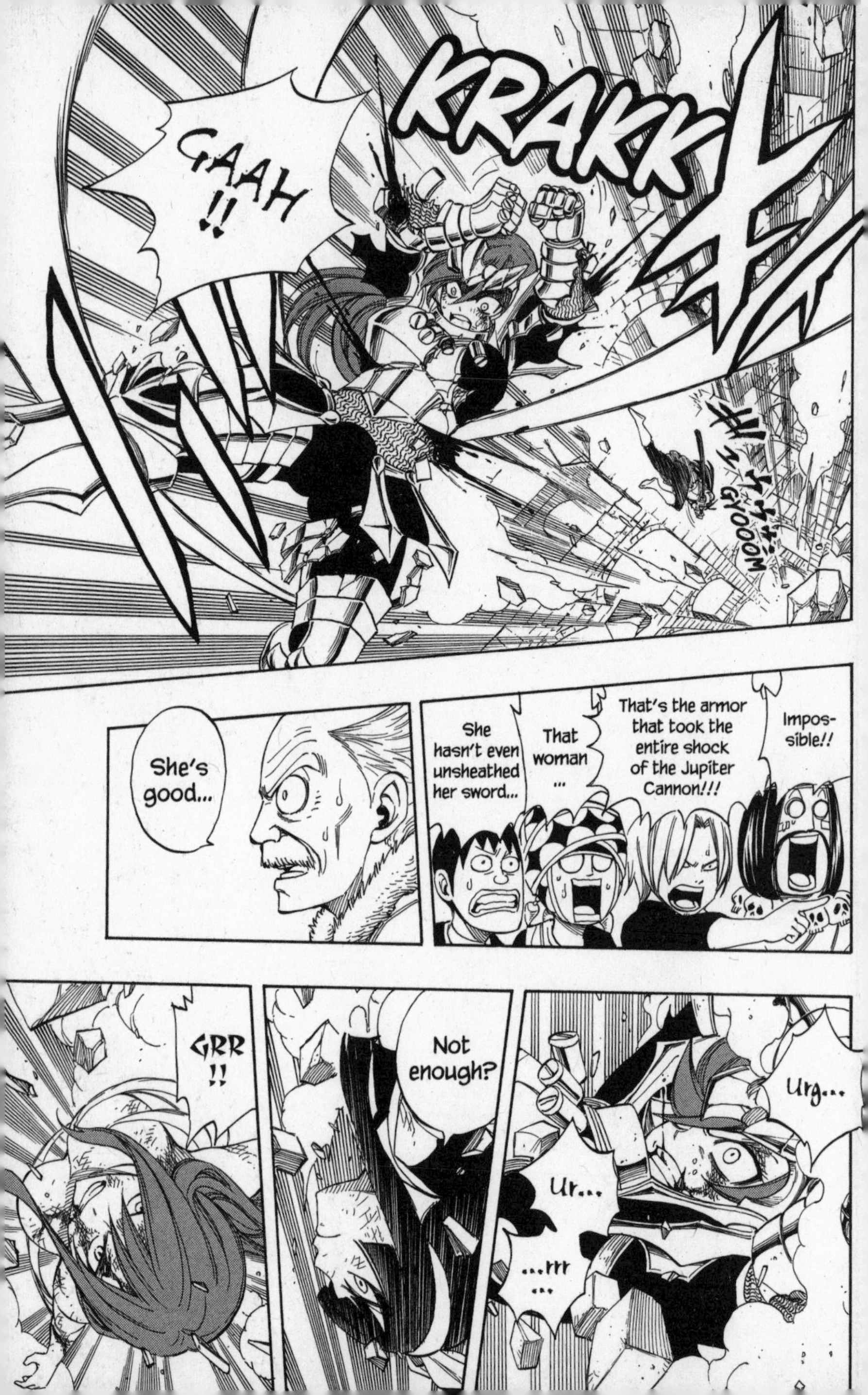
KRAKK
GAAH!!
GYOOOOM
Impossible!!
That's the armor that took the entire shock of the Jupiter Cannon!!!
That woman...
She hasn't even unsheathed her sword...
She's good...
Urg...
Ur...
...rrr...
Not enough?
GRR!!

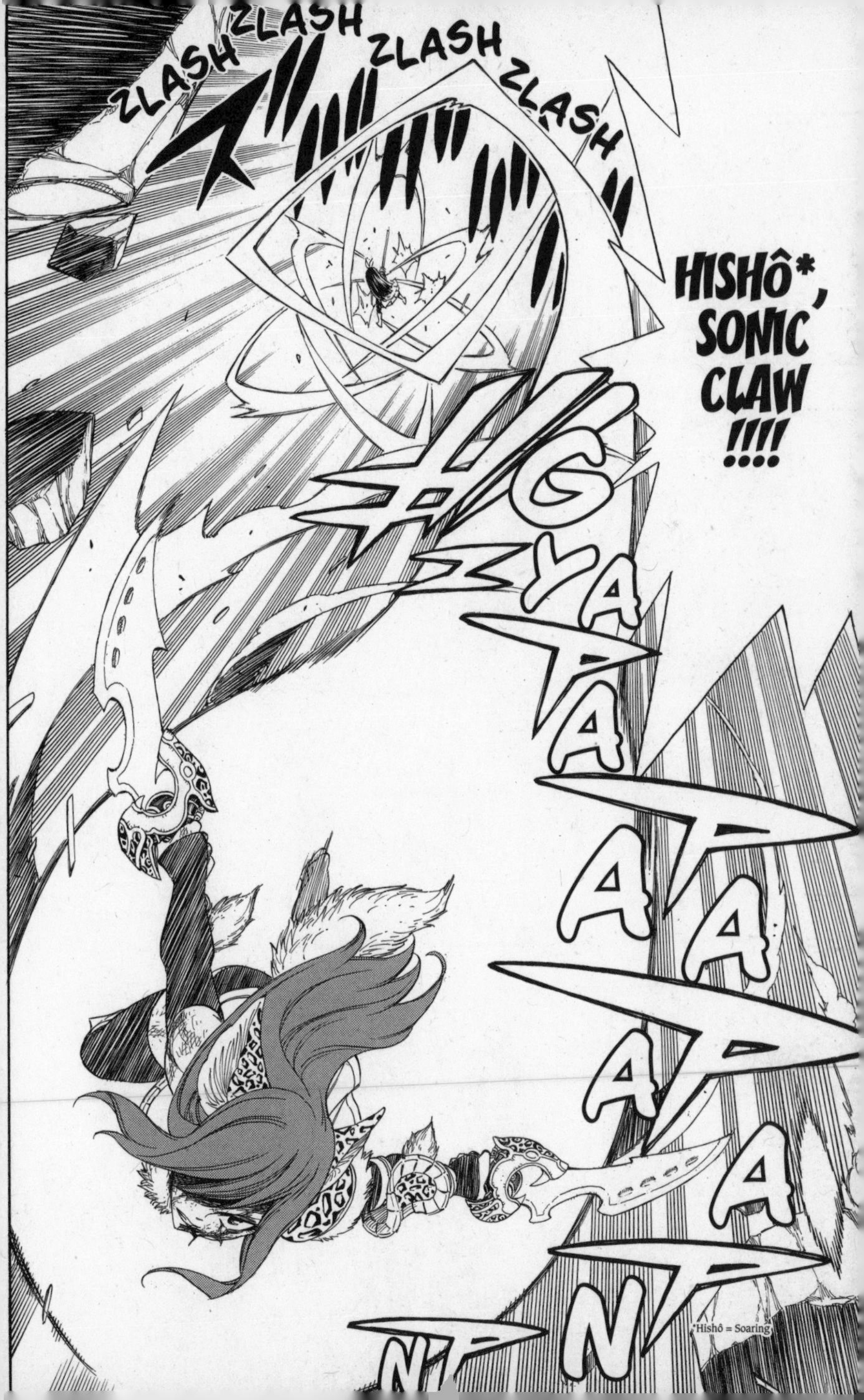
HISHÔ*, SONIC CLAW!!!!
ZLASH ZLASH ZLASH ZLASH ZLASH
HGYAAAAAAAN
*Hishô = Soaring

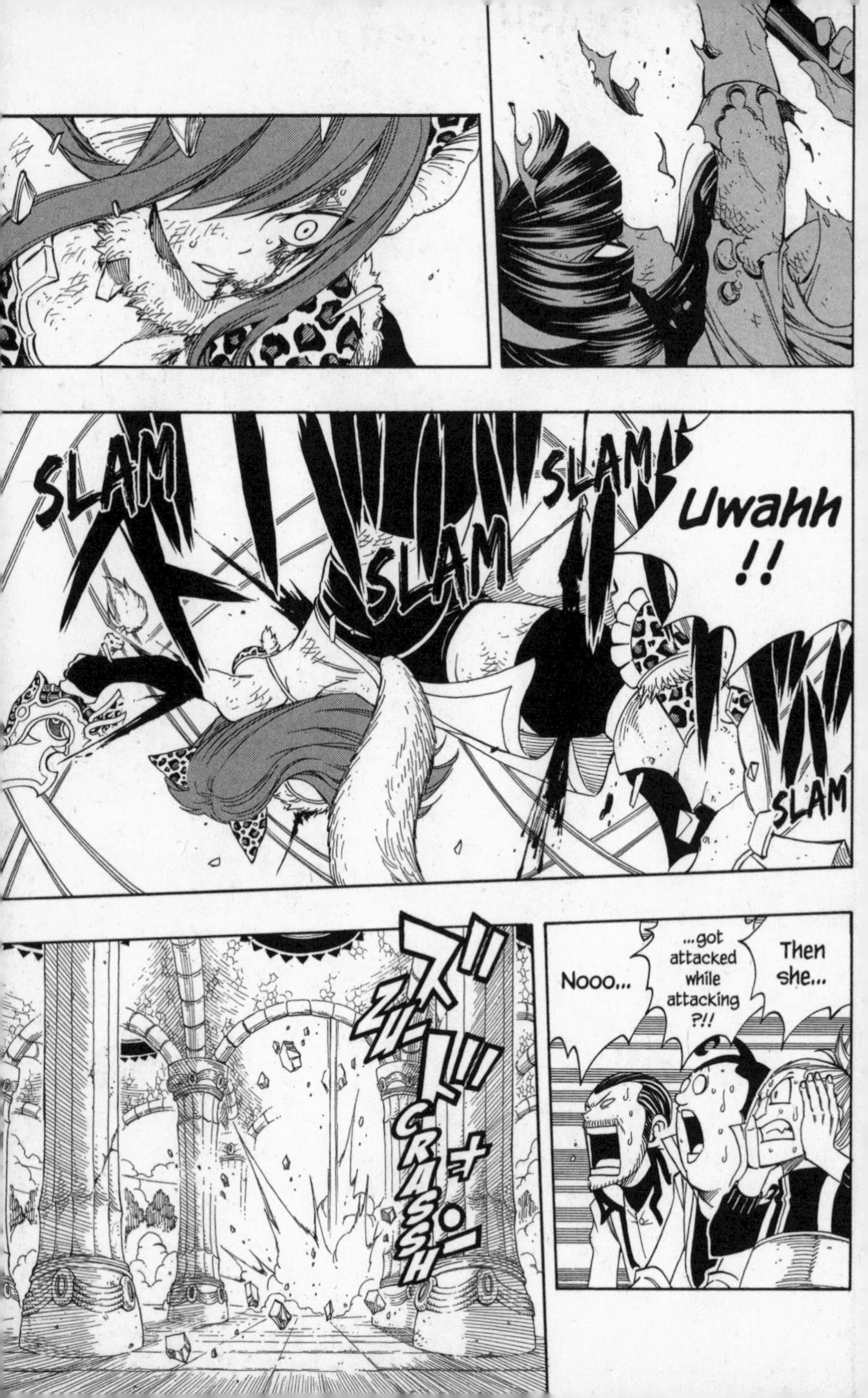

Uwahh !!
SLAM
SLAM
SLAM
SLAM
Then she...
...got attacked while attacking ?!!
Nooo...
CRASH

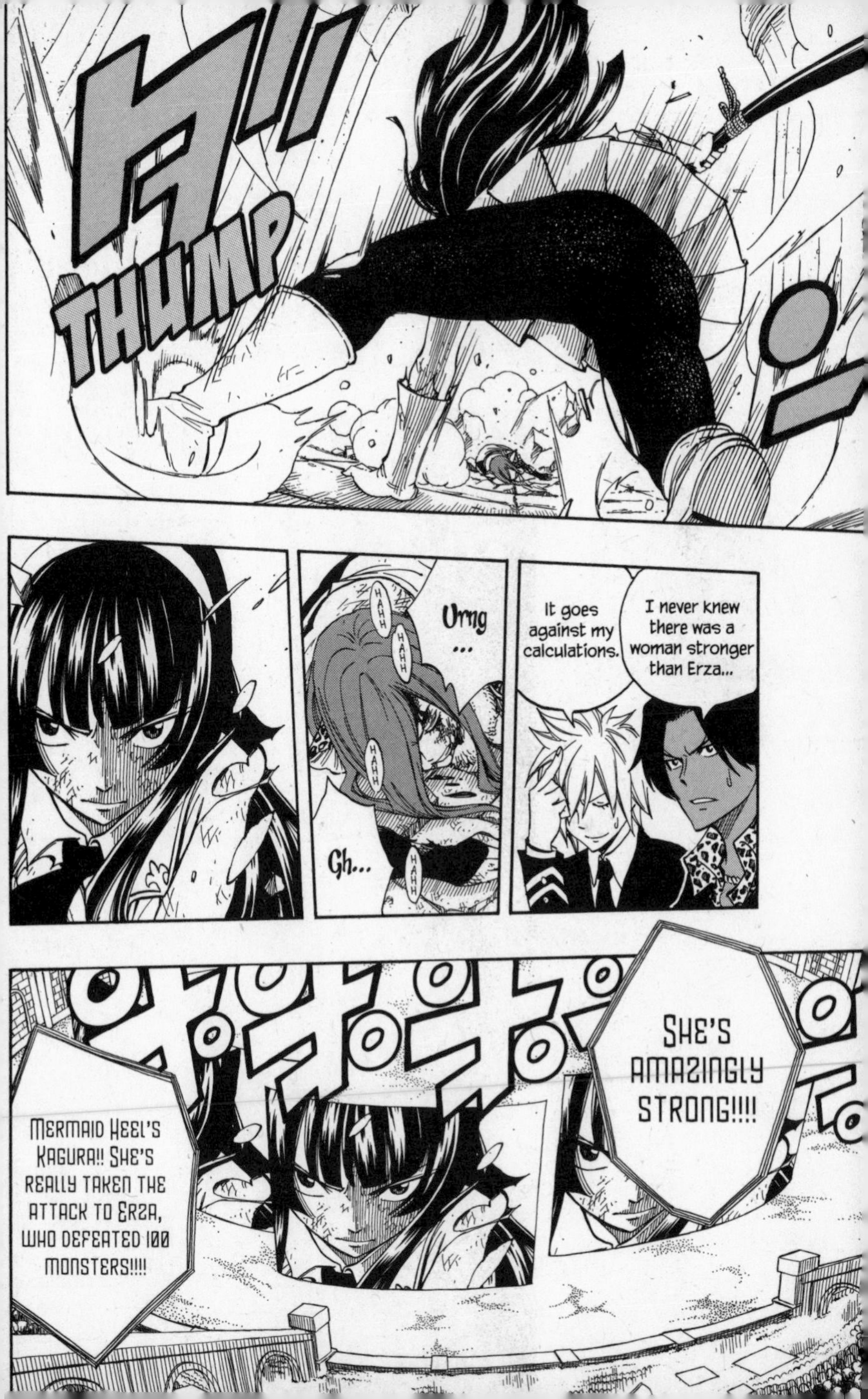
THUMP
I never knew there was a woman stronger than Erza...
It goes against my calculations.
Urng ...
Gh...
SHE'S AMAZINGLY STRONG!!!!
MERMAID HEEL'S KAGURA!! SHE'S REALLY TAKEN THE ATTACK TO ERZA, WHO DEFEATED 100 MONSTERS!!!!

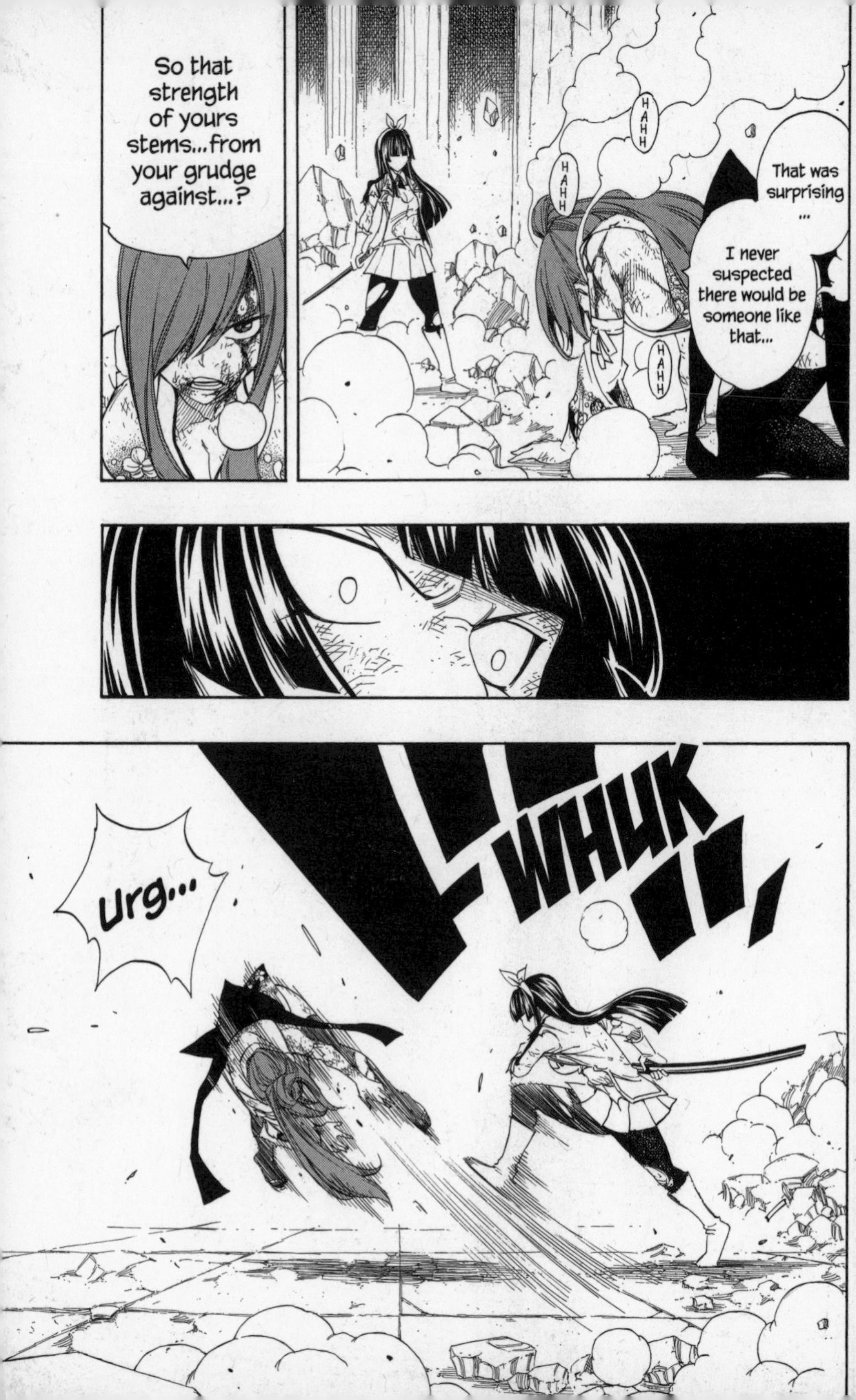
That was surprising ...
I never suspected there would be someone like that...
HAHH
HAHH
HAHH
So that strength of yours stems...from your grudge against...?
WHUK
Urg...

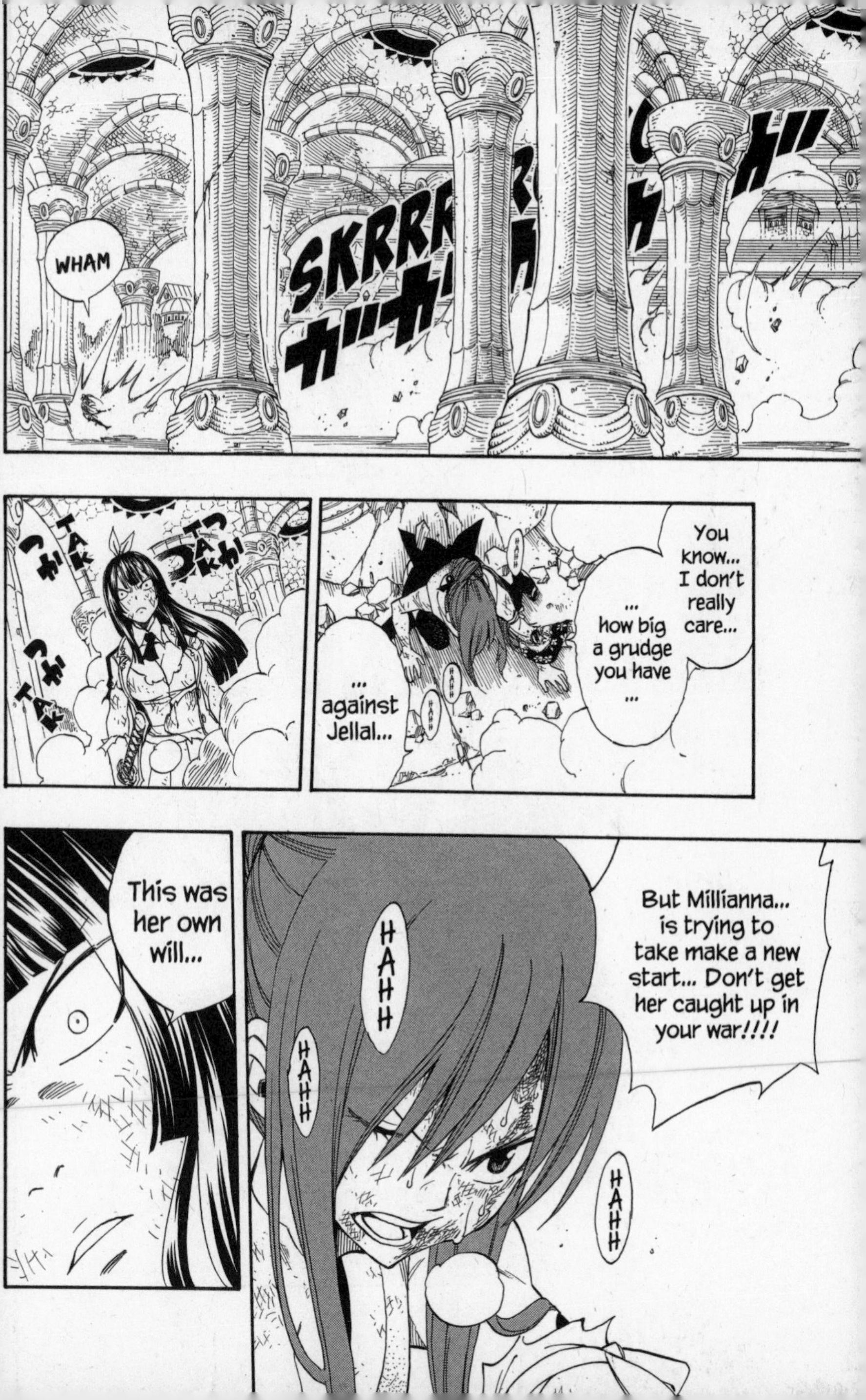
SKRRR
WHAM
You know... I don't really care...
... how big a grudge you have ...
... against Jellal...
HAHH
TAK
TAK
TAK
TAK
But Millianna... is trying to take make a new start... Don't get her caught up in your war!!!!
HAHH
HAHH
HAHH
This was her own will...

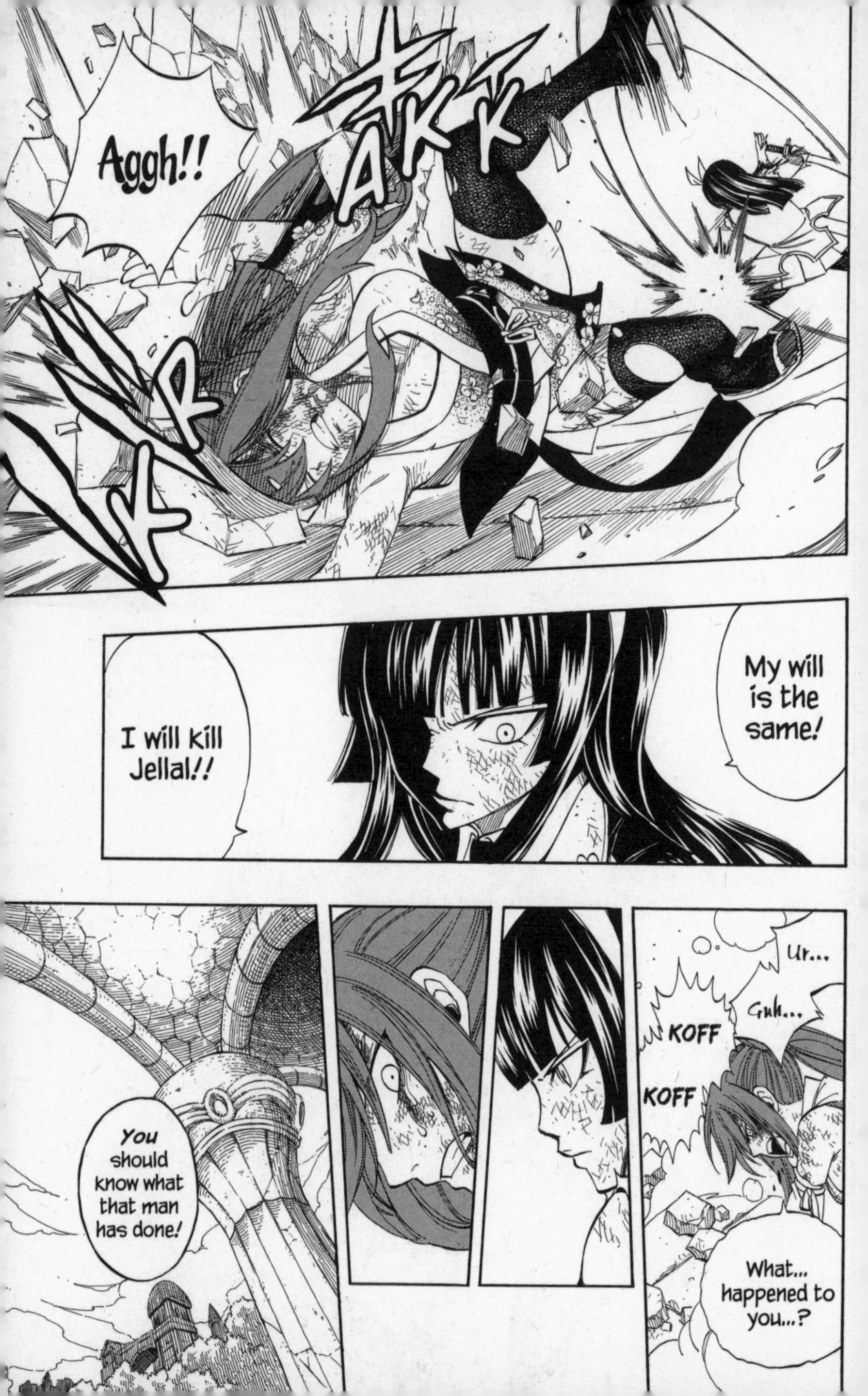
Aggh!!
My will is the same!
I will kill Jellal!!
Ur...
Guh...
KOFF
KOFF
What... happened to you...?
You should know what that man has done!

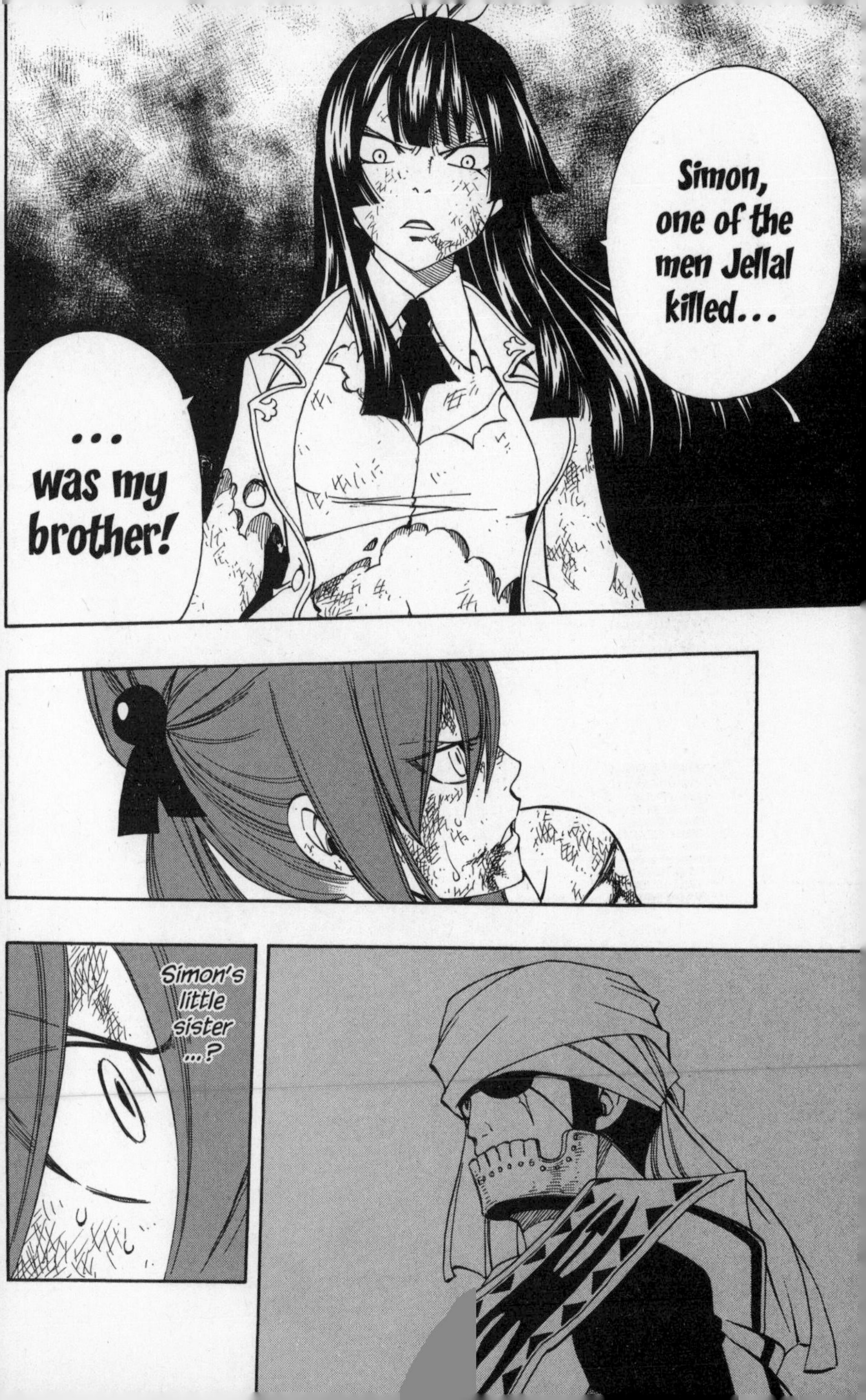
Simon, one of the men Jellal killed...
... was my brother!
Simon's little sister ...?

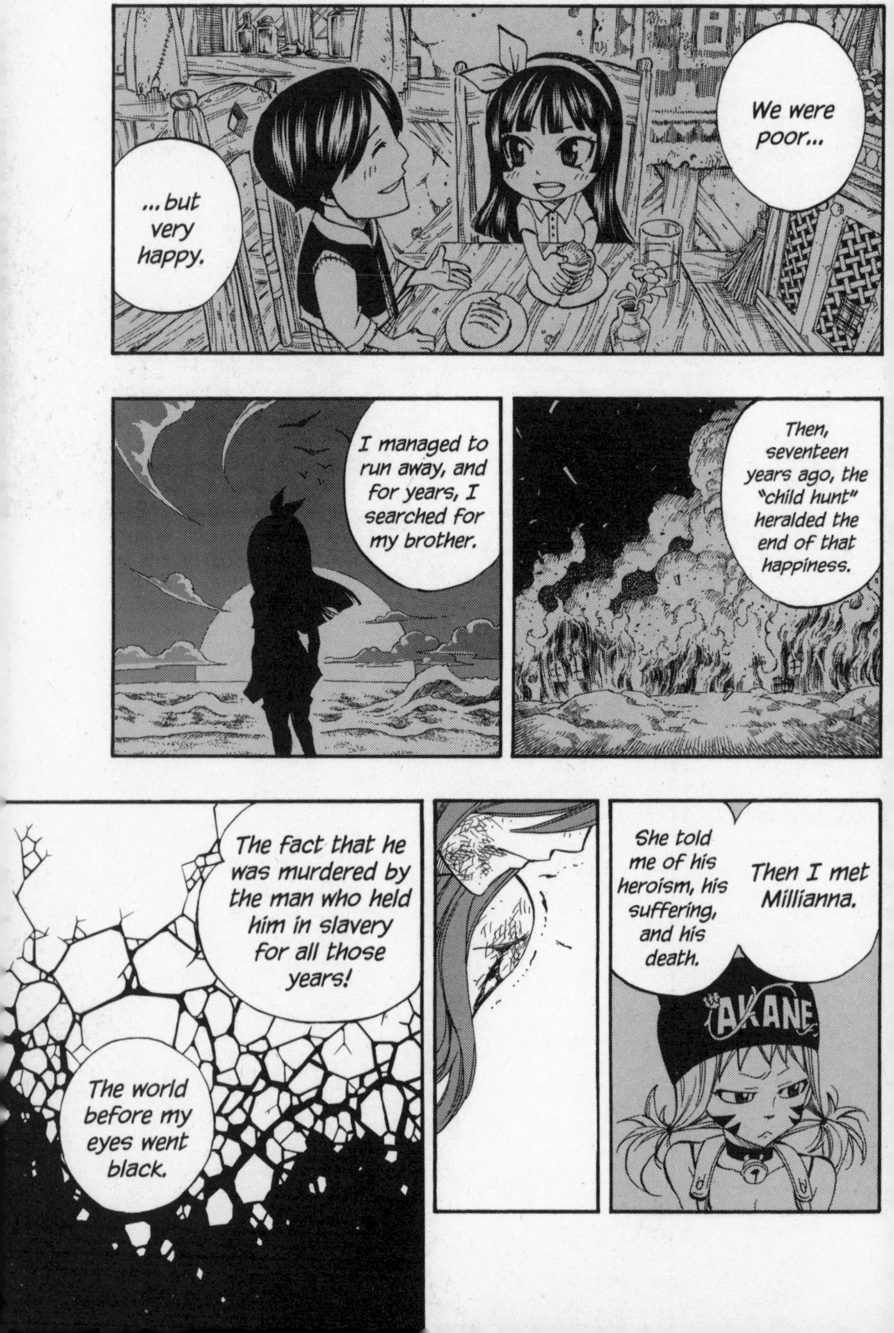
We were poor...
...but very happy.
Then, seventeen years ago, the "child hunt" heralded the end of that happiness.
I managed to run away, and for years, I searched for my brother.
Then I met Millianna.
She told me of his heroism, his suffering, and his death.
AKANE
The fact that he was murdered by the man who held him in slavery for all those years!
The world before my eyes went black.

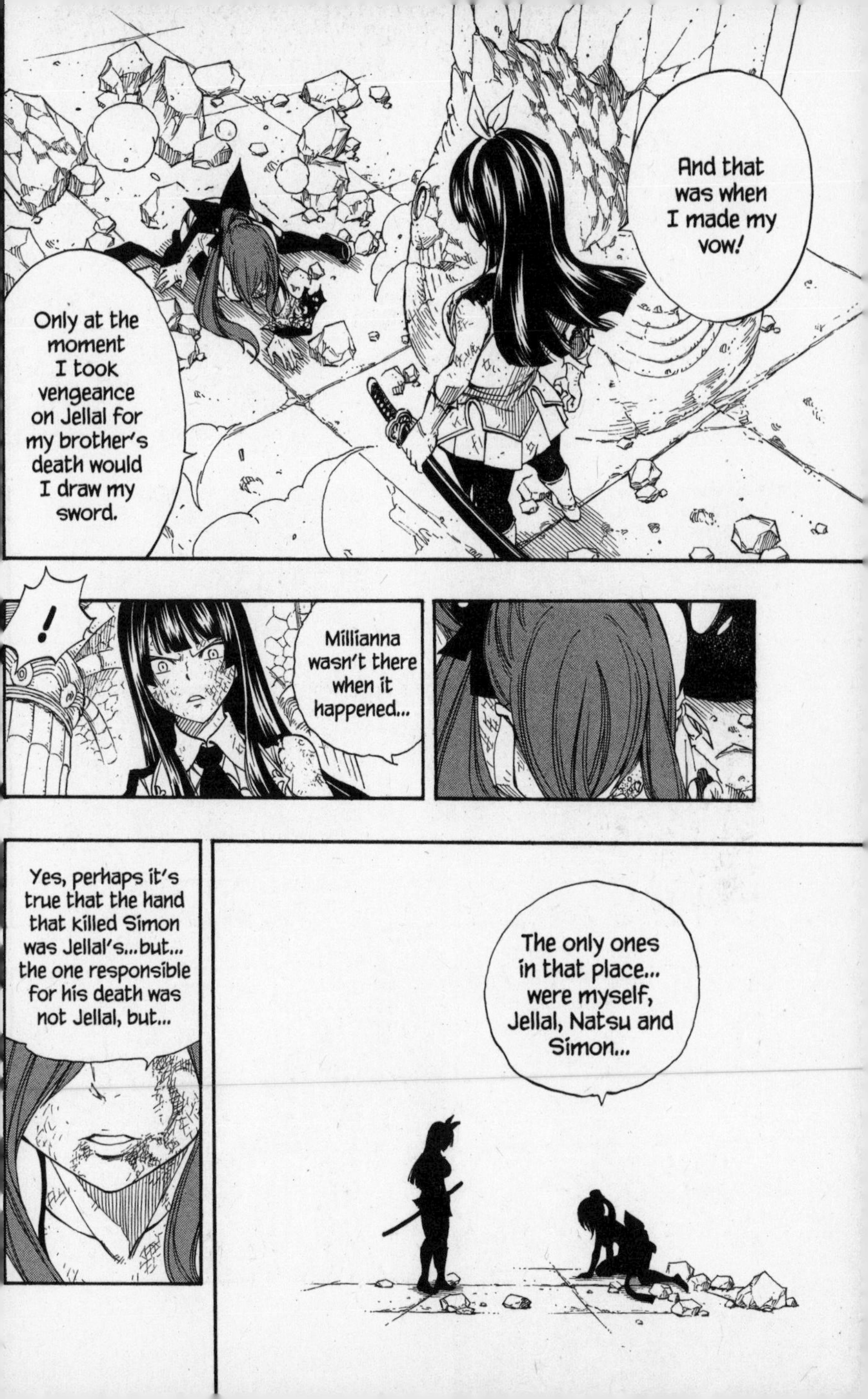
And that was when I made my vow!
Only at the moment I took vengeance on Jellal for my brother's death would I draw my sword.
Millianna wasn't there when it happened...
!
The only ones in that place... were myself, Jellal, Natsu and Simon...
Yes, perhaps it's true that the hand that killed Simon was Jellal's...but... the one responsible for his death was not Jellal, but...

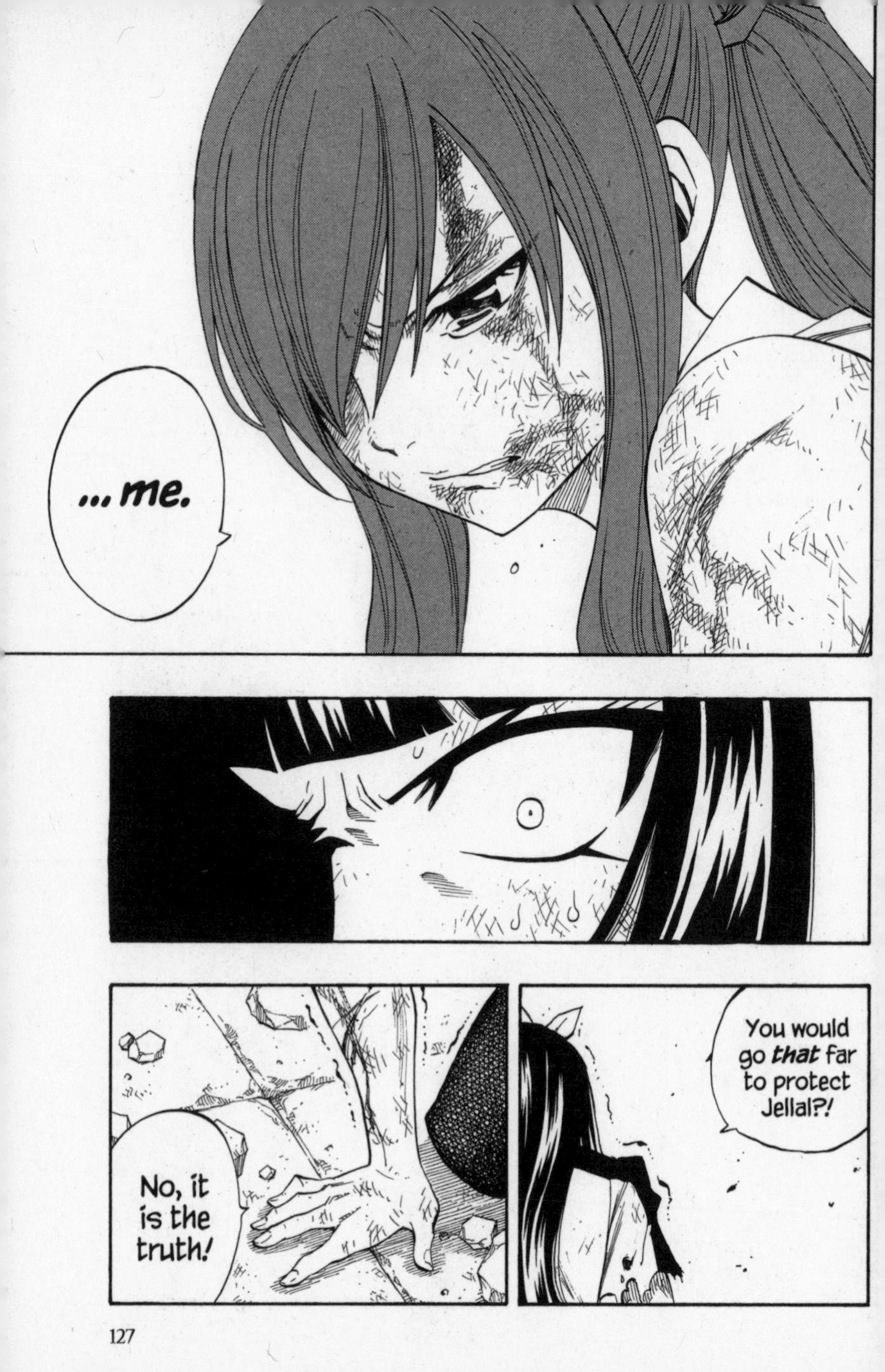
...me.
You would go *that* far to protect Jellal?!
No, it is the truth!

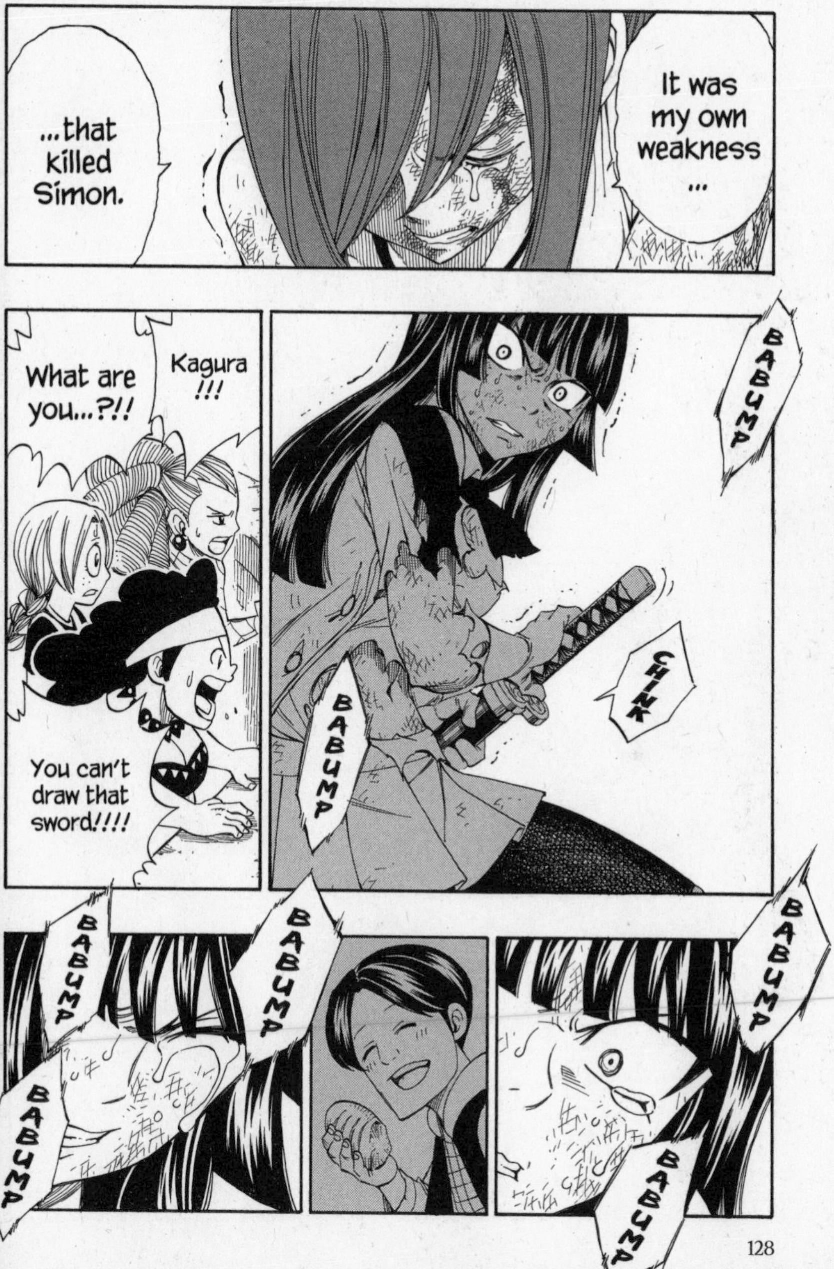
It was my own weakness ...
...that killed Simon.
BABUMP
CHINK
BABUMP
Kagura !!!
What are you...?!!
You can't draw that sword!!!!
BABUMP
BABUMP
BABUMP
BABUMP
BABUMP

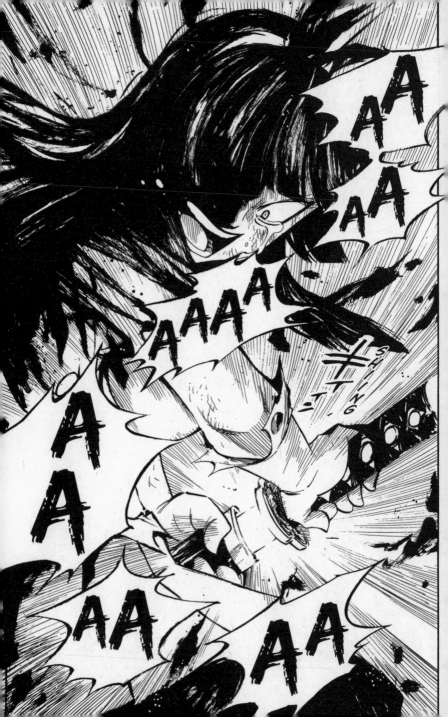

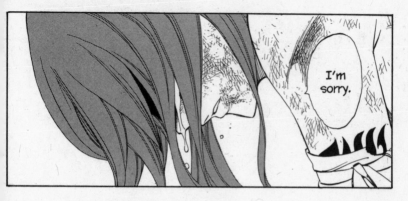

I'm sorry.

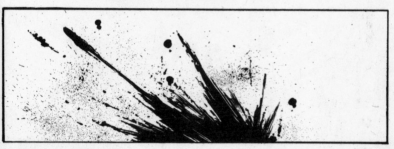

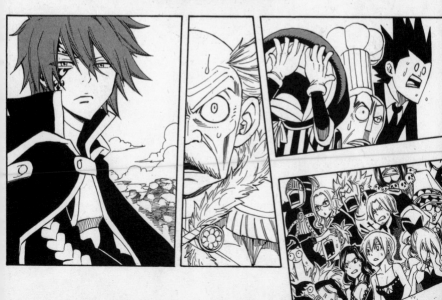

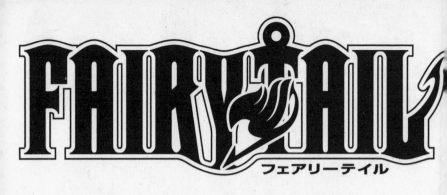

Chapter 315: Rosemary

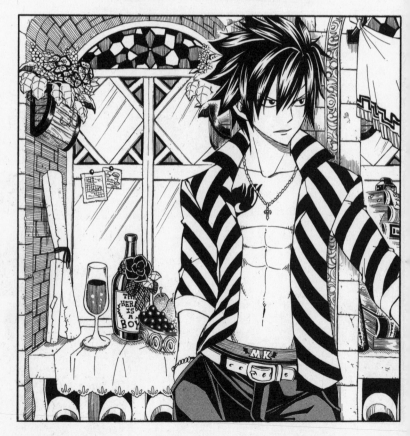

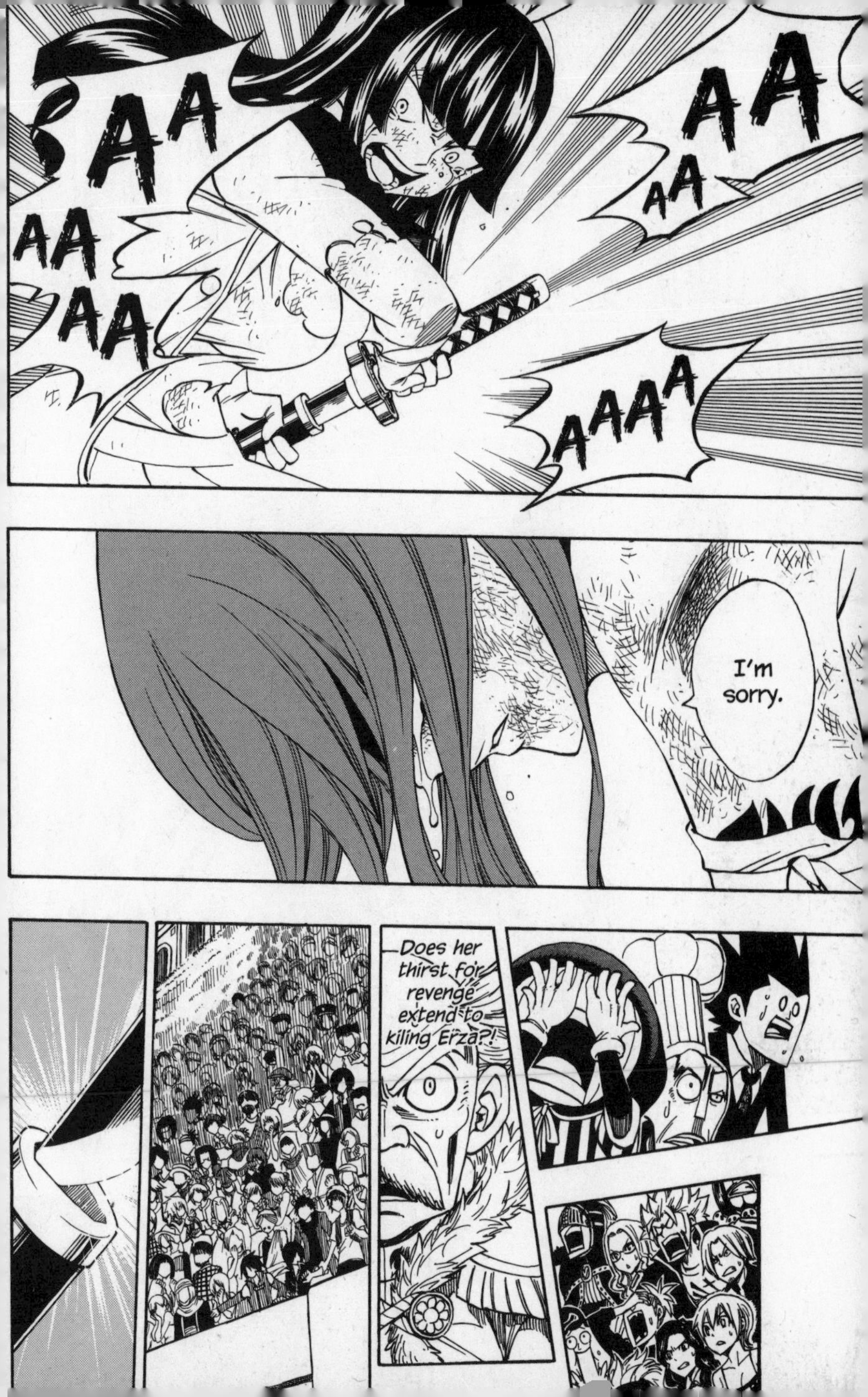
AAAAA
AAAA
AAAAAA
AAAA
I'm sorry.
Does her thirst for revenge extend to kiling Erza?!

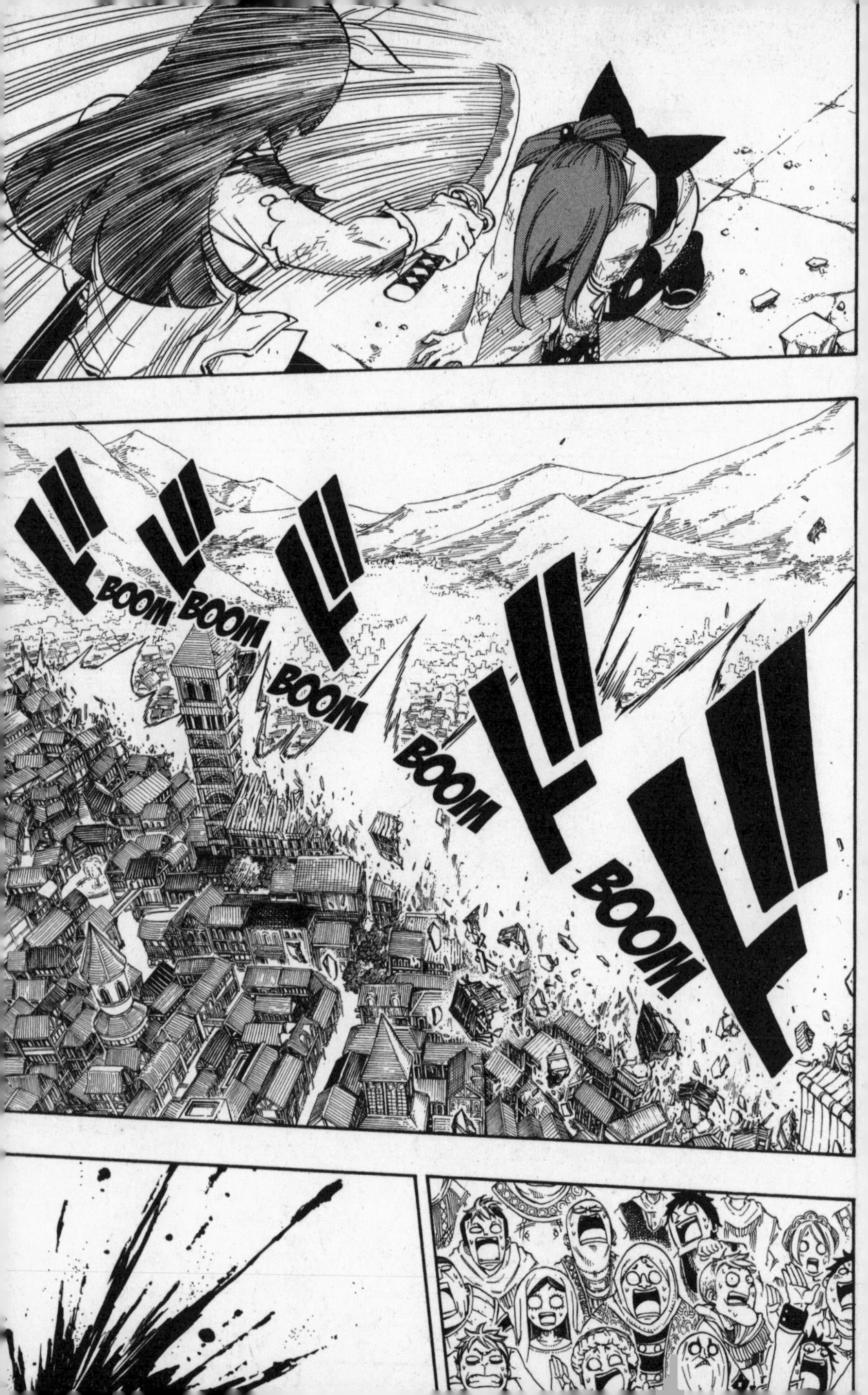
BOOM
BOOM
BOOM
BOOM
BOOM

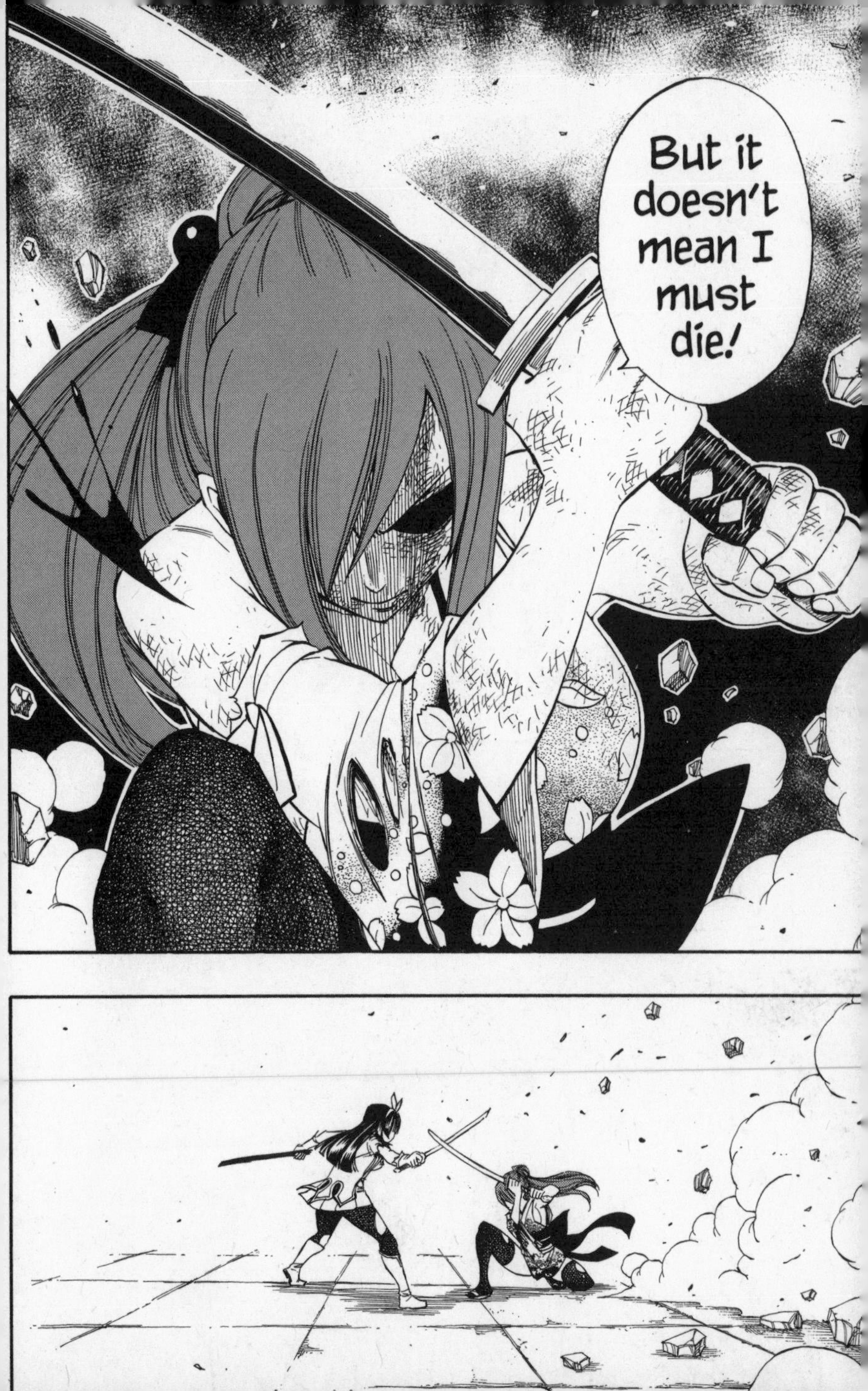
But it doesn't mean I must die!

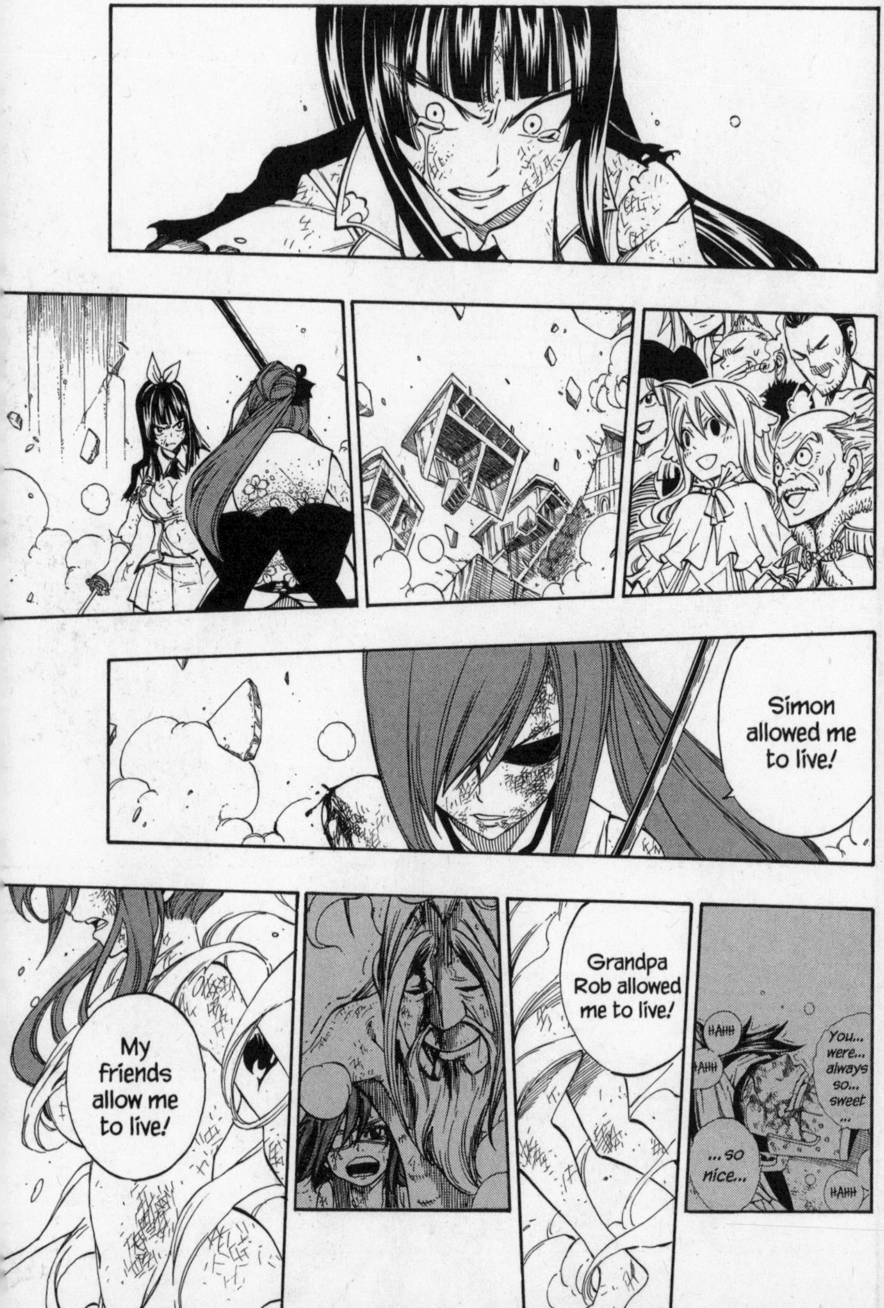
Simon allowed me to live!
You... were... always so... sweet...
HAHH
AHH
HAHH
...so nice...
Grandpa Rob allowed me to live!
My friends allow me to live!

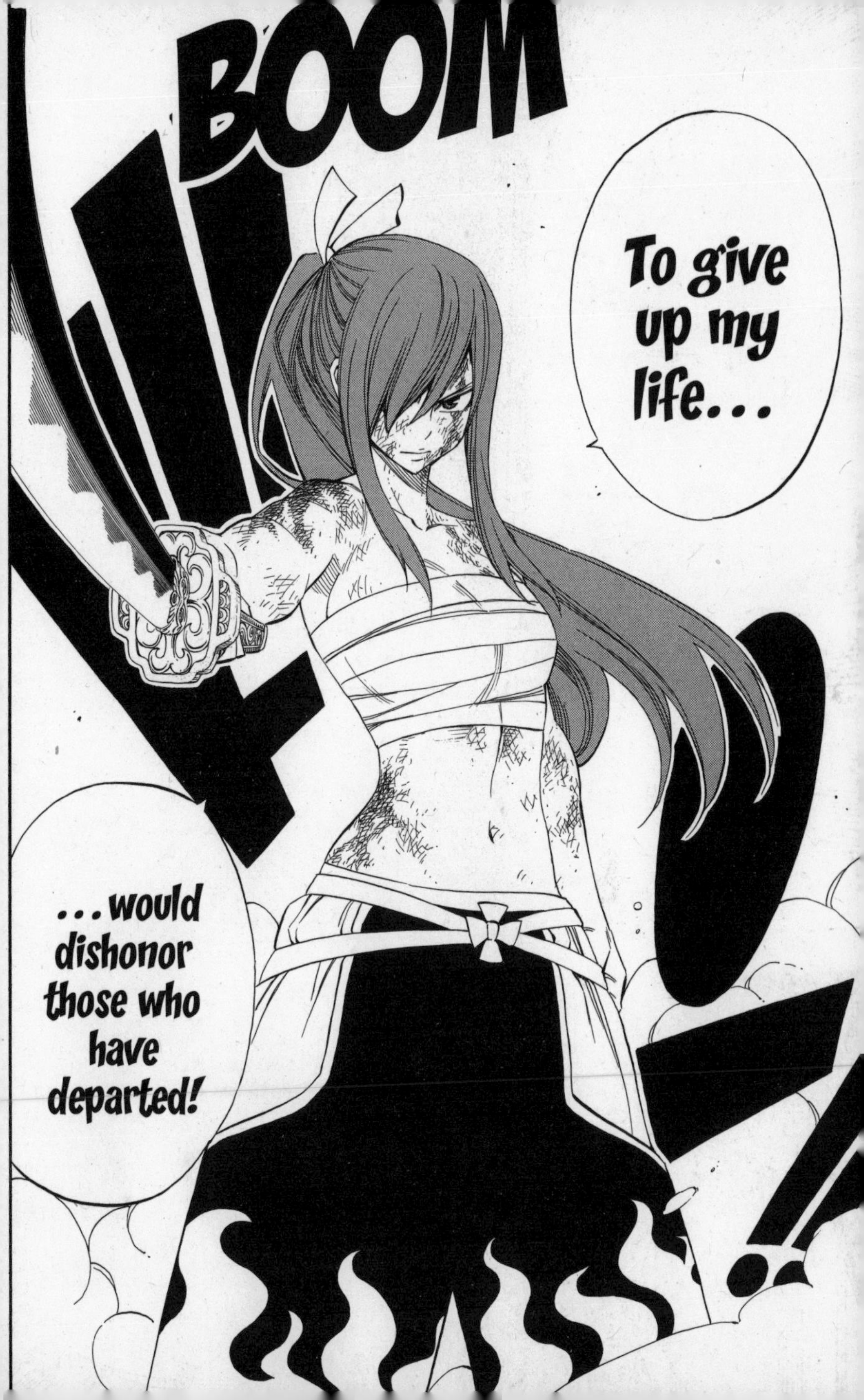
BOOM
To give up my life...
...would dishonor those who have departed!

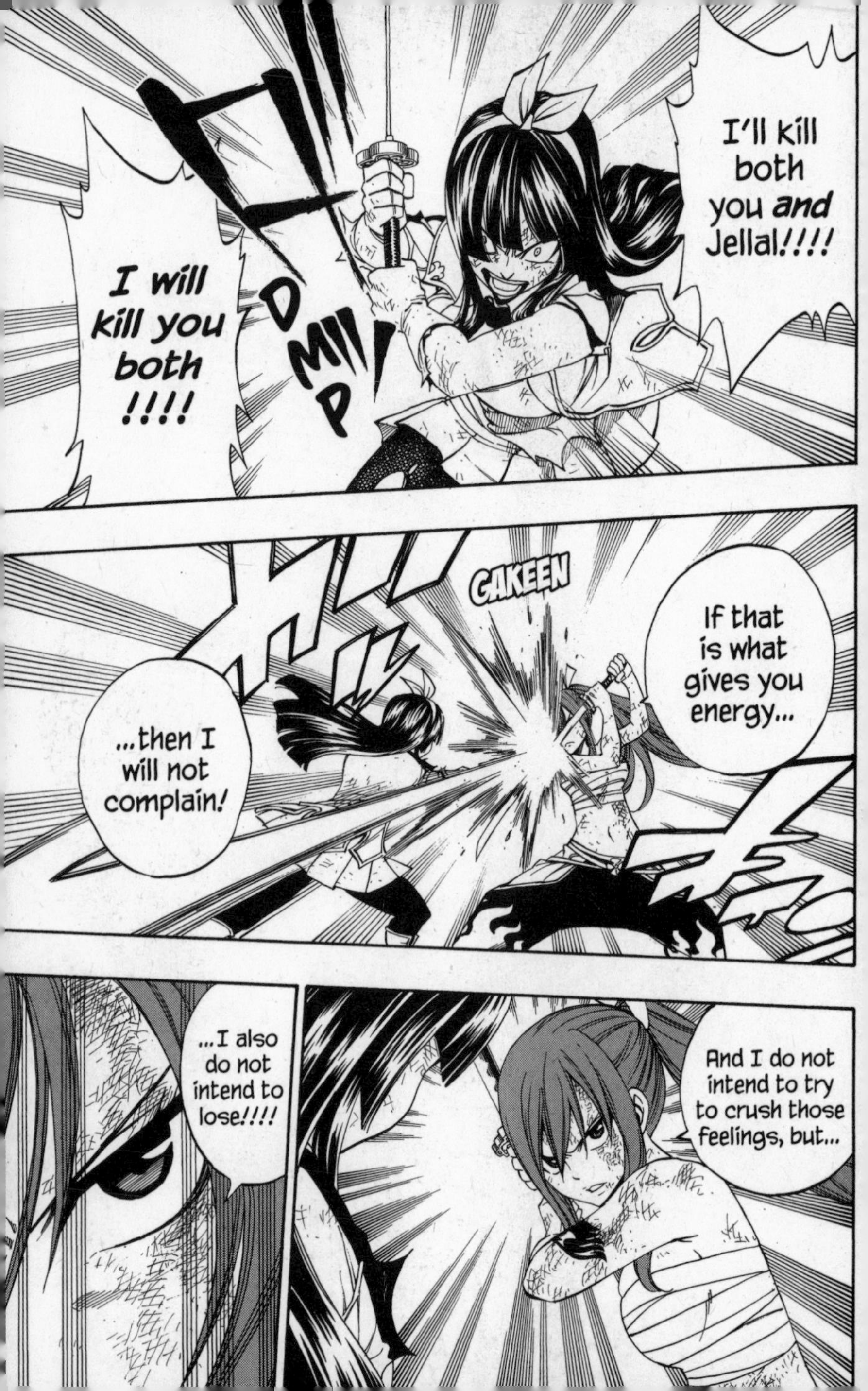
I'll kill both you *and* Jellal!!!!
DMP
I will kill you both !!!!
GAKEEN
If that is what gives you energy...
...then I will not complain!
And I do not intend to try to crush those feelings, but...
...I also do not intend to lose!!!!

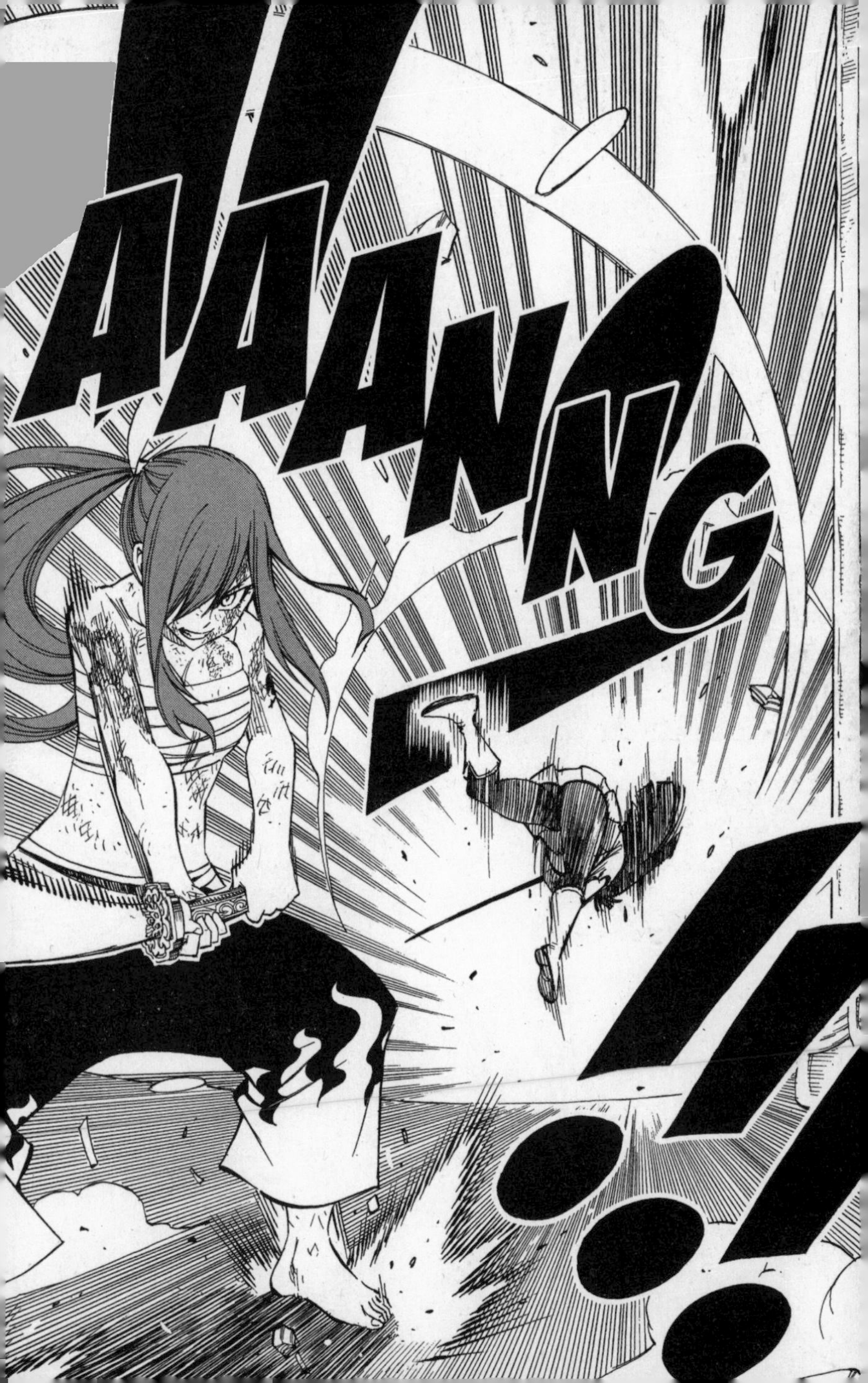
GAAAANNNG!!

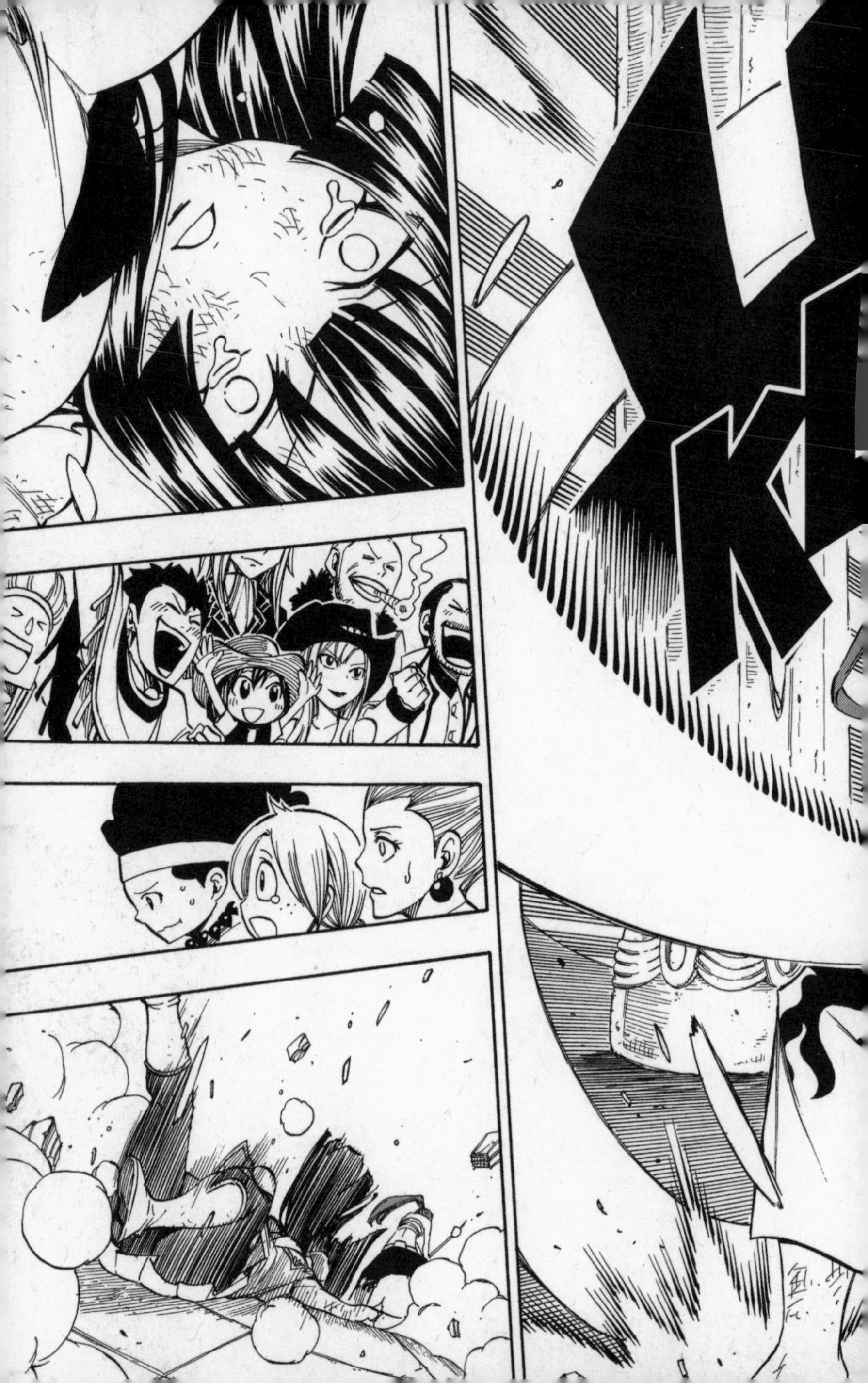

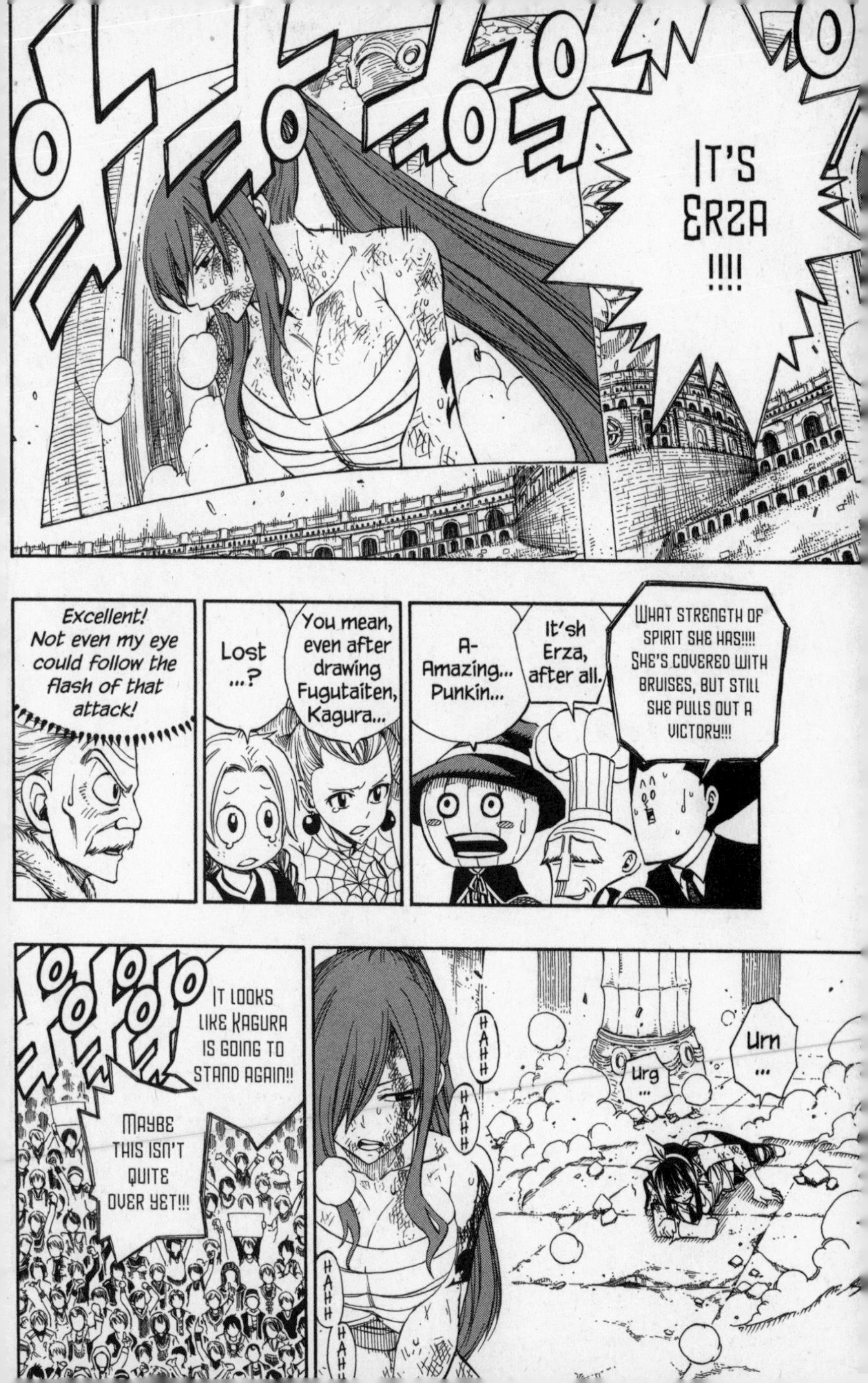
IT'S ERZA !!!!
WHAT STRENGTH OF SPIRIT SHE HAS!!!! SHE'S COVERED WITH BRUISES, BUT STILL SHE PULLS OUT A VICTORY!!!
It'sh Erza, after all.
A-Amazing... Punkin...
You mean, even after drawing Fugutaiten, Kagura...
Lost ...?
Excellent! Not even my eye could follow the flash of that attack!
Urn ...
Urg ...
HAHH
HAHH
HAHH
HAHH
HAHH
IT LOOKS LIKE KAGURA IS GOING TO STAND AGAIN!!
MAYBE THIS ISN'T QUITE OVER YET!!!

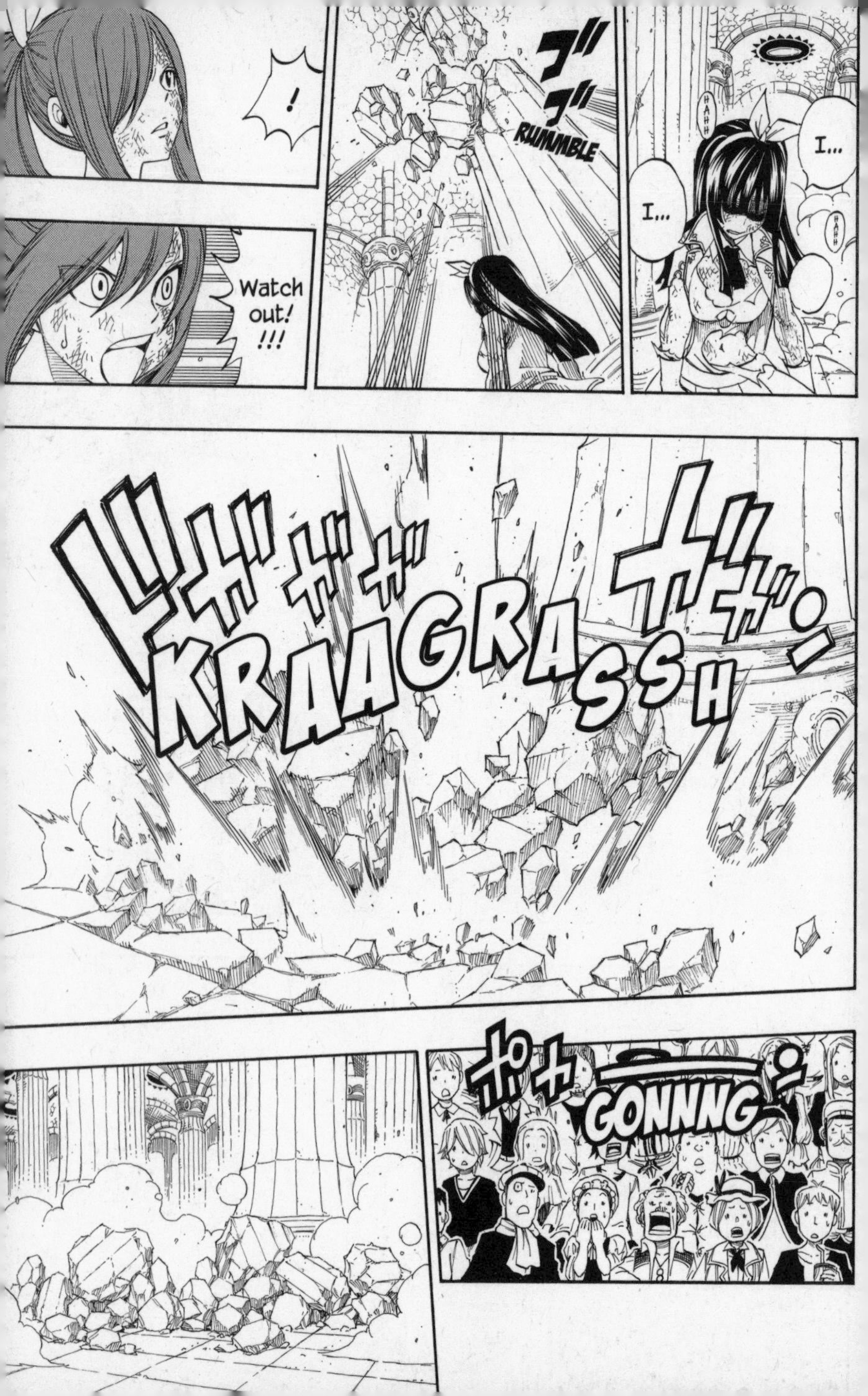
I...
HAHH
HAHH
I...
RUMMBLE
!
Watch out!
!!!
KRAAGRASSH
GONNNG

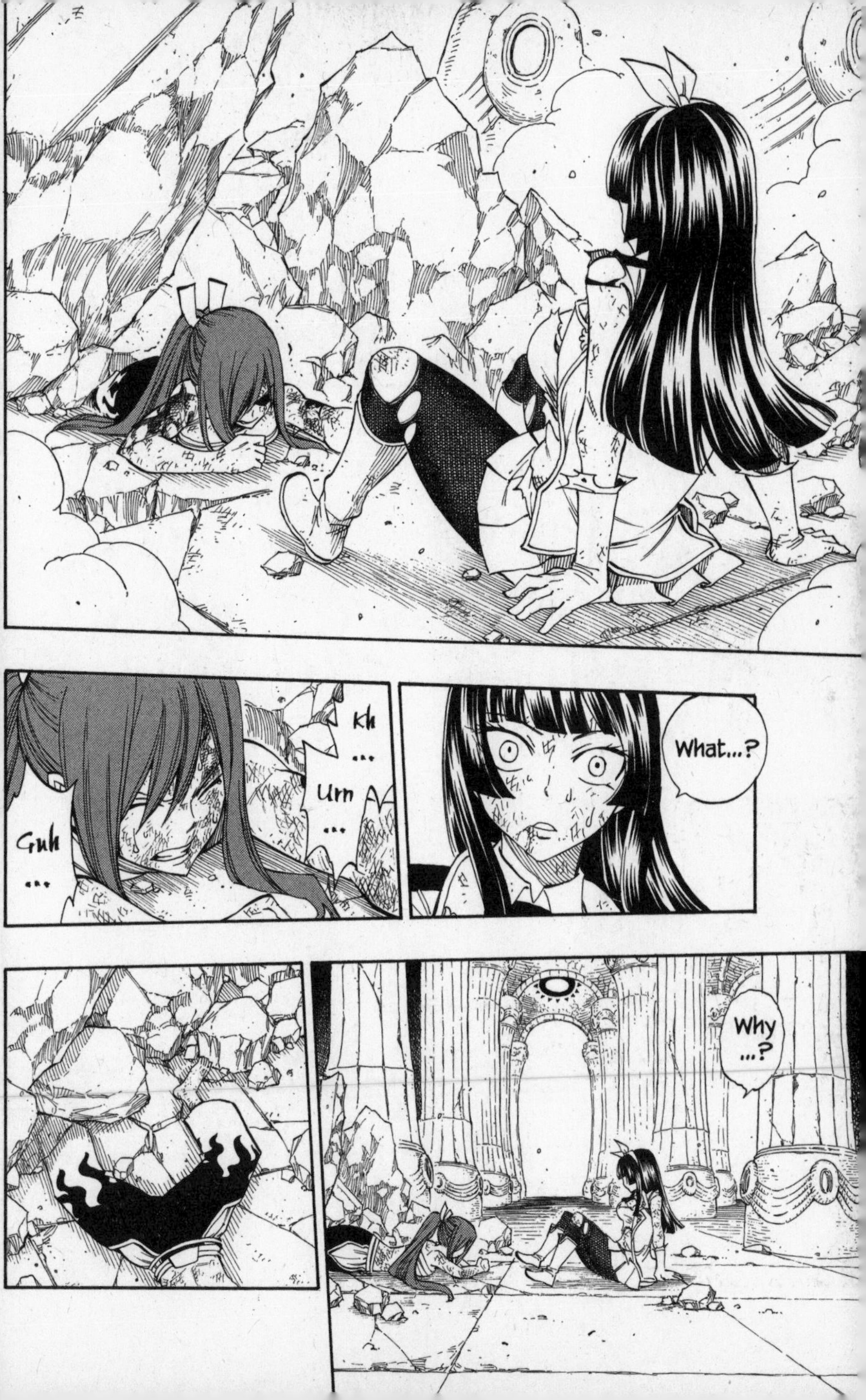
What...?
Kh ... Urn ...
Guh ...
Why ...?

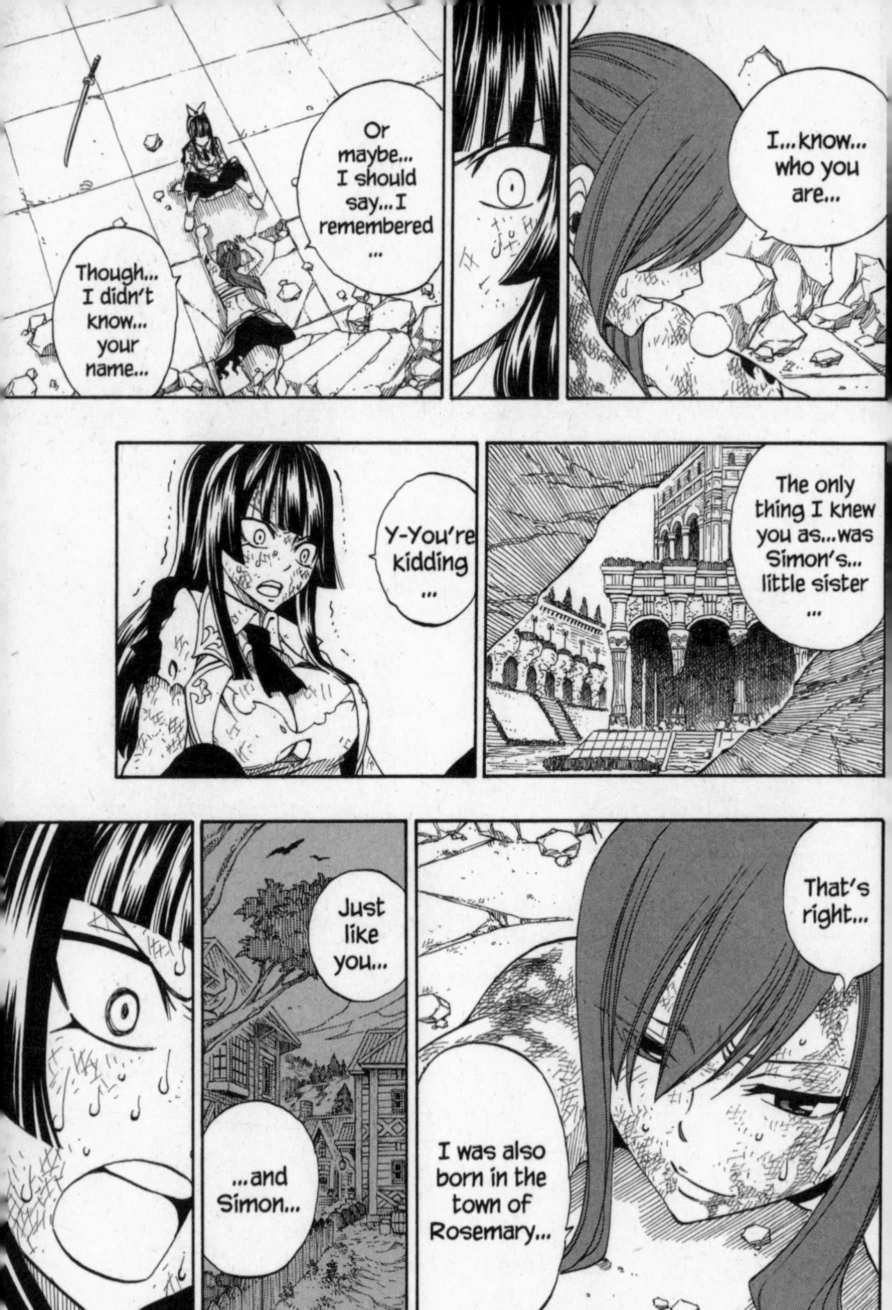
I...know... who you are...
Or maybe... I should say...I remembered ...
Though... I didn't know... your name...
The only thing I knew you as...was Simon's... little sister ...
Y-You're kidding ...
That's right...
I was also born in the town of Rosemary...
Just like you...
...and Simon...

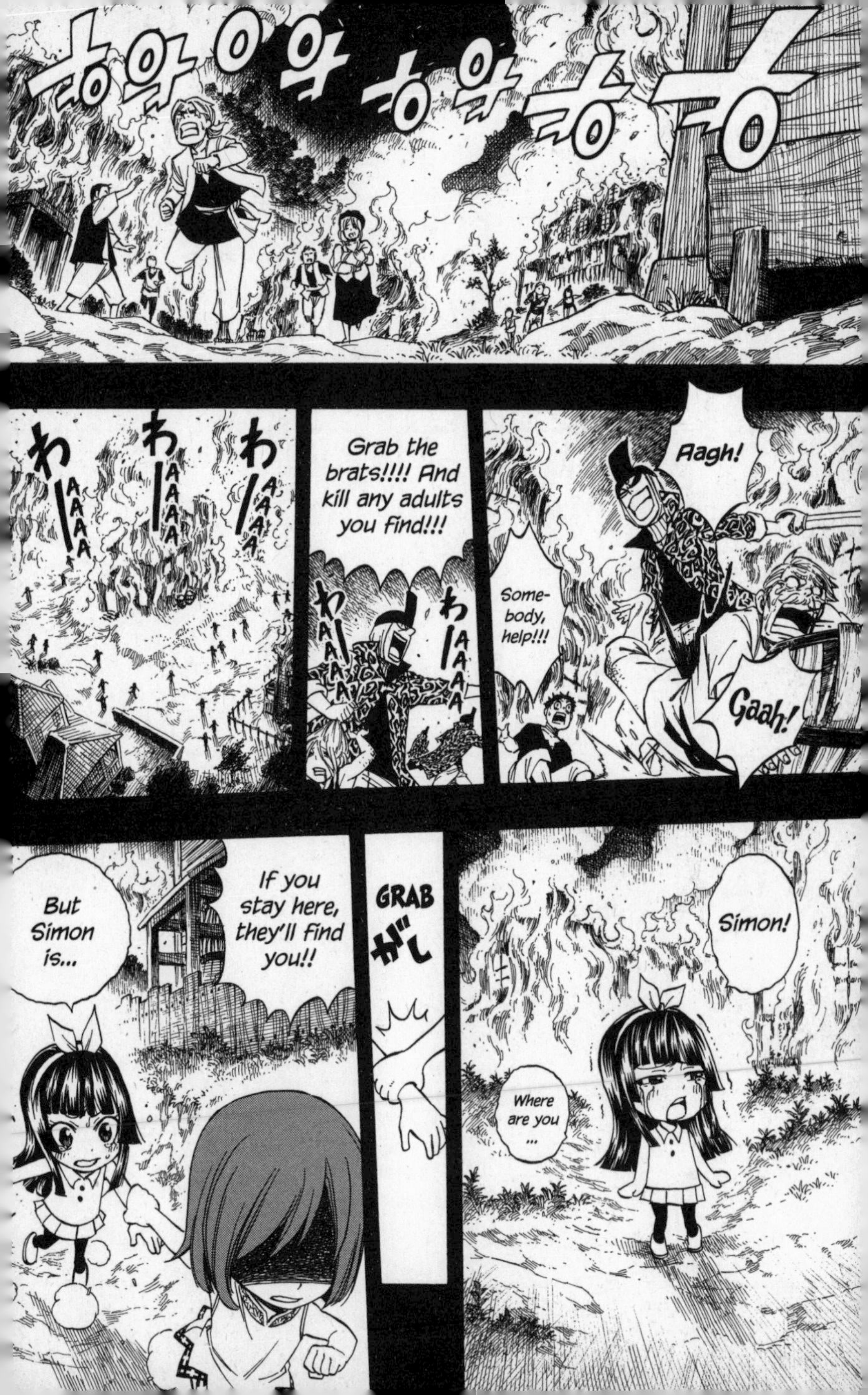
Aagh!
Some-body, help!!!
Gaah!
Grab the brats!!!! And kill any adults you find!!!
わAAAA
わAAAA
わAAAA
わAAAA
わAAAA
Simon!
Where are you ...
GRAB
がし
If you stay here, they'll find you!!
But Simon is...

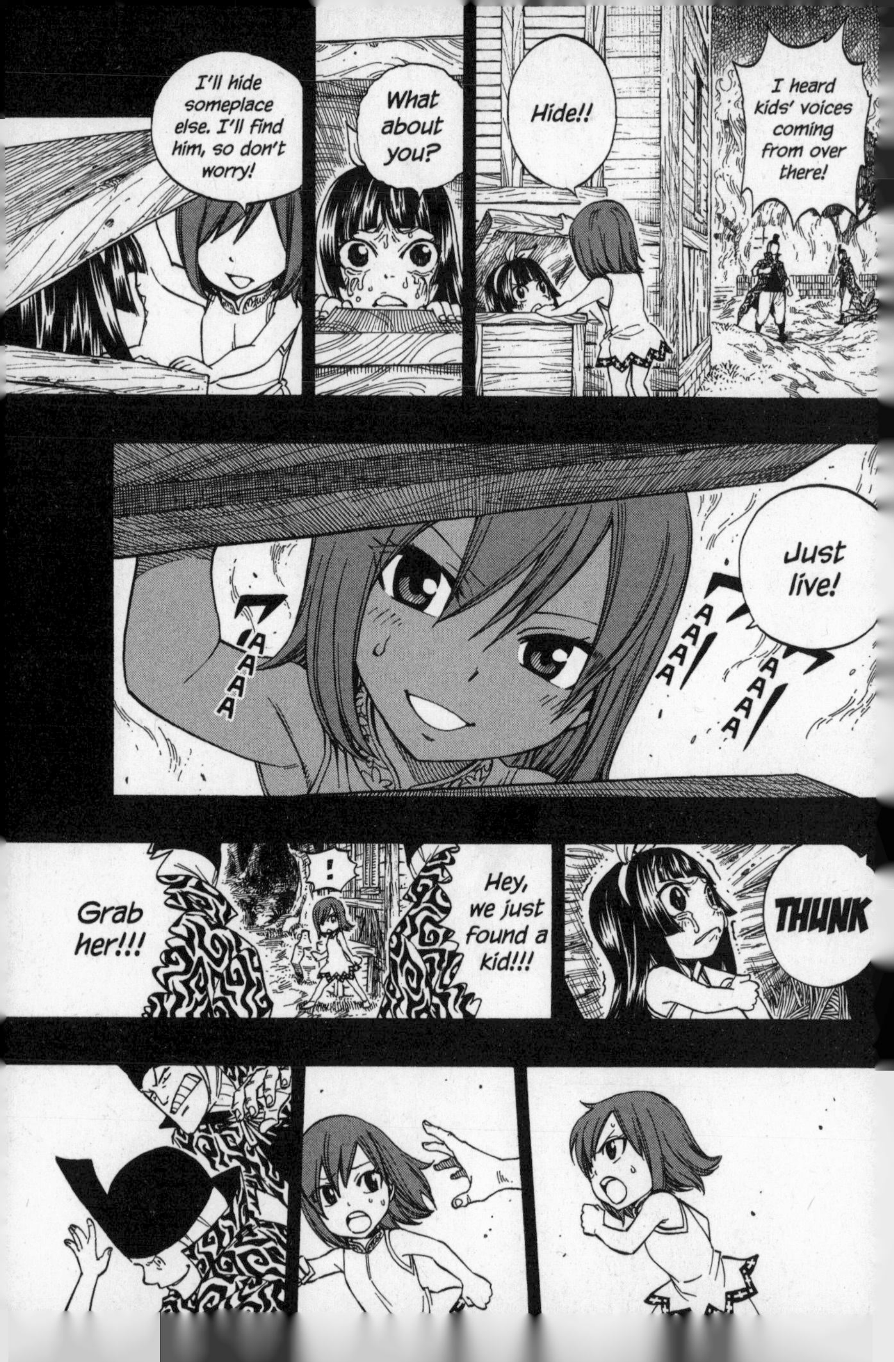
I heard kids' voices coming from over there!
Hide!!
What about you?
I'll hide someplace else. I'll find him, so don't worry!
Just live!
AAAAA
AAAA
AAAAA
THUNK
!
Hey, we just found a kid!!!
Grab her!!!

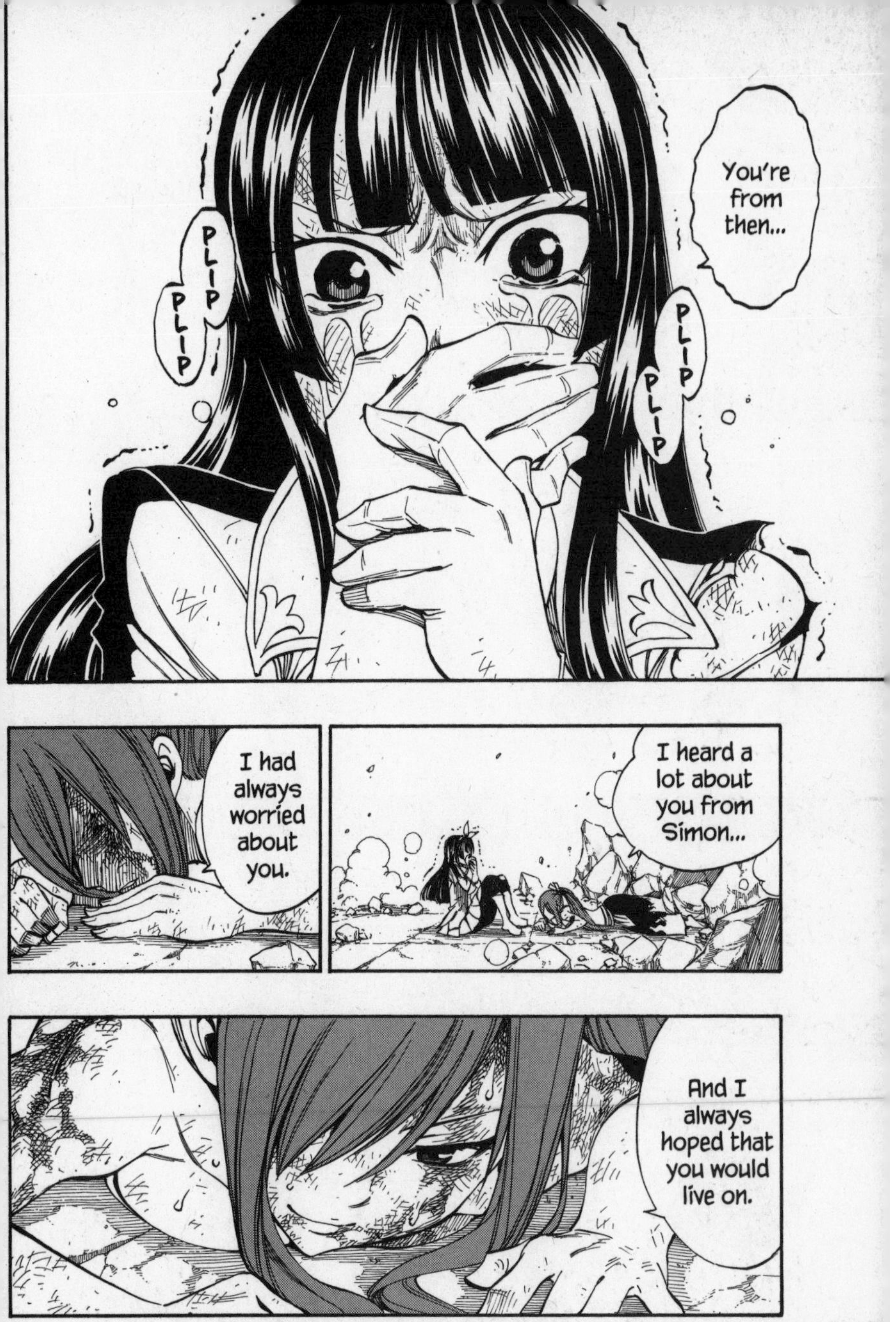
You're from then...
PLIP PLIP
PLIP PLIP
I heard a lot about you from Simon...
I had always worried about you.
And I always hoped that you would live on.

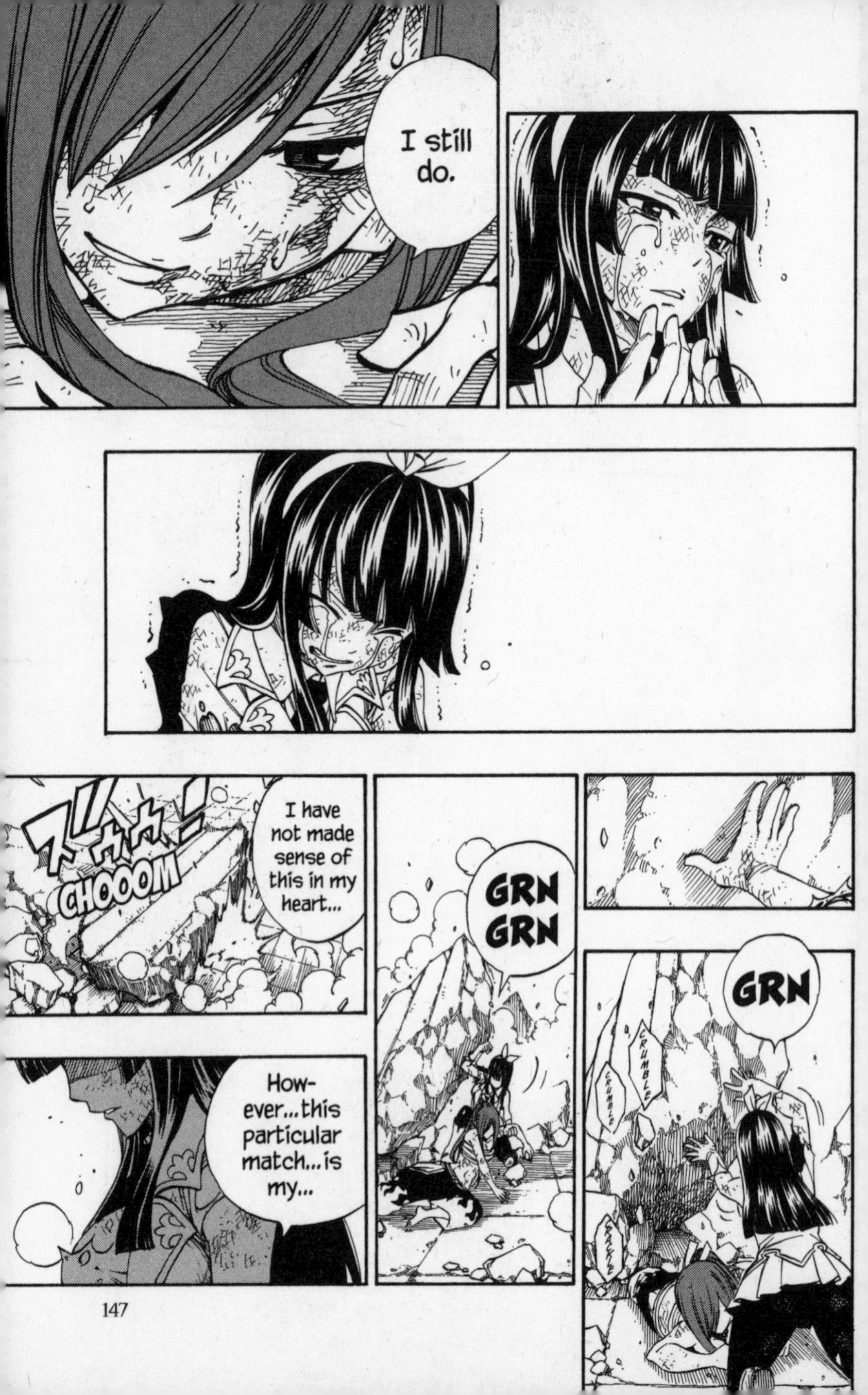
I still do.
GRN
CRUMBLE
CRUMBLE
CRACKLE
GRN GRN
CHOOOM
I have not made sense of this in my heart...
How-ever...this particular match...is my...

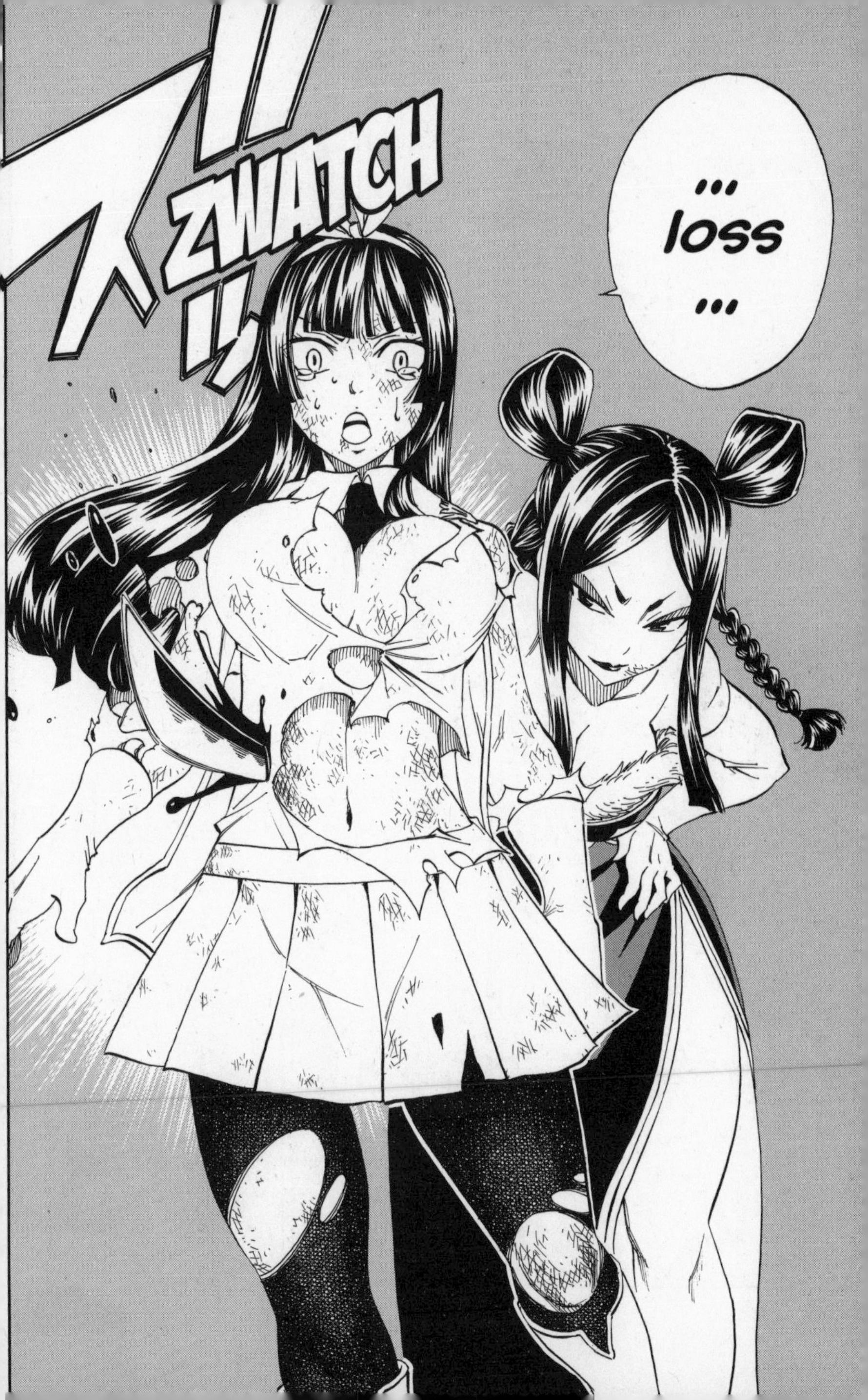
ZWATCH
...loss...

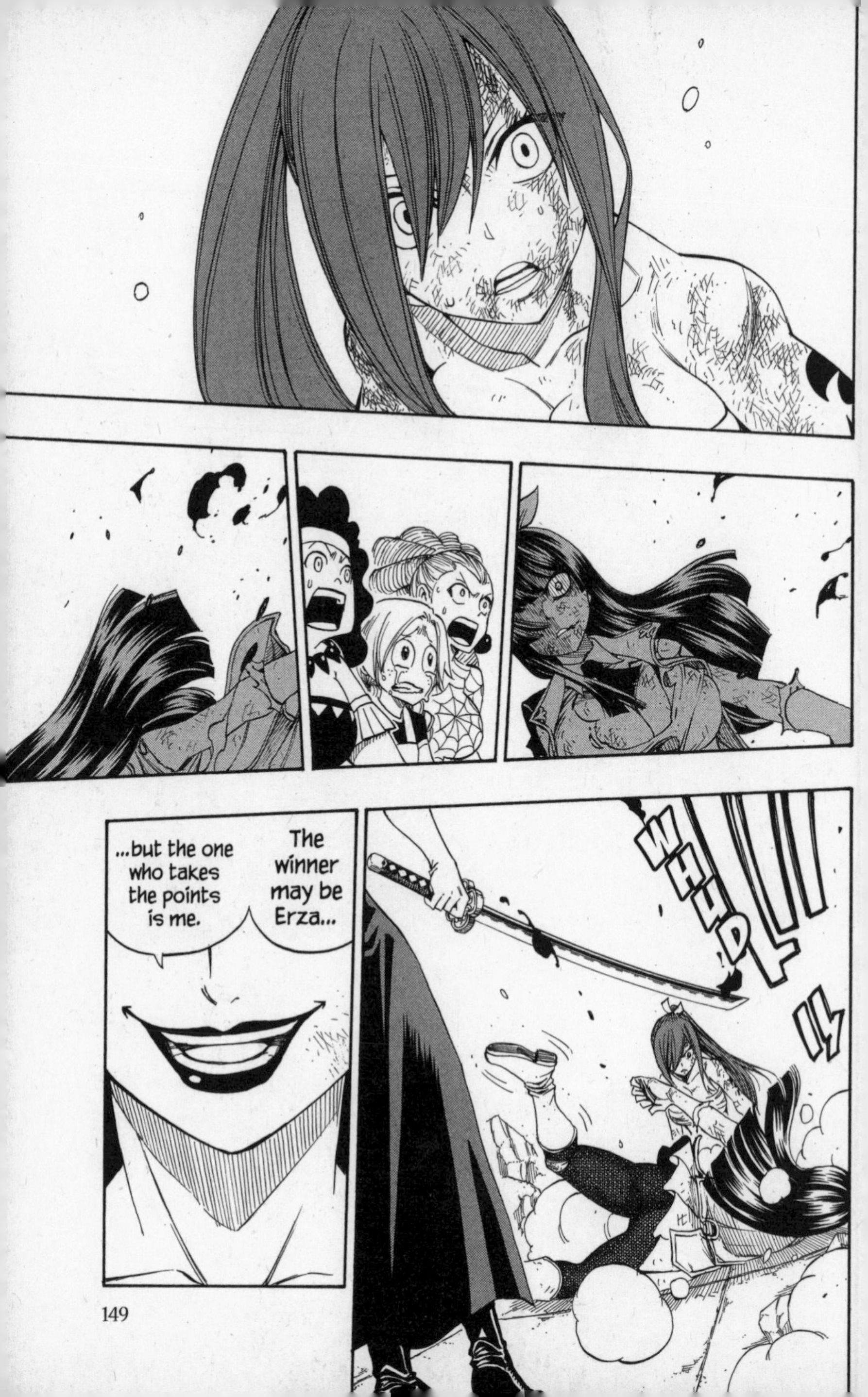
WHUD!!
The winner may be Erza...
...but the one who takes the points is me.

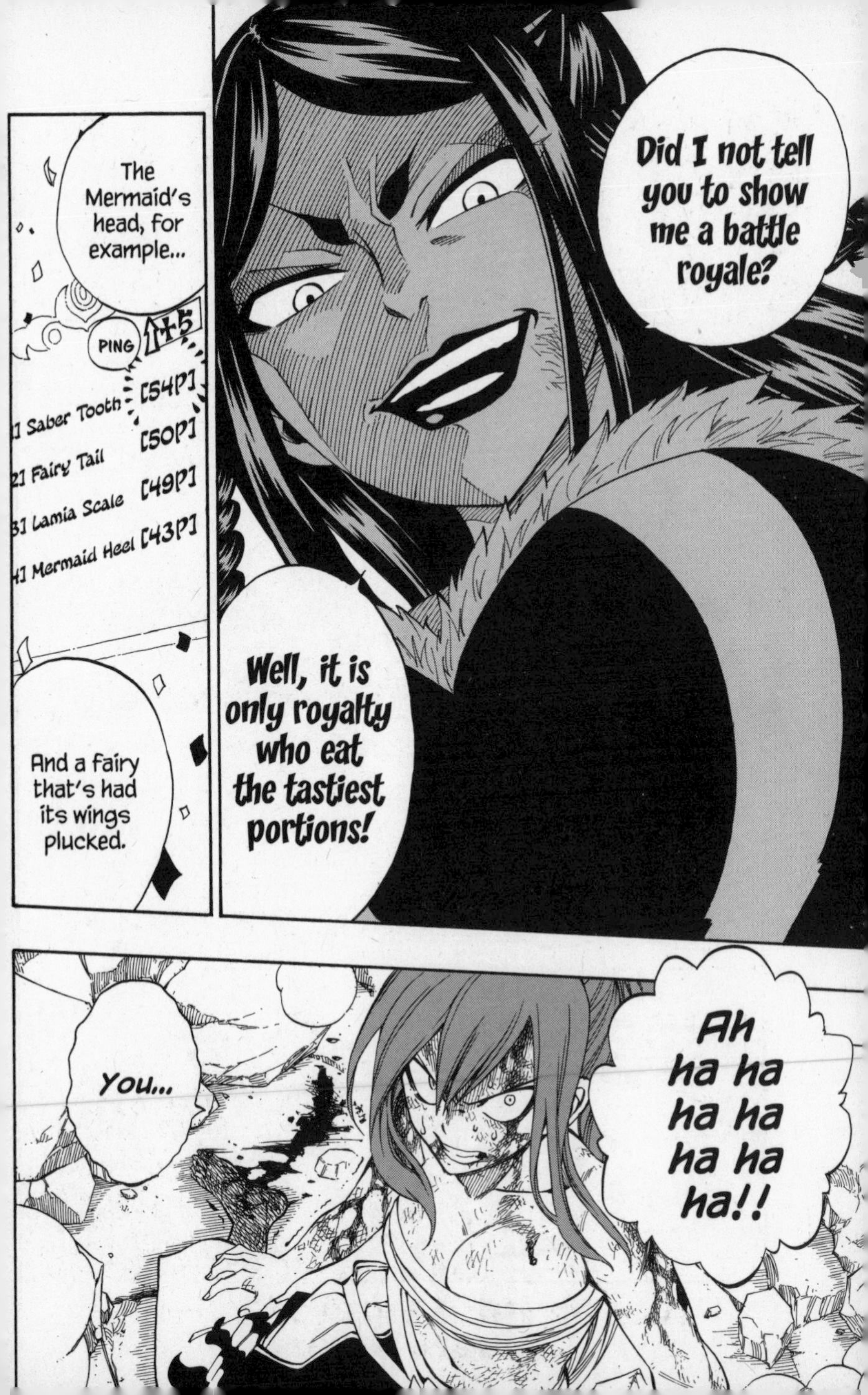
Did I not tell you to show me a battle royale?
Well, it is only royalty who eat the tastiest portions!
The Mermaid's head, for example...
PING
+5
1] Saber Tooth [54P]
2] Fairy Tail [50P]
3] Lamia Scale [49P]
4] Mermaid Heel [43P]
And a fairy that's had its wings plucked.
Ah ha ha ha ha ha ha ha!!
You...

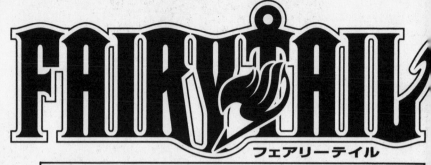

Grand Magic Games Final Day Interim Results

Members left

	Leader	Normal	
1. Saber Tooth	54P	x1	x3
2. Fairy Tail	50P	x1	x4
3. Lamia Scale	49P	x1	x2
4. Mermaid Heel	43P	x0	x1

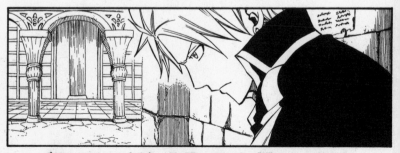

Chapter 316: A Future Hurrying Toward Despair

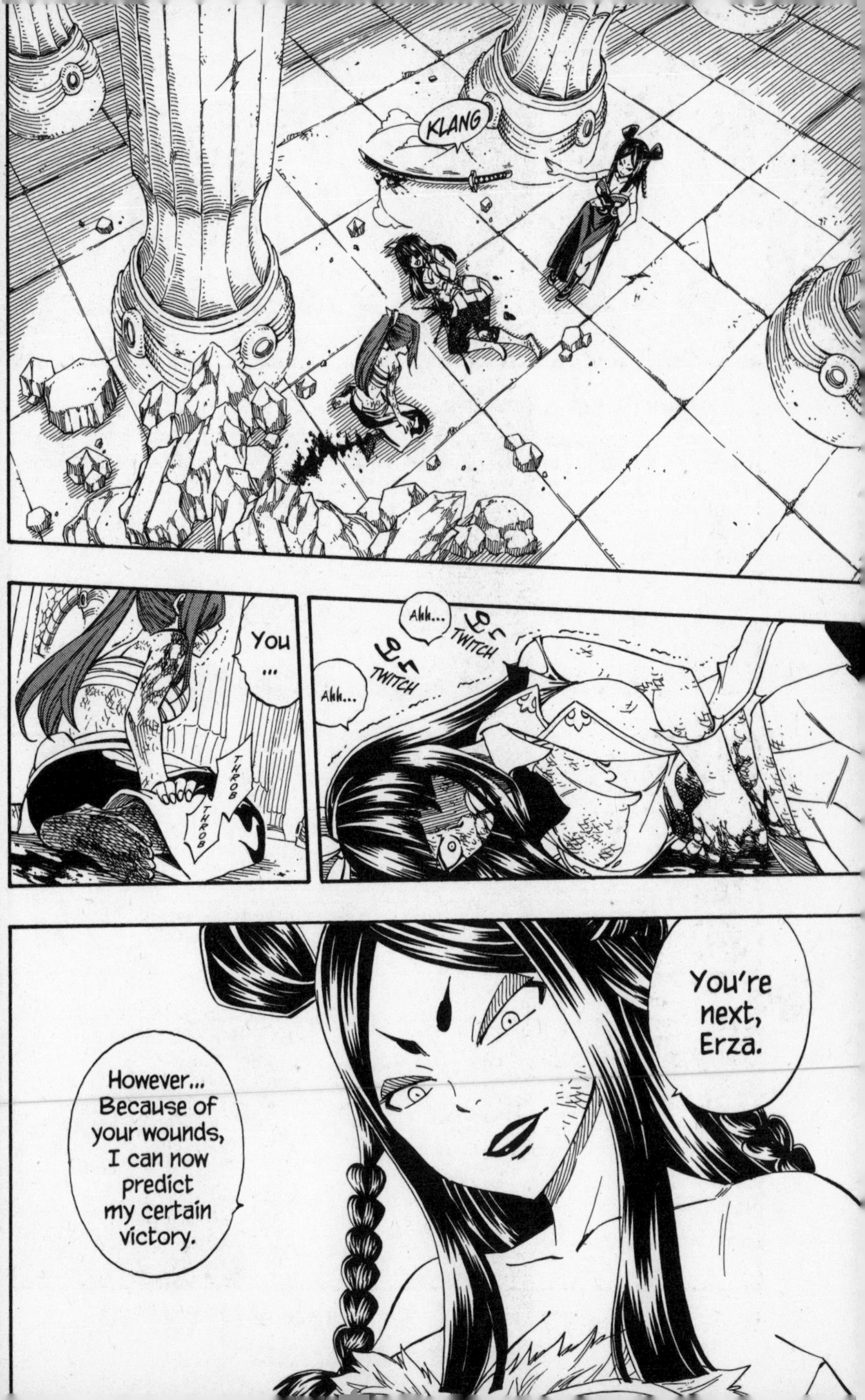
KLANG
Ahh...
TWITCH
Ahh...
TWITCH
You ...
THROB THROB
You're next, Erza.
However... Because of your wounds, I can now predict my certain victory.

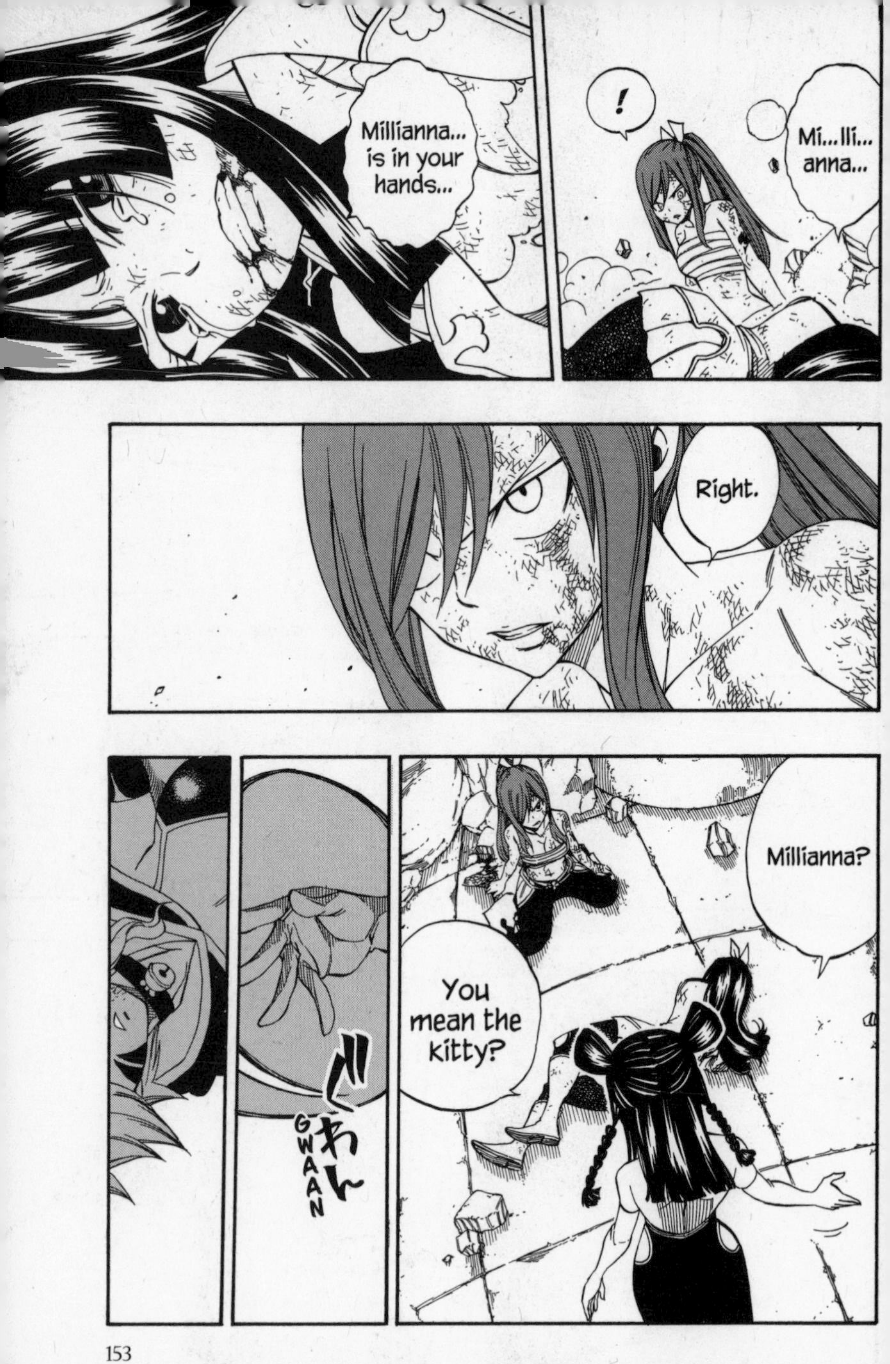
!
Mi...lli... anna...
Millianna... is in your hands...
Right.
Millianna?
You mean the kitty?
ぐわん
GWAAN

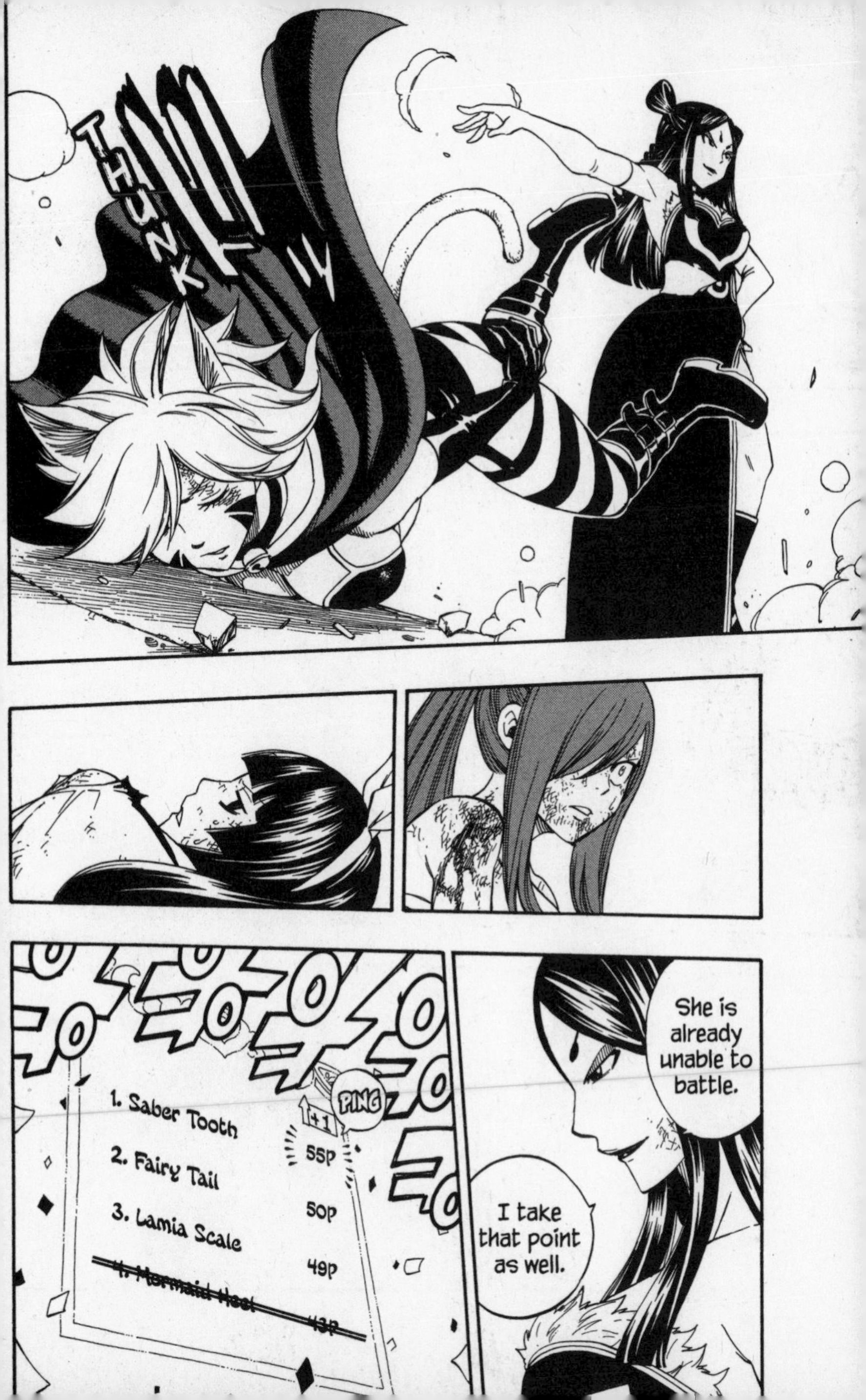
THUNK
She is already unable to battle.
I take that point as well.
PING
+1
1. Saber Tooth
55p
2. Fairy Tail
50p
3. Lamia Scale
49p
4. Mermaid Heel
43p

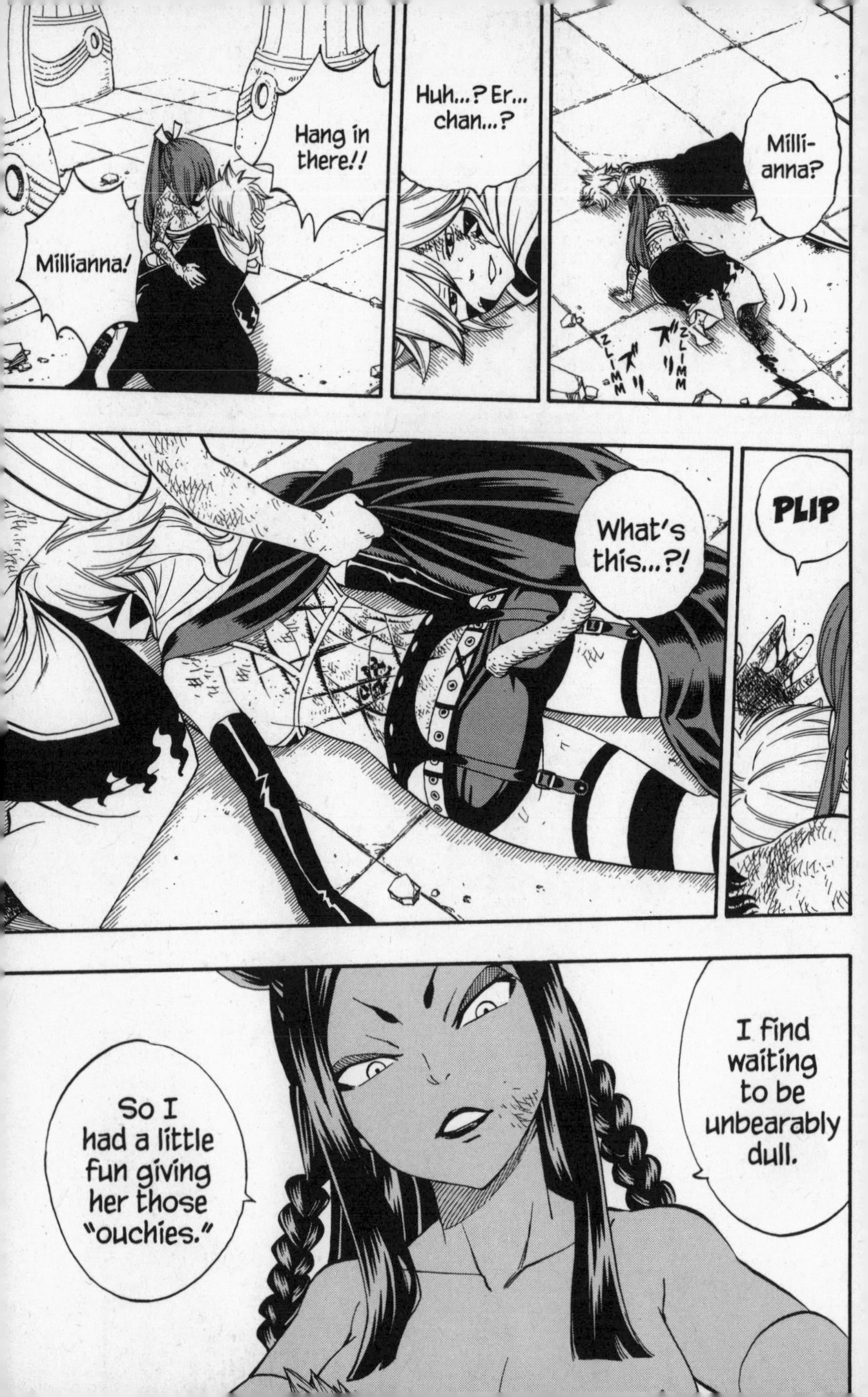

Milli-anna?
ZLIMM
ZLIMM
Huh...? Er... chan...?
Hang in there!!
Millianna!
PLIP
What's this...?!
I find waiting to be unbearably dull.
So I had a little fun giving her those "ouchies."

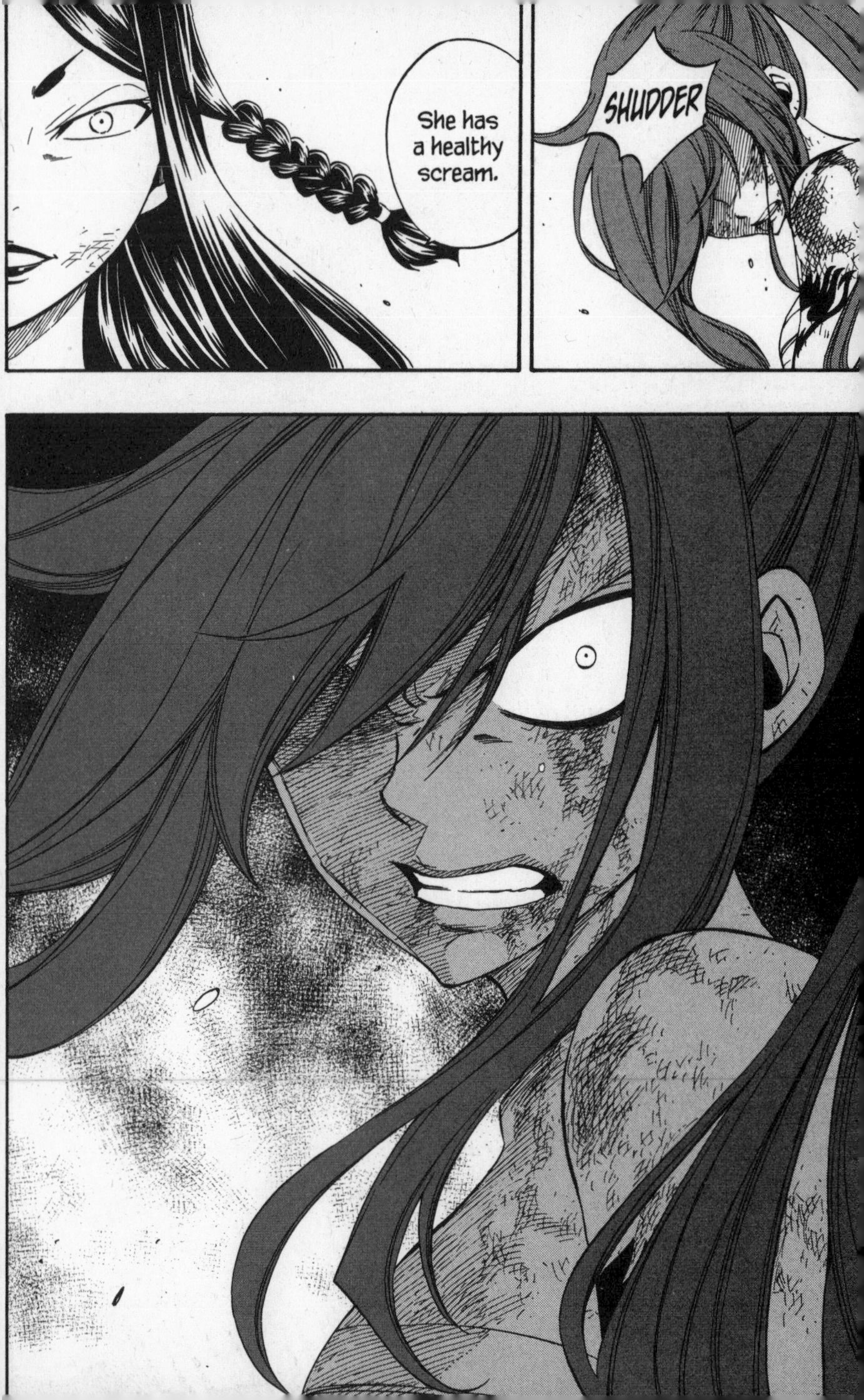
SHUDDER
She has a healthy scream.

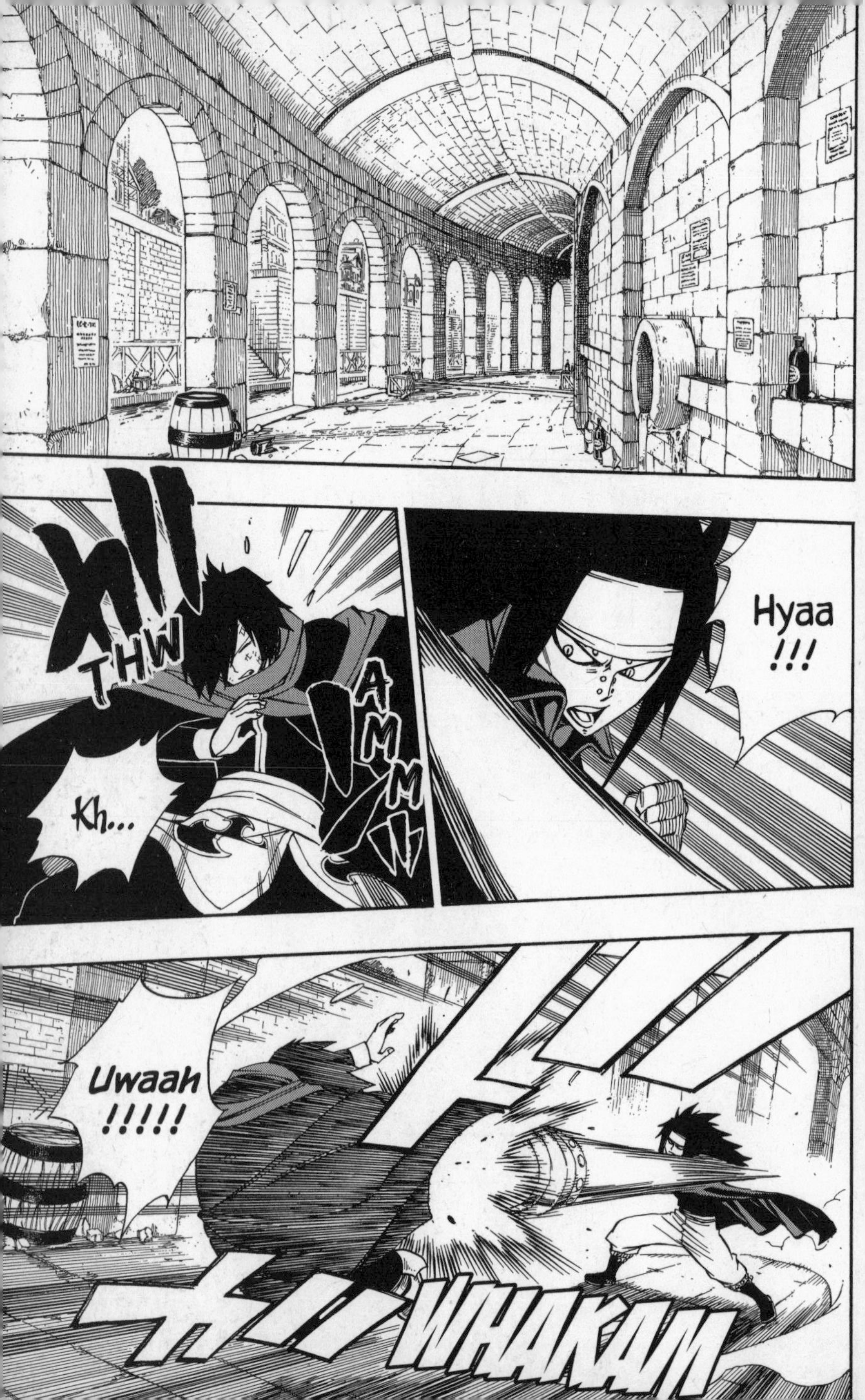
Hyaa
!!!
THWAMM!!
Kh...
Uwaah
!!!!!
WHAKAM

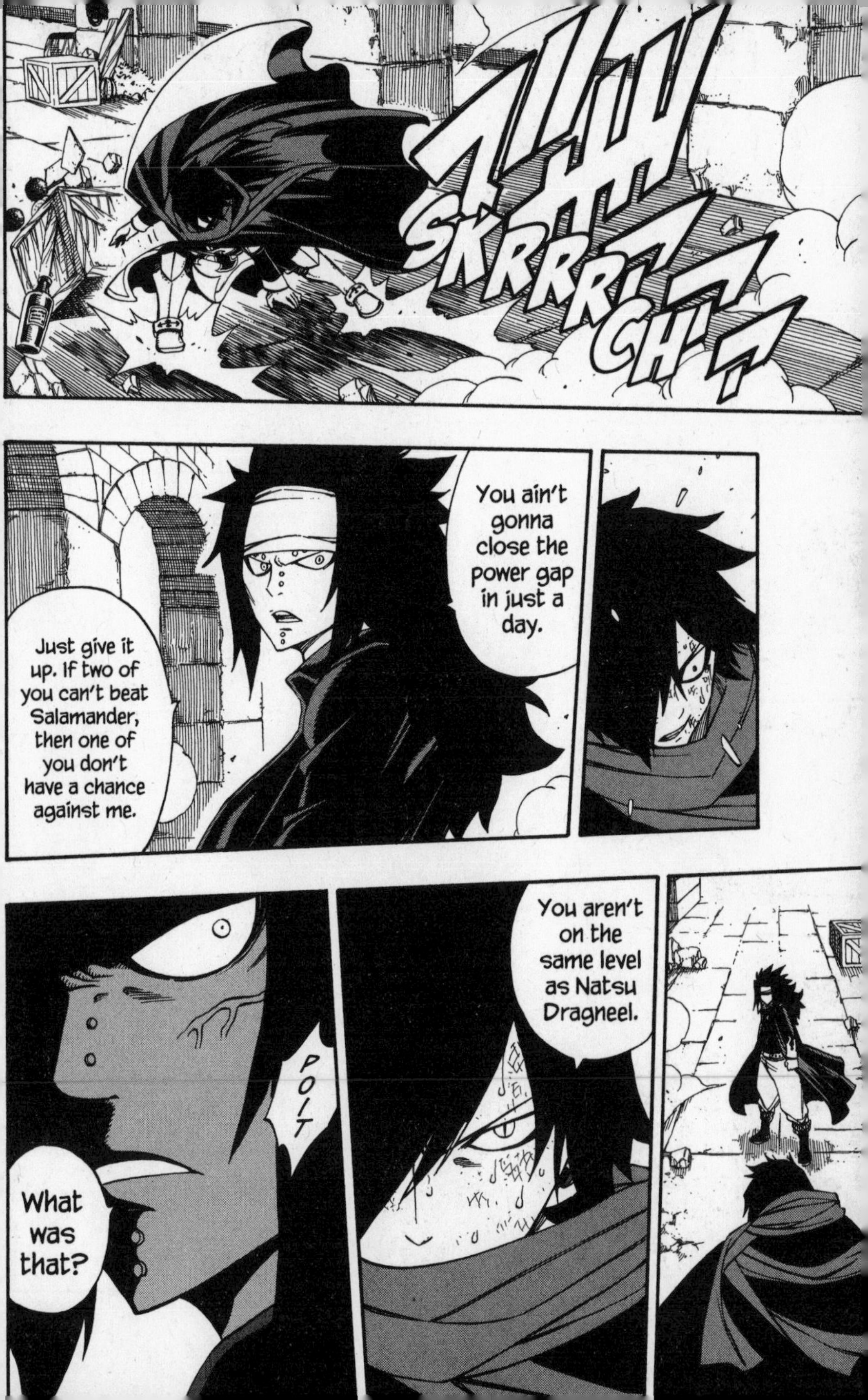
SKRRRICH
You ain't gonna close the power gap in just a day.
Just give it up. If two of you can't beat Salamander, then one of you don't have a chance against me.
You aren't on the same level as Natsu Dragneel.
POIT
What was that?

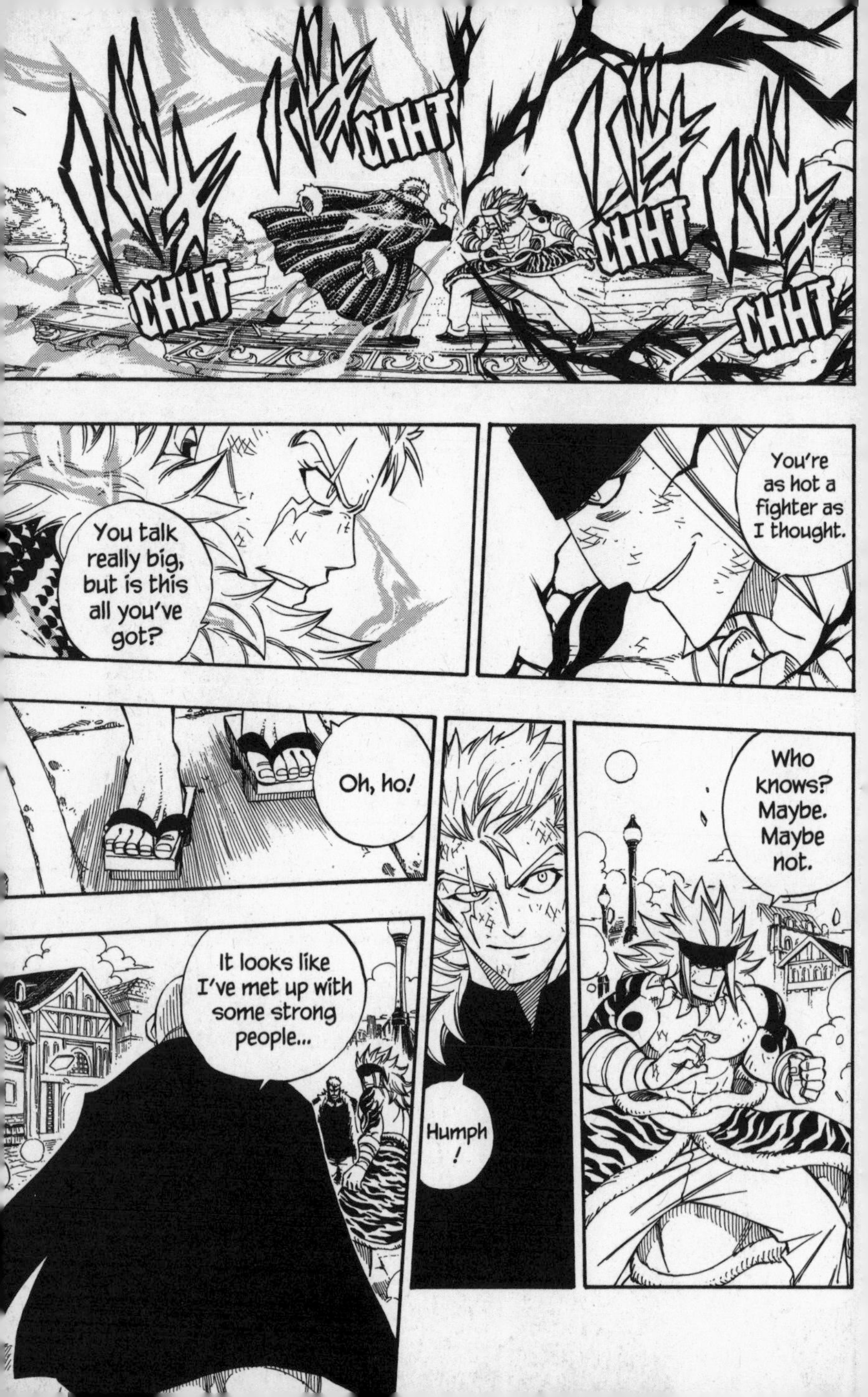
CHHT
CHHT
CHHT
CHHT
You're as hot a fighter as I thought.
You talk really big, but is this all you've got?
Who knows? Maybe. Maybe not.
Humph!
Oh, ho!
It looks like I've met up with some strong people...

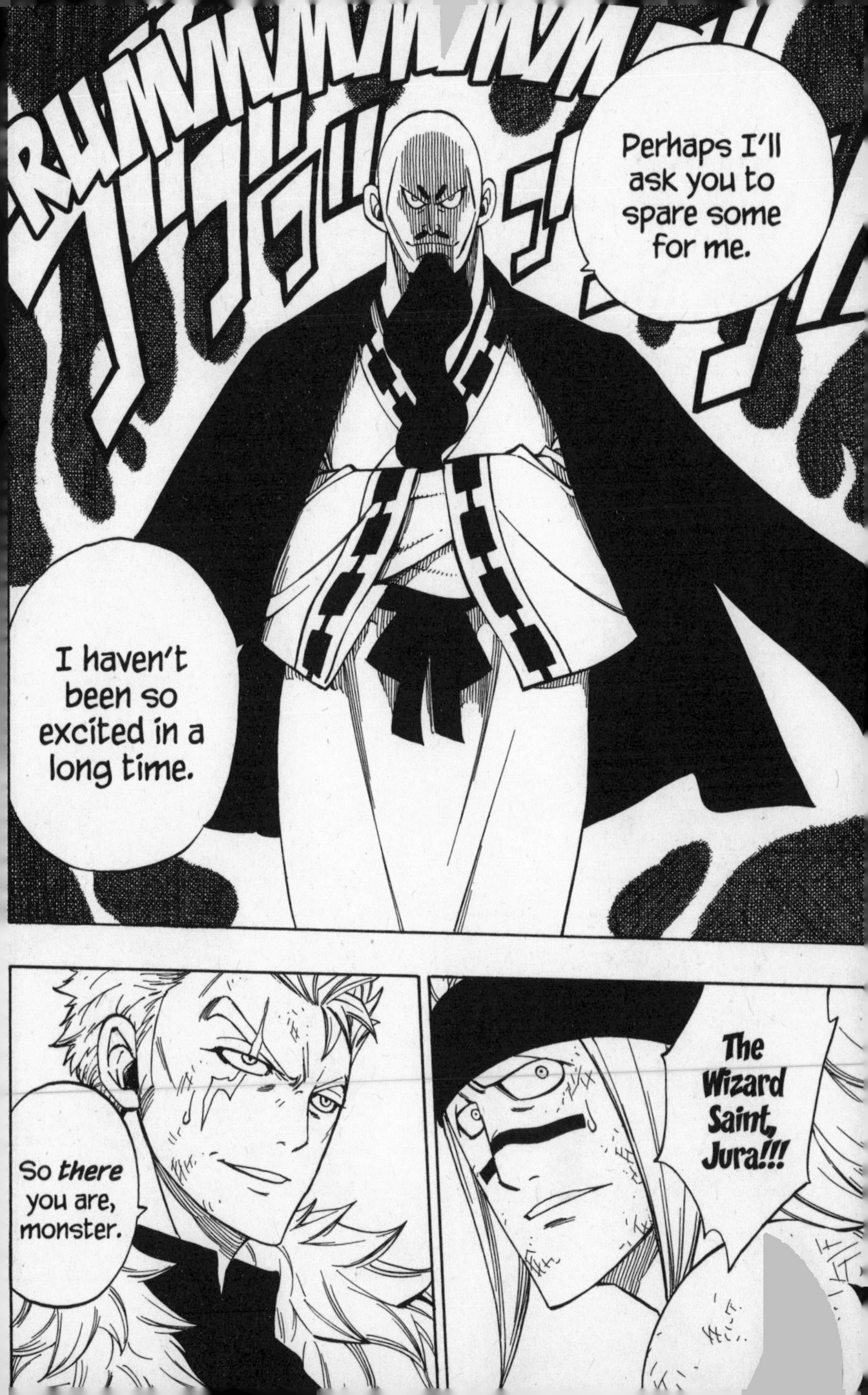
Perhaps I'll ask you to spare some for me.
I haven't been so excited in a long time.
The Wizard Saint, Jura!!!
So *there* you are, monster.

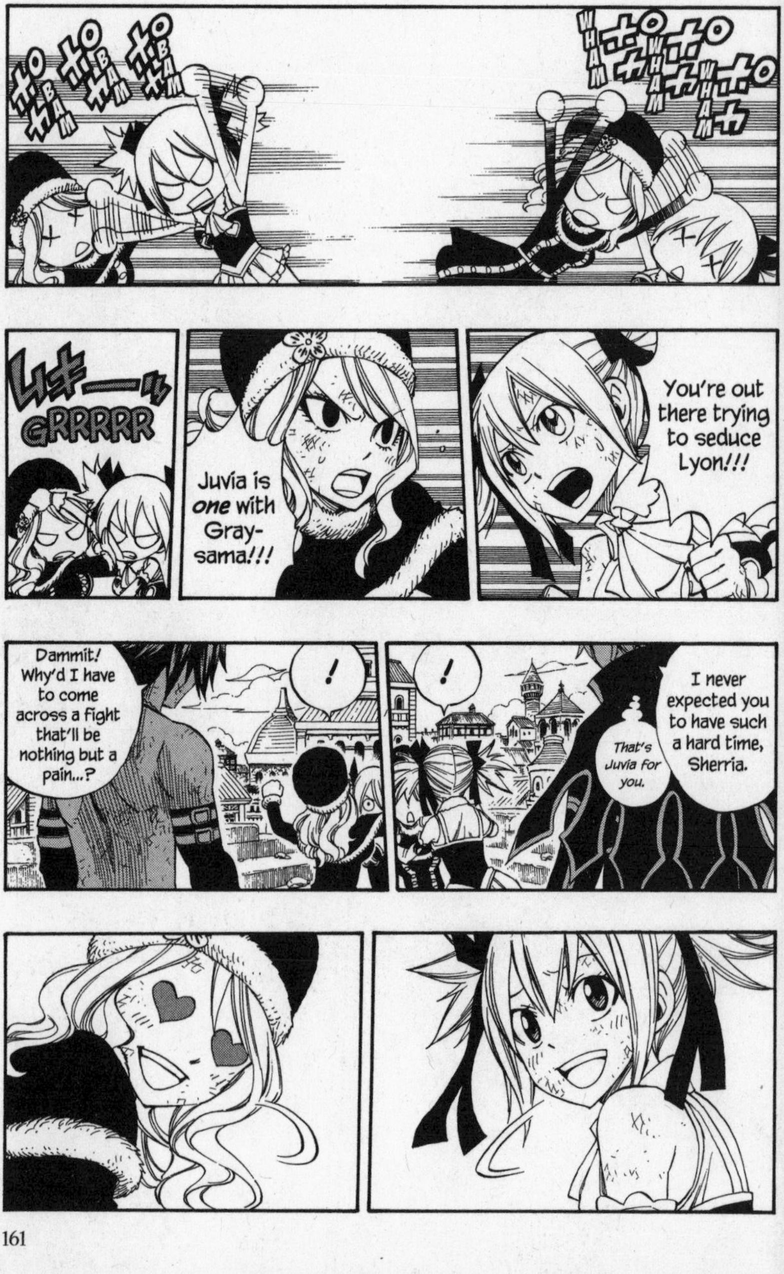
WHAM WHAM WHAM
BAM BAM BAM
You're out there trying to seduce Lyon!!!
Juvia is *one* with Gray-sama!!!
GRRRRR
!
I never expected you to have such a hard time, Sherria.
That's Juvia for you.
!
Dammit! Why'd I have to come across a fight that'll be nothing but a pain...?

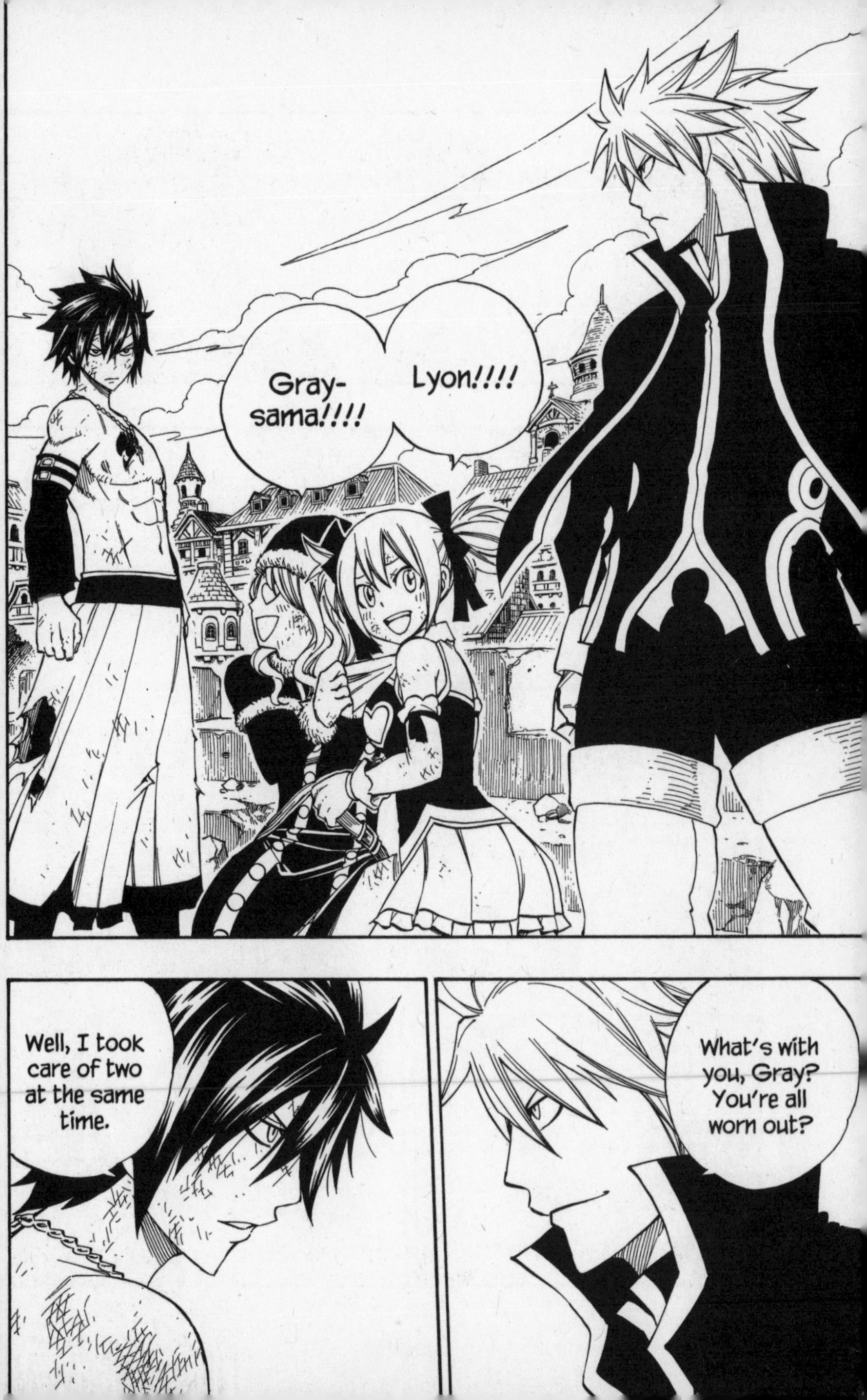
Lyon!!!!
Gray-sama!!!!
What's with you, Gray? You're all worn out?
Well, I took care of two at the same time.

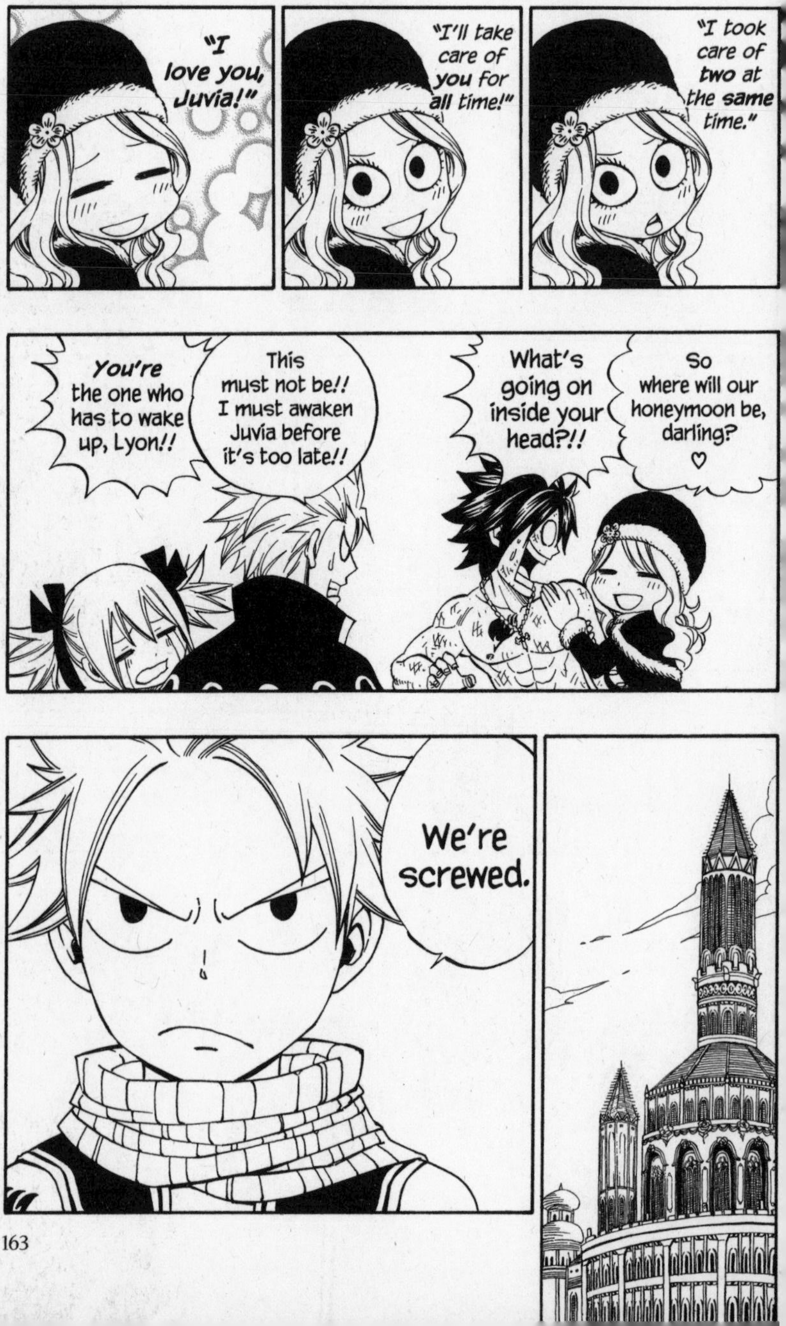
"I took care of two at the same time."
"I'll take care of you for all time!"
"I love you, Juvia!"
So where will our honeymoon be, darling? ♡
What's going on inside your head?!!
This must not be!! I must awaken Juvia before it's too late!!
You're the one who has to wake up, Lyon!!
We're screwed.

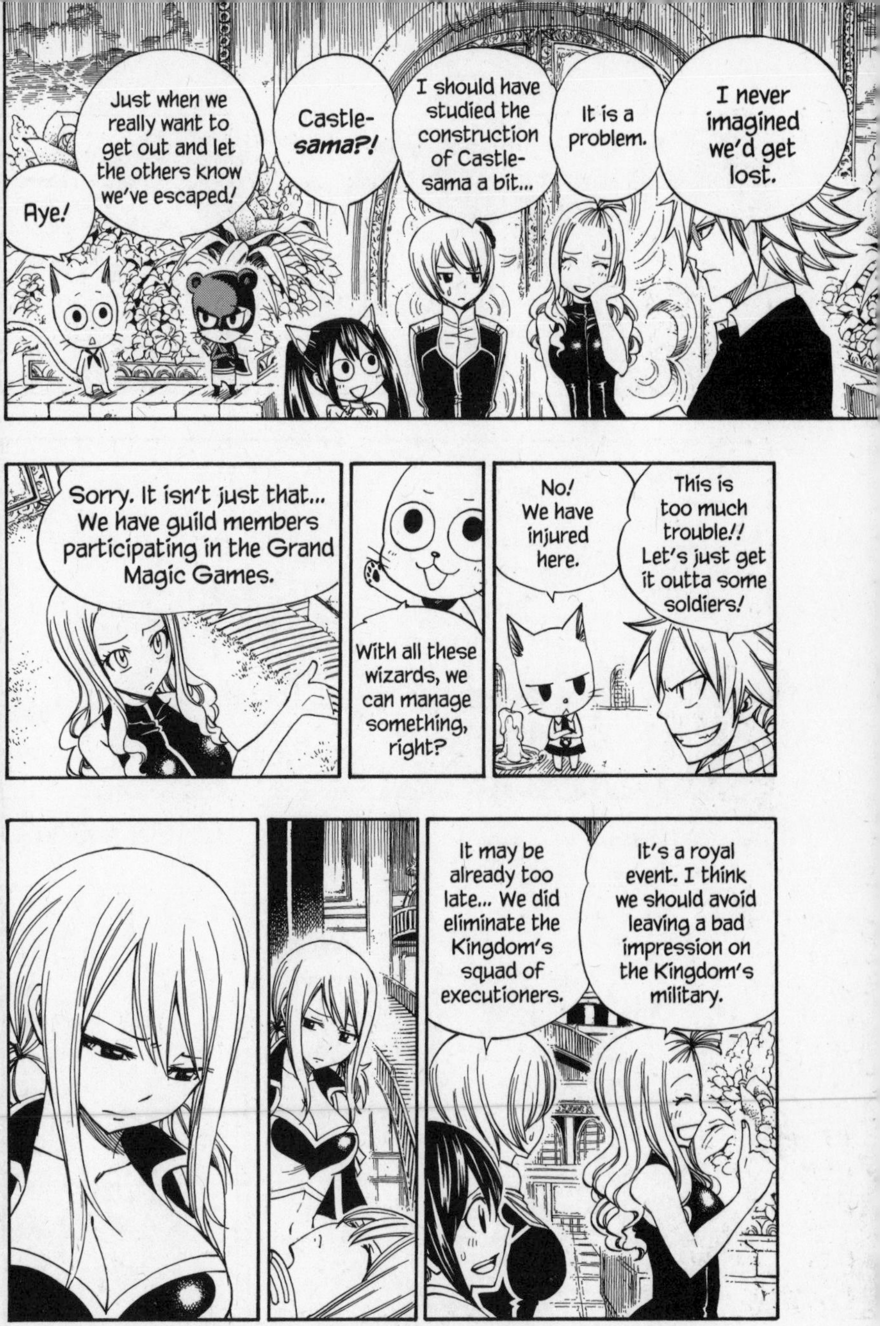
I never imagined we'd get lost.
It is a problem.
I should have studied the construction of Castle-sama a bit...
Castle-*sama?!*
Just when we really want to get out and let the others know we've escaped!
Aye!
This is too much trouble!! Let's just get it outta some soldiers!
No! We have injured here.
With all these wizards, we can manage something, right?
Sorry. It isn't just that... We have guild members participating in the Grand Magic Games.
It's a royal event. I think we should avoid leaving a bad impression on the Kingdom's military.
It may be already too late... We did eliminate the Kingdom's squad of executioners.

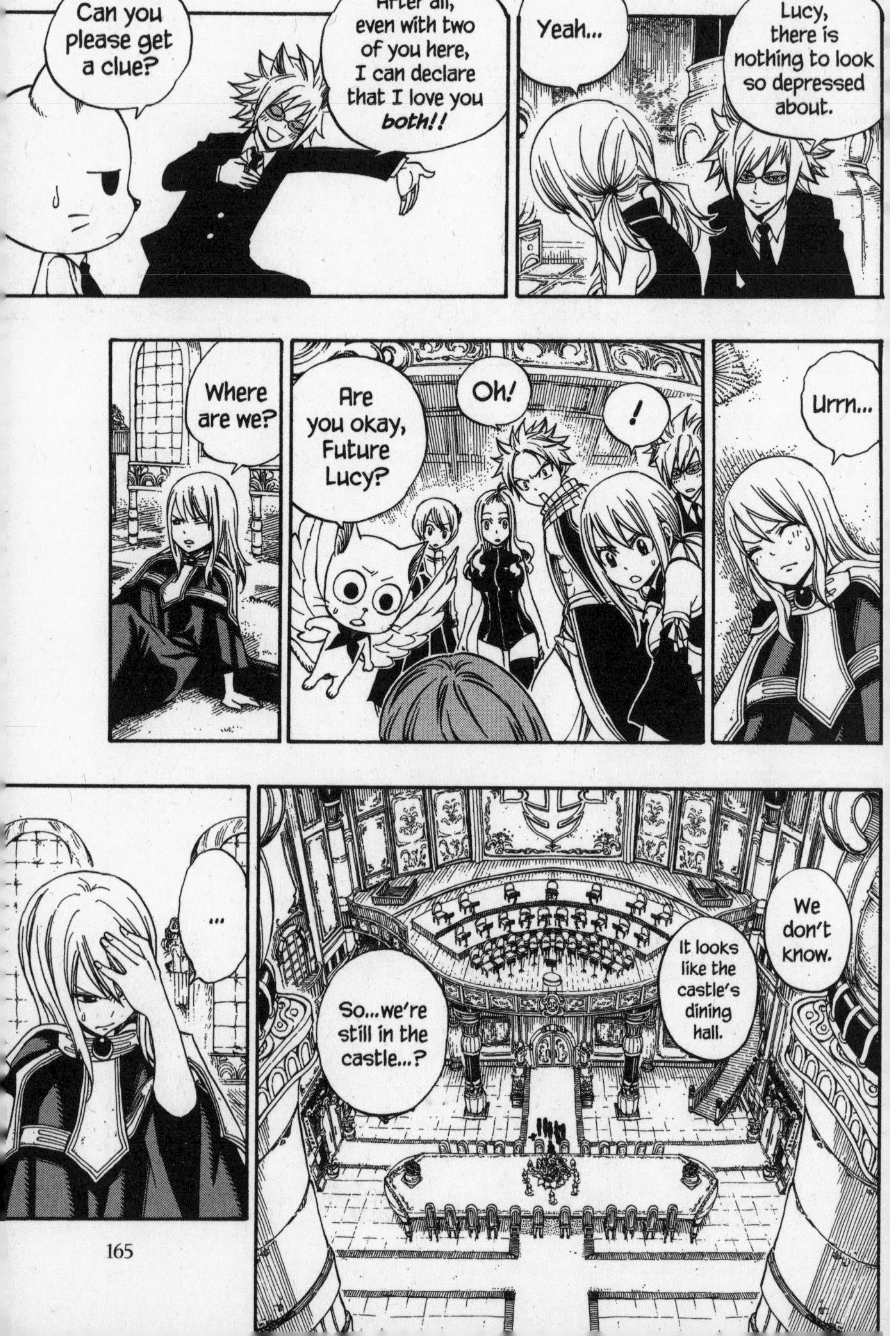
Lucy, there is nothing to look so depressed about.
Yeah...
After all, even with two of you here, I can declare that I love you *both!!*
Can you please get a clue?
Urrn...
!
Oh!
Are you okay, Future Lucy?
Where are we?
We don't know.
It looks like the castle's dining hall.
So...we're still in the castle...?
...

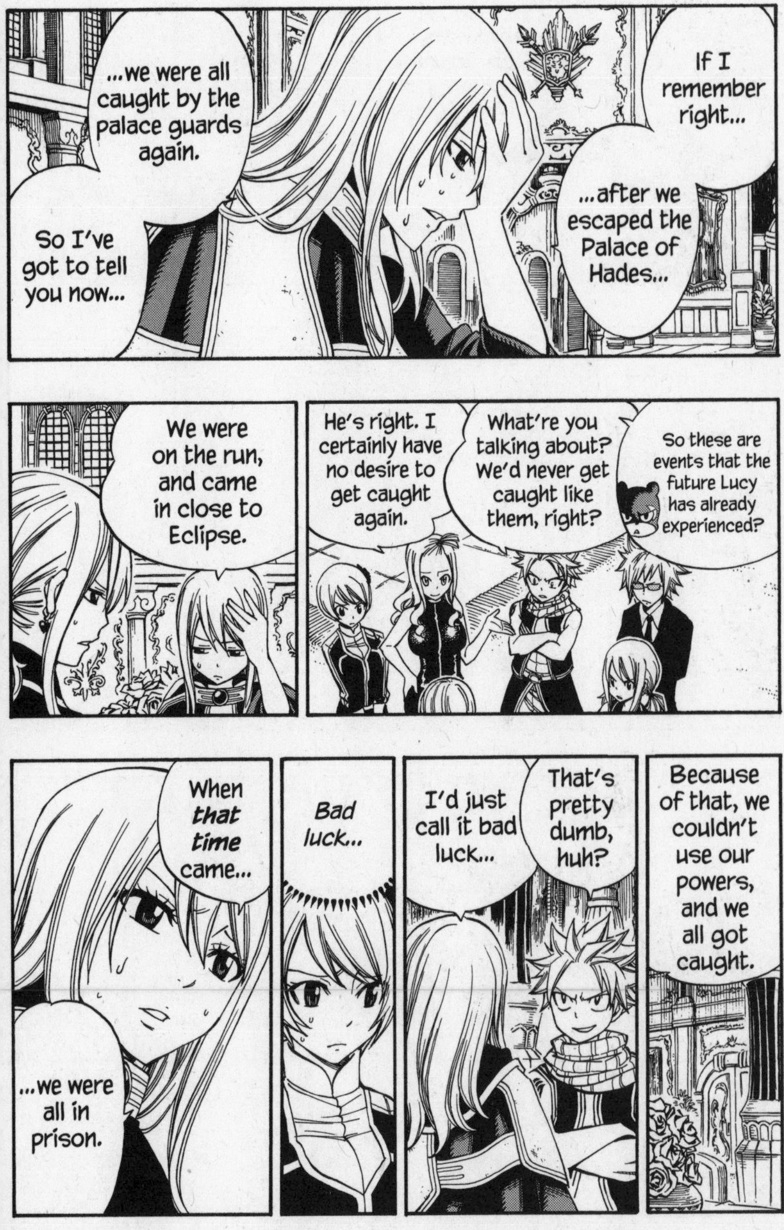
If I remember right...
...after we escaped the Palace of Hades...
...we were all caught by the palace guards again.
So I've got to tell you now...
So these are events that the future Lucy has already experienced?
What're you talking about? We'd never get caught like them, right?
He's right. I certainly have no desire to get caught again.
We were on the run, and came in close to Eclipse.
Because of that, we couldn't use our powers, and we all got caught.
That's pretty dumb, huh?
I'd just call it bad luck...
Bad luck...
When *that time* came...
...we were all in prison.

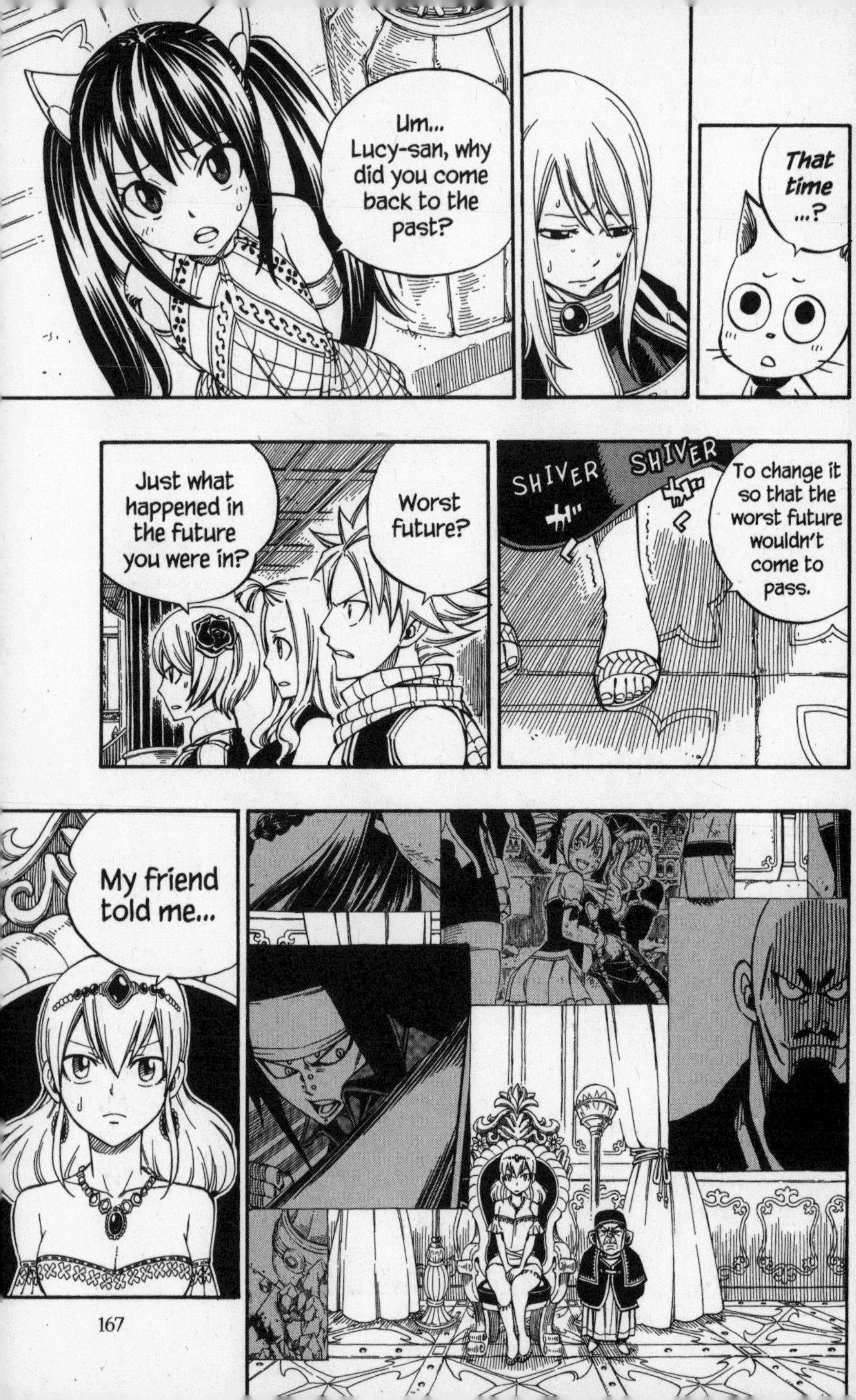

That time ...?
Um... Lucy-san, why did you come back to the past?
SHIVER
SHIVER
To change it so that the worst future wouldn't come to pass.
Worst future?
Just what happened in the future you were in?
My friend told me...

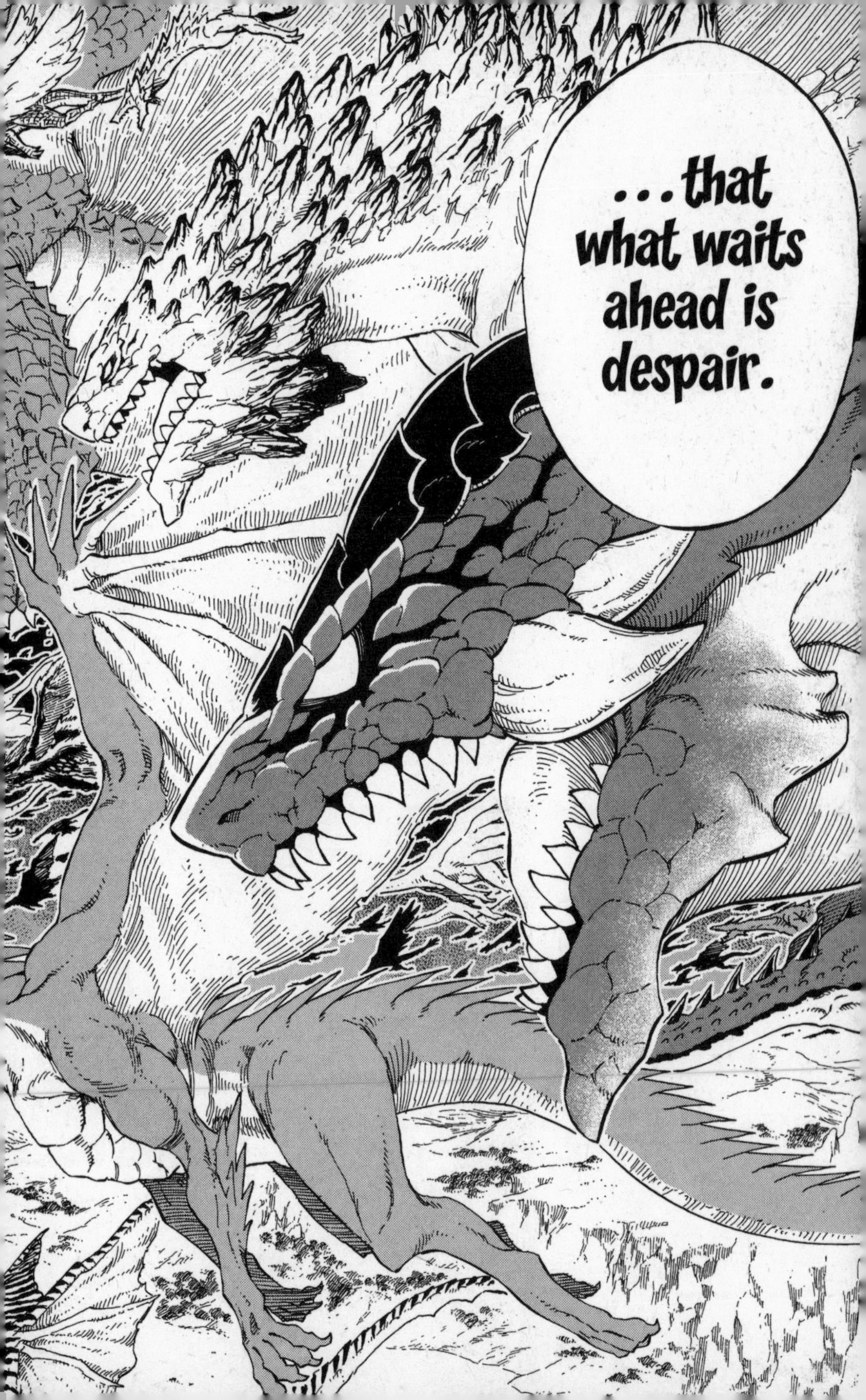
...that what waits ahead is despair.

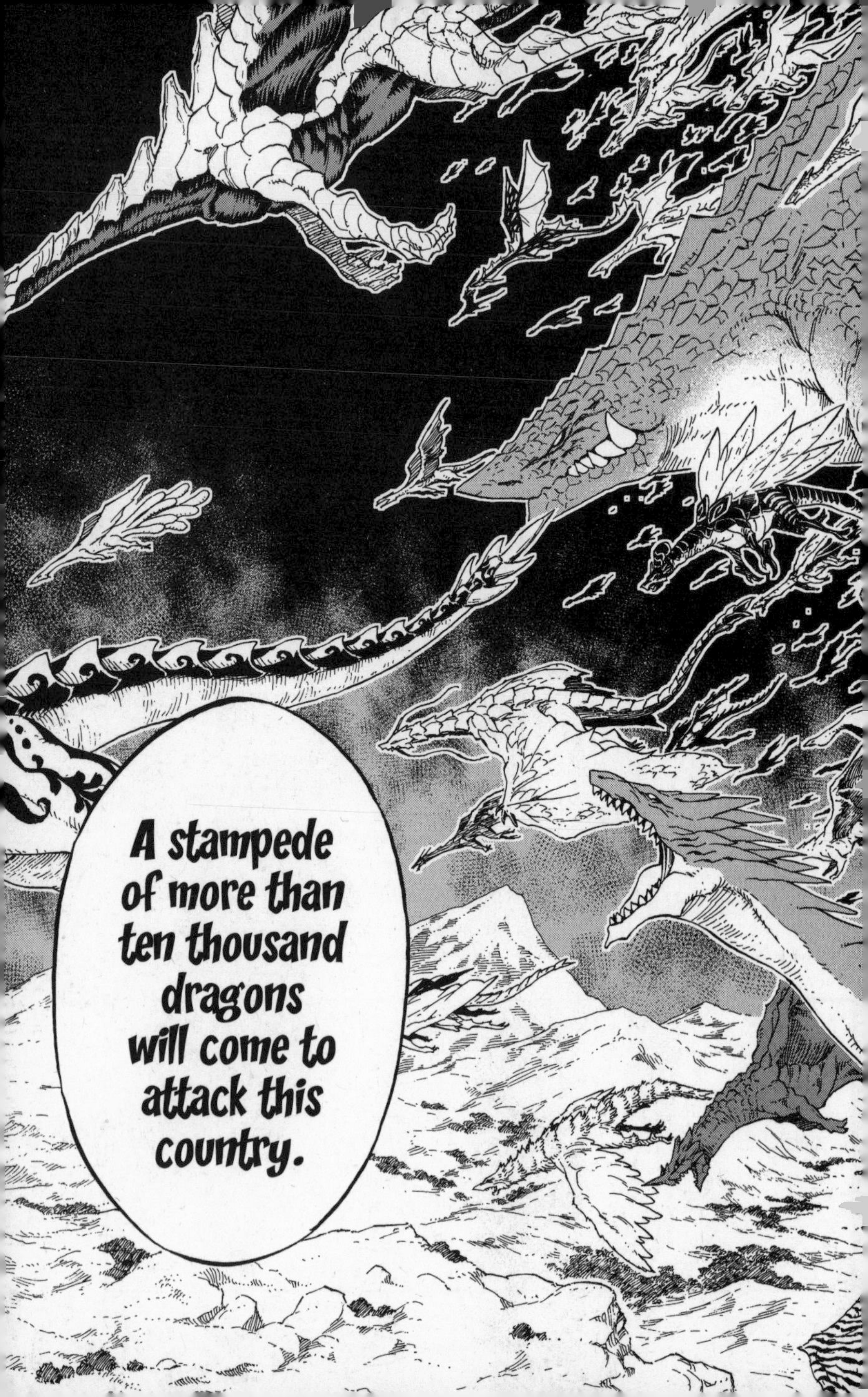
A stampede of more than ten thousand dragons will come to attack this country.

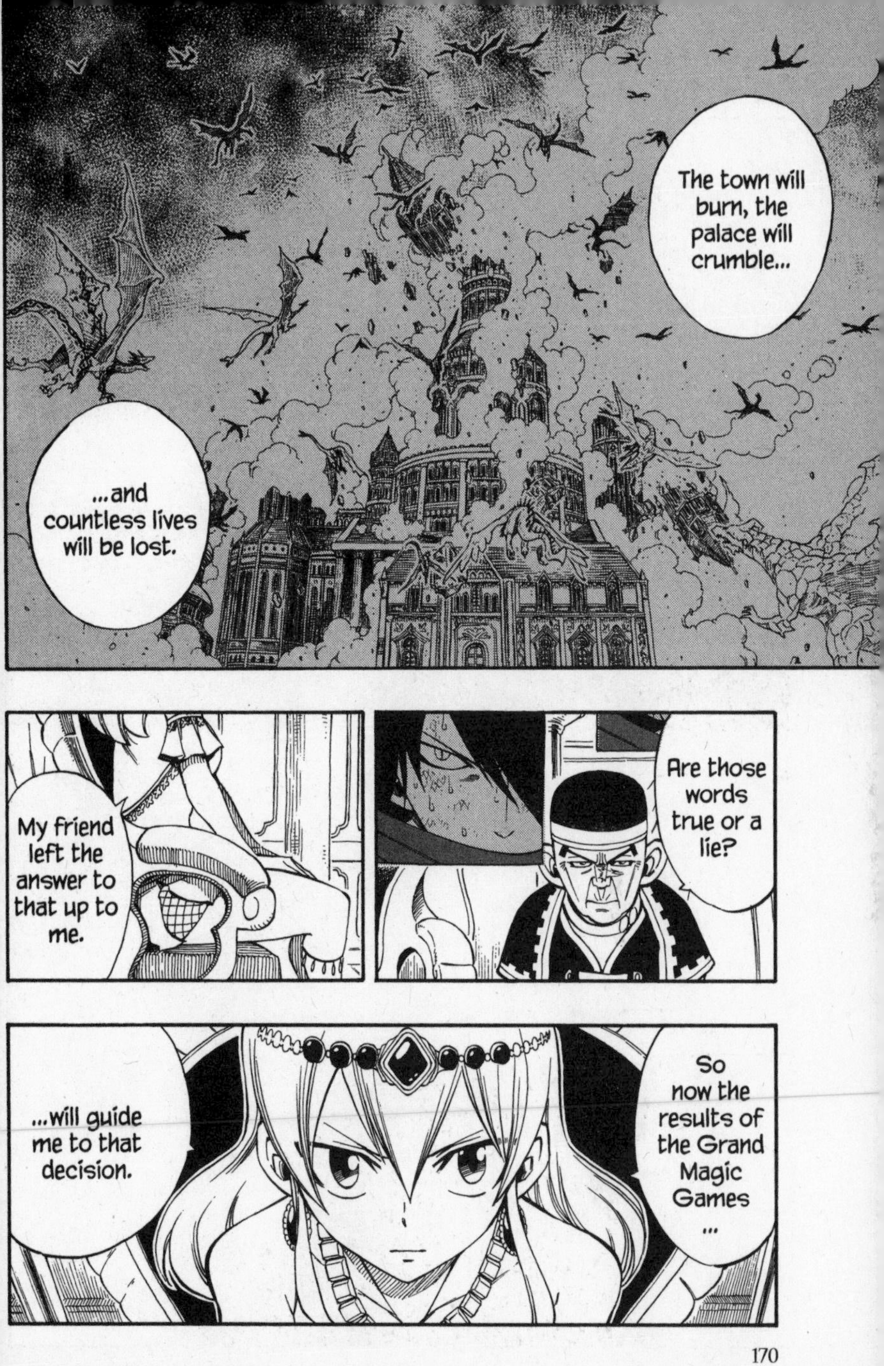
The town will burn, the palace will crumble...
...and countless lives will be lost.
Are those words true or a lie?
My friend left the answer to that up to me.
So now the results of the Grand Magic Games ...
...will guide me to that decision.

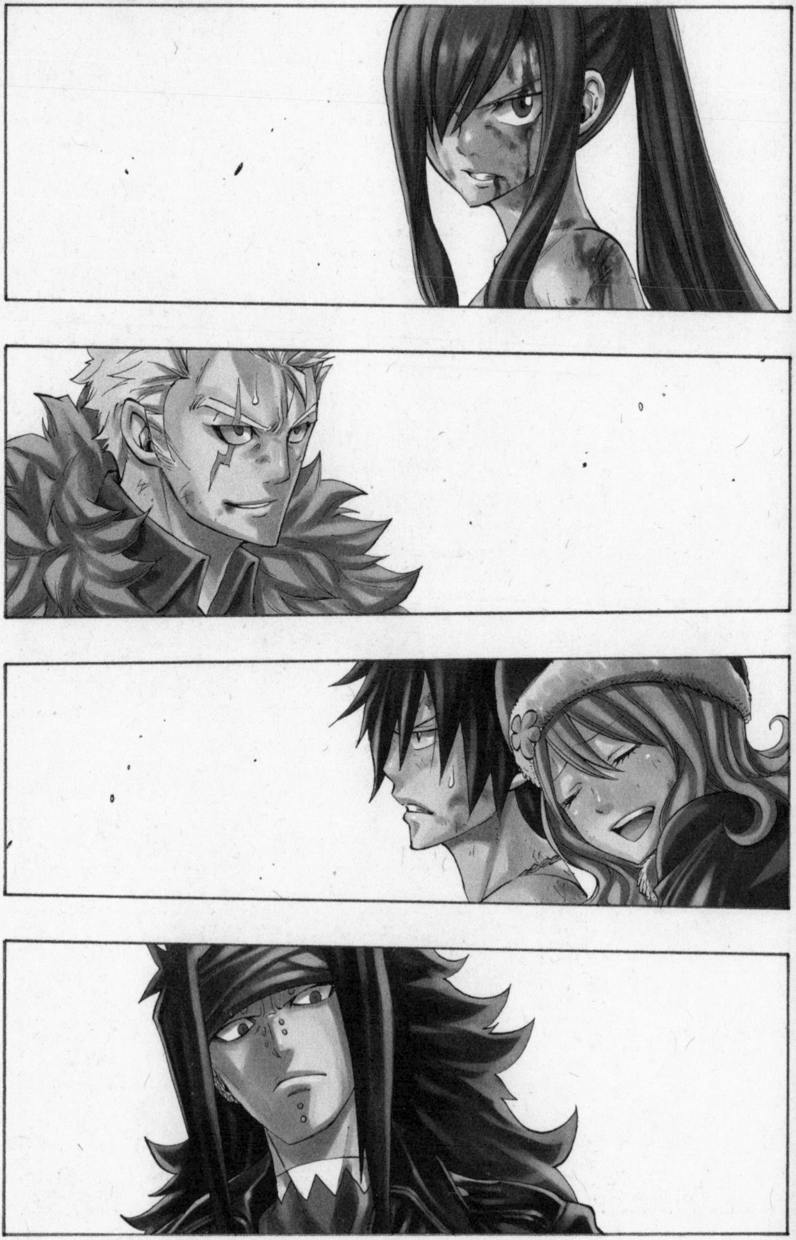

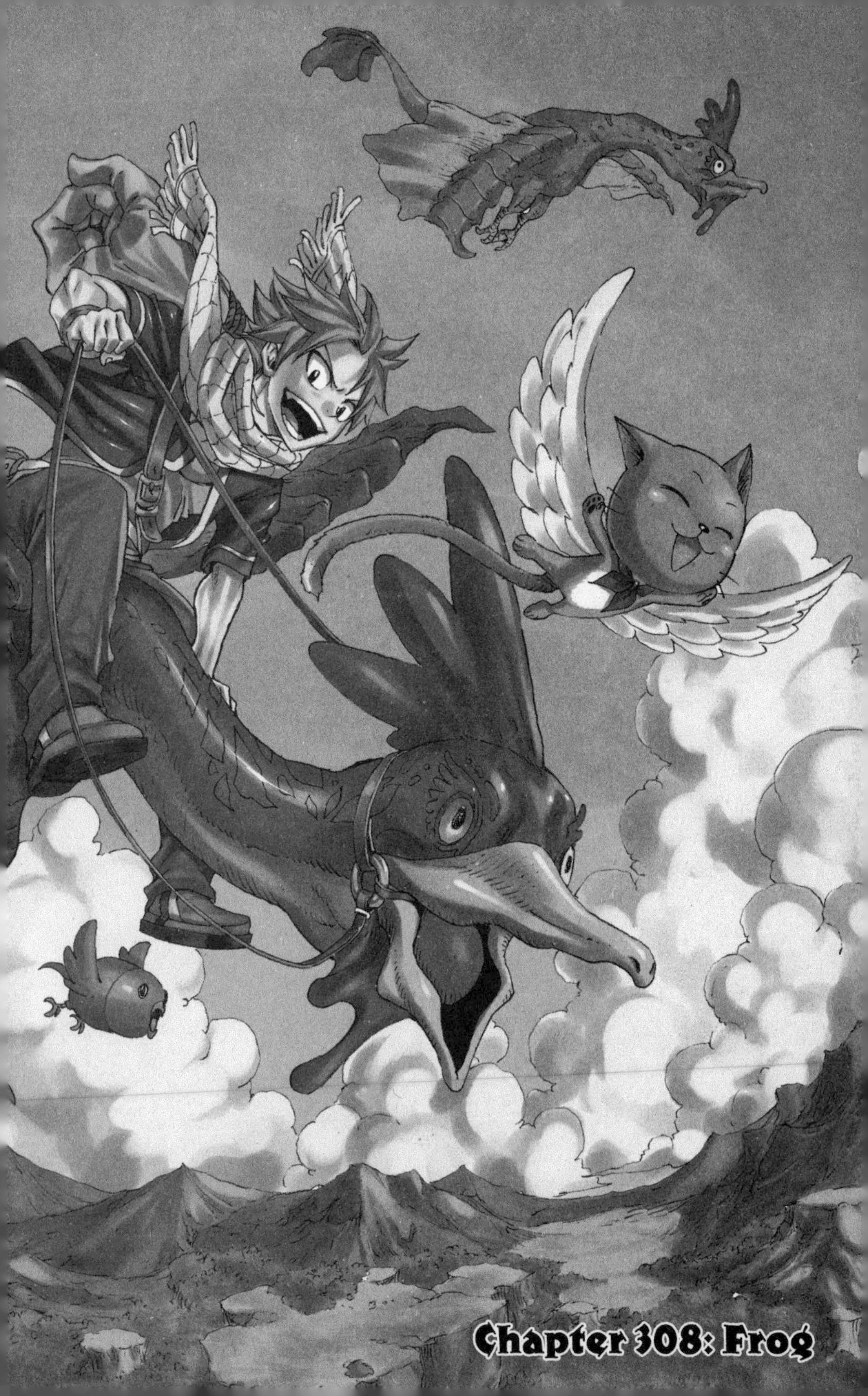

Chapter 308: Frog

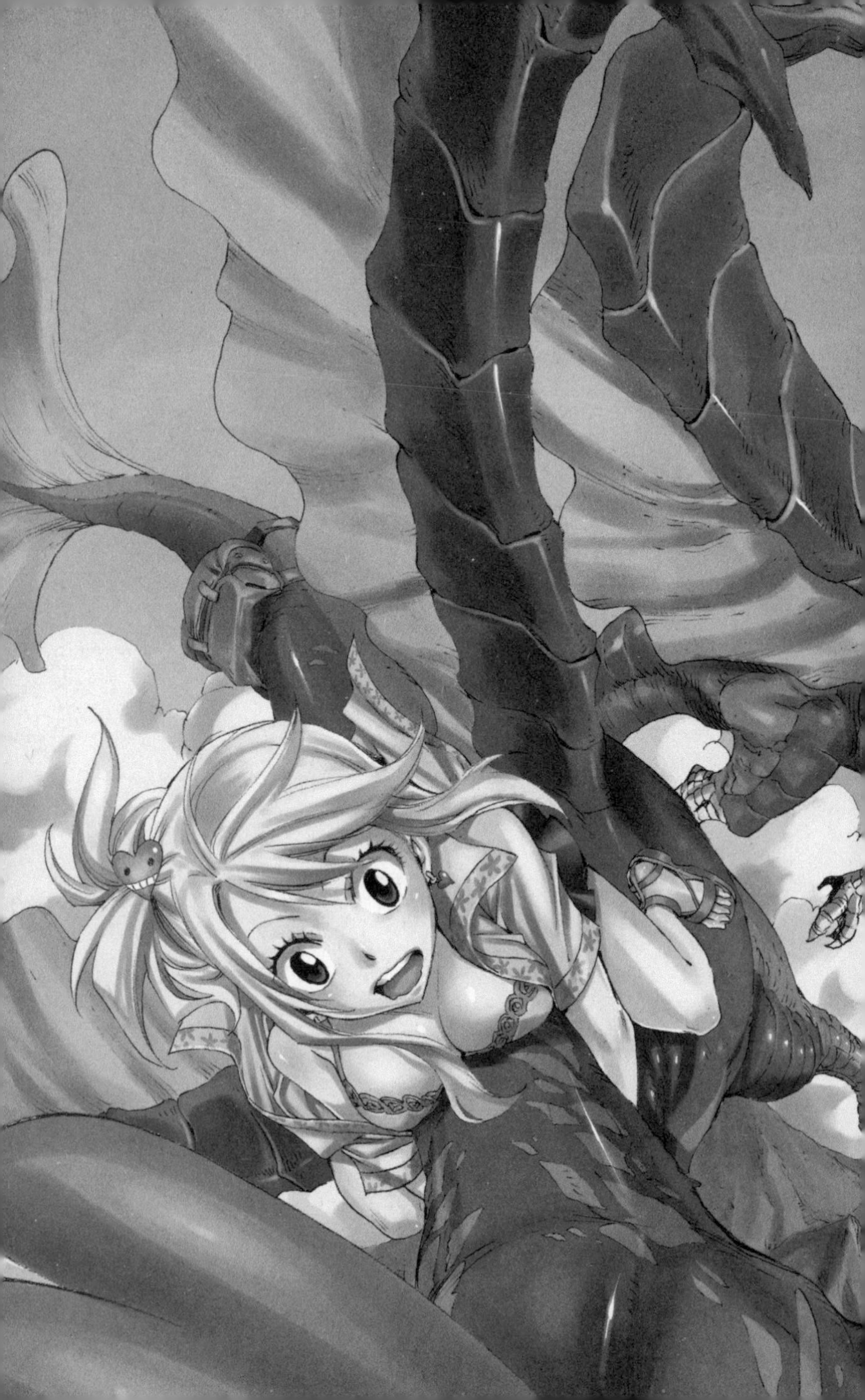

FAIRY TAIL

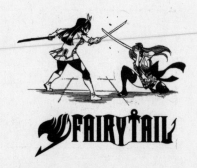

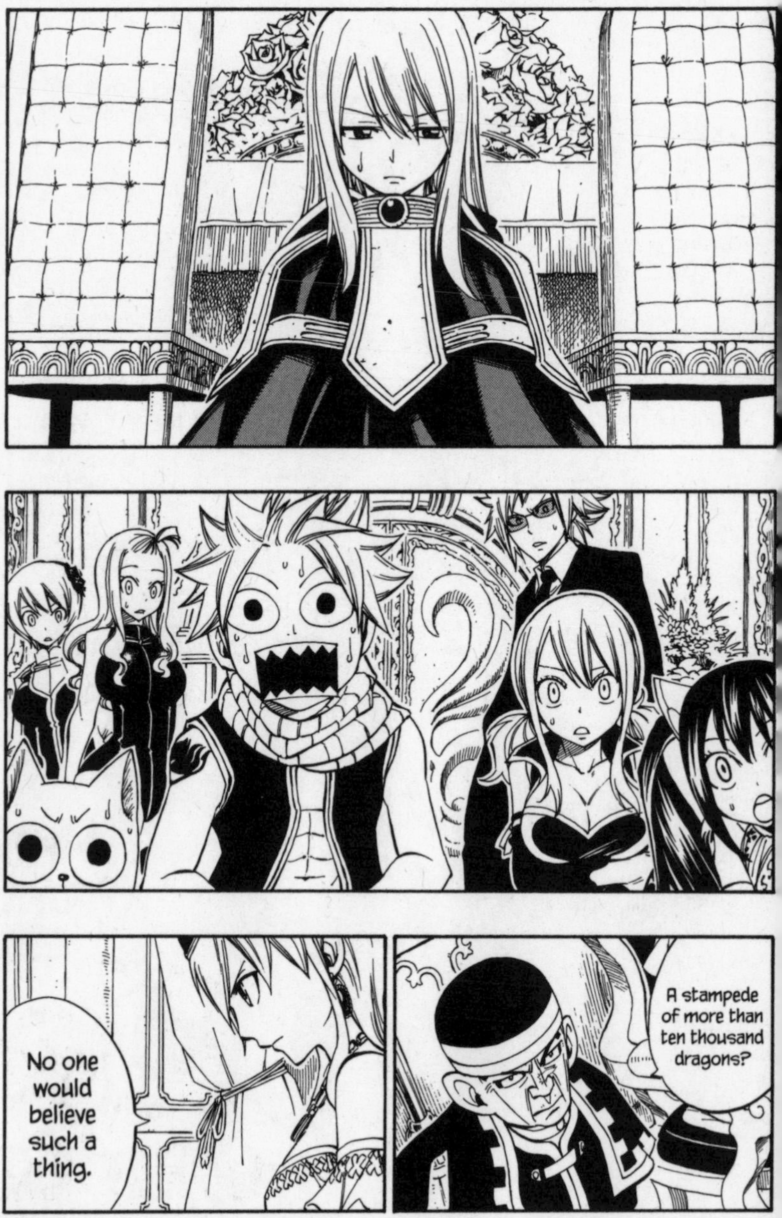
A stampede of more than ten thousand dragons?
No one would believe such a thing.

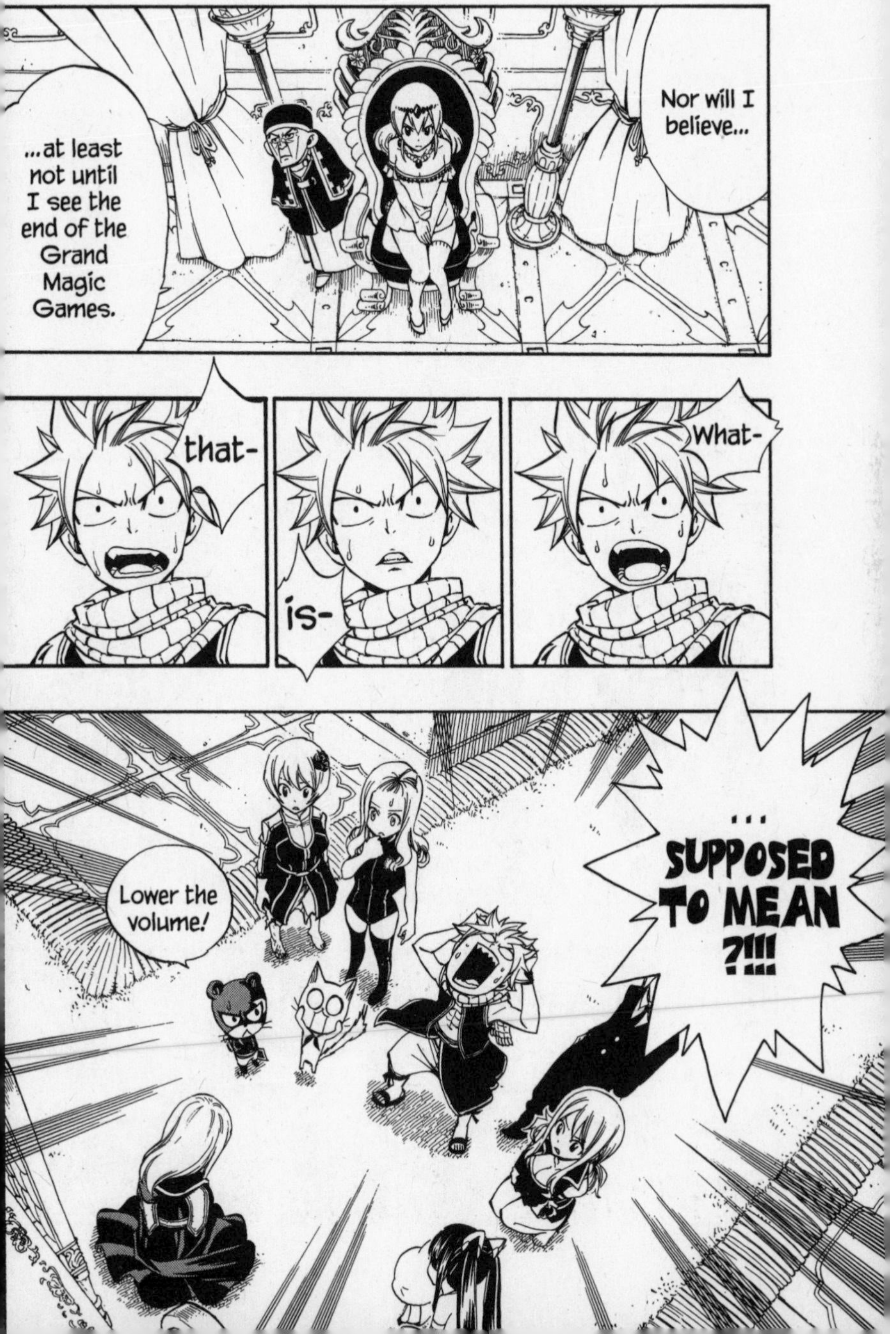
Nor will I believe...
...at least not until I see the end of the Grand Magic Games.
What-
is-
that-
...SUPPOSED TO MEAN ?!!!
Lower the volume!

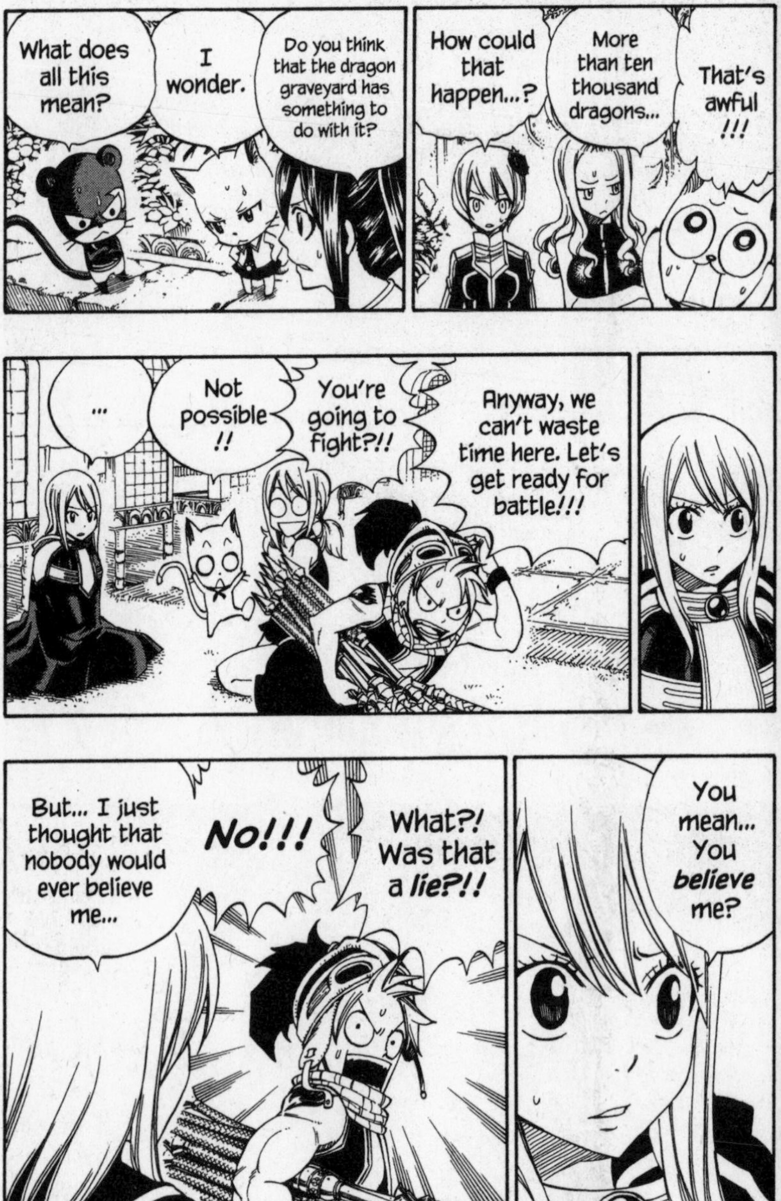
That's awful!!!
More than ten thousand dragons...
How could that happen...?
Do you think that the dragon graveyard has something to do with it?
I wonder.
What does all this mean?
Anyway, we can't waste time here. Let's get ready for battle!!!
You're going to fight?!!
Not possible!!
...
You mean... You *believe* me?
What?! Was that a *lie?!!*
No!!!
But... I just thought that nobody would ever believe me...

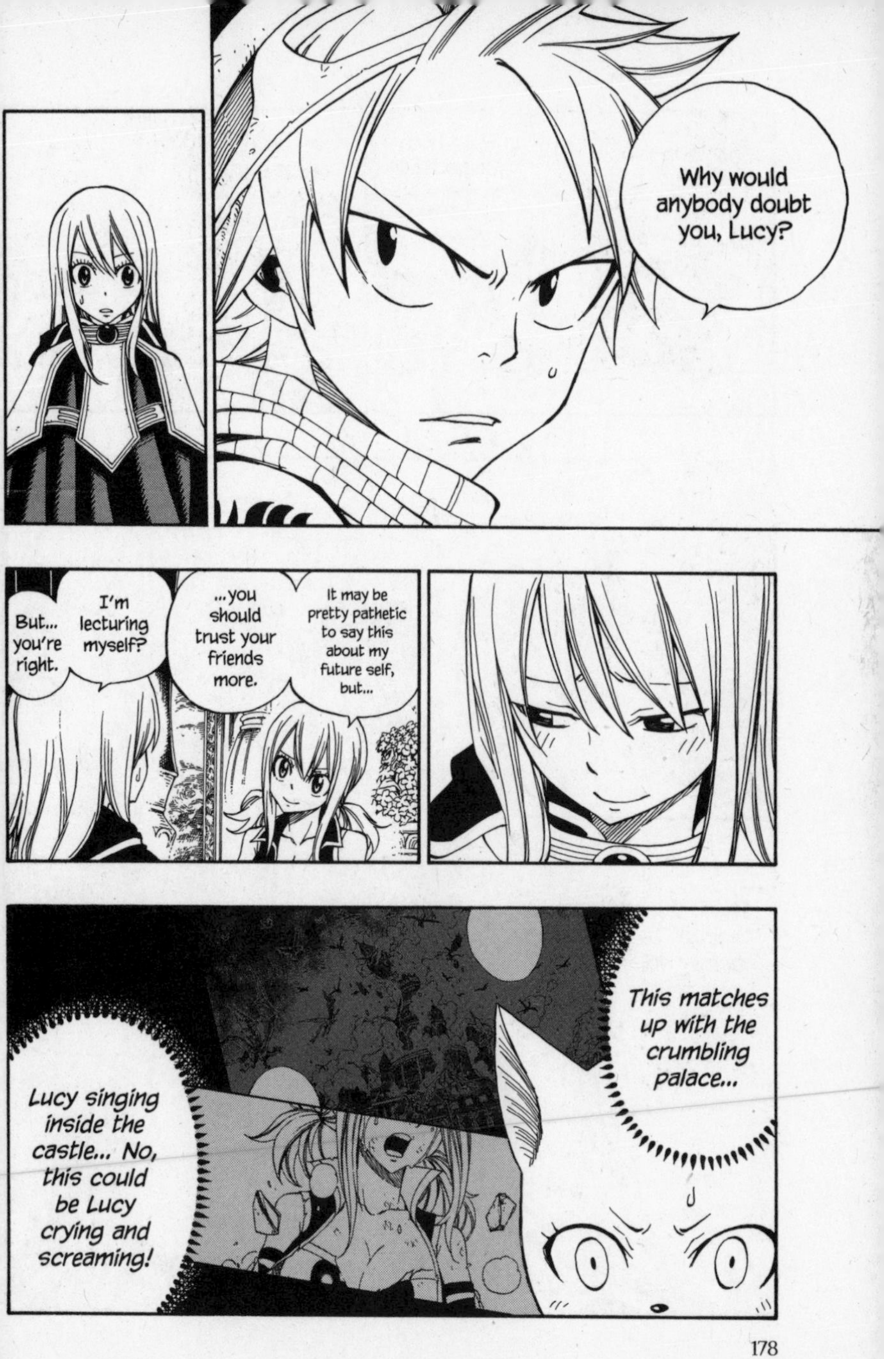
Why would anybody doubt you, Lucy?
It may be pretty pathetic to say this about my future self, but...
...you should trust your friends more.
I'm lecturing myself?
But... you're right.
This matches up with the crumbling palace...
Lucy singing inside the castle... No, this could be Lucy crying and screaming!

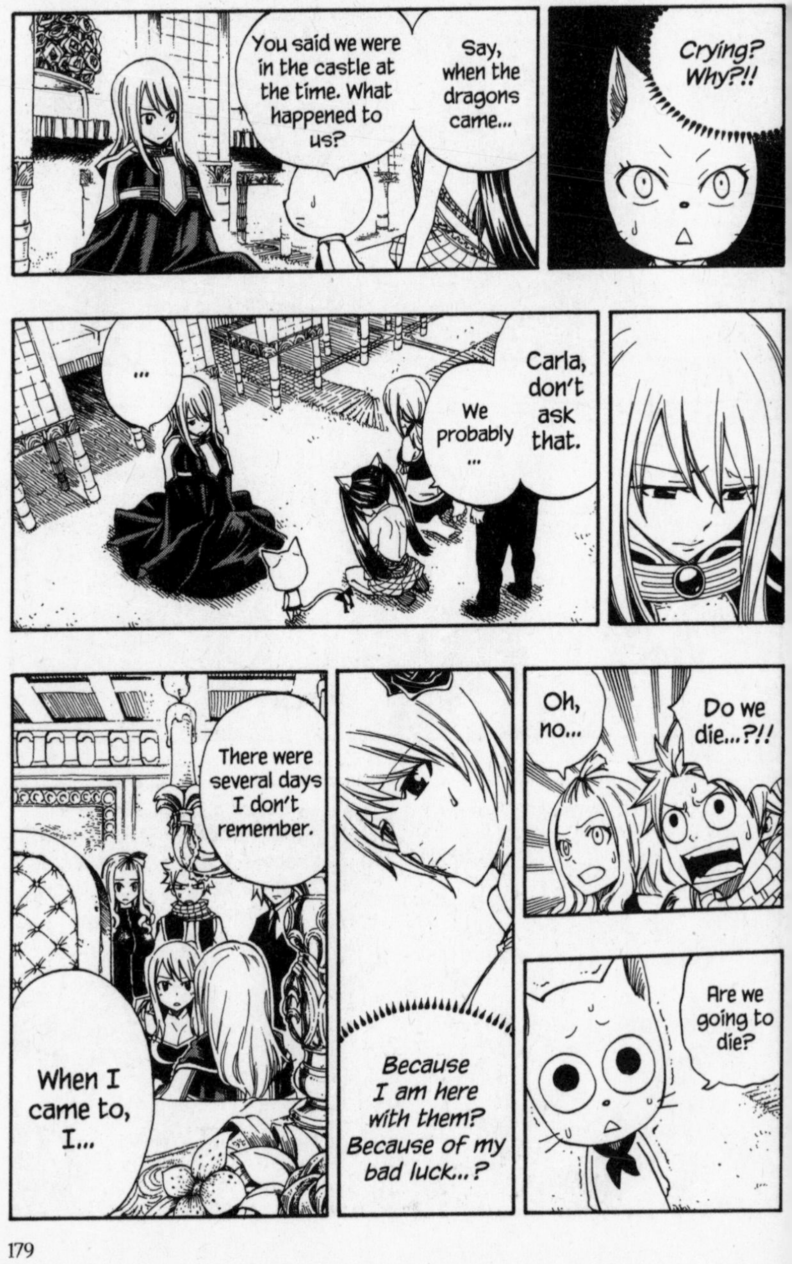
Crying? Why?!!
Say, when the dragons came...
You said we were in the castle at the time. What happened to us?
Carla, don't ask that.
We probably ...
...
Do we die...?!!
Oh, no...
Are we going to die?
Because I am here with them? Because of my bad luck...?
There were several days I don't remember.
When I came to, I...

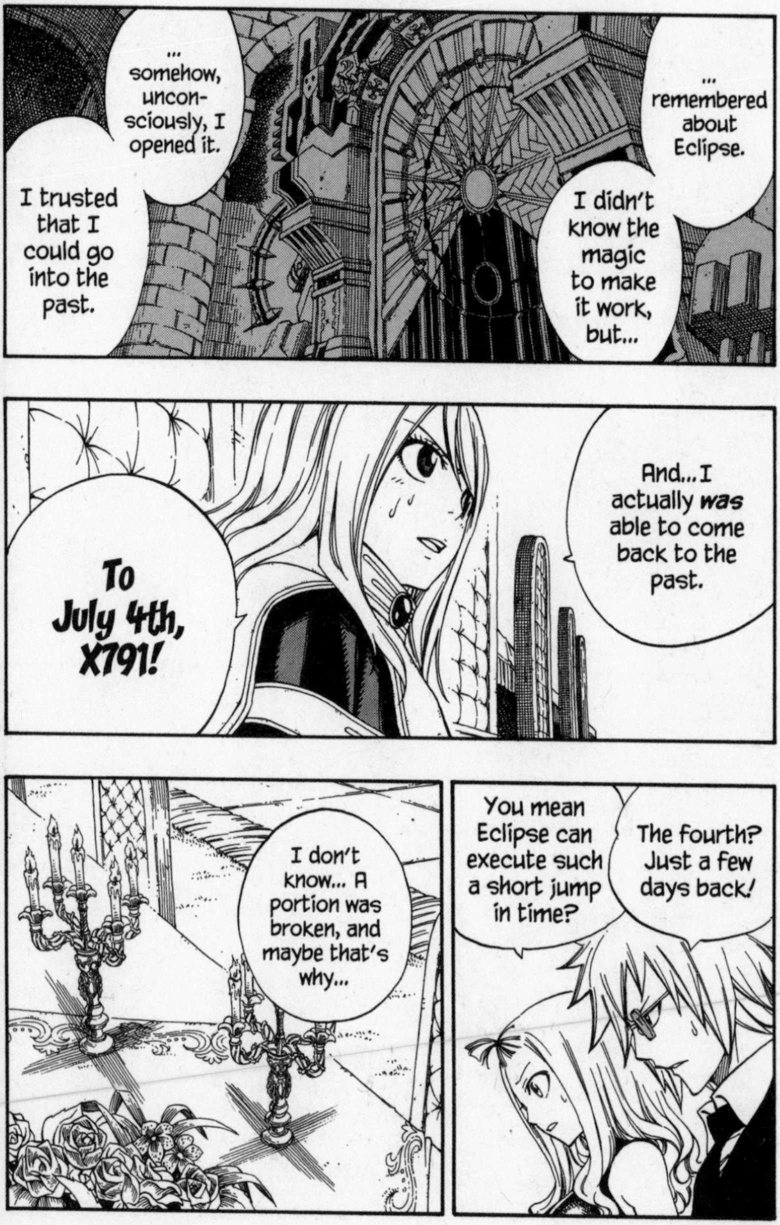
...remembered about Eclipse.
I didn't know the magic to make it work, but...
...somehow, uncon-sciously, I opened it.
I trusted that I could go into the past.
And...I actually *was* able to come back to the past.
To July 4th, X791!
The fourth? Just a few days back!
You mean Eclipse can execute such a short jump in time?
I don't know... A portion was broken, and maybe that's why...

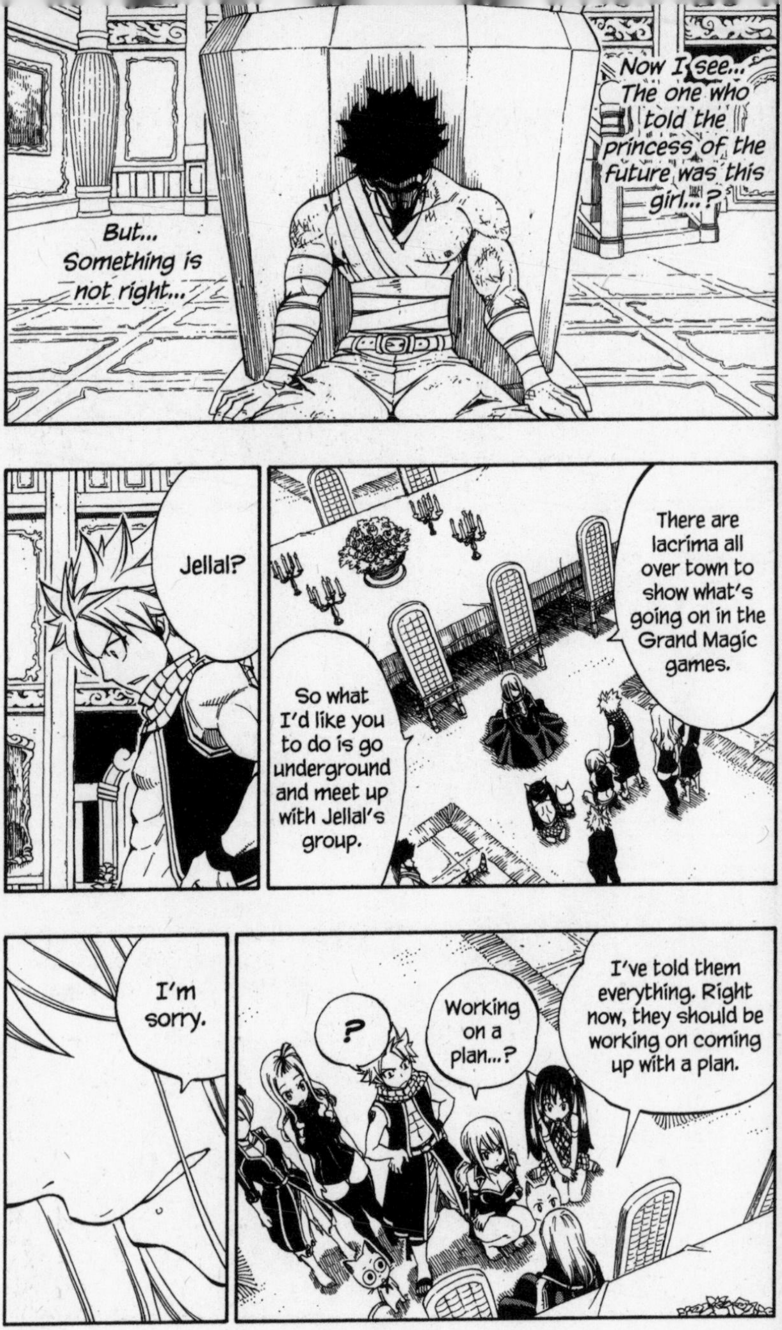
Now I see... The one who told the princess of the future was this girl...?
But... Something is not right...
There are lacrima all over town to show what's going on in the Grand Magic games.
So what I'd like you to do is go underground and meet up with Jellal's group.
Jellal?
I've told them everything. Right now, they should be working on coming up with a plan.
Working on a plan...?
?
I'm sorry.

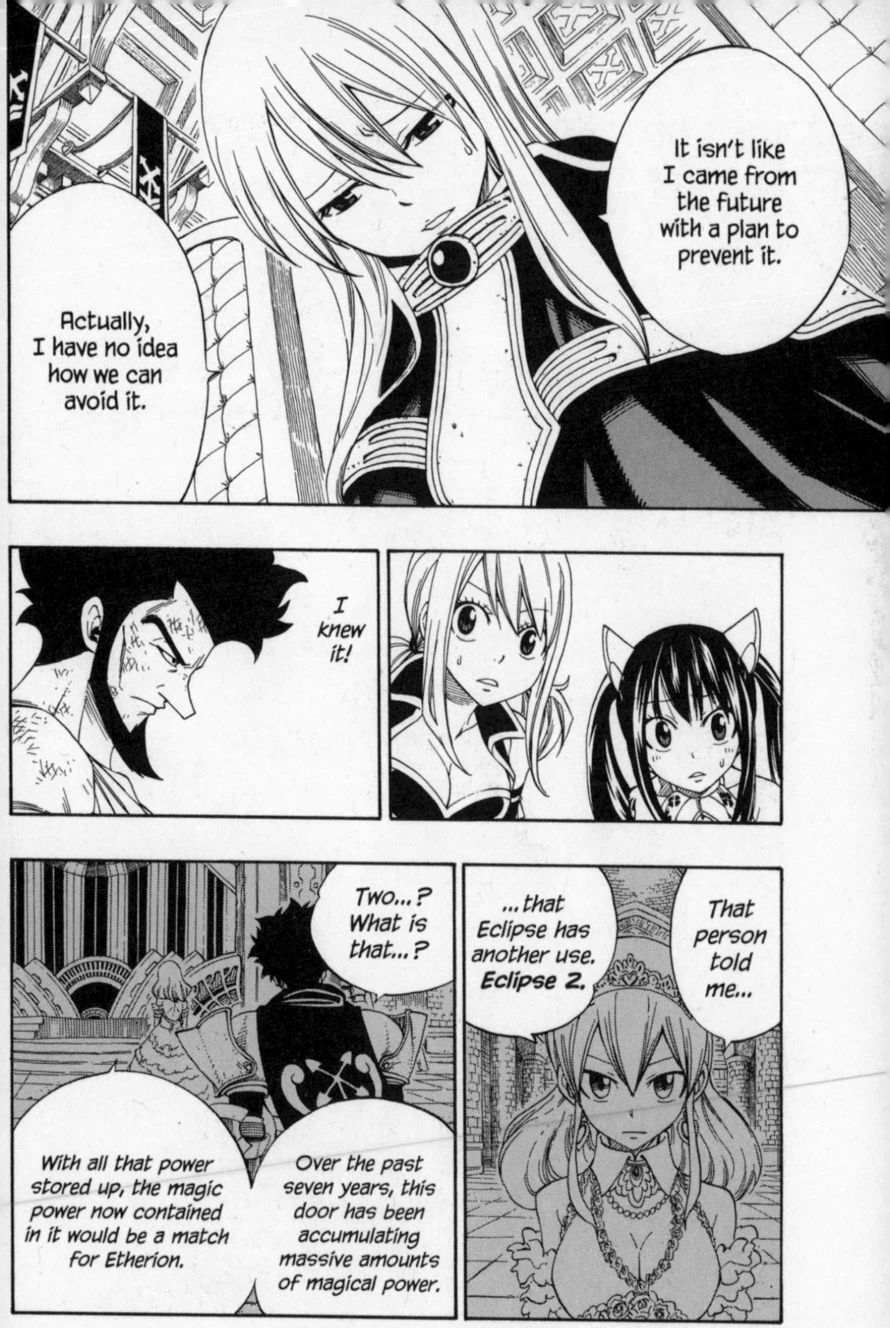
It isn't like I came from the future with a plan to prevent it.
Actually, I have no idea how we can avoid it.
I knew it!
That person told me...
...that Eclipse has another use. **Eclipse 2.**
Two...? What is that...?
Over the past seven years, this door has been accumulating massive amounts of magical power.
With all that power stored up, the magic power now contained in it would be a match for Etherion.

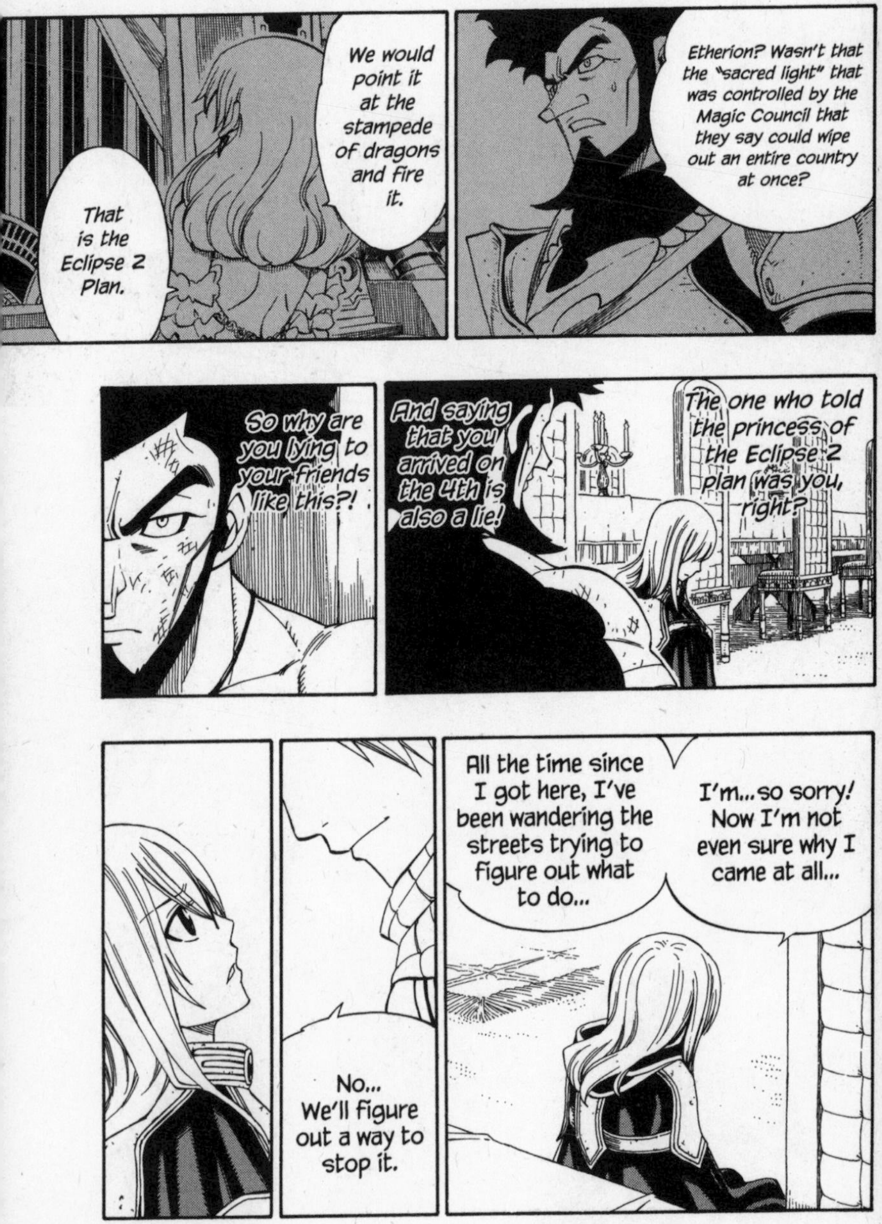
Etherion? Wasn't that the "sacred light" that was controlled by the Magic Council that they say could wipe out an entire country at once?
We would point it at the stampede of dragons and fire it.
That is the Eclipse 2 Plan.
The one who told the princess of the Eclipse 2 plan was you, right?
And saying that you arrived on the 4th is also a lie!
So why are you lying to your friends like this?!
I'm...so sorry! Now I'm not even sure why I came at all...
All the time since I got here, I've been wandering the streets trying to figure out what to do...
No... We'll figure out a way to stop it.

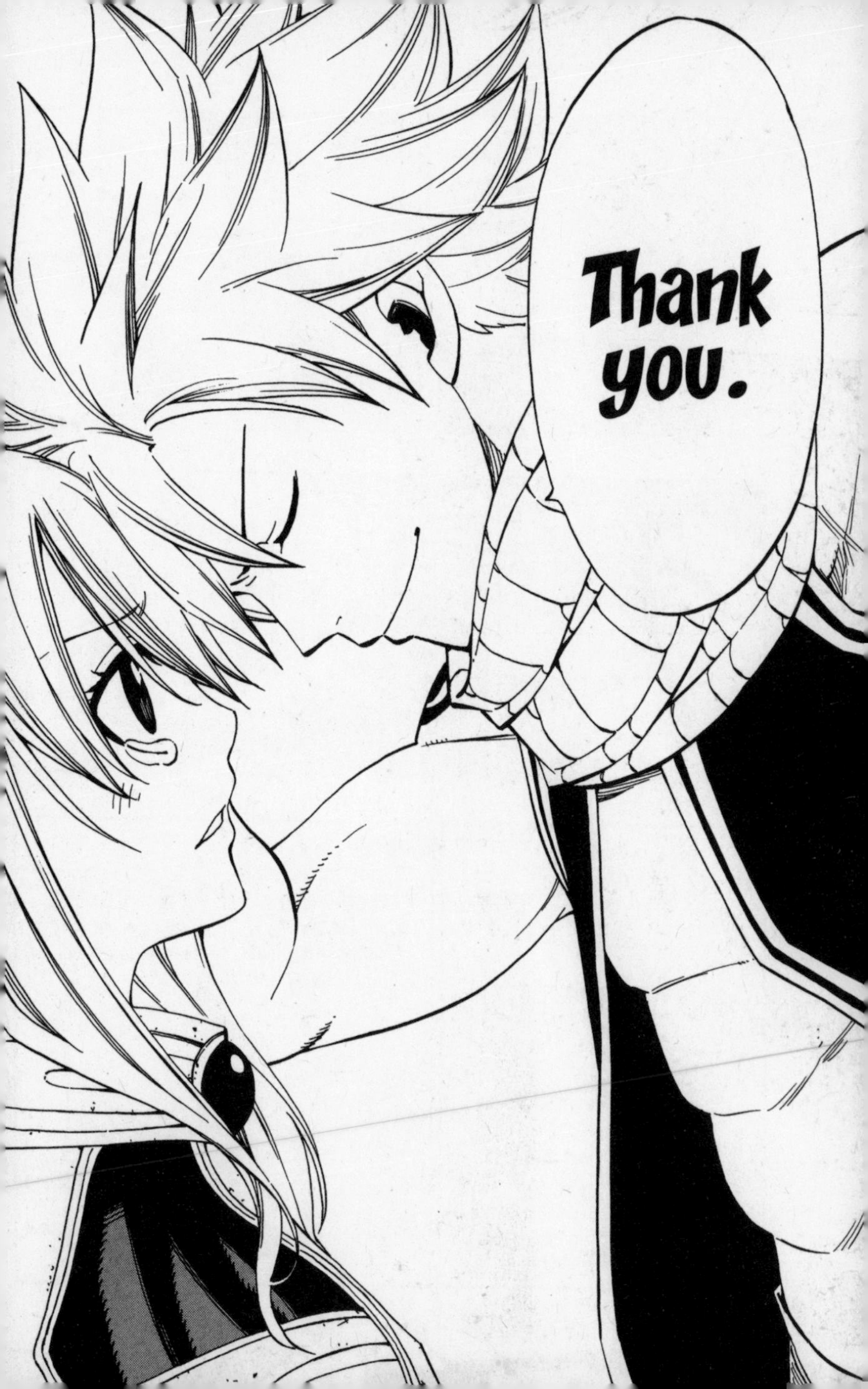
Thank you.

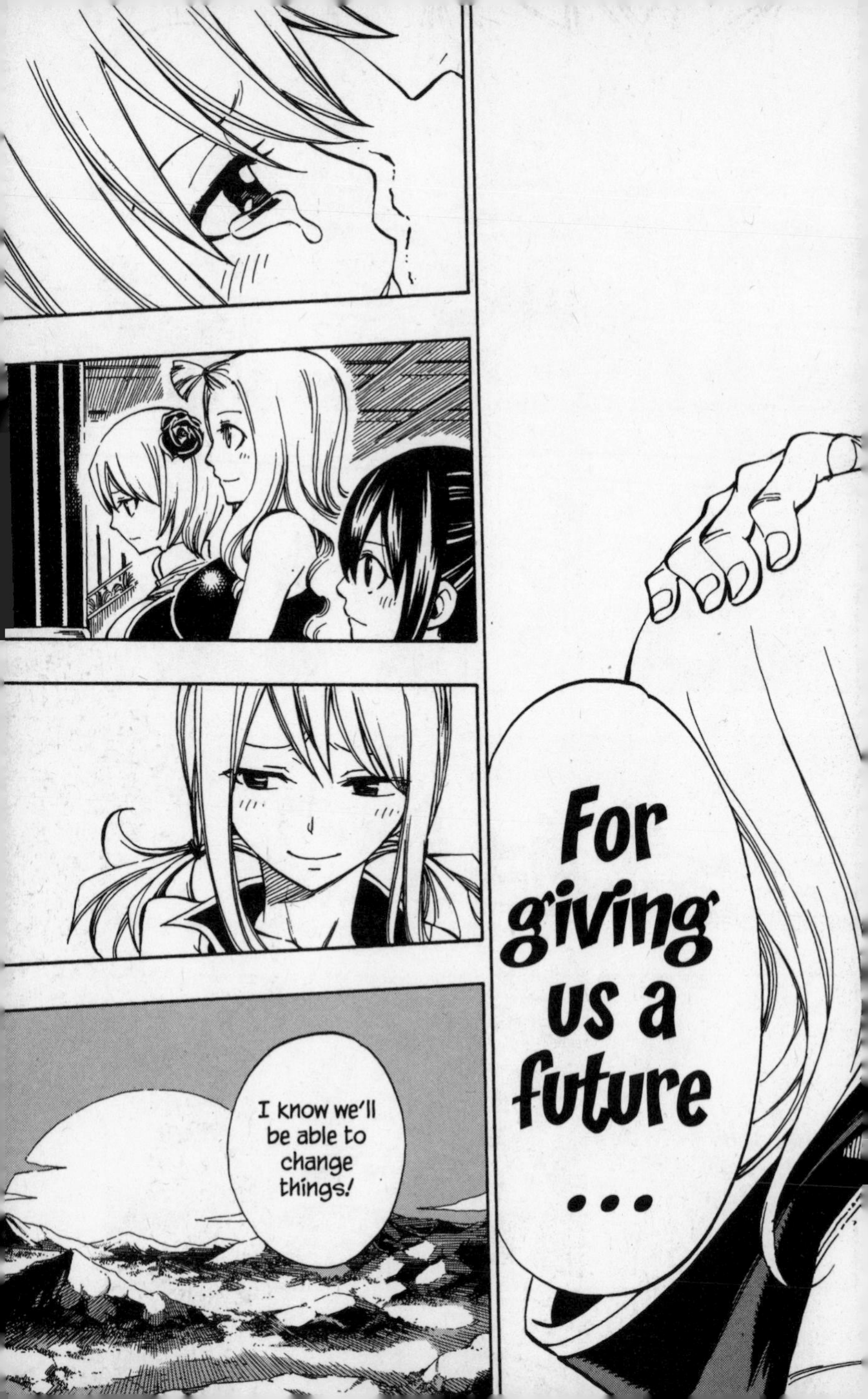
For giving us a future...
I know we'll be able to change things!

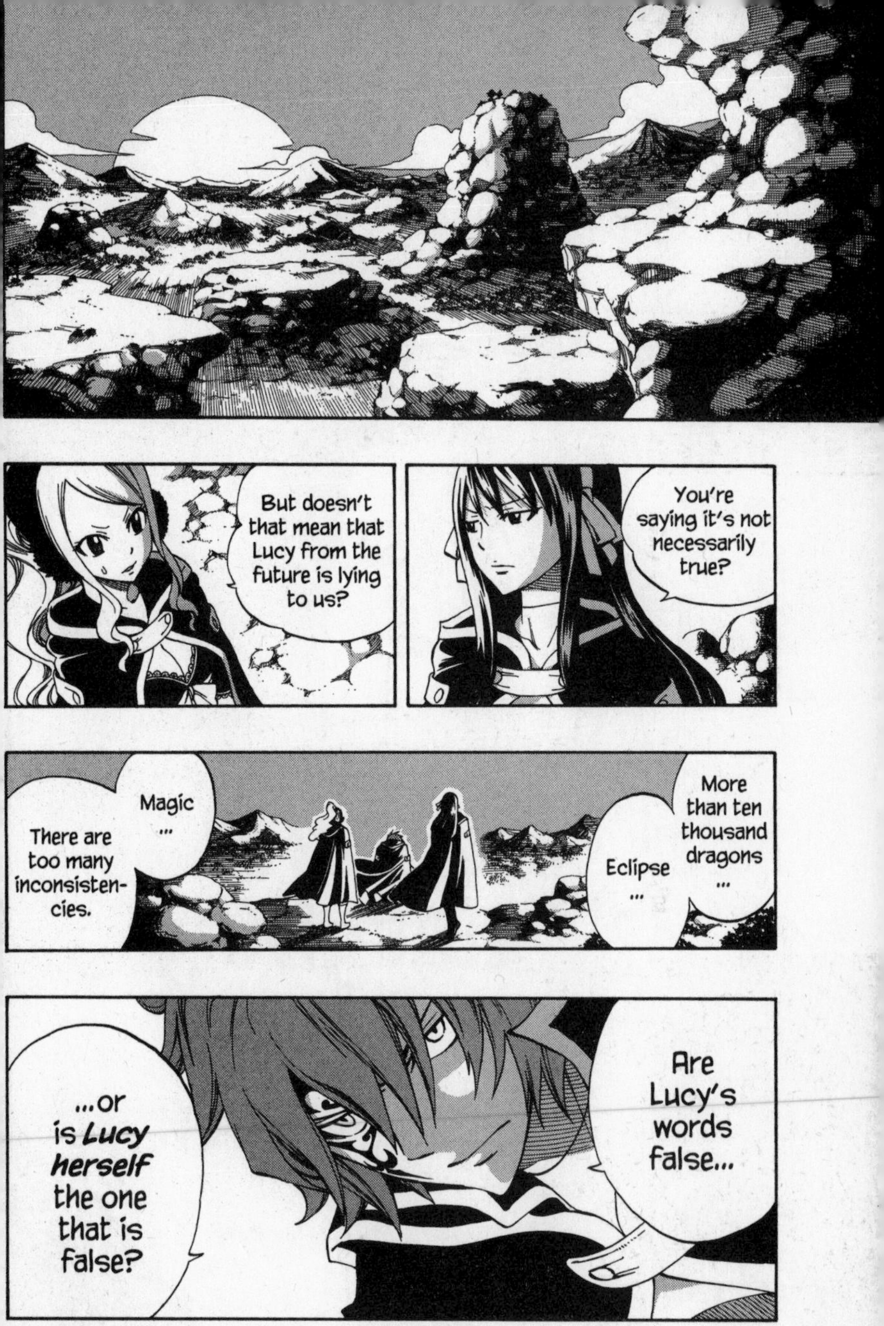
You're saying it's not necessarily true?
But doesn't that mean that Lucy from the future is lying to us?
More than ten thousand dragons ...
Eclipse ...
Magic ...
There are too many inconsisten-cies.
Are Lucy's words false...
...or is *Lucy herself* the one that is false?

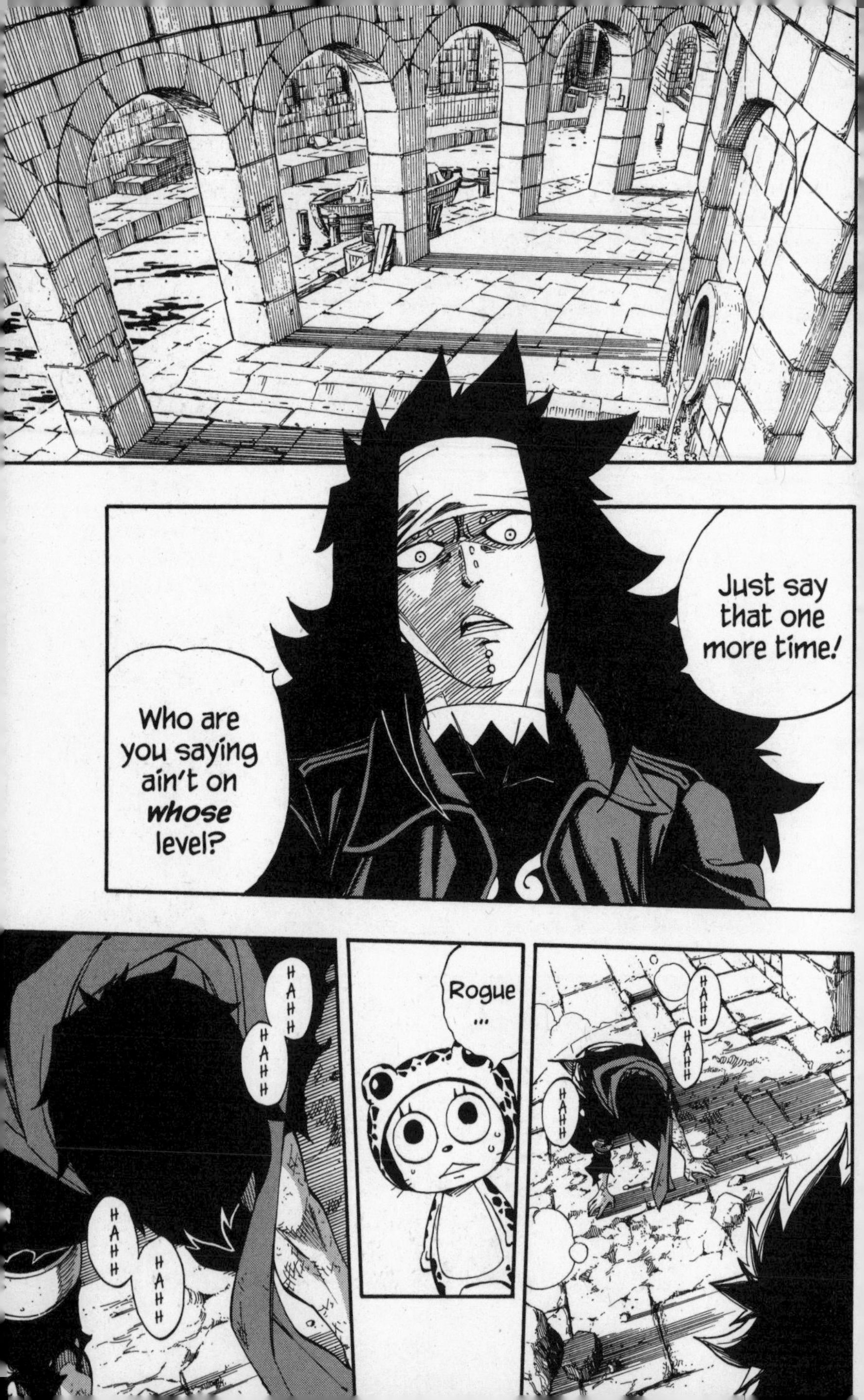
Just say that one more time!
Who are you saying ain't on *whose* level?
HAHH
HAHH
HAHH
Rogue ...
HAHH
HAHH
HAHH
HAHH

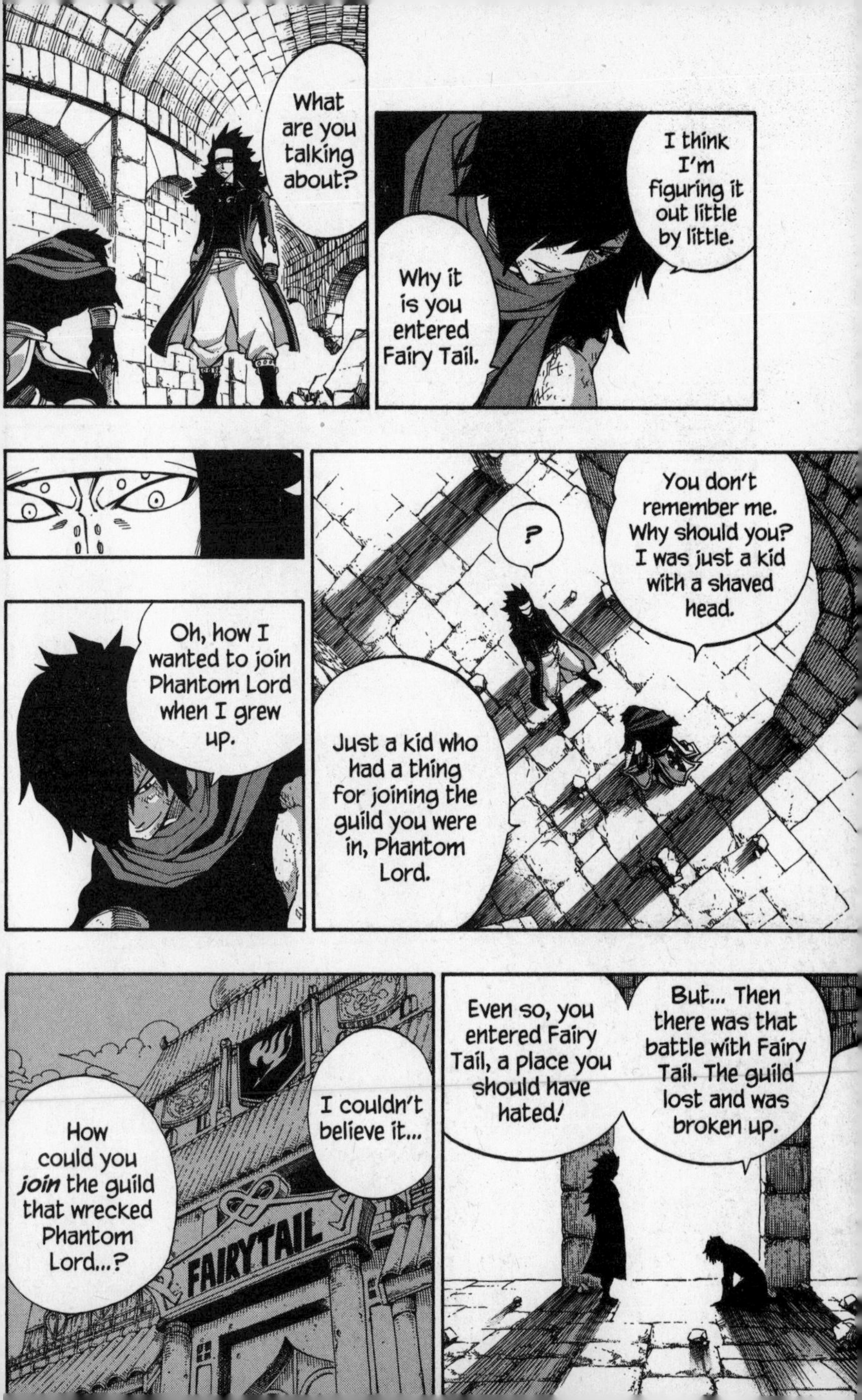
I think I'm figuring it out little by little.
Why it is you entered Fairy Tail.
What are you talking about?
You don't remember me. Why should you? I was just a kid with a shaved head.
?
Just a kid who had a thing for joining the guild you were in, Phantom Lord.
Oh, how I wanted to join Phantom Lord when I grew up.
But... Then there was that battle with Fairy Tail. The guild lost and was broken up.
Even so, you entered Fairy Tail, a place you should have hated!
I couldn't believe it...
FAIRYTAIL
How could you *join* the guild that wrecked Phantom Lord...?

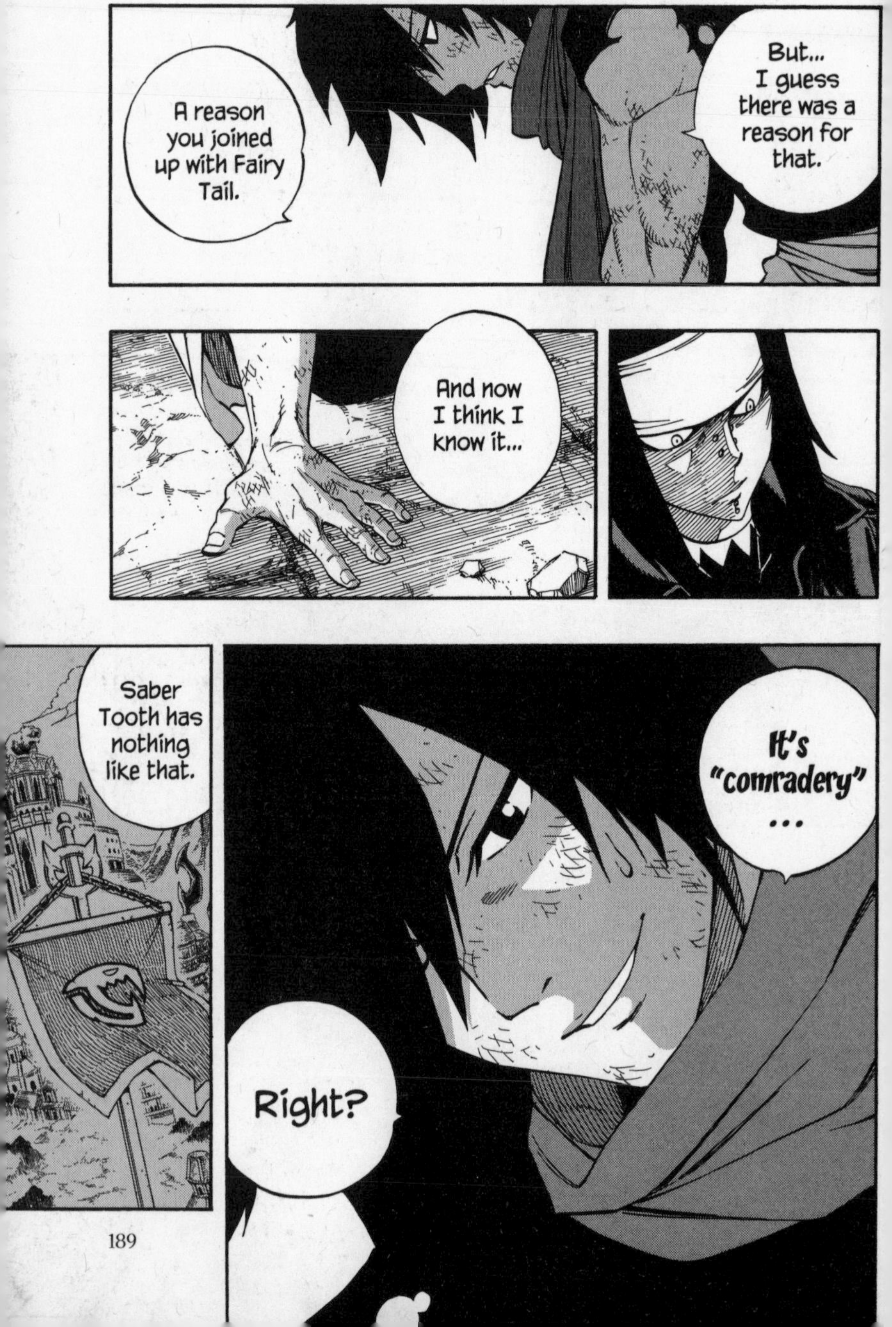
But... I guess there was a reason for that.
A reason you joined up with Fairy Tail.
And now I think I know it...
It's "comradery"...
Right?
Saber Tooth has nothing like that.

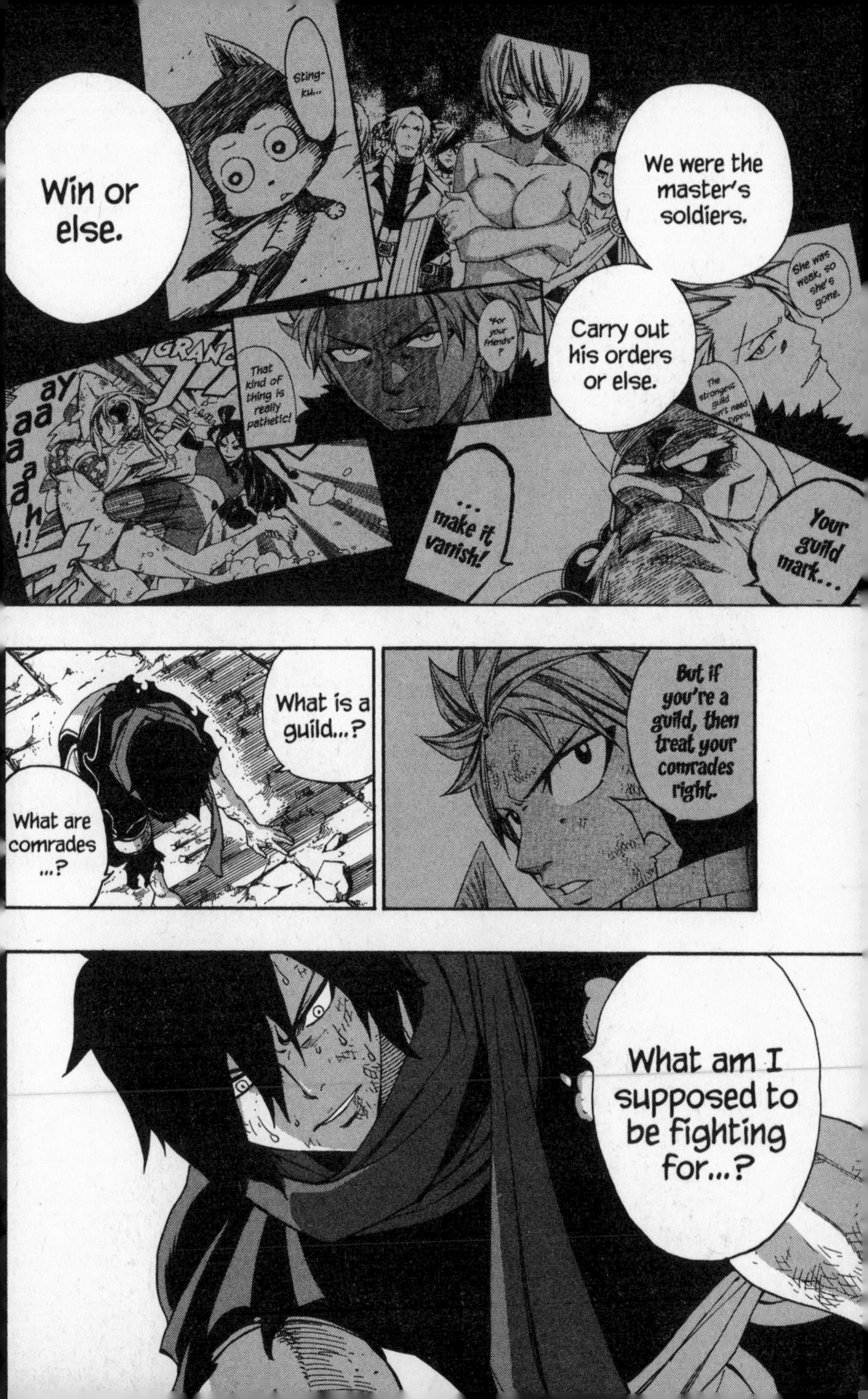

We were the master's soldiers.
She was weak, so she's gone.
Carry out his orders or else.
The strongest guild
Your guild mark...
...make it vanish!
"For your friends"?
That kind of thing is really pathetic!
Sting-kun...
Win or else.
GRAN
aaaaaah!!
But if you're a guild, then treat your comrades right.
What is a guild...?
What are comrades ...?
What am I supposed to be fighting for...?

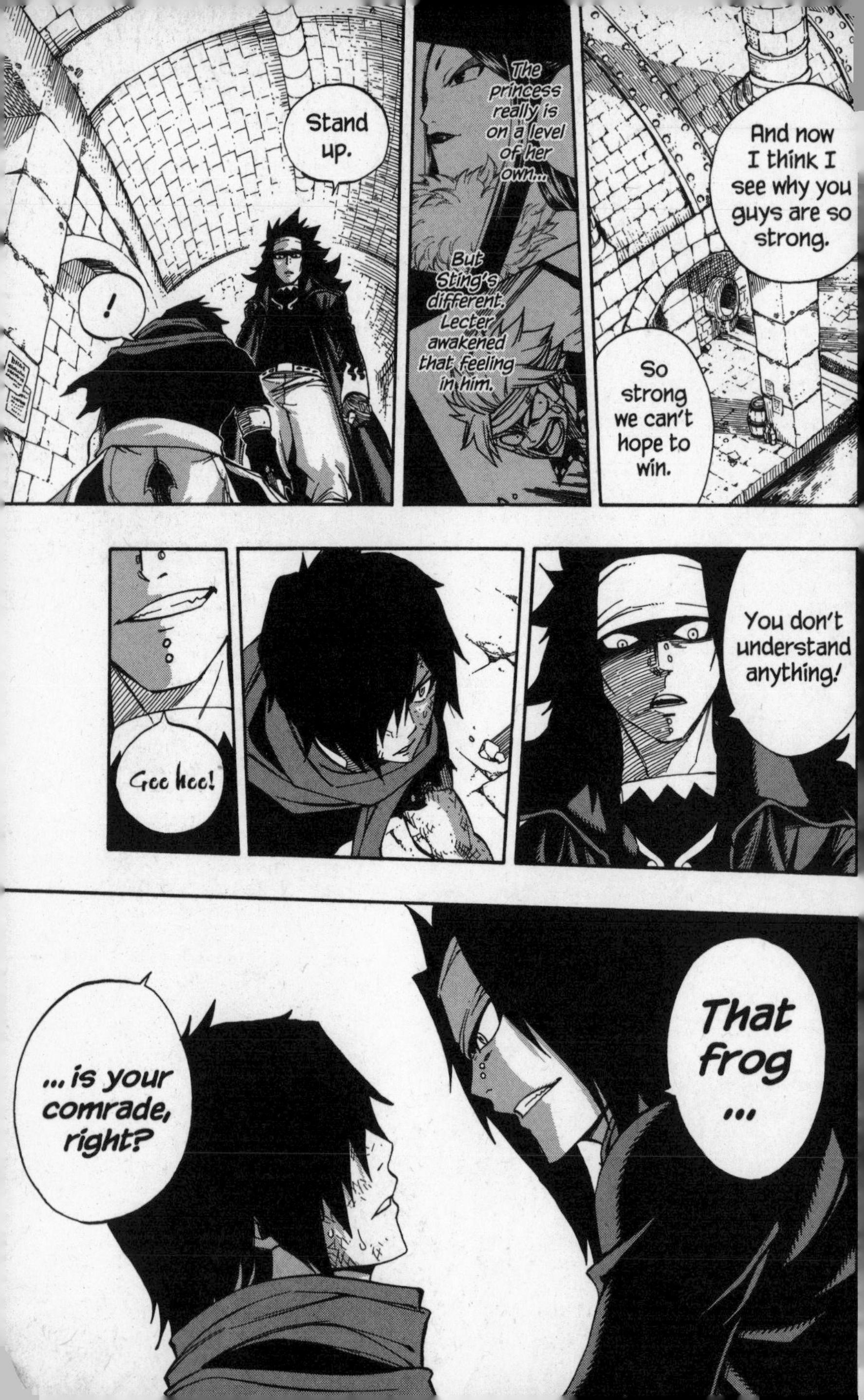
And now I think I see why you guys are so strong.
So strong we can't hope to win.
The princess really is on a level of her own...
But Sting's different. Lecter awakened that feeling in him.
Stand up.
!
You don't understand anything!
Gee hee!
That frog...
...is your comrade, right?

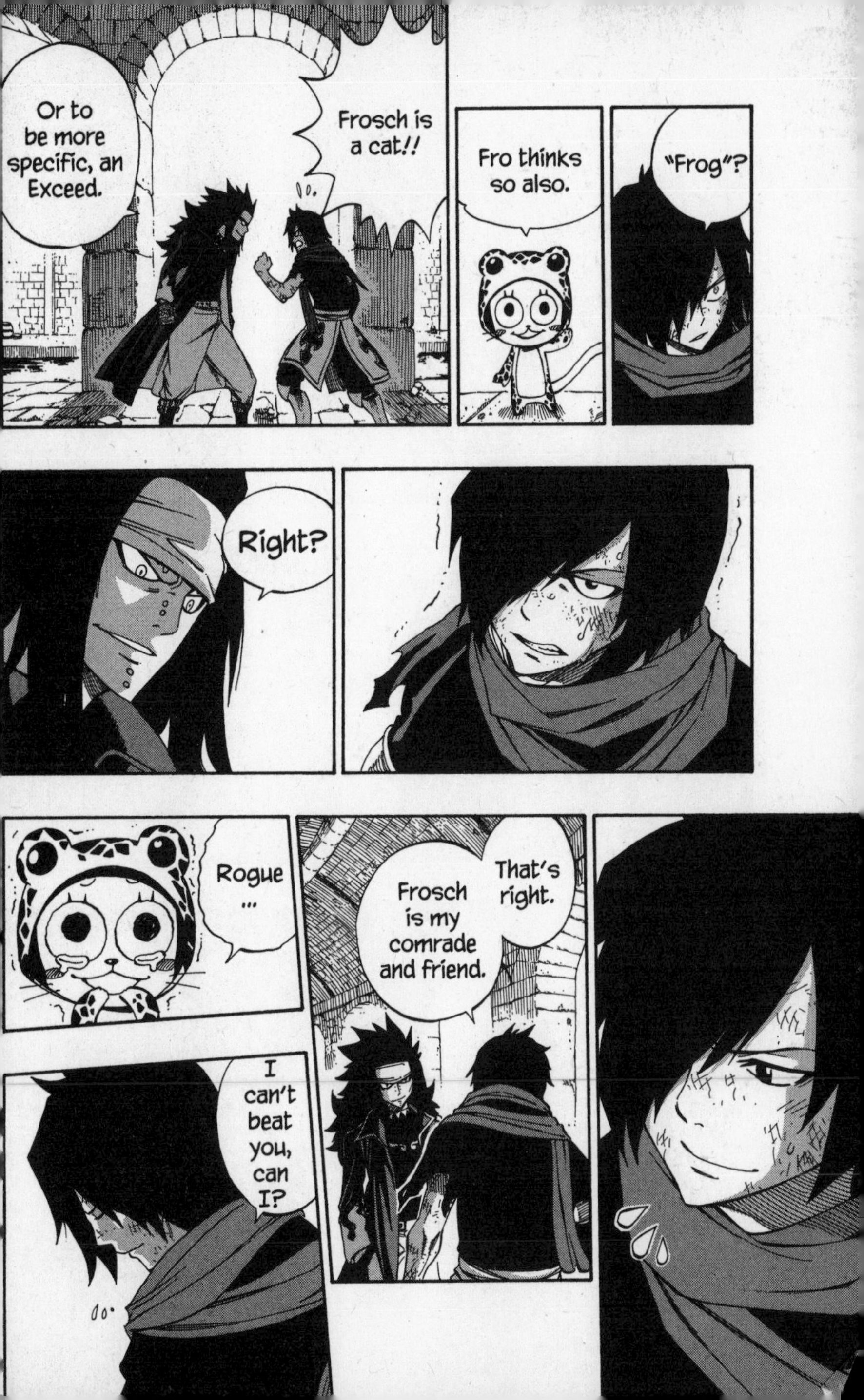
"Frog"?
Fro thinks so also.
Frosch is a cat!!
Or to be more specific, an Exceed.
Right?
That's right.
Frosch is my comrade and friend.
Rogue ...
I can't beat you, can I?

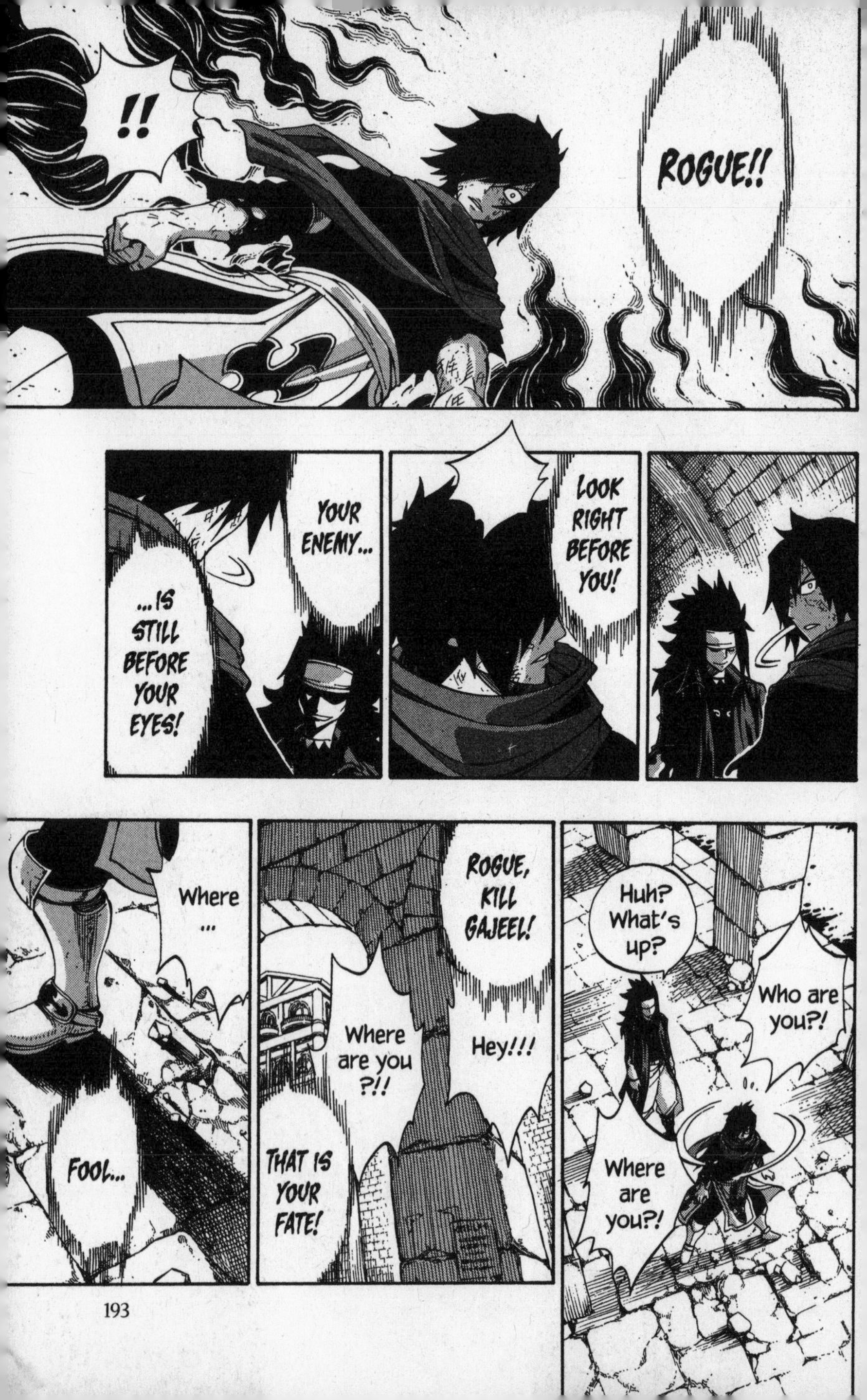
ROGUE!!
!!
LOOK RIGHT BEFORE YOU!
YOUR ENEMY...
...IS STILL BEFORE YOUR EYES!
Huh? What's up?
Who are you?!
Where are you?!
ROGUE, KILL GAJEEL!
Hey!!!
Where are you ?!!
THAT IS YOUR FATE!
Where ...
FOOL...

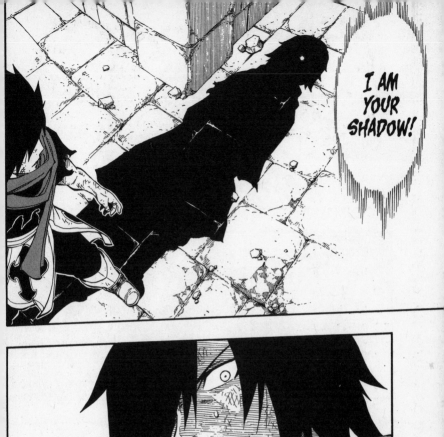

I AM YOUR SHADOW!

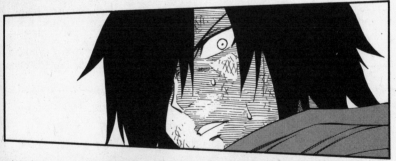

KILL GAJEEL!

I WILL GIVE YOU POWER!

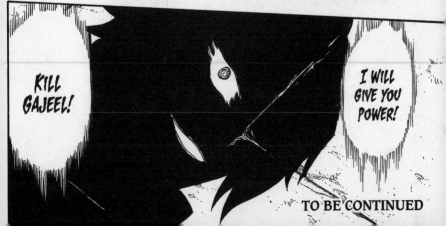

TO BE CONTINUED

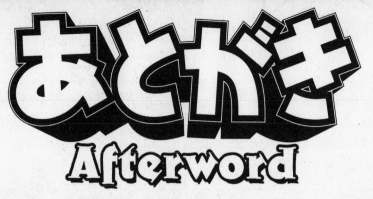

あとがき Afterword

I moved! I see the world a whole new way! And the brand-new feeling is giving me the will to work harder! For a very long time, I've been the type who can never throw anything away. So I took this opportunity and made the decision to toss out everything I don't need.

First, I have always felt it was necessary to keep the individual issues of Magazine, so from my debut until now, I have **fifteen years** worth of Weekly Shonen Magazines, and it filled up an entire room. When I opened up an old Magazine, I'd be flooded with the same feelings I felt at the time. All sorts of feelings are tied up in those...but if I get hooked on that, I'll never see the end of it, so I got rid of them all. We split up the problem over a number of days and sent them all to recycling. There was really a huge load of them.

There were toys that I don't need and old clothes, and unused beds and broken refrigerators, leaving just one thing left to work on. My CDs. A long time ago, I was hooked on collecting CDs. I must have had several thousand CDs, and for most of them, I went ahead and re-bought data versions of them. And if I get the urge, I can convert my present collection to data too, but I still like having the jacket covers and liner notes, so I wasn't able to throw them out.

And manga... Actually, I wasn't able to throw a single book of those away. I brought with me on the move all the books I have, even the ones I thought were boring. You know, I'm still the type who can't throw anything away.

Continued from the left-hand page.

Lucy: Nicknames?

: Right! For example, Mermaid Heel...

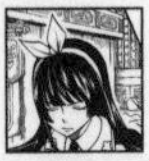
Kagura → White Ribbon.

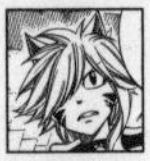
Millianna → Cat Girl.

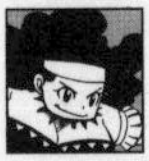
Lislie → Pudgy.

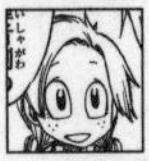
Beth → Freckles.

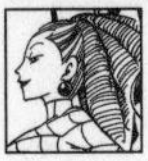
Alaña → Curlyhair

Like that.

: Wow. Not very creative, huh?

Mira: Speaking of names, what about the "Hungry Wolf Knights"?!

Lucy: For the guy who seemed like the leader, I never even heard a name for him...

Mira: There's actually a story behind the members of that group. They were submitted as part of a contest in a book called "Chotto Moorimashita" where readers submitted designs for wizards, and those got used.

Lucy: That's pretty amazing!

Mira: By the way, the winner of that contest was Princess Hisui.

Lucy: And *she's* pretty much a main character!

Mira: I'll bet the designers who won are pretty surprised!

Lucy: What about the name of the Knights' leader?

Mira: He wasn't one of the characters submitted by readers, so he doesn't need a name!

: That's awful!

: Okay, I'll give him a name.

SCYTHE.

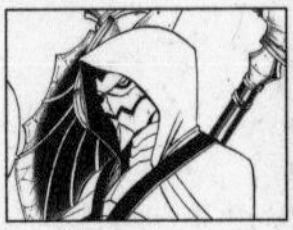

: Zero subtlety!

Mira: It looks like we've made it through another set of questions.

Lucy: Hold it! This time I want the final question to be from me!

: ?

What is the reason that you were dancing?

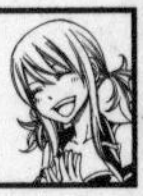

Mira: Heh heh heh. You really want to know?

Lucy: I want to know. What happened with you?

: Ah, well... I thought that I'd surprise you with it later, Lucy.

: What? You mean it was about me?

Mira: Yep! ♥ Actually, Lucy, Carla had a dream about you suddenly becoming nude in front of a huge number of people.

Lucy: A-And what about that would make you want to dance?

Mira: Well, if Carla says she saw it, then it means it will come true! I'm so looking forward to it!♥

Lucy: Nooooo waaaaaay!!!!

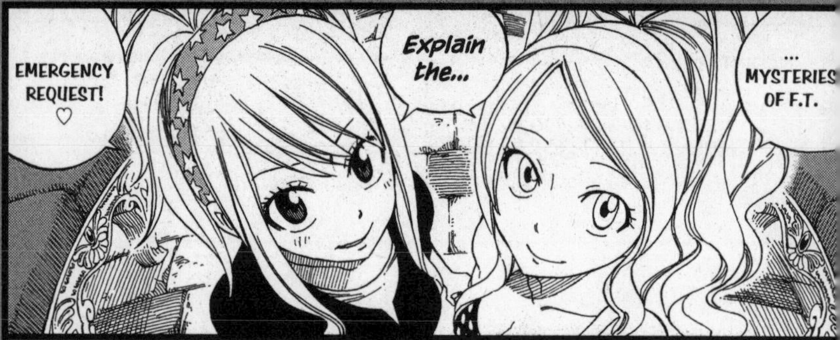
EMERGENCY REQUEST! ♡
Explain the...
... MYSTERIES OF F.T.

At a park in Crocus...

: One, two, right, left...♪ Three, four, five, turn!♪

: What are you doing? What's with the dancing all of a sudden?

Mira: Don't you feel like it too? Come on, Lucy! Dance! Dance!

Lucy: Huhhh?! Did something good happen to you?

Mira: Heh heh heh... Actually...

Lucy: Actually?

Mira: It's a secret!♥

: Whaaaa?!!

Mira: Now for the first question.

Lucy: Huh? You're really *not* going to tell me?!

> ***Why was Loke on the cover of Volume 36? (He wasn't anywhere in the story.)***

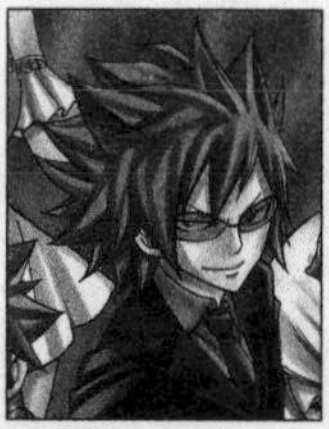

Lucy: Aw, man! So they *did* ask about that.

Mira: I think it was nothing more than a mistake.

Lucy: Loke finally made his entrance in the first chapter of this volume. (Chapter 309).

Mira: And the artist probably just didn't realize, and thought he appeared in the last chapter of Vol. 36.

: But in a way, it was a really big spoiler.

: Next question.

> ***There are so many characters, I can't remember all their names.***

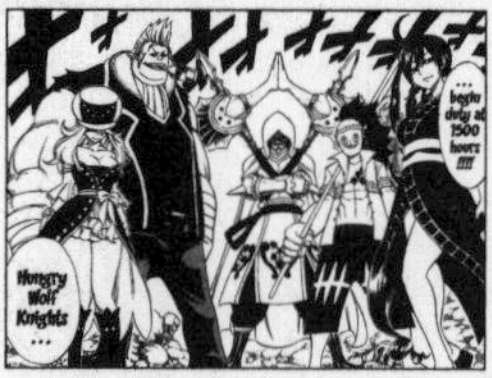
Hungry Wolf Knights...

Lucy: It's certainly true... There are a lot of people in this story arc...

Mira: I don't see a reason to memorize them all.

Lucy: There are a lot of them who don't stick around very long.

Mira: I've been doing my best to remember them by nicknames.

Continued on the right-hand page.

TAIL d'ART

The Fairy Tail Guild is looking for illustrations! Please send in your art on a postcard or at postcard size, and do it in black pen, okay? Those chosen to be published will get a signed mini poster! ♪ Make sure you write your real name and address on the back of your illustration!

Chiba Prefecture, Michael

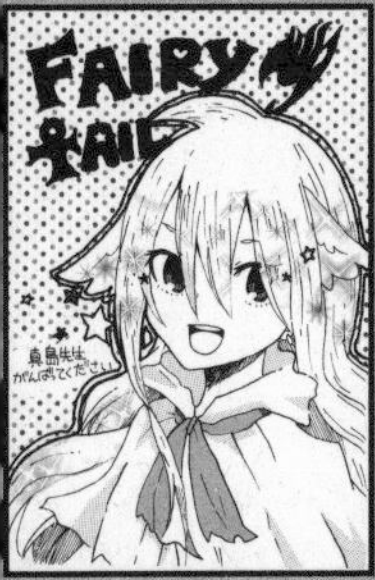
FAIRY TAIL

▲I'm being cheered on by the first master! I'll do my best!

Kanagawa Prefecture, A. S.

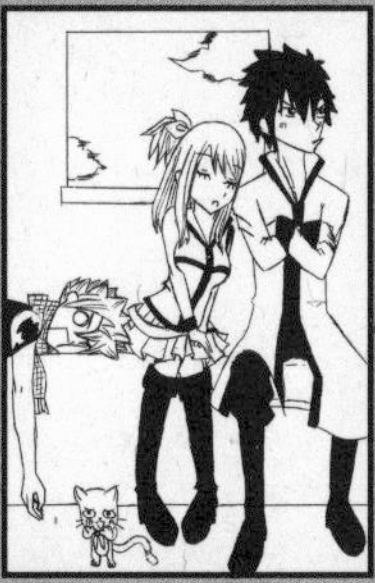

▲Heading somewhere on some kind of vehicle. Natsu looks to be in bad shape.

Shiga Prefecture, Nihimara

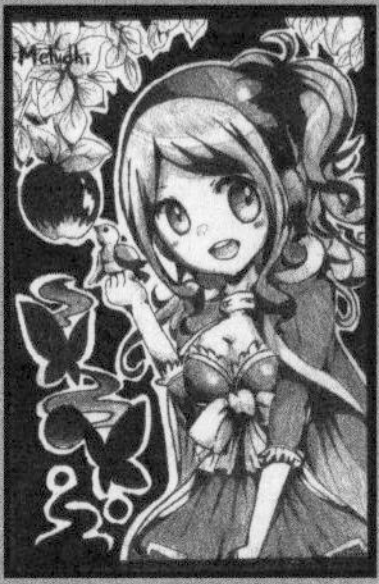

▲This is so cute! She looks good in this kind of outfit even after seven years!

Wakayama Prefecture, Ayaka

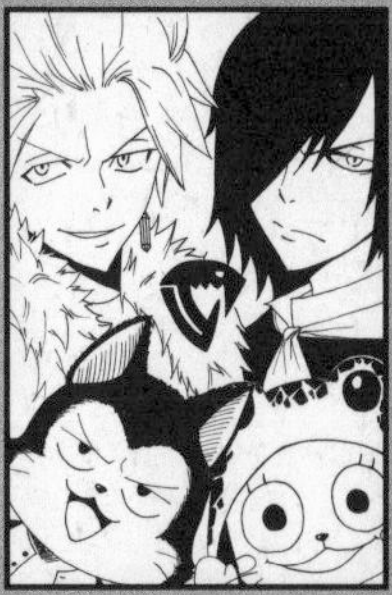

▲The Twin Dragons of Saber and the two cats! Nice!

Tochigi Prefecture, Momoka Kano

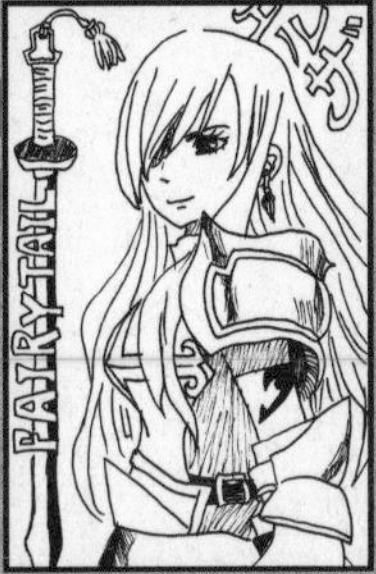
FAIRY TAIL

▲Erza gazing. I wonder what she's looking at.

Gifu Prefecture, Chisato Yumeoka

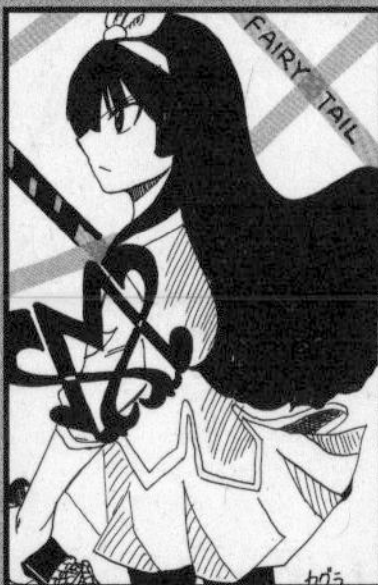
FAIRY TAIL

▲Kagura who has gained quite a bit of popularity. It's been a while since we featured a new strong woman.

Fukuoka Prefecture, Kurukuru

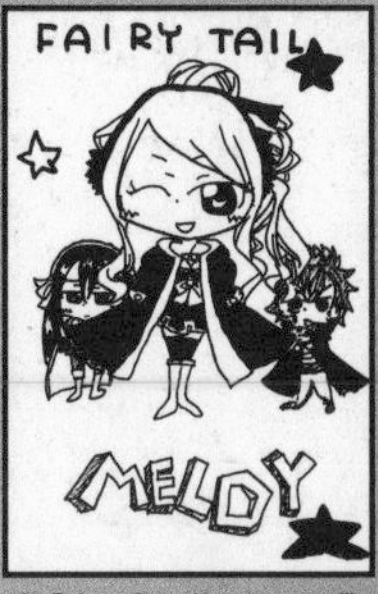
FAIRY TAIL
MELDY

▲Crime Sorcière may still have some work to do yet.

Miyagi Prefecture, Seig's Tool Box

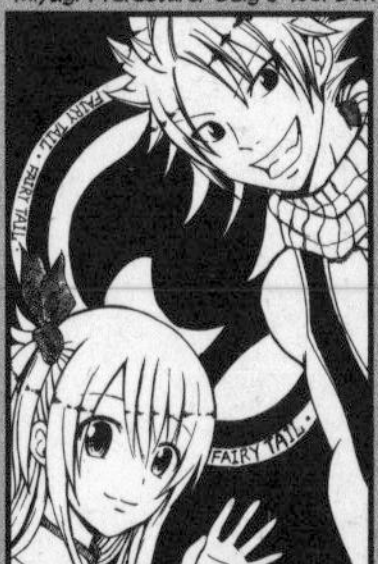
FAIRY TAIL

▲Ah! Very nice line work! Clean and easy on the eyes!

Send to Hiro Mashima, Kodansha Comics
451 Park Ave. South, 7th Floor New York, NY 10016

FAIRY GUILD

Nagasaki Prefecture, Mizuki Tomonaga

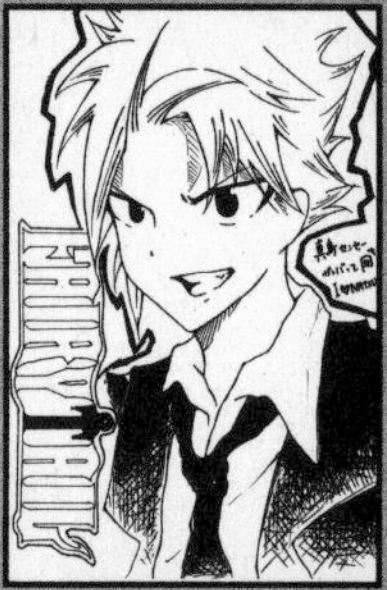
FAIRY TAIL

▲A rare sight of Natsu in a suit. Looking sharp, huh?

Hokkaido, Haruka Murakami

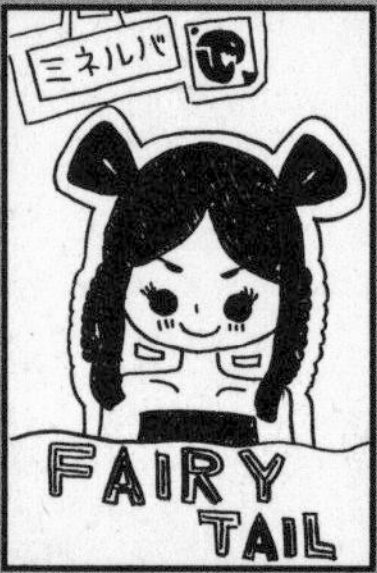
ミネルバ
FAIRY TAIL

▲Drawn like this, and Minerva actually looks cute!

Aichi Prefecture, Tomoka Tani

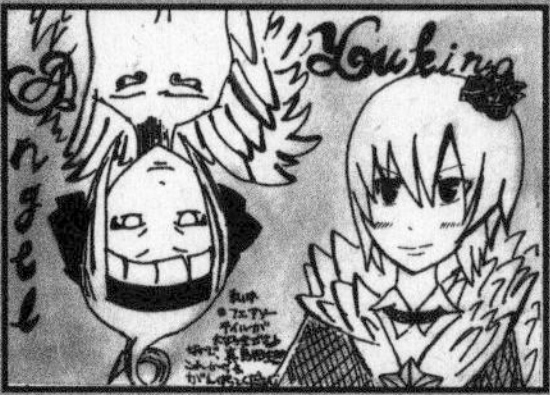
Yukino

Yukino and Angel... Do you think these two might be...?! ▶

Edolas Wendy after such a long time! I hope she's doing great! ◀

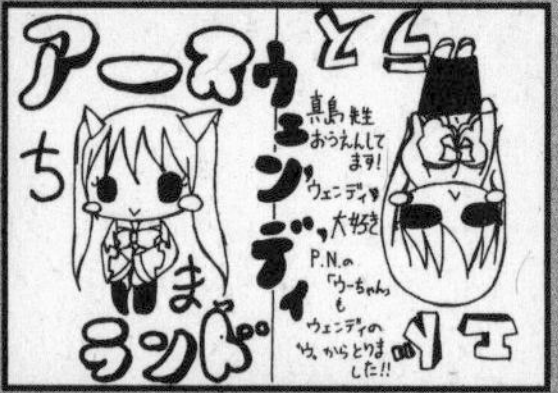
真島先生 おうえんしてます!

Gunma Prefecture, Www-chan

Ibaraki Prefecture, Kuu-tan

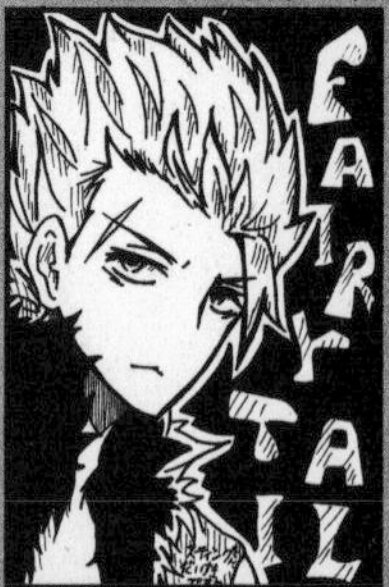
FAIRY TAIL

▲I think that Sting will still have a part to play in this.

Yamanashi Prefecture, Saki Mitsui

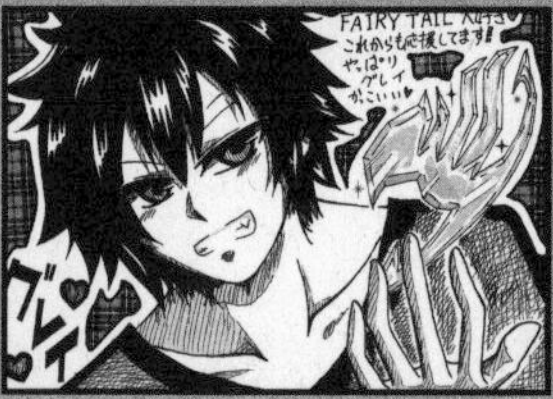

▲ Gray is really an expert at Ice Make for the guild mark.

REJECTION CORNER

Th- They're fused together! But...I never thought it'd be those two!! ▶

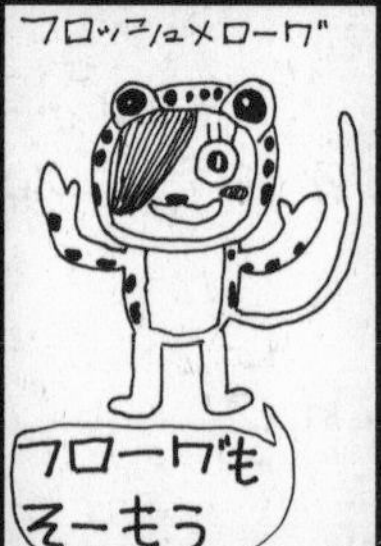
フロッシュメローグ
フローグもそーもう

Hokkaido, Doctor U

By sending in letters or postcards you give us permission to give your name, address, postal code and any other information you include to the author as is. Please keep that in mind.

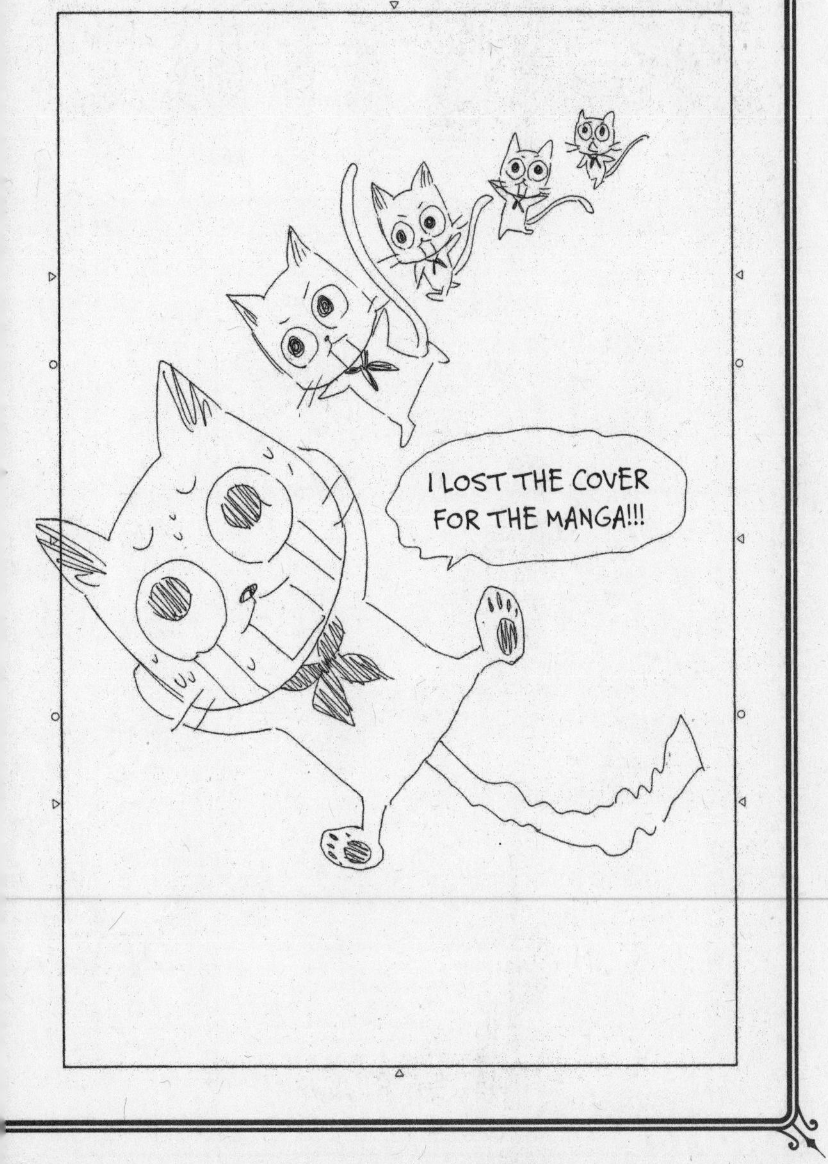
I LOST THE COVER FOR THE MANGA!!!

FAIRY TAIL

フェアリーテイル

37

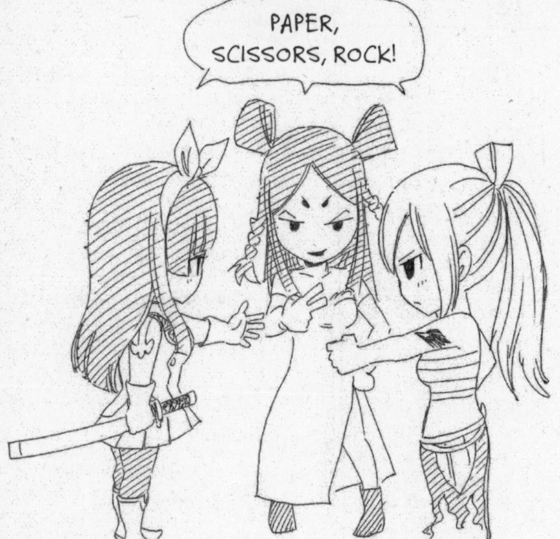
PAPER, SCISSORS, ROCK!

HIRO 真島ヒロ MASHIMA

FROM HIRO MASHIMA

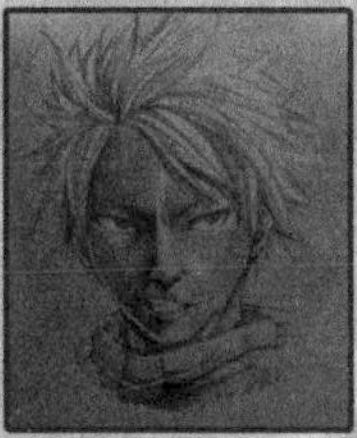

This is a sketch that I put up on Twitter. You may be thinking, "Why are you putting a sketch you did for Twitter in the book?" To me, the borderline between sketches and full-out drawings is very vague. There are sketches that I worked very hard on, and maybe a few dashed-off work illustrations.

Original Jacket Design: Hisao Ogawa

Translation Notes:

Japanese is a tricky language for most Westerners, and translation is often more art than science. For your edification and reading pleasure, here are notes on some of the places where we could have gone in a different direction with our translation of the work, or where a Japanese cultural reference is used.

Page 9, Rinka Renka
This attack name may simply be a meaningless play on sounds on the part of Mashima-sensei. But since Mashima-sensei is also an avid gamer, it may have something to do with the game "Vocaloid." The game "Vocaloid 2" features a female voice, "Rin," and a male voice, "Len." These were described by a game producer as two people who share the same soul. One of their songs was named "Rinka." A later version of Len also had a female version called "Lenka." Since the Japanese language does not discriminate between the "r" and "l" sounds, "renka" and "lenka" sound the same to most Japanese speakers. Vocaloid may be the origin of the magic's name, but it may also just be a coincidence.

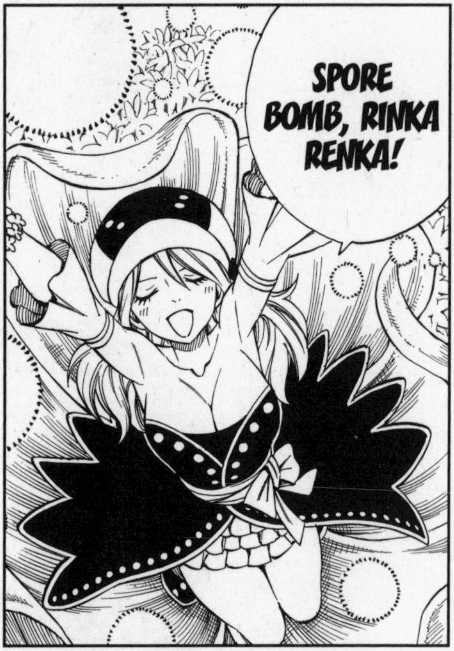
SPORE BOMB, RINKA RENKA!

Page 10, Makura Kamura
This may be another game reference. The Japanese word, *makura* simply means "pillow," and therefore has a lot to do with sleep magic. Kamura (an anagram of *makura*) is the name of a role-playing game made for mobile devices.

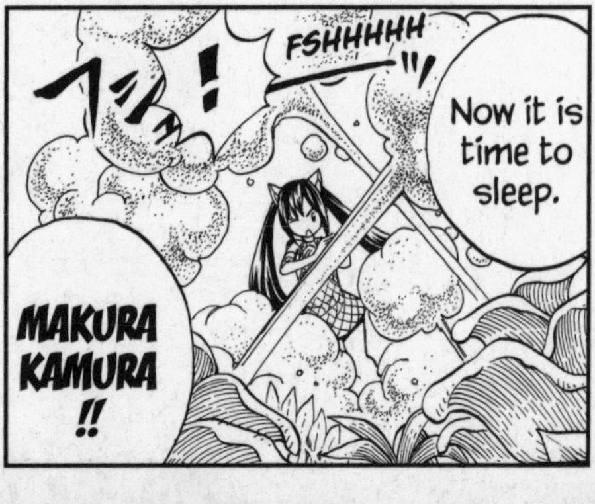
FSHHHHH
Now it is time to sleep.
!
MAKURA KAMURA !!

Page 11, Band

Uosuke (the traditional Japanese fisherman-like character) has a favorite word, "*tai*," and he uses it in his magic as well. Although there is a fish with the Japanese name *tai* ("see bream"), there are many other Japanese words that are pronounced *tai*. One of them is used in his spell, *tai*, meaning "band" or "region."

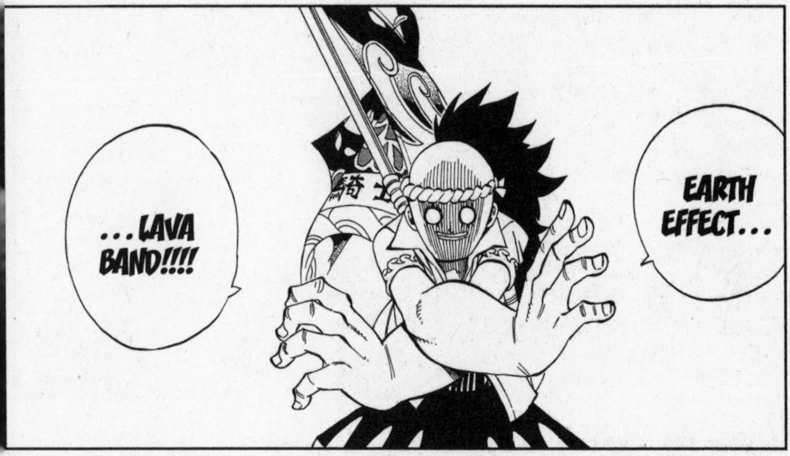
EARTH EFFECT...
...LAVA BAND!!!!

Page 115, Kata

In martial arts, a *kata* is a sequence of moves memorized by the martial artist and performed to show skill and technique. They are mainly used in karate and judo, but also in some other martial arts to hone skills and reflexes.

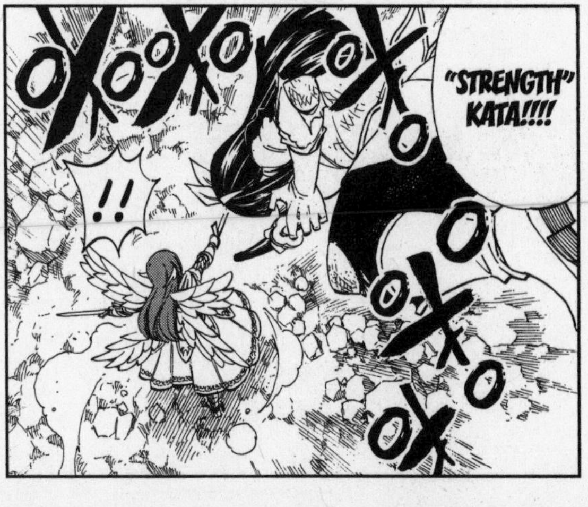
"STRENGTH" KATA!!!!
!!

Page 164, Castle-sama

No, the honorific *-sama* is not generally used for inanimate objects. However the character of Yukino seems to use the honorific *-sama* on everyone, so it's conceivable she might mistakenly use it even on buildings.

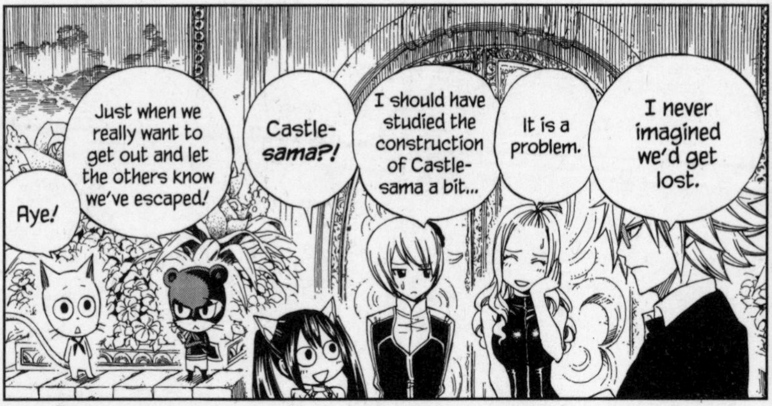

I never imagined we'd get lost.
It is a problem.
I should have studied the construction of Castle-sama a bit...
Castle-*sama?!*
Just when we really want to get out and let the others know we've escaped!
Aye!

Page 200, I lost the cover for the manga!

The Japanese editions come with dust jackets, and these sketches usually appear on the actual paperback underneath the jacket. So a Japanese reader would see this sketch of Happy if he or she lost the dust jacket.

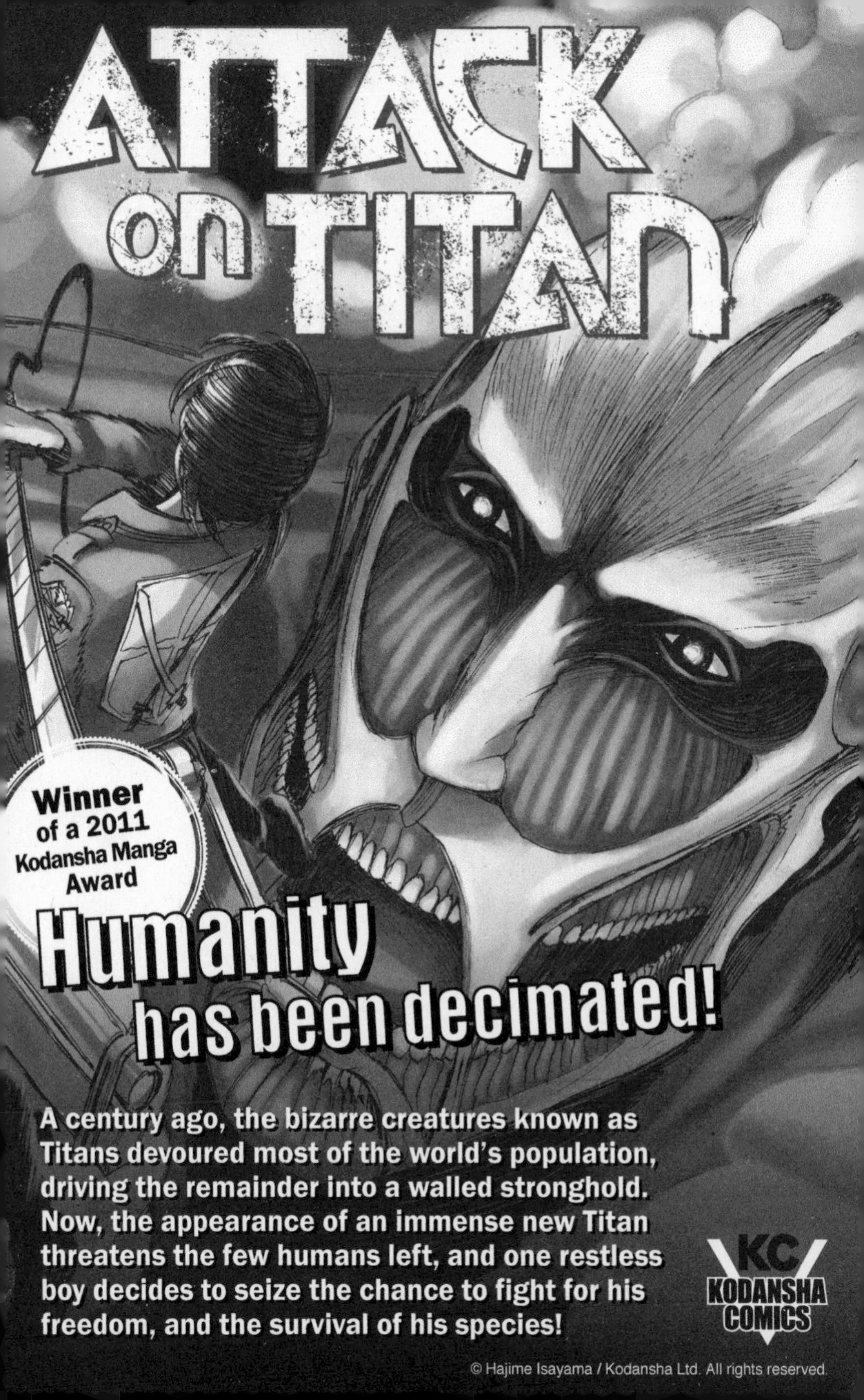

ATTACK ON TITAN

Humanity
has been decimated!

A century ago, the bizarre creatures known as Titans devoured most of the world's population, driving the remainder into a walled stronghold. Now, the appearance of an immense new Titan threatens the few humans left, and one restless boy decides to seize the chance to fight for his freedom, and the survival of his species!

KC
KODANSHA COMICS

Fairy Tail volume 37 is a work of fiction. Names, characters, places, and incidents are the products of the author's imagination or are used fictitiously. Any resemblance to actual events, locales, or persons, living or dead, is entirely coincidental.

A Kodansha Comics Trade Paperback Original.

Published in the United States by Kodansha Comics, an imprint of Kodansha USA Publishing, LLC, New York.

Publication rights for this English edition arranged through Kodansha Ltd., Tokyo.

First published in Japan in 2013 by Kodansha Ltd., Tokyo
ISBN 978-1-61262-433-4

Printed in the United States of America.

www.kodanshacomics.com

9 8 7 6 5 4 3 2 1

Translation: William Flanagan
Lettering: AndWorld Design
Editing: Ben Applegate

TOMARE!

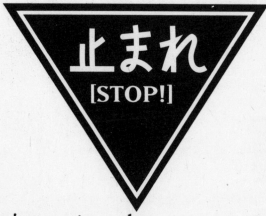

止まれ

[STOP!]

You're going the wrong way!

Manga is a completely different type of reading experience.

To start at the *beginning,* go to the *end!*

That's right! Authentic manga is read the traditional Japanese way— from right to left, exactly the *opposite* of how American books are read. It's easy to follow: Just go to the other end of the book and read each page—and each panel—from right side to left side, starting at the top right. Now you're experiencing manga as it was meant to be!